Sovereign Debt Diplomacies

Sovereign Debt Diplomacies

Rethinking Sovereign Debt from Colonial Empires to Hegemony

Edited by
PIERRE PÉNET and JUAN FLORES ZENDEJAS

OXFORD
UNIVERSITY PRESS

OXFORD
UNIVERSITY PRESS

Great Clarendon Street, Oxford, OX2 6DP,
United Kingdom

Oxford University Press is a department of the University of Oxford.
It furthers the University's objective of excellence in research, scholarship,
and education by publishing worldwide. Oxford is a registered trade mark of
Oxford University Press in the UK and in certain other countries

First Edition published in 2021

Published in the United States of America by Oxford University Press
198 Madison Avenue, New York, NY 10016, United States of America

British Library Cataloguing in Publication Data

Data available

Library of Congress Control Number: 2020950729

ISBN 978–0–19–886635–0

DOI: 10.1093/oso/9780198866350.001.0001

Acknowledgements

One of the nicest things about publishing this volume is the chance to acknowledge the people and institutions who sustained our research. We gratefully acknowledge the financial support of the Swiss National Science Foundation (grants CR11I1_162772, IZSEZ0_179604, 10BP12_198576), the University of Geneva, through its Fonds Général and School of Social Sciences, and the Société Académique de Genève. This support has been instrumental for the development of our work, the organization of the meetings and workshops with our contributors and the publication of this book in Open Access.

We are most grateful to the discussants and attendees who contributed to our first panel on Sovereign debt diplomacies at the 2017 meetings of the Law and Society Association Conference in Mexico City. This volume also benefited tremendously from the insights of the participants in our 2018 Geneva seminar. Besides volume contributors, this event brought together a wonderful team of experts across disciplinary boundaries: Stephanie Blankenburg, Juan Pablo Bohoslavsky, Francesco Corradini, Aline Darbellay, Sebastian Nieto Parra, Makane Moïse Mbengue, Noémi Michel, Boris Samuel, Nathan Sussman and Olivier Vallée. Despite a powerful snow storm and significant travel complications, seminar participants managed to reach Geneva to deliver their presentation while other colleagues participated through videoconferencing. We thank them wholeheartedly for their dedication and commitment.

We are also grateful to three anonymous reviewers and to Carlos Marichal and Aurora Gómez who provided us with valuable comments to previous versions of this manuscript.

Finally, we are indebted to our colleagues at the Paul Bairoch Institute of Economic History: Mary O'Sullivan, Pilar Nogues-Marco, Sabine Pitteloud, Cédric Chambru, Jean Rochat, Sebastian Alvarez, Edoardo Altamura and Jérémy Ducros. Many thanks to them for having contributed to the success of this collective intellectual effort.

Contents

SECTION 3. POSTCOLONIAL TRANSITIONS AND THE HOPES FOR A NEW INTERNATIONAL ECONOMIC ORDER (1960s–80s)

SECTION 4. THE LEGALIZATION OF SOVEREIGN DEBT DISPUTES BETWEEN WISH AND REALITY (1990s–PRESENT)

List of Figures

List of Tables

List of Contributors

Anusha Chari is a Professor of Economics and Finance at the University of North Carolina at Chapel Hill. She is a Research Associate at the National Bureau of Economic Research and the Centre for Economic Policy Research. She received a PhD in International Finance from UCLA and a BA in Philosophy, Politics and Economics at Balliol College at Oxford and Economics at the University of Delhi. She has held faculty positions at the University of Chicago's Booth School of Business, the University of Michigan, and The Haas School of Business at Berkeley. Professor Chari was a special advisor to the Indian Prime Minister's Economic Advisory Council and member of an Advisory Group of Eminent Persons on G20 Issues. Her research is in the fields of open-economy macroeconomics and international finance.

Giselle Datz is Associate Professor of Government and International Affairs at Virginia Tech. Her research focuses on sovereign debt restructuring, pension, and financial system reforms. Some of her work has been published by *Review of Political Economy*, *New Political Economy*, *Latin American Politics and Society*, and *Government and Opposition*.

Laura de la Villa is a PhD candidate at the Paul Bairoch Institute of Economic History at the University of Geneva. She works on sovereign debt restructurings occurred during the 1940s and 1950s under the supervision of Professor Juan Flores Zendejas. She collaborates on the project Sovereign Debt Diplomacies with Professors Flores Zendejas and Pénet.

Quentin Deforge holds a PhD in Political Science from Paris Dauphine University (2019). He is now a postdoctoral fellow at EHESS (Centre Alexandre-Koyré). His work focuses on the socio-history of development policies, especially regarding the emergence of governance policies in the 90s.

Nicolas Degive is a PhD student in Financial History at the Centre E. Bernheim, Solvay Brussels School of Economics and Management, Université Libre de Bruxelles. His dissertation is directed by Kim Oosterlinck and is focused on sovereign debt issued by colonies during the first half of the twentieth century. He is also a teaching assistant in corporate finance and financial markets.

Gustavo Del Angel is Professor at the Department of Economics, CIDE (Mexico). He specializes in bank history and banking, mainly of Mexico. Gustavo has been affiliated to the Hoover Institution at Stanford University, the Centro Espinosa Yglesias, Banco de México, and the Université de Paris 3. He holds a PhD from Stanford University.

Juan Flores Zendejas is Associate Professor of Economic History at the University of Geneva. His main research interests are the history of financial crises, the rise of European stock exchanges in the late nineteenth-century and Latin American international financial development across the nineteenth and twentieth centuries. He has published in several leading academic journals such as the *Business History Review*, the *Economic History*

Review, the *European Review of Economic* Histor,y and *Law and Contemporary Problems.* Prior to joining the University of Geneva in 2008, Flores Zendejas was Research Fellow at University Carlos III in Madrid and invited scholar in several European universities. Additionally, he has worked several years for the Mexican government and as consultant for OECD.

Felipe Ford Cole is a JD-PhD candidate at the Northwestern University Pritzker School of Law and Department of History. His research examines the legal and financial history of the United States and Latin America across the nineteenth and twentieth centuries and focuses on topics in sovereign debt and international investment law.

Mitu Gulati is a Professor of Law at Duke University. Gulati's primary research interests are in the historical evolution of sovereign debt contracts and in the mechanics of sovereign debt restructurings. His current research focus is on the pricing and restructuring of government guaranteed debt. He has authored articles in the *Journal of Legal Studies*, the *Review of Finance*, and *Law and Social Inquiry*.

Ryan Leary is an associate at the Brattle Group with experience working on investment-related cases, with an emphasis on suitability analysis. He received his PhD in Economics from the University of North Carolina at Chapel Hill, where he focused his academic research on empirical international finance. His work has been published by the National Bureau of Economic Research. Prior to receiving his PhD, Dr Leary held positions at the Congressional Budget Office and the Federal Reserve Board of Governors.

Benjamin Lemoine is a Researcher in Political Science and Sociology at the French National Centre for Scientific Research (CNRS). He is based at IRISSO at Paris Dauphine University and specializes in the analysis of state financialization processes, through sovereign debt, accounting, and financial law. He recently published 'Bankrupcy Politics. Public services and the law of survival', (with Pierre-André Juven), *Actes de la recherche en sciences sociales* 221 (March 2018), and 'Democracy and the political representation of investors: On French sovereign debt transactions and elections', in Marc Lenglet (eds.) *The Making of Finance: Conventions, Devices and Regulation* (Routledge, 2018) and *L'ordre de la dette, Enquête sur les infortunes de l'État et la prospérité des marchés* (La Découverte, 2016).

Odette Lienau is a Professor of Law at Cornell University, where she also co-directs the International Law/International Relations Colloquium and is a Faculty Member in the Graduate Field of Government. Her research and teaching interests include international economic law, international law and international relations, bankruptcy and debtor–creditor relations, and political and legal theory. Her scholarship seeks to understand the broader norms and principles that underpin international market rules and that impact expectations about appropriate behaviour for businesses, governments, and other actors. Her book, *Rethinking Sovereign Debt: Politics, Reputation, and Legitimacy in Modern Finance* (Harvard University Press, 2014, winner of a Book Award from the American Society of International Law), challenges the conventional wisdom that all states, including those emerging from a major regime change, must repay debt or suffer reputational consequences. She contends that this practice is not essential for functioning capital markets, and locates the twentieth-century consolidation of the repayment rule in contingent actions taken by government officials, international financial institutions, and private market actors. Her articles and chapter contributions have been published or are forthcoming with the *Harvard International Law Journal, the Yale Journal of International Law, the Hastings Law Journal*, and Oxford University Press, among others. She has consulted for the United Nations Conference on Trade and Development on the establishment of a sovereign debt workout mechanism, and is a Term Member of the Council on Foreign Relations.

Grégoire Mallard is Professor in the Department of Anthropology and Sociology and Director of Research at the Graduate Institute of International and Development Studies (Geneva). After earning his PhD at Princeton University in 2008, Professor Mallard was Assistant Professor of Sociology at Northwestern University for five years. He is the author of *Fallout: Nuclear Diplomacy in an Age of Global Fracture* (University of Chicago Press, 2014) and co-editor of *Contractual Knowledge: One Hundred Years of Legal Experimentation in Global Markets* (Cambridge University Press, 2016) and *Global Science and National Sovereignty: Studies in Historical Sociology of Science* (Routledge, 2008). His latest book, *Gift Exchange: The Transnational History of a Political Idea* (Cambridge University Press, 2019), received the 2020 Best Book Award of the History of Sociology Section of the American Sociological Association. His other publications focus on prediction, the role of knowledge and ignorance in diplomacy, and the study of harmonization as a social process (see http://www.gregoiremallard.com) In 2016, he has been the recipient of an ERC starting grant (2017–22) for his new project titled *Bombs, Banks and Sanctions*.

Kim Oosterlinck is Professor of Finance at the Solvay Brussels School of Economics and Management (Université libre de Bruxelles) and Research Fellow at the CEPR. He holds a Master's in management, a Master's in Art History and Archaeology, and a PhD in Economics and Management from the Université libre de Bruxelles (ULB). His main research interests are sovereign bond valuation, financial history, and art market investments. He has published in several leading academic journals such as the *American Economic Review*, the *Economic Journal*, the *Journal of Economic History*, the *Journal of Monetary Economics*, and the *Review of Finance*. He just published, with Yale University Press, a book on the Repudiation of Russian Sovereign Bonds.

Ugo Panizza is Professor of International Economics at the Graduate Institute Geneva and Director of the Institute's Centre for Finance and Development. Ugo Panizza has been a Visiting Professor at the Institute since 2008, a position he held in addition to being the Chief of the Debt and Finance Analysis Unit at the United Nations Conference on Trade and Development. Professor Panizza's research interests include international finance, sovereign debt, banking, and political economy. He has extensive work and research experience in Latin America and the Middle East and North Africa. He is Vice-President of the Centre for Economic Policy Research (CEPR). Professor Panizza's recent work includes a series of important articles on the costs of sovereign defaults, on the links between public debt and economic growth, and research with Professor Arcand and Enrico Berkes, of the IMF, on the threshold above which financial development no longer has a positive effect on economic growth. Together with Barry Eichengreen of the

University of California, Berkeley and Ricardo Hausmann of Harvard's Kennedy School, he worked on the causes and consequences of 'original sin' in international finance. He has also worked with Eichengreen on capital account liberalization and bond market development. Professor Panizza's research is wide-ranging and has covered areas such as income inequality, public sector labour market, and the relationship between religion and the education gender gap.

Pierre Pénet holds a PhD in Sociology from Northwestern University and Sciences Po Paris (2014). He is a CNRS researcher at the École Normale Supérieure Paris-Saclay (IDHES) and a former Fellow at the Paris Institute for Advanced Study (2019–20). His expertise straddles the boundaries of economic sociology and the history of quantification. He has worked extensively on topics of credit rating agencies, the European debt crisis, austerity programmes, and the legal doctrine of odious debt. His work has been published by the *British Journal of Sociology*, *European Journal of Sociology*, *Poetics*, *Sociologie du Travail*, etc. His forthcoming book on financial prophecies will study the economists who claim to have predicted the 2008 financial crisis.

Lorena Pérez-Hernández is Researcher at the Fundacion Rafael Preciado (Mexico). She specializes in political historiography and political history of Mexico. Lorena in the past was affiliated to the Centro Gomez Morin, the UNAM, and the UAM. She holds a PhD from the Metropolitan University (UAM) in Mexico.

Christian Suter is Professor of Sociology at the University of Neuchâtel. He is the current editor of the *Swiss Journal of Sociology* and *International Journal of Comparative Sociology*. His main research interests are sovereign debt and financial history. His book *Debt Cycles in the World-Economy: Foreign loans, financial crises, and debt settlements, 1820–1990* (1992) influenced later studies in economics and history on sovereign debt, most notably Carmen Reinhart and Kenneth Rogoff's latest opus *This Time is Different: Eight Centuries of Financial Folly* (2009).

Ali Coşkun Tunçer is Associate Professor in Economic History at University College London (UCL). He received his PhD from the London School of Economics in 2011. Prior to joining UCL, he taught and worked as a researcher at the LSE and European University Institute. His research focuses on the history of financial markets, the evolution of international financial and monetary institutions, and long-term economic change in the Middle East and Southeastern Europe. Coşkun is currently co-investigator on a British Academy-funded research project investigating sovereign debt in the first age of globalization.

Michael Waibel studied Law at the universities of Vienna, Paris II Pantheon-Assas Harvard Law School, and Economics at the London School of Economics. He worked at the European Central Bank, the World Bank, and the International Monetary Fund. He has been a Professor of International Law at the University of Vienna since 2019. Previously, he taught for a decade at the University of Cambridge, and was from 2015 until 2019 Co-deputy Director of the Lauterpacht Centre for International Law and Director of Studies at Jesus College. In 2010–11 he was the Schmidheiny Visiting Assistant Professor in Law and

Economics at the University of St Gallen. In 2019, he was Nomura Visiting Professor of International Financial Systems at Harvard Law School. The focus of his research is international law, international economic law, and international dispute settlement. He received the Deák Prize of the American Society of International Law, the Book Prize of the European Society of International Law, and a Leverhulme Prize for his research.

Introduction

Sovereign Debt Diplomacies

Pierre Pénet and Juan Flores Zendejas

> Every seventh year you shall practice remission of debts [Shmita]. This shall be the nature of the remission: every creditor shall remit the due that he claims from his fellow; he shall not dun [request debt payment from] his fellow or kinsman, for the remission proclaimed is of the Lord.
>
> Deuteronomy 15:1–2

In Jewish scriptures, *Shmita* laws require that all debts be cancelled once every seven sabbatical years, roughly every fifty years. Shmita, literally meaning 'release', celebrates ancient Jewish economic policies of debt forgiveness. The social basis of Shmita policy is to proclaim the liberation of forced labour and the surrender of property to give the poor a financial reset opportunity. In ancient times, it was common for subsistence farmers to sell themselves into servitude as a means of paying off debts. Breaking the cycle of debt and indenture was a main focus of Shmita laws.

While the mechanics of the ancient Shmita (most notably, its routine nature) may be foreign to modern sensibilities, the values behind the policy speak directly to an important fact about modern debtor–creditor relations: debt binds debtors and creditors, bringing them into dependency relations (Goodhart & Hudson, 2018). For centuries, debt has been one way for lenders to win social influence and political power. Indebtedness typically creates duties and obligations that can alter the social destiny of debtors. Yet, the entangling nature of debt contracts also affects creditors: after debt is contracted, lenders become to a certain degree obliged to their debtors, and they may develop a financial interest in their survival, even if they do not share their worldviews, or agree with how debtors spend their borrowed funds.

To be sure, debt entanglements are not always controversial. As a rule, debtors repay their debts and financial obligations are simply assumed. In this case, debt

Pierre Pénet and Juan Flores Zendejas, *Introduction: Sovereign Debt Diplomacies* In: *Sovereign Debt Diplomacies: Rethinking Sovereign Debt from Colonial Empires to Hegemony.* Edited by: Pierre Pénet and Juan Flores Zendejas, Oxford University Press (2021). © Oxford University Press. DOI: 10.1093/oso/9780198866350.003.0001

entanglements get 'forgotten about', as they remain buried in contractual agreements. But when repayment becomes problematic, because of a changing or uncertain political or financial context, parties rediscover the controversial reality of debt entanglements. Conflicts are waged and creditors and debtors revisit prior agreements in the light of present difficulties. Central to debt disputes is the question of how and whether debt contracts can be unmade and who should bear the cost of breaching promises.

In this book we concentrate on one particular type of debtor–creditor interactions. These are the interactions between sovereign borrowers, namely the governments of a nation state and their state-controlled entities, and international creditors—bondholders, banks, international organizations, and foreign states. According to textbook accounts, nations enter into a contractual agreement with foreign creditors to fund activities which they cannot otherwise finance. But foreign debt is not just about borrowing and lending money, it is also about making allies, projecting power, and exporting norms. More often than not, the pure financial transaction that debt is often understood to be is in fact a more complex and composite object. Sovereign debt creates bonds and interdependences between creditors and debtors who eventually become part of a constituency of interests organized along financial *and* non-financial dimensions. From contracting to defaulting, the life cycle of sovereign debt has a political complexion: witness how the development of sovereign debt markets over the past centuries has intersected with the rise and fall of colonial regimes, warfare, regime change, and, more generally, the history of diplomatic relations.

Creditor–debtor relations in the sovereign sector evidence processes and problems strikingly similar to those we can observe in the world of personal and corporate debt. In all matters related to debt, one recurring issue is how and whether contracts should be breached when their binding nature undermines the welfare or the very existence of the contracting parties. In the world of personal debt, debtor prisons have ceased to exist in the mid-nineteenth century (Coleman, 1999) and bankruptcy frameworks allow individual debtors to break free from over-indebtedness. Corporations can also reorganize in the shadow of international bankruptcy code (Halliday & Carruthers, 2009). But nothing comparable to an insolvency law exists for the resolution of sovereign debt crises. International bankruptcy rules for sovereigns are the unicorn that regulators and scholars have been chasing since the 1930s but without success. Recent attempts to adopt a comprehensive restructuring mechanism have failed (Setser, 2005). Odious debt, the legal doctrine often cited in civil society circles to justify the cancellation of debt, has only a narrow perimeter and is not nearly the legal solution that could provide a comprehensive framework to regulate sovereign debt disputes (Buchheit, Gulati & Thompson, 2007). In the contemporary world, there is no orderly exit to sovereign debt disputes.

This points to a structural problem: in the absence a transnational framework of debt dispute management, sovereign debt disputes often foster an anarchic system of competing interests and suboptimal outcomes for both creditors and debtors (Stiglitz & Heymann, 2014). There is a striking contrast between the $22 trillion worth of sovereign bonds outstanding in 2019 and the paucity of rules governing international lending and borrowing. Without formal rules to regulate defaults, creditor–debtor relationships have been unstable and controversial: sovereign debt disputes often produce disorganized tactics on the parts of creditors and debtors to force or block repayment, causing fantastic disruptions in global finance, with distributional effects on the well-being of citizenry, such as in the recent debt restructurings of Argentina ($82 billion, 2001), Greece ($138 billion, 2012), and Puerto Rico ($72 billion, 2016).

I.1 Debts, Defaults, Disputes

This volume is about conflicts and disputes. Sovereign debt disputes are as old as state borrowing itself. How, to what extent, and under what conditions sovereign debt should be repaid are consequential and controversial questions that have concerned a large number of nations from Germany and Greece to Russia, Mexico, and Argentina. The ambition of this book is to take stock of the normative, moral, and political issues raised by debt disputes since the rise of foreign debt markets in early nineteenth century. We should already make clear at this early stage that this volume is not a problem-solving exercise. Volume contributions are mostly devoid of reformative pretension. And when the authors venture into suggesting reforms to enhance the current sovereign debt regime, it is without assuming that conflicts arising in matters of sovereign debt can be fully erased. Our collective starting point is the observation that the meaning of debt, the sanctity of contracts, and the extent to which debt can and should be repaid have been controversial subjects and will remain so in the years to come. Debt conflicts are inherent to sovereign indebtedness, rather than anomalies that could be cured.

In some sense, this volume picks up where most debt studies leave off; namely, we seek to trace and evaluate the concrete actions that creditors take to defend their interests after their expectations of repayment are compromised. Recent research has greatly expanded our comprehension of the sort of legal and financial precautions that investors take upon lending (Gulati & Scott, 2012). Detailed emphasis on contractual clauses and methods of risk analysis is warranted because they structure expectations of repayment and, without them, there would not be lending at all (Mallard & Sgard, 2016). But one lesson of history is that legal contracts and risk models do not guarantee repayment, far from it. Sovereign debt disputes are akin to events during which, Keynes (1937, p. 215) observed, 'the practice of calmness and immobility, of certainty and security, suddenly breaks down' Keynes (Ibid) further noted that during such unsettling events: 'all these pretty, polite techniques, made for a well-panelled Board Room and a nicely regulated market, are liable to collapse.' This volume invites more focused consideration on the range of tactics and methods to extract repayment such as moral suasion, political influence, informal threats, instruments of foreign interference, behind-the-scenes exchanges at international summits, military controls, etc.

Our empirical analysis concentrates on one critical issue on which generations of creditors have reflected, namely: what methods and tactics of debt collection can be deployed when the preferred mechanisms of repayment are no longer available? The history of sovereign debt disputes suggests that debt collection practices have varied greatly in terms of availability, acceptability, and efficacy. Consider Britain's use of military power against Egypt in 1882 to force repayment of defaulted loans. Such display of power could not have possibly occurred against, say, the US states of Virginia and Maryland, which also defaulted on British creditors in the 1840s. Nor could it happen today: defaulters are no longer bombarded and, quite fortunately, captains of gunboats no longer have a say in debt disputes. Consider, alternatively, that actors that were once marginal or insignificant, such as vulture funds and extraterritorial courts, have become key players in recent debt disputes. Finally, witness the great variability in debt dispute outcomes: the stance of forbearance adopted by international creditors towards Germany and Japan after the Second World War looks quite exotic if we bear in mind the drastic conditions recently imposed on Greece by international creditors in exchange of new loans. The provisional conclusion that can be drawn from history is that different actors and entities have deployed different set of tools and methods of dispute resolution with different outcomes.

I.2 Sovereign Debt Diplomacies

This volume traces important changes in the ways debtors and creditors have managed and settled sovereign debt disputes since the early nineteenth century. In order to delineate and identify analytically this complex research object, we develop the concept of *sovereign debt diplomacy*. When a state is unable to fulfil its financial obligations, lenders engage into diplomatic actions to remedy broken contracts. Our interest in diplomacy stems from the observation that in the world of sovereign debt, few things proceed from the automatic application of rules. Debt disputes are typically negotiated not litigated (Waibel, 2010). We define sovereign debt diplomacy as the interface between two orders, on the one hand, *practical expectations* about repayment and, on the other, *normative models* about the meaning of debt, sovereignty, and the limits placed on the continuity of debt contracts. Practical expectations derive from the 'contractual knowledge' (Mallard & Sgard, 2016) acquired upstream of the lending process, when debtors and creditors agree on a course of future behaviour regarding the terms of lending and debt repayment. Normative models refer to broader cognitive, political, and legal frames defining the range of acceptable behaviour in debt markets. These models shape what is being deliberated and the type of outcome that sovereign debt disputes generate. Thus, the diplomatic actions of creditors and debtors involved in debt disputes can be situated in this interface of practical expectations and normative models.

In our definition of sovereign debt diplomacy, we find four components: (1) *risk analysis*, or a set of trusted methods and devices that creditors use to price risks; (2) *legal clauses*, or the standardized provisions that govern debt contracts and determine the legal fate of creditors when repayment is compromised; (3) *bargaining power*, or the private tools and forums that creditors use to increase coordination and press for repayment; and (4) a *conception of state responsibility*, or a worldview that allows a state to interpret the actions of others and to reflect upon its responsibility to intervene in financial affairs. A sovereign debt diplomacy is therefore a composite mix of risk analysis, legal clauses, private coordination mechanisms, and state power.

Risk analysis includes the tools and methods that creditors mobilize upstream of the lending process to evaluate the creditworthiness of borrowers. These shape creditors' expectations of repayment and therefore make debt contracting possible. *Legal clauses* provide a second entry to the question of creditors' expectations. Debt being contracts, the general expectation is that all debt must be repaid, no matter the circumstances. Lenders and borrowers can rely on contractual terms and conditions when forming contracts to legally compel borrowers to do certain things and prevent them from doing others. Legal clauses contain boilerplate language that help parties better define their relationship, especially if the terms of the contracts become contested (Gulati & Scott, 2012). For instance, lenders can require the consent of borrowers to maintain the value of their debt with gold clauses. Today, some of the most common legal clause is the arbitration clause that requires the parties to resolve their disputes through an arbitration process. A focus on legal clauses allows capturing the growing importance of international and domestic courts as platforms of debt dispute adjudication.

Risk analysis and legal clauses are techniques of 'uncertainty absorption' (March & Simon, 1958, p. 165). They make investments predictable and debt contracting possible. But debtors do not always conform to what's expected from them. Attention to *bargaining power* is thus warranted to understand the type of action that actors resort to when faced with the perils of default. Bargaining power is the capacity to act strategically and collectively, the form of which has varied across historical and geographical context. Creditors can organize themselves in bondholder committees to threaten defaulters with the loss of market access. More recently, vulture funds have threatened debtor countries with costly litigation if they do not comply with the terms of lending. Besides self-organization, bargaining power also derives from the capacity to lobby the 'official sector'—the state and their officials—to intervene on their behalf.

The history of sovereign defaults and restructuring episodes highlights various elements of change and continuity in the role of states. State have assumed various roles from that of a passive monitoring institution to that of an active enforcer of creditors' claims and property rights. The choice of a role depends ultimately on how states represent their responsibility in global financial affairs. Depending on prevailing *conceptions of state responsibility*, states can act upon creditors' request for help, but they can also choose to alter the normal workings of creditor coordination, for instance, when states perceive that debt repayment poses a threat to international security. In particular, we assess conceptions of state responsibility against the historical thread of colonialism, from the building of colonial empires to decolonization. As we will show, conceptions of state responsibility emerged and solidified to a large extent in relation to the threads of colonial history, from the building of colonial empires to the decolonization era.

To summarize, a sovereign debt diplomacy refers to a composite set of tools for managing debt disputes which are shared between actors and deemed acceptable according to institutional models of international conduct. This framework brings to the picture a new method to analyse debt disputes. In our view, the concept of sovereign debt diplomacy has two main virtues. First, its analytical premises are resolutely *pragmatic*. A diplomatic perspective suggests that financial disputes cannot be easily reduced to legal contracts or any standardized blueprint of action. Therefore, the unfolding and outcome of debt disputes requires that careful attention be paid to the point of view of actors and how they make sense of broken contracts. With this diplomatic perspective, we aim to move research on sovereign debt disputes beyond the traditional opposition of payment versus default. While the legalistic approach of sovereign debt holds that states are bound by the principle of *pacta sunt servanda* ('agreements must be kept') and that any deviation from repayment is problematic, a diplomatic perspective suggests that repayment is not always the ultimate goal or even the measuring rod of 'success' for the parties involved in debt disputes.

Our diplomatic approach is also *pluralist*. We have opted for the plural term debt diplomacies to allow a sustained reflection on the varieties of sovereign debt diplomacies across historical and geographical contexts. With this volume, we intend to join a small but growing scholarly effort to rethink sovereign debt from an interdisciplinary viewpoint (Flandreau, 2016; Lienau, 2014; Mallard & Sgard, 2016). This volume integrates insights from research in 'law and society', economic history, sociology, political science, and studies in economics and finance to evaluate the variety of diplomatic engagements that debt disputes have elicited since the nineteenth century and their outcomes for debtors and creditors. Ultimately, this interdisciplinary perspective applied to sovereign debt not only improves our understanding of the past but also makes it accessible and legible in terms that resonate with non-expert populations.

I.3 Analytical and Methodological Contributions

This volume innovates both analytically and methodologically. Analytically, it extends the literature on sovereign debt in four directions. First, we bring history and, in particular, colonial history, to the fore of the investigation. Economists often consider the post-1980 globalization period as a mostly novel era, and they often fall short of providing a measure of this novelty against previous historical experiences. This is unfortunate because there is a lot to be learnt about recent debt disputes from earlier comparable events during the nineteenth century and mid-twentieth century. *Circa* 1820, Western creditors began to lend to overseas nations, most commonly Latin American and Mediterranean countries. Creditors adjusted to the context of increasing market integration and capital expansion with institutional innovations that durably structured debtor–creditor interactions. The first globalization era also coincided with the rapid expansion of colonial empires, a process that intersected with and contributed to the expansion debt markets. With this focus on history and in particular colonial history, we aim to show that debt disputes and colonial empires were co-produced during the nineteenth century and that this co-production of finance and politics continues to shape current debates about sovereign debt.

Second, we add a 'law and society' dimension to research on sovereign debt. Against the conventional understanding that international law emerged more or less naturally, socio-legal studies suggest that legal tools to redress against defaulters were slow in coming and their historical development since the nineteenth century has been irregular (Gulati & Scott, 2012; Lienau, 2014; Mallard & Sgard, 2016; Mann, 2002; Waibel, 2011). For instance, until 1914, legal methods of enforcement like arbitration clauses were not meant to be open to litigation but served to enlist the participation of creditor states in sovereign debt disputes (Weidemaier, 2010). A socio-legal perspective is also useful to capture the historical circumstances that enabled or constrained the availability of legal recourses in disputes over broken contracts. For instance, US legislative decisions to weaken the doctrine of sovereign immunity in the 1950s raised the profile of law in debt disputes by giving creditors a legitimate claim to bring a recalcitrant debtor before a court of law. But on the other hand, the anti-vulture funds legislations passed in Europe after 2008 amount to a significant reversal (Datz, this volume). These new laws testify to the recent efforts to impose limits on creditors' uncompromising and legalistic behaviour in negotiations over broken contracts. Overall, we add a law and society perspective to show that sovereign debt contracts continue to elicit flexible conceptions of repayment and that the use and meaning of legal recourses against sovereign debtors are neither self-evident nor irreversible.

Third is a contribution about the role of states in sovereign debt disputes. States are central players in debt diplomacies because they are vested with the authority to define the rules of market exchange. They possess tools that private actors do not have; namely the military force and the capacity to pass legislations and sign commercial treaties. States also entertain close ties with and considerable influence on international organizations (e.g. the IMF, World Bank, and UNCTAD) and specialized intergovernmental forums (e.g. the Paris Club), whose general norms and guidance (e.g. conditionality frameworks) shape the behaviour of debtors and creditors and, ultimately, impact the resolution and outcome of debt disputes. The capacity of states to define the rules of market exchange has always granted them with considerable influence in debt management. Upstream of the lending process, the influence of states can be observed in the propensity of creditors to invest in domestic assets (Obstfeld & Rogoff, 2000). During colonial times, this 'home-bias' also applied to investments in colonized countries, which were then considered as 'domestic' territories (Flandreau, 2006). Under such circumstances, investors are under strong incentives to invest where domestic laws are recognized and in countries with which their state has a special relation (e.g. empire, formal or informal). When operating under the umbrella of state power, creditors develop strong expectations that they will be bailed out, should problems emerge.

If states are so important in our volume, it is also because they have the legitimacy to uphold the sanctity of contracts. The influence of states often extends into shaping the meaning of debt disputes and their outcome. When private bargaining power proves insufficient against defaulters, investors typically turn to their states to intervene. State behaviour can be represented along a continuum between defending private property rights and taking a special interest in the survival of indebted countries, thus frustrating creditors' hopes of repayment. We argue that the position of state action in this continuum has fluctuated according to how states interpret their responsibility to intervene in financial affairs. Before granting support to private creditors, powerful states like the US and European powers typically weigh the interests of private creditors against their own range of objectives and targets, including national economic interests, international cooperation and peacebuilding efforts, and global security concerns. Investigating state actions is therefore paramount to our quest to understand why the norm of debt repayment has been politically and historically variable. The originality of this volume is to assess state actions against the historical thread of colonialism, from the building of colonial empires to decolonization. As we intend to show, conceptions of state responsibility have emerged and evolved to a large extent in relation to the threads of colonial history, from the building of colonial empires to the decolonization era.

This brings us to our fourth and last contribution on colonial history. This volume fills an important gap in recent debt historiographies. None of the recent textbooks on sovereign debt (for instance Eichengreen & Lindert, 1989; Jochnick & Preston, 2006; Kolb, 2011; Tomz, 2007; Roos, 2019) have designated sections on empires or colonial rules. This trend stands in stark contrast to older Marxist literature on capitalism and imperialism. Scholars such as Jean Bouvier, René Girault, or Jacques Thobie analysed and contrasted mainly the British and French experiences through the lens of commercial expansionism and imperialism.[1] For these authors, government loans were a central component of a general strategy promoted by imperial states to secure new markets and natural resources. Their work followed directly from the early studies published by Lenin (1939) and Hobson (1902). More recently however, economic historians have engaged with colonialism only reluctantly or *en passant*, giving credence to the idea that colonialism is not a development that deserves to be treated on its own.[2] In our view, this has led to suboptimal developments in recent scholarship. We contend that sovereign debt disputes have at once reflected and shaped colonial processes. First, the nineteenth century was the century of colonial empires so much that debt disputes rarely occurred without explicit reference to the colonial context of that time. As we shall see in this volume, for a cluster of Latin American, North African, and Eastern Mediterranean countries, over-indebtedness led to imperial responses, the form of which varied between the imposition of full-fledged colonial rule and informal empire effects. The tangled histories of sovereign debt and colonialism were also clear during the breakdown of colonial empires in the 1960s and 1970s, when the continuity in debt repayment once again became a controversial issue, most particularly in northern and sub-Saharan Africa.

This volume also focuses on the distinctive contributions made by legal scholars from the Global South. In the late nineteenth and early twentieth centuries, imperial projects met with the resistance of legal scholars from Latin America who perceived that they could enlist international law to protect debtor countries from creditors' uncompromising behaviour in negotiations over broken contracts. Conflicting interpretations of international law (as a method to force repayment or as a resource that protects debtors) resurfaced during the postcolonial transitions of the 1960s and 1970s, in particular in the legal proposals made by Mohammed Bedjaoui to organize a 'New International Economic Order'. Even if these proposals were not ultimately conclusive, they further raised the profile of international law in debt disputes and, as such, their legacy can still be felt in current debates.

If the history of debt disputes is one where colonial history plays a central role, where does that leave us after 1970? Even though colonial empires have ceased to

[1] A general summary can be found in Bouvier, Girault & Thobie (1986).

[2] An exception is the remarkable work of Hudson (2017), analysing the joint development of financial markets and colonial practices from the late nineteenth century to the Great Depression.

exist, global asymmetries of power in debt disputes have not disappeared. The return of international debt disputes has left scholars ponder the question of the applicability of colonial experiences to assess the current predicament of sovereign debt affecting countries such as Argentina, Greece, Venezuela, and Puerto Rico. Our volume imports insights from, and contributes to the body of research currently developed in the Humanities under the label 'colonial and postcolonial studies'. Scholars of postcolonial studies have claimed a 'neo-colonial' perspective on the post–Cold War international financial order (Amin, 2001; Shohat, 1992). Sovereign debt has been seen by others as a tool of 'imperialism after empire' (Robinson, 1984). Decades after the collapse of colonial empires, this volume assesses the merits and limits of neo-colonial frames on recent debt developments. As we do not want to raise the reader's expectations in relation to the charge of neo-colonialism, the available evidence sustains only modest support for this thesis. As we shall see, serious doubts can be raised regarding the capacity of international creditor to exert the sort of colonial control that nineteenth century debtor country experienced.

To summarize, this volume traces important changes in the ways debtors and creditors have managed sovereign debt disputes since the early nineteenth century. With our diplomatic perspective, our key objective is to identify regularities and departures in the practical responses that sovereign debt defaults have elicited from different actors across geographical and historical contexts.

Methodologically, our analysis of change is harnessed at the micro-level. Tracing two centuries of change in sovereign debt disputes warrants a meticulous inspection of 'small' decisions and local actors. Our diplomatic perspective is rooted at the micro-level, but it does not ignore the existence of institutional logics. Indeed, the unfolding and outcomes of sovereign debt disputes can be ascribed to broader institutional models and schemas that both enable and restrict the range of possible actions against recalcitrant debtors. We thus follow an 'institutionally embedded' view (Carruthers, 1996; Fligstein, 2002) to situate sovereign debt disputes against prevailing models and schemas that constrain agency. Key to this logic of embeddedness are not just hard (formal) rules or state-level policies and legislations but also softer institutional norms and legal frames promoted by international organizations, multilateral forums, and private actors (Abbott & Snydal, 2000; Graz & Nolke, 2007). These norms and frames provide cognitive stability for market participants and guide them into selecting their preferred options in a conflict over debt repayment. Nevertheless, institutions change. Change in diplomatic models of engagement can follow 'critical junctures' (Capoccia & Kelemen, 2007) like a war or a 'loud' event that make old models impracticable. In the parlance of Thomas Kuhn (1970), critical junctures are 'paradigmatic shifts', moment during which prior habits are breached and routine become unsettled. Such cases of change brought about by seismic events require actors to rebuild what has been destroyed and create new models of action.

How do we understand change in sovereign debt diplomacies? In new institutional theory, attempts to change or displace prevailing models are characterized as acts of 'institutional entrepreneurship' (DiMaggio, 1988; Seo & Creed, 2002). Institutional theory also suggests that how and why such entrepreneurial efforts succeed is not clear without a micro-perspective on the processes by which institutional entrepreneurs (e.g. lawyers, creditors, negotiating parties) mobilize interpretative resources and discourses to make comprehensible the desirability and relevance of change (Fligstein, 1997).[3] To summarize, our comparative-historical analysis of changes affecting institutional models of debt dispute resolution is harnessed at the micro-level.

Following these analytical and methodological premises, we have asked our team of contributors to consider the following research questions:

- Actors, instruments, and outcomes:
  Who are the key public and private actors involved in sovereign debt disputes? What methods and tactics of debt collection are deployed when contracts are breached? What is the outcome of such methods for both creditors and debtors? To answer these questions, we have directed our contributors to provide contextual information to explain why actors acted the way they did. We have also directed them to uncover, as far as possible, traces of doubts and hesitations in the negotiation stances favoured by debtors and creditors. The pay-off of this exercise is to suggest that sovereign debt disputes are diplomatic exchanges and that the resolution of debt disputes seldom proceed from the automatic application of rules.
- Patterns of historical change:
  Can we observe regularities and departures in the identity of negotiating actors and in the methods they use to remedy broken contracts? Are there any principles restricting the scope of legitimate methods of contractual enforcement? We have directed our contributors to pay close attention to individual agency, discourses and representations, local innovations, and, whenever possible, to document the processes by which local decisions became solidified into stable, models of debt dispute settlement. With this focus on local actors and decisions, we seek to avoid a teleological perspective on institutional change.
- Global asymmetries of power and colonial history:
  Can we identify colonial or imperial forms of agency in sovereign debt disputes? To what extent sovereign debt disputes reflect and reproduce global asymmetries of power between the developed world and the Global

[3] Such insights drawn from new-institutionalism are valuable to 'old' institutionalist approaches which tend to focus on institutional stability at the expense of institutional change, which they often have difficulty explaining. A nice synthesis of these theoretical debates is provided by Thelen (1999).

South? We have also asked contributors writing on more recent cases to elaborate on the relevance to use neo-colonial or hegemonic tropes to characterize recent cases of sovereign debt disputes. Some contributions address head on the narratives of colonial history and postcolonial developments. Others chose to engage with such narratives in more indirect ways or at a distance. But each volume contribution pushes the analysis forward in some way, drawing from different disciplines and historical periods.

To answer these questions, this volume examines a selection of episodes of debt disputes. Practical reasons motivate our choice to extract a sample of case studies, as it is of course impractical to chronicle in one volume the 296 external default episodes since 1800 listed in Reinhart & Rogoff (2009). And even if it were, such a panoramic approach would be ill-suited to the pursuit of our research goals. Our starting point has been to recognize that sovereign defaults are a perennial feature of sovereign borrowing. Based on this observation, the main objective with this volume is to survey meaningful regularities and changes in the management of sovereign debt dispute across different historical periods. To do so, we extracted several important cases of debt dispute from the four main clusters of sovereign defaults since 1820: nineteenth-century default episodes, interwar defaults, defaults arising from postcolonial transitions in the 1960s and 1970s, and post-1990s cases. Thinking in terms of historical clusters is helpful to capture meaningful similarities with regards to risk analysis, legal clauses, bargaining power, and conceptions of state responsibility, the four components of sovereign debt diplomacies. Our key objective here is to offer avenues of research forward to identify historical regularities and articulate a sense of unity in the long and messy history of sovereign debt disputes. A cluster-perspective is not only useful to think *synchronically* about how cases of debt dispute may 'rhyme' and present comparable features, it also provides a relevant method to recognize *diachronic* patterns of change with regards to the actors involved in debt disputes, their preferred methods of dispute resolution and the settlement outcomes. As will become clear in the following chapter, the analysis of defaults loses accuracy and precision when methods and tactics of dispute resolution are viewed ahistorically, without sufficient reference to the context of precedence and logics of path dependency between historical contexts.

References

Abbott, K. W. & Snidal, D. (2000). 'Hard and Soft Law in International Governance'. *International Organization*, 54(3), 421–56.

Amin, S. (2001). 'Imperialism and Globalization'. *Monthly Review*, 53(2), 6–24.

Bouvier, J., Girault, R. & Thobie, J. (1986). *L'impérialisme à la Française, 1914–1960,* Paris: La découverte.

Buchheit, L. C., Gulati, G. M. & Thompson, R. B. (2007). 'The Dilemma of Odious Debts'. *Duke Law Journal,* 56(5), 1201–62.

Capoccia, G. & Kelemen, R. D. (2007). 'The Study of Critical Junctures: Theory, Narrative, and Counterfactuals in Historical Institutionalism'. *World Politics,* 59(3), 341–69.

Carruthers, B. (1996). *City of Capital: Politics and Markets in the English Financial Revolution.* Princeton: Princeton University Press.

Coleman, P. J. (1999). *Debtors and Creditors in America: Insolvency, Imprisonment for Debt, and Bankruptcy, 1607–1900.* Washington, DC: Beard Books.

DiMaggio, P. J. (1988). 'Interest and Agency in Institutional Theory', in L. G. Zucker (Ed.), *Institutional Patterns and Organizations: Culture and Environment* (pp. 3–21). Cambridge: Ballinger.

Eichengreen, B. & Lindert, P. (1989). *The International Debt Crisis in Historical Perspective*: MIT Press.

Flandreau, M. (2006). 'Home Biases, Nineteenth Century Style'. *Journal of the European Economic Association,* 4(2–3), 634–43.

Flandreau, M. (2016). *Anthropologists in the Stock Exchange: A Financial History of Victorian Science.* Chicago: University of Chicago Press.

Fligstein, N. (1997). 'Social Skill and Institutional Theory'. *American Behavioral Scientist,* 40(4), 397–405.

Fligstein, N. (2002). *The Architecture of Markets: An Economic Sociology of Twenty-First-Century Capitalist Societies.* Princeton: Princeton University Press.

Goodhart, C. & Hudson, M. (2018). 'Could/Should Jubilee Debt Cancellations be Reintroduced Today?', *CEPR Discussion Paper No. DP12605.*

Graz, J.-C. & Nölke, A. (Eds.). (2007). *Transnational Private Governance and Its Limits.* London: Routledge.

Gulati, M. & Scott, R. E. (2012). *The Three and a Half Minute Transaction: Boilerplate and the Limits of Contract Design.* Chicago: University of Chicago Press.

Halliday, T. C. & Carruthers, B. G. (2009). *Bankrupt: Global Lawmaking and Systemic Financial Crisis.* Stanford: Stanford University Press.

Hobson, J. A. (1902). *Imperialism: A Study.* London: JNisbet.

Hudson, P. J. (2017). *Bankers and Empire: How Wall Street Colonized the Caribbean.* Chicago: University of Chicago Press.

Jochnick, C. & Preston, F. A. (2006). *Sovereign Debt at the Crossroads: Challenges and Proposals for Resolving the Third World Debt Crisis.* New York: Oxford University Press.

Keynes, J. M. (1937). 'The General Theory of Employment'. *The Quarterly Journal of Economics,* 51(2), 209–23.

Kolb, R. W. (2011). *Sovereign Debt: From Safety to Default.* Hoboken, N.J.: John Wiley & Sons.

Kuhn, T. S. (1970). *The Structure of Scientific Revolutions.* Chicago: University of Chicago Press.

Lenin, V. (1939). *Imperialism, the Highest Stage of Capitalism: A Popular Outline.* Rev. translation. Little Lenin Library. New York: International Publishers.

Lienau, O. (2014). *Rethinking Sovereign Debt: Debt and Reputation in the Twentieth Century.* Cambridge: Harvard University Press.

Mallard, G., & Sgard, J. (2016). *Contractual Knowledge: One Hundred Years of Legal Experimentation in Global Markets.* Cambridge: Cambridge University Press.

Mann, B. H. (2002). *Republic of Debtors.* Cambridge, MA: Harvard University Press.

March, J. G. & Simon, H. A. (1958). *Organizations.* Cambridge, MA: Wiley.

Obstfeld, M. & Rogoff, K. (2000). 'The Six Major Puzzles in International Macroeconomics: is There a Common Cause?' *NBER Macroeconomics Annual*, 15, 339–90.

Reinhart, C. M. & Rogoff, K. S. (2009). *This Time is Different: Eight Centuries of Financial Folly.* Princeton: Princeton University Press.

Robinson, R. (1984). 'Imperial Theory and the Question of Imperialism after Empire'. *The Journal of Imperial and Commonwealth History*, 12(2), 42–54.

Roos, J. E. (2019). *Why Not Default?: The Political Economy of Sovereign Debt.* Princeton: Princeton University Press.

Seo, M.-G. & Creed, W. D. (2002). 'Institutional Contradictions, Praxis, and Institutional Change: A Dialectical Perspective'. *Academy of Management Review*, 27(2), 222–47.

Setser, B. (2005). 'The Political Economy of the SDRM'. *IPD Task Force on Sovereign Debt.*

Shohat, E. (1992). 'Notes on the "Post-Colonial"'. *Social Text*, 31/32, 99–113.

Stiglitz, J. E. & Heymann, D. (2014). *Life after Debt: The Origins and Resolutions of Debt Crisis.* London: Palgrave Macmillan.

Thelen, K. (1999). 'Historical Institutionalism in Comparative Politics'. *Annual Review of Political Science*, 2(1), 369–404.

Tomz, M. (2007). *Reputation and International Cooperation. Sovereign Debt across Three Centuries.* Princeton: Princeton University Press.

Waibel, M. (2010). 'The Diplomatic Channel', in J. Crawford, A. Pellet (Eds.), *The Law of International Responsability* (pp. 1085–98). Oxford: Oxford University Press.

Waibel, M. (2011). *Sovereign Defaults before International Courts and Tribunals.* Cambridge: Cambridge University Press.

Weidemaier, M. C. (2010). 'Contracting for State Intervention: The Origins of Sovereign Debt Arbitration'. *Law and Contemporary Problems*, 73(4), 335–55.

1

Rethinking Sovereign Debt from Colonial Empires to Hegemony

Pierre Pénet and Juan Flores Zendejas

1.1 Imperial Solutions to Sovereign Debt Crises (1820–1933)

During the nineteenth century, free trade and financial integration contributed to what is often referred to as the first globalization wave (1820–1914) (Flandreau, 2013; Flandreau & Zumer, 2004; Mauro et al., 2006). As creditors began to expand the reach of their operations by investing in the bonds of foreign nations, sometime from overseas, lending became more perilous. For instance, British investors often knew little about the Latin American countries whose bonds they were purchasing.[1] Nineteenth-century cross-border lending exemplifies the problem of information asymmetries familiar to economists (Stiglitz, 2000). In this case, uncertainties were compounded by the fact that lenders in the sovereign sector could not mitigate default risk by collateralizing their loans: as a rule, ownership of public assets cannot be transferred to foreigners. To reduce the anxiety of long-distance investing, investors began to seek information pertaining to the trust and credit profile of foreign borrowers. Since investors did not always possess sufficient organizational capabilities and resources to examine the facts, risk analysis was delegated to intermediaries, in particular merchant banks. As informational third parties, merchant banks performed the important function of certifying the credit of debtors, thus providing a practicable solution to the problem of uncertainty in sovereign lending (Flandreau & Flores, 2009). Such banks owned a 'brand' that could grant borrowing states market access on more favourable terms. Gradually, the notion of creditworthiness became cardinal in international lending and borrowing.

Technologies of risk assessment played a cardinal role in the building of nineteenth-century debt markets (Carruthers, 2013). The tools of risk analysis which have become so ubiquitous recently can be traced back to the nineteenth

[1] The controversy about Poyais provides a good testimony of how difficult it was for creditors to invest abroad without reliable information to rely on. Poyais, as it turned out, was a fictitious country (Clavel, 2020).

Pierre Pénet and Juan Flores Zendejas, *Rethinking Sovereign Debt from Colonial Empires to Hegemony* In: *Sovereign Debt Diplomacies: Rethinking Sovereign Debt from Colonial Empires to Hegemony.* Edited by: Pierre Pénet and Juan Flores Zendejas, Oxford University Press (2021). © Oxford University Press. DOI: 10.1093/oso/9780198866350.003.0002

century (Gaillard, 2012). At first crude, rough, and quasi-intuitive, these tools were then made more complex by international organizations: the League of Nations during the interwar and then (after 1945) by Bretton Woods institutions like the IMF and the World Bank and bilateral aid agencies like USAID (Kelber & Monnet, 2014; Pauly & Ferran, 1997, pp. 67–8). Even the private rating agencies, which have assumed an ever-increasing role in country risk analysis since the 1980s (Sinclair, 2005), were founded at the turn of the last century (Pénet, 2019).[2]

Risk analysis equipped creditors and shaped their repayment expectations. At the same time, dynamics of trust and reputation also shaped countries' perceptions of what it meant to be sovereign. As measures of creditworthiness entered and disciplined the subjectivities of debtor countries, repaying debt became integral to how nations saw themselves as belonging in the realm of civilization. Prominent lawyers also came to view the non-repayment of debt as a violation of the civilizational standard (Borchard, 1951; Moore & Wharton, 1906). Such cultural and moral framing of state responsibility continues to remain pervasive in current debates.

However, creditworthiness alone was often not sufficient to discipline debtor states. To protect themselves against risks of default, nineteenth-century creditors organized themselves into bondholder committees. Such committees furnished creditors with their most efficient method against recalcitrant debtors. They derived their authority from their capacity to sponsor market access to preferred customers and to refuse to list new bonds from a creditor in default (Flandreau, 2013; Hautcoeur & Riva, 2012). Given the prominence of London as the main international financial centre, the most important of such committees was the British Corporation of Foreign Bondholders (CFB) (Mauro & Yafeh, 2003). Thereafter, other CFBs-type organizations emerged in other European financial centres. CFBs also advised debtors countries, offering them additional loans in exchange of the repayment of extant ones, thus developing early conditionality frameworks that were later refined by the IMF and World Bank (Babb & Carruthers, 2008).

In most cases, this mixture of market sanctions and moral suasion exerted on debtor states were quite effective. Countries avoided defaulting on their financial obligations for fear of losing market access. Tomz finds that CFBs raised significantly the costs of defaulting by making it virtually impossible for defaulters to raise new capital (Tomz, 2006, pp. 17–19). CFBs often managed to bring defaulters back to the table of negotiation, thereby securing comparatively positive results for investors, as compared to instances of debt disputes in which these organizations did not participate (Esteves, 2013). Disputes were also solved with the

[2] Moody's issued its first sovereign risk report in 1900 and its first rating of foreign government bonds in 1918. Poor's (in 1922), Standard Statistics, and Fitch (in 1924) also began rating a small number of sovereigns. In 1920, Moody's rated 189 foreign bonds and ten countries (Pénet, 2014, p. 73).

collaboration of major merchant banks, such as Baring or Rothschild, whose dominant position in London's sovereign debt market permitted them to promise market access to governments that acceded to renegotiate unpaid debts (Flandreau & Flores, 2012).

In light of the above, many historiographies of nineteenth-century debt markets conclude with the observation that the expansion of international capital flows generated adequate market solutions to the problem of information asymmetries. While not under-estimating the performance of market tools of debt dispute resolution, it is hard to miss that such solutions were not always satisfactory. When financial uncertainties overwhelmed market-based solutions, creditors were left with little alternative but to seize control over a defaulter's customs or tax collection system. Such forceful extraction of repayment could produce desired results more expediently than market-based solutions, but these required coercive tools like military power which only states possessed.

This volume provides a close examination of the essential role of creditor states in the building of modern sovereign debt markets. The nineteenth-century context, often lauded as the triumph of self-regulating markets, actually turns out to be radically different upon closer inspection. Karl Polanyi famously saw the nineteenth-century rise of international markets as the outcome of 'conscious and often violent intervention on the part of government which imposed the market organization on society for noneconomic ends' (Polanyi, [1944] 2001, p. 258). The fast expansion of international capital markets was an achievement in which the British government participated in no small part. First of all, the British administration supported the overseas operations of its financial sector. British diplomats provided bondholder committees with some degree of cooperation with respect to routine tasks. They also served as liaison in the country where they operated. Besides such brokerage function, the British government occasionally lent military support to private creditors against defaulters. Based on the above, we claim that it is nearly impossible to understand the nineteenth-century development of global debt markets without taking into account the cycles of asymmetries of power between nations, which sovereign debt disputes both reflected and reproduced. On the one hand, creditors from the North benefited awesomely from the colonial wars waged by their home states on their behalf. On the other, private capital was an essential cog in the exploitative and extractive system that supported the building and maintaining of colonial empires.

In this volume, we emphasize imperial aspects in the rise of sovereign debt markets in Latin America and the Eastern Mediterranean, two regions of the world which clearly illustrated the interlinkages between debt disputes and imperial practice. Two directions of research are explored. First, we identify sovereign debt as a powerful tool of colonial empire-building. In the nineteenth century, capital market expansion encouraged the creditors of industrialized countries to invest heavily abroad. This influx of foreign capital dangerously inflated the debt of peripheral countries, bringing them closer to insolvency. When default became a tangible threat, private creditors assisted by powerful states like Britain and France could resort to monetary and fiscal controls to ensure continuity in commercial and financial relations with countries mired into financial trouble. Scholars have used the concept of 'informal empire' (Hopkins, 1994; Knight, 2008) to characterize this imposition of foreign controls without territorial occupation (see Flores Zendejas & Cole in this volume). And in such cases that controls were insufficient, more punitive methods were available, such as the use of gunboats or the threatened use of them by imperial powers (Mitchener & Weidenmier, 2005). Two representative cases are Egypt and Tunisia, where the suspension of debt repayments provided justification for European powers to assert colonial control. Military invasion then led to full-fledged colonization (see Coşkun Tunçer in this volume). Colonial solutions to debt defaults led to new institutional relations with creditors, as colonial powers offered explicit imperial guarantees against private investment losses. Yet, colonial guarantees began to show signs of weakening after the First World War. For instance, in the 1930s, investors reassessed the likelihood that Britain, then facing financial turmoil, could honour its guarantee of Indian's debts (see Degive & Oosterlinck in this volume).

To be sure, such episodes of gunboat diplomacy were rather infrequent (Flores, 2012; Tomz, 2006, pp. 114–57).[3] States seldom intervened in debt disputes, performing only a passive, subsidiary role (Lipson, 1985). States were often reluctant to intervene to prevent moral hazard (Platt, 1968). For instance, the British government invoked on many occasions the so-called Palmerston doctrine—'When people choose to lend money to a foreign country, they [do] so at their own risk' (Williams, 1924, p. 18)—to deny state protection of private interests. This pledge of state neutrality was also reflected in US Secretary of State Bryan's dictum: 'When you go abroad you have to take your chances' (Howland, 1928, p. 183). Public protection of private capital was therefore flexible, as it laid entirely within the political discretion of government (Waibel, 2011, p. 23). While states seldom intervened in debt disputes, they could act as the sword arm of private creditors when they found political and diplomatic interest to do so, as Britain and France found in Egypt and Tunisia, respectively. Far from mechanical, creditor state support required a great deal of persuasion from bondholders. It is this particular form of state protection of private capital, which we call *imperial debt diplomacies*, that this volume emphasizes.

The other avenue of research concerns the nineteenth-century development of international law which was connected in important ways to state power and

[3] Between 1860 and 1913, we have computed forty-five defaults (to loans issued in London and Paris). Among them, ten led to some forms of foreign control, including colonial rule. Direct military interventions were exercised in only four cases (Mexico, Egypt, Tunisia, and Venezuela). Sources: Suter (1990), the Corporation of Foreign Bondholders Annual Reports, and Gleditsch (2004).

imperial policies. As international debt markets developed during the nineteenth century, important innovations took place in the world of debt contracting. Gradually, creditors inserted legal clauses in contracts to better define the duties of debtors, especially if repayment became contested (Flores Zendejas, 2016). Yet, in the nineteenth century, creditors had not yet forged the expectation that defaults could be adjudicated by an international court. The idea that extraterritorial courts could provide a relevant remedy to debt disputes was entirely foreign to the nineteenth-century investor. In fact, legal clauses did not open to litigation but served as a trigger to activate state power (Weidemaier, 2010). Up until 1914, creditors used legal discourses to convince their states to intervene on their behalf and force defaulters to repay their debt. Under such circumstances, we argue that the development of legal clauses was connected in important ways to imperial debt diplomacies.

1.2 Debt Disputes in the Age of Financial Repression: When Repayment Takes a Backseat (1933–70s)

The first financial globalization was brought to a close by the First World War and the Great Depression (James & James, 2009). The mechanisms that had bolstered international trade and capital flows during the nineteenth century were critically and durably weakened. During the war, the decline of international trade and capital flows eroded creditors' bargaining power. The threat to block a country's future debt issuances was persuasive only in a context of continuous sovereign debt borrowing. With the global retreat of external debt markets, debt issuances came to a halt and CFBs lost their dissuasive authority on defaulters (Jorgensen & Sachs, 1988). We also know from prior research that legal recourses like collective action clauses (CACs) or gold clauses did not perform as expected by creditors because the interwar context was too thinly legalized (Weidemaier, Gulati & Gelpern, 2016).

In the light of these constraints, creditor governments and market actors launched an effort to rebuild the international economic system around new actors and forums of debt dispute adjudication. The League of Nations was empowered with a public coordination role in the management of trade and debt disputes, thus filling the private role previously assumed by CFBs. The League intervened in 1923 to help Austria deal with its financial problems (Flores Zendejas & Decorzant, 2016). There, the League ensured repayment using methods previously used in the nineteenth century, assuming direct control over Austria's fiscal and monetary institutions. The League would apply the same receipt in other Eastern European countries. While this experience has met with relative success, the League was too fragile to bring coordination and stability to rapidly multiplying international debt disputes. Beginning in 1931, the majority of states had no alternative but to suspend interest payments on their foreign obligations. The economic consequences of the Great Depression combined with the rising political uncertainties in the years leading up to the Second World War would effectively postpone the negotiations between borrowers and bondholders to after 1945 (Eichengreen, 1991; Eichengreen & Portes, 1989). Even the countries which did not suspend repayment had to take protective measures. In 1933, in an effort to escape the Great Depression, Roosevelt announced plans to take the US off the gold standard and devalue the dollar. This decision, which involved cancelling all gold clauses inserted in past contracts, was widely interpreted by investors as a tacit form of debt repudiation (Edwards, 2018).

International debt markets did not return to pre-war levels until the 1980s, a period often characterized in the literature as the second financial globalization (Artis & Okubo, 2009; Bordo & Flandreau, 2003; Giddens, 2001). This period of transition between the first and the second globalization has not yet received the attention it deserves. In particular, while many economic historians and legal scholars have focused on the interwar years and the Great Depression in particular, the post-1945 context has remained largely unattended.[4] This is a pity because these three decades—otherwise known as the 'Glorious Thirty'—have witnessed the development of durable changes affecting creditor–debtor interactions in the sovereign sector, in particular with respect to conceptions of state responsibility and legal recourses (two components of sovereign debt diplomacies as highlighted in the introduction). With its focus on the post-war years, this volume extends the discussion on sovereign debt in two directions.

First, it examines important changes in the way sovereign debtors and creditors settled debt disputes in the turmoil of the post-1945 context. For debtors and creditors, the post-war settlement of debt disputes represented an enormous task not only because of the sheer amount of debt in default but also because old methods of debt settlement no longer applied. When the question of debt repayment resurfaced in 1945, capital markets were virtually shut down. In the face of uncooperative behaviour from defaulting and recalcitrant governments, the threat to block market access was no longer dissuasive. Having abandoned bond markets, states borrowed domestically or through public lending schemes such as Export Promotion Agencies or multilateral organizations. With CFBs in disarray, creditors sought diplomatic support from their government to remedy broken agreements. Yet, faced with the prospect of war (and after 1945 with the task of rebuilding the international order), powerful states (the US, the UK, and France) operated under a markedly different conception of state responsibility. Creditor states were not prepared to sponsor claims of debt repayment without

[4] Lienau (2014) is a notable exception.

considering as well other concerns such as peace, international trade, reparation, and the building of a new international order. In the 1940s and 1950s, the US, the UK, and France took steps to significantly reduced the foreign debts of Egypt, Mexico, Germany, and Japan—to name a few—sometimes resorting to unilateral actions that hurt the interests of private creditors (see Del Angel & Pérez-Hernàndez and De la Villa in this volume). Debt forbearance guided state action towards defaulters because debt had become a secondary concern to the most pressing issue of bolstering diplomatic and trade ties with foreign allies.

We call this new regime of sovereign debt disputes *interstate debt diplomacies* because the locus of debt talks shifted to the interstate level and dispute resolution became firmly anchored within the ambit of state authority. After 1945, the functional control over international enforcement of sovereign debt claims was effectively transferred from creditor committees to creditor states. As states became the contractual enforcers of private debt claims, debt acquired a public and diplomatic meaning. From assuming the role of protector of private capital and debt contracts during the long nineteenth century (until 1914), states came to assume an alternative role as debt relief provider during the Cold War period. In the hands of states as ultimate enforcers, bond contracts lost their universal validity because their value became contingent upon diplomatic recognition. As a result, the sanctity of debt contracts was durably undermined. Debt became one layer or tranche of interests in the bundle of interests (peace, commercial interests, etc.) which a state was prepared to defend during interstate negotiations. This observation did not apply only to the high-profile cases of Mexico and Germany (in the 1940s and 1950s, respectively) but to the majority of debt restructuring cases after the Second World War (see Flores Zendejas, Pénet & Suter in this volume).

It is an understatement to say that creditors did not appreciate states meddling into their affairs, especially when state involvement led to significant haircuts imposed on their claims. But creditors were left with no other choice than to seek the mediation of their governments to press their rights. Of course, when debtor states were cooperative, creditors could still rely on the mediation provided by bondholder committees to reach a settlement. In Japan, for instance, US and British creditors obtained the resumption of debt service at the full contractual rates. But when a defaulting state had neither the will nor the capacity to repay, foreign creditors depended ultimately on brokerage resources from their representative states.

The second contribution concerns the ambiguous development of international law in post-1945 debt disputes. The post-war era fathered new habits and modes of legal reasoning. After 1945, state support being mostly unavailable, creditors began to contemplate making international courts the prime enforcers of broken contracts. In other words, what creditors could no longer obtain through the diplomatic channel (and through imperial policies), they began to pursue through legal methods. Creditors began to raise the expectation—and we claim that this was a novel expectation—that they could elevate their claims to legal forums without the mediation of the creditor state. Although it is important to acknowledge that creditors raised new expectations that repayment could be pursued through legal means, it is also important to notice that this expectation was not immediately consequential. Debtor states being sovereign entities, international courts frequently denied jurisdiction. The 1950s dispute between French bondholders and Norway is interesting along those lines. When Norway refused to recognize the gold clause inserted into bond contracts, French creditors attempted to elevate debt claims against Norway to the International Court of Justice. But the Court was not receptive to French bondholders' claims because it deemed the dispute an interstate issue. The chance of successful legal action was limited under the principle of sovereign immunity which made it virtually impossible for bondholders to sue sovereign debtors.

The US legislative decisions to weaken the doctrine of sovereign immunity in the 1950s gave creditors a legitimate claim to bring a debtor state before a court of law. These decisions can be interpreted as a way to rebuild creditors' authority in the post-1945 context, when states' support to private creditors against defaulters grew weaker. In other words, we argue that twentieth-century development of international law was grafted onto the changing realities of state power, which were themselves linked to colonial history. We also suggest that the rising profile of international law in debt disputes was not a deliberate outcome sought by policymakers but rather an inadvertent outcome of states' attempts to solve other problems—among others, fostering national economic interests, international cooperation, and peacebuilding efforts during the Cold War and postcolonial context.[5]

1.3 Postcolonial Transitions and the Hopes for a New International Economic Order (1960s–80s)

The profile of international law was further enhanced during the postcolonial debt disputes of the 1960–70s. Postcolonial transitions gave rise to a new discourse in international public law, bringing into question the legitimacy and legality of sovereign debts contracted during the colonial times (Anghie, 2007, pp. 196–244; Mallard, 2019). Interestingly, the driving force of legal developments were actors from the South. In the 1960s, legal entrepreneurs from former colonies began to wage a battle to bring into the legal realm matters that were not previously deemed

[5] This contribution reads very much like Krippner's (2011) argument that states created conditions conducive to the rise of financial markets during the 1960–70s, although this shift was not deliberate but the inadvertent result of economic, social, and political dilemmas that confronted policymakers.

legal. In substance, their quest entailed making the debt claims of former colonial powers conditional upon broader legal matters such as the meaning of sovereignty and the responsibility of lenders. Postcolonial debates are fascinating because they reflect an effort to make international law a resource not for creditors but for countries facing problems of over-indebtedness. Today, legal recourses are often construed as contractual resources to protect creditors' claims against recalcitrant debtors. But historical developments remind us that international law was not always confined to being a tool of redress available to creditors. During postcolonial transitions, legal recourses were also construed as a resource to emancipate debtor countries from the chains of colonial debt.

To be sure, this fundamental ambiguity that lies at the very heart of Cold War legal debates is not new and goes back to the initial formulation of the doctrine of odious debts during the interwar. The starting point of every modern discussion of odious debt is the work of the Russian lawyer Alexander Sack. When Sack published his influential treatise on odious debt (Sack, 1927), the examples of debt repudiation seemed to increase at a dangerous rate with the dissolution of the Austro-Hungarian and Ottoman empires and the Bolshevik revolution of 1917. In these cases, the process of debt collection was compromised because the states that had contracted the debts had ceased to exist. As a rule, Sack did not oppose the norm of repayment, as he endorsed the idea that debts were binding legal contracts and therefore had to be repaid. But his great innovation was to claim that certain debts should be treated differently from others, based on their origins and purpose (King, 2016; Pénet, 2018b).

The debate on odious debt resumed during the 1960–70s against the backdrop of the fall of colonial empires. Integral to what we call *postcolonial debt diplomacies* are the efforts from lawyers in debtor countries to weaponize international law on behalf of former colonies in order to place legal limits on the continuity of debt contracts. Mohamed Bedjaoui's effort to establish a Convention on the law of State Succession in respect to State Property, Archives and Debts was a central aspect in this debate (see Mallard & Waibel in this volume). Although his Convention (signed in 1983) has not yet been ratified, it would be misleading to judge Bedjaoui's legacy as one of failure. His influence on current debates is probably stronger than what we can assume if we take ratification as the main criterion of success. In fact, Bedjaoui's attempt to establish a 'New International Economic Order', was a source of inspiration for UNCTAD policies and it can be credited with having substantially influenced development economists and debt campaign movements in the 1960s–70s before it became the subject of countervailing measures (see Deforge & Lemoine in this volume). Even more, the principle of non-transmissibility of state debt pioneered in late nineteenth-century Latin America (see Flores Zendejas & Cole in this volume) and refined during postcolonial transitions (see Mallard and Waibel in this volume) is now available to the legal public as a recourse in present and future debt debates (see Gulati & Panizza in this volume).

1.4 Post-Cold War Sovereign Debt Disputes: Hegemony or Fragmentation?

The breakdown of Bretton Woods capital controls in 1971 and the ensuing deregulation of financial markets in the 1980s contributed to restore a lively sovereign debt market. Syndicated banking grew during the 1970s and soon government loans returned to pre-1914 levels. These trends converging in early 1980s are often referred to as the second era of globalization (Artis & Okubo, 2009; Bordo & Flandreau, 2003; Giddens, 2001). The initial momentum of financial liberalization accelerated with the widespread policy shift towards deregulation, as epitomized by the variety of changes in the law that both the Thatcher and Reagan administrations promoted in Great Britain and the United States, respectively (Boyer, 1996; Helleiner, 1996; Loriaux, 1997). With the loosening up of some key New Deal and post-war financial regulations, market actors gained greater freedom in their financial operations. Of course, political factors were instrumental to create these new investment opportunities, but they are insufficient to explain how creditors turned these opportunities into actual investment decisions.

Consistent with our focus on sovereign debt diplomacies, this volume concentrates on actual investment practices as defined in the interface between two orders: practical expectations about repayment and normative models about the meaning of sovereignty and debt and the limits placed on the continuity of debt contracts. The diplomatic action of creditors and debtors during the post-1980s context involves elements of change and continuity from the previous three regimes in several aspects.

The first aspect concerns risk analysis, the first component of sovereign debt diplomacies. Financial deregulation encouraged the multiplication of new entrants seeking access to capital markets. The opportunities associated with deregulation generated a significant increase in borrower diversity. Sovereign borrowers with poor or no credit history gained market access and began to raise capital by selling securities. The revival of external debt markets brought about uncertainties typical of investment decisions made at a distance. While deregulation and internationalization allowed investors to enter into new financial territories and capture highly lucrative investment opportunities, the prospect of making investment decisions overseas generated new financial uncertainties. It was thus crucial for lenders to turn the uncertainties that the breakdown of capital controls and the ensuing liberalization of capital markets had opened up into calculable risk and, therefore, actual investment opportunities (Eaton & Gersovitz, 1981; Eaton, Gersovitz & Stiglitz, 1986). This pattern of deregulation and internationalization increased the propensity of market actors to use credit ratings in investment decisions (Sinclair, 2005). During the 1980s, credit rating agencies (CRAs) became pivotal knowledge intermediaries for lending and borrowing transactions. The number of countries seeking a rating to access international capital markets grew exponentially from a mere fifteen in 1980 to over a hundred in 1998 (Pénet, 2014, p. 146).

The second aspect—and perhaps the most debated one in recent debt studies—concerns the increasing legalization of sovereign debt markets. The Foreign Sovereign Immunities Act of 1976 gave a more restrictive interpretation of the principles protecting sovereign debtors and allowed debtors to sue a foreign government in US courts (Brownlie, 2003, p. 325). The US repeal of sovereign debt immunity provided impetus for debtor litigation and arbitration as means to sanction recalcitrant borrowers (Buchheit, 1995). Since the 1970s, the legal tools governing the management and repayment of public debt have grown more diverse and sophisticated. Creditors and third parties (e.g., courts, communities of experts, international organizations, central banks) have invested considerable efforts and resources to design mechanisms of enforcement and sanctions. This was expected to improve the continuity in debt repayment or, at the least, allow sovereign defaults to occur in a somewhat orderly fashion. Yet, despite these efforts, there is no conclusive evidence that countries end up repaying their debt in full and in time any more than before. Far from adding more certainty and predictability into the financial world, the increasing legalization of sovereign debt markets has been credited with generating additional financial uncertainties. Studies in law and society have noted that international law is not nearly as triumphant as it is usually felt. Not only litigation delays the resolution process (Trebesch, 2008) but it also weakens the prospect of effective resolution (Bi, Chamon & Zettelmeyer, 2011; Krueger, 2002). Another recent development is arbitration, in particular the initiative to take a defaulting country before the International Centre for Settlement of Investment Disputes (ICSID). This legal option has also yet to produce the desired results (Waibel, 2007). This is not to say that international law is not consequential in sovereign debt. But its function in the stabilization of creditor–debtor interactions is ambiguous—some would say more wish than reality.

The third defining feature concerns the multilateral tools and forums that creditors use to increase coordination and press for repayment. Central to the management of post-1980s debt disputes is the International Monetary Fund's (the IMF or 'the Fund') conditionality framework. When a country is unable to service its debt, it can turn to the Fund for loans, provided that its debt is deemed sustainable by IMF experts. Conditionality is the activity of making the provision of financial resources contingent on a set of policy conditions that the recipient country must consent before aid disbursement (Flores Zendejas, 2016). UNCTAD, the Paris Club, the World Bank, regional development banks, and bilateral organizations also use conditionality frameworks in their country financing operations (Babb & Carruthers, 2008). At the IMF, conditionality-setting is typically understood by sociologists and political scientists as an 'epistemic' activity, shaped by internal experts and their belief systems and ideational filters (Clift, 2018; Nelson, 2017). A useful counterpoint to this epistemic approach comes from studies showing the prevalence of state interests in the IO system (Kentikelenis & Seabrooke, 2017; Knill, Bayerlein, Enkler & Grohs, 2018). From the 1980s onward, powerful shareholders like the US and Europe traditionally seek to influence IMF's programmes in terms of their own political, geopolitical, or even military interests (Stone, 2002). Multilateral forums such as the IMF work as a strong vehicle of state interests (Abbott & Snidal, 1998; Pénet, 2018a; Strange, 1996). And in many cases, states act through international organization to help private creditors recover their loans. The role of international organizations in sovereign debt disputes has turned controversial since the Argentinian crisis of the early 2000s. Organizations like UNCTAD have criticized the heavy social and economic costs that IMF arrangements often impose on debtor countries. As suggested in this volume, these critiques are reminiscent of debates which arose during postcolonial transitions about the mandate of international organizations and their responsibility to bring about an international financial order more representative of the economic interests of the developing world.

The last aspect concerns the perceptions of sovereign debt problems by powerful states. After the end of the Cold War, solving private debt crises was no longer a preferred way to make allies because there was no global enemy left. After the demise of the Soviet Union, Western states ceased to defend the interest of debtor nations as a way to bolster their diplomatic standing. In the past two decades, sovereign debt has remained a state-to-state exchange only on rare occasions, for instance, China's lending in Africa or Russia's lending in Venezuela. That said, Western states did not quite assume a passive and subsidiary role in debt disputes. Since the 1980s, states have reverted to their nineteenth-century role of protectors of private capital (Abdelal, 2007), offering their mediation to help banks remedy broken contracts.

So where does that leave us? To some, the current regime is a direct continuation of imperial practices (Amin, 2001; Toussaint, 1999). While sovereign debt remains a binding mechanism that can result in the subjugation of debtor states to their creditors, we claim, however, that the current context is only superficially similar to what we call imperial debt diplomacies. State actions no longer entail the use of military tools like gunboats against defaulters. Gunboats have disappeared, and violence is no longer an acceptable means of recovering debt. In our view, this is sufficient to justify distinguishing the current predicament of sovereign debt from the imperial debt diplomacies that prevailed in the nineteenth century. Nonetheless, the current context is uniquely unforgiving of irregularities of debt repayment, a feature that contrasts strongly with the interstate (1933–1970s) and postcolonial (1960s–80s) regimes of debt diplomacies.

To characterize the post-1980s context, we prefer an alternative narrative that borrows from classical as well as more recent studies of financial hegemony

(Kindleberger, 1986; Strange, 1987; Yeates, 2002). The frame of hegemony builds on the observation that creditors continue to exert tremendous power on debtor states through indebtedness. But the means of coercion have changed to a significant extent. Debt repayment mobilizes multilateral organizations like the IMF, the World Bank, and the Paris Club, whose practices of conditionality are hard to resist, even by Western countries, such as Greece recently (Pénet, 2018a). Hegemonic norms and rules of financial exchange may appear softer and more respectful of the sovereignty of debtor countries than colonial tools of debt dispute. But they are not less consequential. In many ways, one can observe that the former has a universal reach which no colonial empire (for instance the British Empire before 1914) ever had before. Structural adjustment policies, austerity programmes, and privatization plans have been likened to the 'Washington consensus' (Williamson, 1990). But in reality, these prescriptions enjoy universal appeal well beyond US policies. The requirements of austerity, privatization, and liberalization have become integral to the world consensus about how to manage fiscal policies from Africa to South America and East Asia (Bear, 2015; Stiglitz, 2002). Even more, these requirements rank as axiomatic in Europe, as was evidenced in the terms and conditions that the European Commission and European Central Bank imposed on southern European countries during the European debt crisis (Blyth, 2013; Dyson, 2014).

The three essential features of what we call *hegemonic debt diplomacies* are deterritorialization, universality, and uniformity. The current regime is deterritorialized because diplomatic involvement in debt disputes no longer reflects the preference of a territorial centrality, be it a powerful state or a capital (e.g., London, Paris, Washington). Unlike previous regimes, the current regime appears more universal in reach. The British Empire was immense and Britain the only nation to ascend to truly global power. But it was not quite hegemonic insofar as there was a strong competitor, the French Empire, and that it did not encompass important regions of the globe like China and Japan. The US ascendance to global power after 1945 was not any more universal. During the Cold War, the Soviet Union kept exclusive economic ties with its satellite states and other regions of the world such as India and Northern Africa. The expansion of Western capital markets also excluded the People's Republic of China and its sphere of influence in Asia. And recall that, until the 1980s, the New International Economic Order initiative (NIEO) led by Third World countries entertained the promise that a counter-model for the organization of global financial affairs was possible. But the NIEO did not survive the rise of Washington Consensus policies in the 1980s and 1990s.

The current regime is also unprecedented in terms of its uniformity. Today, borrowing nations are beholden to market forces in a way not seen in the post-war years (Boyer & Drache, 2005). Debtor–creditor relationships are anchored in global metrics of performance and indicators of good governance (Davis, Fisher, Kingsbury & Merry, 2012; Ralph, 2015). Private credit ratings offer a good example of 'governance by indicators' with respect to financial and investment decisions (Pénet & Mallard, 2014). Such deterritorialized tools and norms have contributed to naturalize market discipline and creditors' expectations of repayment (Arewa et al., 2018; Lemoine, 2016). Be it the IMF, the US Federal Reserve, the Eurozone financial institutions, or even the globalized elites from the Global South, the baseline expectation is that debt must be repaid, no matter the costs.

Despite this disagreement over the neo-colonial character of current sovereign debt markets, we wish to emphasize several methodological affinities with post-colonial studies. Our colonial perspective on sovereign debt and, in particular, the 'history from below' approach that many volume contributors have adopted resonates with the work of de Sousa Santos & Rodríguez-Garavito (2005) and Jaffe (2015). This approach is key to understand the paradox whereby the economic elites of formerly Third World nations have come to accept, and even in some cases, promoted conservative policies of international debt management. Understanding how and why debtor countries gave their assent to structural adjustment policies, austerity programmes and privatization plans are instrumental to better understanding how the current hegemonic regime of sovereign debt disputes came into being and how it is reproduced. With a focus on subaltern agency (Spivak, 1988), this volume usefully complements the traditional elite perspective on financial imperialism favoured by the Cambridge school of empire history and by many scholars in the globalization studies.

This volume also identifies important cracks in the current sovereign debt regime. Hegemonic debt diplomacies have not erased 'global legal pluralism' or the 'distinctive institutional and normative characteristics which shape the production implementation and enforcement of rules' (Snyder, 1999, p. 372). First, the constraints imposed on debtor countries by international organizations and market actors have produced contestation, resistance, and opposition (Yeates, 2002). Creditor states and large investors themselves have recently showed signs of exasperation at the legalistic behaviour adopted by vulture funds in debt disputes. In Europe, new anti-vulture funds legislations represent an important step forward in the regulation of opportunistic behaviour created by the legalization of sovereign debt (see Datz in this volume). The adoption of bail-in rules following the 2008 crisis are another example. We suggest that these new developments require additional research.

The return of the legal doctrine of odious debt is another important development that warrants closer scrutiny in research. Since the legal treatise published by Alexander Sack (1927), the term broadly refers to the debts of a nation incurred against the interests of its population. Debts are odious and should not be repaid when they were incurred by irregular regimes and for improper uses (King, 2016). Odious debt has made a spectacular comeback in the international conversation about Venezuelan debt (see Gulati & Panizza in this volume). The legal doctrine has been used to admonish the decision of US creditors to lend to the Maduro government. The scope and application criteria of odious debt have elicited considerable interest and debate among academic and civil society circles in recent years (Nehru & Thomas, 2009). Some are calling for a broader and more flexible doctrine in recognition of the fact that most states currently burdened with crushing debt are democratic states (Pénet, 2018b). This lively debate on odious debt, and more broadly, on the problem of debt repayment, testifies to the fact that the universal sanctity and validity of debt contracts remains a contested subject in the current sovereign debt regime.

Overall, the current development of international law is more ambiguous than it seems if we consider that political actors retain significant authority to impose limits on creditors' uncompromising and legalistic behaviour in negotiations over broken contracts. Furthermore, another source of ambiguity lies in the identification of the beneficiaries of the growing legalization of sovereign debt. We argue in this volume that investors and bondholders are not the only actors benefiting from such legalization. As evidence in the recent discussions surrounding odious debt, international law is a development that may also benefit debtors, since it limits creditors' claims against politically unsettled countries. The same applies to legal clauses which not only benefit creditors (who use them to enhance their expectations of repayment) but also debtors, in particular the 'quasi-sovereign' states which can find legal clauses a source of stability during times of uncertainty (see Chari and Leary in this volume).

1.5 Organization of the Volume

This volume is organized into four sections, each one analysing a cluster of sovereign debt disputes according to a mode diplomatic involvement: the nineteenth-century default episodes (imperial debt diplomacies), the interwar wave of defaults (interstate debt diplomacies), defaults arising from postcolonial transitions in the 1960s–70s (postcolonial debt diplomacies), and post-1980s cases (hegemonic debt diplomacies). This chronological organization is meant to display contextual similarities and variations in sovereign debt diplomacies and highlight logics of path dependency between contexts. Some volume contributions offer a thick analysis of a single case of sovereign debt dispute while others survey a larger number of cases. As we explain below, the selected cases were chosen on the basis of their representativeness in the period concerned.

Imperial Debt Diplomacies (1820–1933)

The first section unpacks the nineteenth-century relationships between sovereign debt markets and colonial history. This section covers several prominent cases of debt default which prompted imperial powers to expand and consolidate colonial rule. Scholars in the colonial and postcolonial studies have typically assessed the building of empires in the broader political context of civilizing missions and their consequences on people, bodies, and cultures (Conklin, 1997; Cooper & Stoler, 1997). The first section of this volume complements these studies by surveying financial drivers to empire-building projects.

The first two chapters by Flores Zendejas and Cole and by Coşkun Tunçer compare the imperial responses to sovereign debt defaults and their effects on defaulters in Latin America and the Mediterranean region. Drawing on archival data, Flores Zendejas and Cole (chapter 2) attempt a broad survey of the role of Britain and private intermediaries in controlling and limiting the sovereignty of Latin American nations during the first globalization wave beginning in 1820. Following an 'informal empire' perspective, they show that British merchant banks played the central role as mediators and arbitrators between defaulting states and international creditors. The originality of this chapter is to survey the development of new legal methods of contractual enforcement pioneered by European states and creditors such as the use of diplomatic conventions for debt repayment or the adoption of direct contracting, a kind of settlement in which the holders of defaulting bonds could obtain physical assets and shares of companies in the services or transportation sectors. Flores Zendejas and Cole suggest that while prior debt dispute cases were often considered on a case-by-case basis, it was in late nineteenth century that European states (in particular Britain) and Latin American debtor states codified for the first time legal templates for the resolution of disputes over broken contracts.

Ultimately, Flores Zendejas and Cole show that Latin American debt disputes were seldom accompanied by armed interventions. Because of geographical distance and the (relative) absence of European geopolitical interests in Latin America, European states mostly refrained from military intervention and limited bondholder support to the diplomatic arena. Only on rare occasions—France and England in Mexico (1862) and Britain, Germany, and Italy in Venezuela (1902)—did European States use the military force against defaulting countries. But they show that these episodes were primarily motivated by geopolitical interests and territorial disputes and only remotely concerned with debt collection. These interventions produced important debates among European and Latin American jurists about the legality of such military interventions and the applicability of legal remedies to prevent them. These debates did not prevent further foreign interventions, this time by the US in Central America in the early twentieth century, but they are valuable to study in this volume because they would later serve as focal points in twentieth century debates about sovereign debt.

In chapter 3, Coşkun Tunçer compares the process of debt build-up, default, and establishment of colonial rule in Egypt and Tunisia. There, defaults led to military interventions and territorial conquests by the dominant powers—the

French in Tunisia and British in Egypt. Drawing on archival data, he argues that the building of colonial rule was a gradual process. The first stage in the process involved bondholder committees' attempts to impose fiscal controls on defaulting nations and force extraction of repayment. But financial controls were not an efficient method because of local opposition to harsh tax. Such attempts often being unsuccessful, bondholders would then, in a second stage, ask their governments for support. Coşkun Tunçer's analysis of governmental responses to creditors' requests for assistance therefore complicates how we understand nineteenth-century colonial expansion in the Eastern Mediterranean. In particular, he shows that British and French colonial expansion in Egypt and Tunisia did not follow a preconceived plan. Instead, territorial expansion was the outcome of a series of contingent decisions and local improvisations.

While the first two contributions examine debt as an empire-building instrument, chapter 4 concentrates on the weakening effects of imperialism on government debt markets during the interwar years, using India and Australia as cases in point. Degive and Oosterlinck's main objective is to test the 'empire effect', i.e., the impact of colonial status on borrowing costs. The literature on empire effects has yet to produce a consensus as to how and whether colonial status affects borrowing costs. For some, membership to the British Empire led to privileged capital market access and lower borrowing costs, partly due to an implicit imperial guarantee to the loans issued by the colonial governments (Accominotti, Flandreau & Rezzik, 2011). The empirical evidence remains controversial, in part because studies have focused exclusively on the nineteenth century. Oosterlinck and Degive innovate by adopting an interwar perspective on empire effects. The interwar context is valuable because colonial guarantors faced their own sets of economic difficulties and because the rise of independence movements in the colonies made a default a real possibility, thus undermining the strength of the colonial guarantee and shifting foreign investors' perceptions of the creditworthiness of colonized territories.

Their main finding is that the British colonial rule offered a guarantee against high borrowing costs, albeit this function was not uniform across countries. Investors developed rival interpretations about the credibility of the colonial guarantee. Oosterlinck and Degive hint at two understandings of the British colonial guarantee: *protection against repudiation* in India and *protection against economic default* in Australia. To understand these differences, the authors depart from a conventional understanding of investors' behaviour as shaped primarily by tools of risk analysis and legal clauses. They show that these differences were patterned onto the political and diplomatic realities of British Empire in the two countries. In India, investors were less concerned about the colony's ability to pay than about the threat of independence and political repudiation, which became credible in the 1930s. In Australia, prices reflected the country's own macroeconomic fragilities. The coexistence of different pricing rationalities within the

British Empire is a fascinating finding that revisits how we understand the complex financial realities within the British Empire. Ultimately, the notion of implicit guarantee and the various interpretations that it produces suggests that, from the British Empire to the Eurozone debt crisis, the role of the official sector as protector of private capital has always elicited competing understandings.

Interstate Debt Diplomacies (1933–70s)

The three chapters in this section examine important changes in the way sovereign debtors and creditors settled debt disputes in the turmoil of the Second World War and in the post-war context. Our assessment of post-war debt diplomacies concentrates on the context immediately preceding and following the war, a crucial period in the history of sovereign debt which is often neglected by historians.[6] The post-war context provides empirical illustration of the claim made by Lienau (2014) that the norm of debt repayment is politically and historically variable. The three chapters show that the sanctity of debt contracts varies according to the identity of the agent charged with conducting debt talks. So long as private creditors were the main negotiator agents, debt talks were strictly restricted to one background expectation: repayment. But as states began to assume a more explicit role as enforcer of debt contracts after the Great Depression, negotiating on behalf of their domestic bondholders, debt acquired a broader public and diplomatic meaning. Creditor states did not give consideration to debt repayment without considering as well other concerns such as peace, trade, reparation, and the building of a new international order. As a result, the sanctity of debt contracts was durably undermined. No longer universal, the value of debt claims became contingent upon creditor states' recognition.

Chapters 5 and 6 trace two cases of interstate debt diplomacies. Del Angel and Pérez-Hernández focus on the little-known Mexico debt agreement of 1942 and De la Villa revisits the 1953 London Debt Agreement on German Debts (LDA). The German and Mexican cases stand out from the rest of dispute settlements of that time because their debt overhang was restructured in a unitary fashion.[7] In chapter 5, Del Angel and Pérez-Hernández examine the conditions that allowed a resolution so favourable to a government that had been negotiating for decades with creditors without success. The originality of this chapter is to provide the

[6] The early interwar period and, in particular, the question of German reparations, is not covered in this volume. But the legacy of interwar problems is visible in our analysis of post-war debt disputes. For instance, the spirit of forbearance that prevailed at the London Conference on German debts can be explained in part by the concern shared by creditors not to repeat the mistakes of the Versailles Treaty, which Germans regarded as a national humiliation.

[7] In comparison, the restructuration of Japanese debt led to separate agreements with US, British, and French bondholders. As for the defaulted debts of Russia and China, they would not be addressed until the end of the twentieth century.

perspective of the Mexican debtor. Previous literature has emphasized the US government's strategic interest to forbear Mexican debt as the main driver behind decisions to cancel Mexican debt (Borchard, 1951). This externalist reading gives President Roosevelt the leading role: it was he who coerced US creditors into accepting major losses in order to build strong diplomatic and commercial interests with Mexico. While this political argument is essential, it provides only a partial explanation. More problematic in this story is that Mexico is often featured on the receiving end of decisions taken in Washington. In contrast, Del Angel and Pérez-Hernández follow an internalist 'state capacity' argument that recalls the perspective pioneered by Skocpol and Finegold (1982). They observe that since the onset of the Mexican Revolution, the government of Mexico was weak and therefore lacked international credibility to remedy its long and problematic history with US creditors. Important changes in leadership at the Ministry of Finance in the 1930s improved the negotiation position of Mexico. In particular, he highlights the role of the Mexican elite and business groups in placing debt negotiations in a broader set of bilateral negotiations, including the signature of trade agreements and the thorny question of state compensation for expropriations of US citizens and nationalization of oil companies during the Mexican revolution. This grand bargain proposed by Mexican elites played a major role in the normalization of Mexico–US bilateral relationships.

Germany was another prominent case of debt forbearance. In chapter 6, De la Villa shows that creditor states enforced a 'principle-based' approach in their restructuration of German debt. The three principles that facilitated the outcome of the LDA were: 1) capacity to repay, 2) equality of treatment, and 3) majority acceptance. The main innovation of the LDA, she suggests, was to prioritize the economic recovery of Germany over creditors' claims of repayment. De la Villa argues that these principles should not be equated with plain and simple discretionary politics. To be sure, the negotiations between Germany and foreign creditors took place under Allied control and according to the principles settled by foreign powers. But creditors were not entirely passive. They were, in fact, an important contributing force in shaping the outcome of the LDA. This is an interesting claim given that much of the literature on debt disputes has been attracted either by the figure of the inflexible creditor (claiming that debt must be repaid in time and in full) or that of the rogue state (evading their legal obligations). De la Villa identifies in the LDA a peculiar equilibrium where creditors and states were willing to meet each other halfway between full repayment and default. To the current observer, it is quite amazing to observe that creditors were willing to settle for less, without even putting up a legal fight. Having lost most of their bargaining power, private creditors were ready to accept losses on their investments that most current creditors (think, for instance, German creditors to Greece) would deem unacceptable. Therefore, the German case evidences an important fact about the norm debt repayment: far from being stable and inevitable, the debt continuity norm is inherently political and historically variable.

One may legitimately ask whether the experience of Mexico and Germany can find generalization in the post–Second World War context. Drawing on archival data collected on a broad sample of high-profile cases of debt restructuring, Flores Zendejas, Pénet, and Suter show in chapter 7 that, as states gradually became the contractual enforcers of private debt claims after the Second World War, debt contracts 'took the backseat' to other concerns perceived as more important such as peace, trade, reparation, and the building of a new international order. For major powers like the US, France, and Britain, the resumption of international trade—rather than the resumption of capital markets—was seen as the essential objective of debt negotiations. Thus, the unpaid debt that remained from the 1930s wave of defaults lost strategic relevance in the eyes of financial powers. This new order of priority enhanced the bargaining power of defaulters and weakened the position of bondholders. Under this new conception of state responsibility which emphasized the rebuilding of the international order, the previous relationship between sovereign debt and imperialism also vanished.

Additionally, Flores Zendejas, Pénet, and Suter show how private creditors sought to challenge the outcome of interstate debt disputes, notably in relation to equality of treatment between creditors. They emphasize several cases of creditors attempting to elevate debt disputes to international legal forums. Although such attempts failed, they are significant because they foreshadow many aspects and problems in the current debate about debt dispute adjudication. Finally, the authors assess the efficiency of interstate tools of debt settlements against metrics of performance. They find that interstate diplomacies resulted in longer periods of debt negotiations and higher losses for bondholders than during the previous financial periods.

Overall, this interstate regime of debt diplomacy accounts for an intermediate phase in the history of sovereign debt disputes between what we called imperial debt diplomacies and the post-1980s period of hegemonic debt diplomacies. The post-war context was marked by the role of states in limiting the bargaining power of creditors and creditors' lower expectations of repayment. The repayment difficulties facing creditors continued throughout the postcolonial transitions of the 1960–70s when the contractual claims contracted during colonial times became contested with the breakdown of European empires.

Postcolonial Debt Diplomacies (1960s–80s)

The entangled histories of sovereign debt and colonialism returned to the surface during the breakdown of colonial empires, when the continuity in debt repayment became a controversial issue. Postcolonial transitions raised the issue of debt continuity in the context of state succession. Postcolonial transitions pointed to a difficult trade-off for newly independent states: if they repaid their debt, self-determination could run the risk of becoming de facto illusory because these states would be burdened with unsustainable debt. At the same time, for these newly independent states, paying off debt was a prerequisite for being recognized by the international community and gaining capital market access. This trade-off between de facto and *de jure* sovereignty was implicit in the legal debate on state succession that opened in the 1960s.

Chapters 8 and 9 by Mallard and Waibel can be read in tandem. They show that postcolonial transitions gave rise to a new discourse in international public law on the legitimacy and legality of sovereign debts contracted during colonial times. The legal debate was polarized into two positions embodied by Daniel Patrick O'Connell and Mohammed Bedjaoui, the two foremost scholars on the law of state succession. Mallard and Waibel trace the intellectual trajectories of Bedjaoui and O'Connell, respectively, highlighting their theoretical contributions to legal philosophies on state succession and, more broadly, how postcolonial transitions affected the historical developments of the legal profession.

In chapter 8, Mallard concentrates on Mohamed Bedjaoui, whose work at the International Law Commission (ILC) had a major influence on legal philosophies of state succession. An Algerian legal scholar trained in France, Bedjaoui was also a member of the Provisional Government of the Algerian Republic during the War of Independence. At the ILC (1965–82), Bedjaoui was tasked with identifying existing trends in state succession and the issues it raised in matters of public property, archives, and debts. Bedjaoui, perceiving that extant international laws had been written by former metropolises to protect their economic interests in the postcolonial era, set to work on a convention. Bedjaoui endorsed the idea that the colonizer's obligations are extinguished on independence. This 'clean slate' theory (in the words of Waibel) provides that no state debt of the predecessor state shall pass to the successor state, unless an agreement between the newly independent state and the predecessor state provides otherwise.

Waibel's contribution on Daniel Patrick O'Connell (chapter 9) usefully complements Mallard's study. If Bedjaoui was a proponent of clean slate theory, O'Connell (trained in the UK and Chichele Professor of International Law at Oxford University) was a foremost proponent of the 'equitable doctrine' holding that creditors retain 'acquired rights' that allow them to claim compensation for debts incurred by predecessor governments. This doctrinal conflict between Bedjaoui and O'Connell reflected larger political interests and asymmetries of power between the North and the South. Mallard and Waibel provide a detailed description of the rivalry between these two approaches, and, through them, the competition between *people* (networks of lawyers) and *places* (the particular forums where doctrines were elaborated).

While Mallard and Waibel work from a history of ideas perspective, their contribution is valuable to this volume because they are also interested in the international diffusion of legal ideas and their impact on actual negotiation practices. At first glance, Bedjaoui and O'Connell do not seem to have made a lasting impact in the legal world. The main outcome of Bedjaoui's legal activism was the 1983 Vienna Convention on the Succession of States in Respect of State Property, Archives and Debts. This Convention has neither attracted broad state participation nor has it had a major impact on subsequent state practice. O'Connell's equitable doctrine also failed to become part of customary international law. Waibel reflects on the problem of failure and asks: who has an interest in the absence of a legally ratified convention on colonial debts? This is a key question whose relevance extends to the recent failed IMF proposal (Krueger, 2002) to establish a sovereign debt restructuring mechanism (SDRM). As Waibel suggests, the crux of the matter is deceptively simple but crucial to recall: state practice is tangled, conflicted, and, as such, it resists codification. In light of the complexity of the problems involved with state succession, the solutions adopted have so far remained highly case specific.

The legacy of Bedjaoui and O'Connell is deeply ambiguous, as their proposals were not codified into hard, legal principles of international debt restructuration (although it should be noted that Bedjaoui had a direct influence on the debt dispute between Algeria and France). Yet, it would be misleading to judge their legacy as one of failure. Their influence on current debates is probably stronger than what we can assume if we take ratification as the main criterion of success. Deforge and Lemoine (chapter 10) show that the legal innovations arising from postcolonial transitions, in particular Bedjaoui's attempt to establish a 'New International Economic Order', deeply influenced the United Nations Conference on Trade and Development (UNCTAD), the Geneva-based organization founded in 1964 and whose history is closely linked to the history of postcolonial transitions. Bedjaoui's work was a source of inspiration for UNCTAD policies and it can be credited with having substantially influenced development economists and debt campaign movements in the 1960s–70s before it became the subject of countervailing measures. Drawing on archival sources and international diplomatic cables, Deforge and Lemoine explain how and why UNCTAD's projects for structural reform of the international financial architecture were contested and ultimately rejected in the late 1970s. Such defeats were a blow to the transformative goals that UNCTAD had initially set out to achieve. The author shows that in the 1980s, UNCTAD gradually became a technical agency and its mandate restricted to providing technical assistance to developing countries during their negotiations with the Paris Club. Overall, rather than providing a more symmetric relationship between the North and the South, the authors argue that UNCTAD is merely restating the 'good governance' prescriptions which conventional wisdom sees necessary to attract foreign capital (e.g., creating a 'business-friendly' environment).

The originality of this chapter is to accommodate the perspective of developing countries as agents of political and social change. Deforge and Lemoine suggest that the hegemony of market recipes to financial uncertainties owes much to the disappearance of a 'non-aligned' movement. The paucity of cooperation mechanisms between developing countries is in stark contrast with the situation that prevailed in the 1960s–70s, when political linkages between developing countries triggered off-market forms of exchange. For instance, foreign loans extended by the Soviet Union to developing countries were not premised on the sort of market-based evaluations of creditworthiness that prevail today but on principles of political solidarity and strategic forms of interstate coordination. What transpires in Deforge and Lemoine is that developing nations now seem reluctant or even unwilling to propose an alternative framework challenging the current market-based sovereign debt regime. These forms of solidarity have vanished and debt is now fully embedded into market-based rationalities. Ultimately, internal changes at UNCTAD and broader ideological shifts affecting developing nations go hand in hand with reproducing the current market-based regime.

As we are coming to the end of this section, we can legitimately wonder if the hopes of an alternative system for the organization of global financial have been quashed. Deforge and Lemoine suggest that the dogma of the necessary uniformity of national regimes under the supervision of transnational actors has become hard to resist. Yet, the last section of our volume offers an alternative, perhaps more optimistic, outlook on the current sovereign debt regime.

Hegemonic Debt Diplomacies? (1990s–present)

The last section concludes the cycle of legal and political innovations in sovereign debt that began during the postcolonial context. Volume contributions are complementary because each focus on a particular facet of the current hegemony of legal actors in debt disputes, which some have referred to as the increasing 'legalization' of sovereign debt. Each of the three chapters provides a different viewpoint on the current development of international law and its ambiguous effects on sovereign debt disputes since the 1990s.

In chapter 11, Datz demonstrates that state legislators retain significant authority to impose limits on creditors' legalistic behaviour in negotiations over broken contracts. Her main focus is on anti-vulture funds legislations in Britain, France, and Belgium. Since the 1990s, legal manoeuvres by holdout creditors have been a source of financial uncertainty for both debtor countries and large investors. In Argentina, for instance, the uncompromising behaviour adopted by vulture funds disrupted the debt restructuring that the majority of bondholders wish to make. National legislators have reacted to such legal tactics with legislative and contractual changes. These efforts suggest that lessons can be learnt, even if reform can be slow in the making. Datz claims that anti-vulture funds legislations reaffirm the importance of 'place' in what have been usually conceived as global, footloose bond finance. National lawmakers have attempted to counter the growing deterritorialization of sovereign debt with domestic policies designed to protect domestic financial players against the uncertainty produced by vulture funds. She suggests that the global significance of international norm-providers does not diminish the relevance of states in sovereign debt disputes. The literature has often suggested that private creditors still need the state on their side to facilitate its operations and maximize expectations of repayment when countries are unable to assume their financial obligations (Evans, 1997; Pooley, 1991). As Datz shows, the role of states also extends into drafting legislations. Thirty years after the financial deregulation reforms of the 1990s, states are 'back in' with national anti-vulture funds legislation to curb a haphazard system of debt adjudication that lacks a universal set of rules. She suggests that the current anti-vulture funds legislations represent a step backward, namely a way to re-embed litigation firmly within the perimeter of the state.

It remains to be seen what effects—if any—these legislations will have on creditor–debtor interactions and on vulture funds whose power could be, after all, fragile and reversible. But these initiatives already suggest several important insights into current debates about sovereign debt. First, a fascinating aspect in Datz's chapter is the fact that such countervailing measures are originating from European governments, acting as institutional entrepreneurs. Back in the 1960s, the proponents for a New International Economic Order were countries of the South, mostly postcolonial states. Today, EU anti-vulture funds legislations can be understood as a countervailing action against US judges (Judge Griesa most particularly) and, more broadly, the idea hegemonic in the current debt regime that debt must be repaid regardless of the costs of repayment on debtor states. Datz concludes her investigation by suggesting that a geographical rift has recently opened between Europe and the US over the meaning of international law. Second, this chapter suggests that domestic tools afford key solutions to global problems. Anti-vulture funds legislations demonstrate that state legislation remains relevant to bring about important transformations in the world of sovereign debt.

In chapter 12, Gulati and Panizza examine the current ambiguity of international law from a different angle. Their chapter takes up the classic question of odious debt to understand whether successor governments can be held liable for debts issued by a former administration. Their case is Venezuela, an already much discussed case and one that will likely become more controversial in the years to come. The scope and application criteria of odious debt have elicited considerable interest and debate among academic and civil society circles in recent years (Nehru & Thomas, 2009; Pénet, 2018b; Toussaint, 2017) but there continues to be a great deal of scepticism among lawyers about whether odious debt can find recognition in international customary law (Buchheit, Gulati & Thompson, 2007;

King, 2016). This chapter suggests, quite innovatively, that the doctrine of odious debt could take a more prominent role in sovereign debt markets.

The true originality of the chapter is to address the question of odious debt 'in-the-making'. Most studies of odious debt tend to adopt a rear-view-mirror approach, using old cases to explore the legal meaning of odious debt, and its costs and benefits on international law. This chapter adopts a different perspective: the authors look at how possible accusations of unauthorized, invalid, and illegitimate debt are shaping investors' decisions to invest in bonds. Venezuela offers an experimental case to analyse how investors price bonds which might be odious but whose character of odiousness was not yet formally recognized by a court of law. Drawing on quantitative methods, they show that, although the legal basis for repudiation is very uncertain in Venezuela, the threat of odiousness was nevertheless internalized in bond prices, thanks in no small part to the activism of Harvard economist and former Venezuelan Minister of Planning Ricardo Hausmann.

The Hausmann–Gorky effect makes up for an interesting case of legal performativity.[8] Around the globe, lawyers affect markets by saying what markets are and what they should do. But, despite these facts, lawyers are still largely thought of as professionals whose activity is restricted to the courtroom. Gulati and Panizza boldly challenge this view by showing that odious debt does not need to be legally enforceable to produce real-world effects. Simply that investors might believe the threat of odiousness is a credible one would thus be sufficient to make the debt odious. Ultimately, this contribution shows that international law remains fundamentally an ambiguous development in the contemporary debt world, being at once a development that bolsters and limits creditors' claims against recalcitrant debtors. Whereas Mallard's and Waibel's chapters surveyed the failed attempts to adopt comprehensive laws on state succession, Gulati and Panizza offer a more optimistic outlook by showing that odious debt can find meaningful application even outside the courtroom. Altogether, this chapter engages into a relevant debate about the meaning of law and the role of lawyers and 'legal entrepreneurs' in the world of sovereign debt from Sack to Bedjaoui and O'Connell and Hausmann.

In chapter 13, Anusha Chari and Ryan Leary investigate how credit risk affects the pricing of contractual provisions. The authors demonstrate the significance of legal clauses in the current functioning of sovereign debt markets. Their case is the Puerto Rican debt restructuring, the most significant municipal restructuring in US history. Puerto Rico offers an experimental case to analyse how 'quasi-sovereign' entities deal with sovereign debt disputes. Quasi-sovereignty is problematic for the issuing state because it sends mixed signals to investors (Gelpern,

[8] The influential concept of performativity comes from economic sociology and has so far been applied to financial models (Callon, 1998; MacKenzie, 2006). Gulati and Panizza's contribution extends this concept to legal clauses.

2011). This problem typically concerns formerly colonized territories or peripheral countries. The case of Puerto Rico is useful to compare with Greece: both countries belong in a larger constituency of interests (the Eurozone, the US, a regional monetary union) but do not control monetary institutions, which undermines policy reactivity after a financial shock. Drawing on results from the inspection of the yields and legal components of over 4,000 Puerto Rican bonds spanning a decade, the authors show that legal clauses are most valued by bondholders when credit risk is highest. For the borrowing country, legal clauses also afford a protection against higher yields when a restructuring becomes more likely. This contribution can be read in tandem with the previous chapter as providing an interesting avenue of research on the benefits of legal clauses not just for creditors (who use them to enhance their expectations of repayment) but also for debtors who can find in them a source of stability during times of uncertainty.

The concluding remarks (chapter 14) by Odette Lienau reflect back on this volume and ponder the relevance of investigating sovereign debt from a diplomatic perspective, from the building of colonial empires to the recent debates about hegemony. She begins by noting that the terms that we have used to characterize debt diplomacies (colonial, postcolonial, hegemonic) are very much alive in the contemporary world since they are regularly used by activists and resonant with broader populations. Beyond the popular salience of these terms, Lienau suggests that these terms have value for scholarship because they connect 'to the search for a responsible actor in international financial relations'. Finding a responsible governing actor is often difficult in global financial affairs, particularly in sovereign debt, where creditor–debtor relationships involve multiple forums and mechanisms of powers.

Ultimately, Lienau suggests that there may be value in asking two layers of questions that align with the idea of sovereign debt diplomacies. The first, taken up more directly by this volume's contributions, involves a study of sovereign debt in light of the concepts of (neo)colonialism, (neo)imperialism, and hegemony in ways that blur disciplinary boundaries and that adopt pragmatic rather than formalistic approaches to these issues. A second layer, implicitly suggested by volume contributors, takes up more explicitly the matter of how these politically laden terms themselves frame discussions of sovereign debt in ways that have impact in the world.

References

Abbott, K. W. & Snidal, D. (1998). 'Why States Act Through Formal International Organizations'. *Journal of conflict resolution*, 42(1), 3–32.

Abdelal, R. (2007). *Capital Rules: The Construction of Global Finance*. Cambridge, MA, Harvard University Press.

Accominotti, O., Flandreau, M. & Rezzik, R. (2011). 'The Spread of Empire: Clio and The Measurement of Colonial Borrowing Costs'. *The Economic History Review*, 64 (2), 385–407.

Amin, S. (2001). 'Imperialism and Globalization'. *Monthly Review*, 53(2), 6–24.

Anghie, A. (2007). *Imperialism, Sovereignty and the Making of International Law* (Vol. 37). New York, Cambridge University Press.

Arewa, O., Baccaro, L., Balachandran, G., Büthe, T., Mallard, G., Nightingale, A., Pénet, P., Pestre, D. & Roberts, A. (2018). 'Governing Capital, Labor and Nature in a Changing World'. In IPSP (Ed.), *International Report on Social Progress* (pp. 491–522). Cambridge, Cambridge University Press.

Artis, M. & Okubo, T. (2009). 'Globalization and Business Cycle Transmission'. *The North American Journal of Economics and Finance*, 20(2), 91–9.

Babb, S. L. & Carruthers, B. G. (2008). 'Conditionality: Forms, Function, and History'. *Annual Review of Law and Social Science*, 4, 13–29.

Bear, L. (2015). *Navigating austerity: Currents of debt along a South Asian river.* Stanford, Stanford University Press.

Bi, R., Chamon, M. & Zettelmeyer, J. (2011). 'The Problem that wasn't: Coordination Failures in Sovereign Debt Restructurings'. *IMF Working Papers*, 1–28.

Blyth, M. (2013). *Austerity: The History of a Dangerous Idea.* New York, Oxford University Press.

Borchard, E. (1951). *State Insolvency and Foreign Bondholders. Volume I. General Principles.* New Haven: Yale University Press.

Bordo, M. D. & Flandreau, M. (2003). 'Core, Periphery, Exchange Rate Regimes, and Globalization'. In *Globalization in Historical Perspective* (pp. 417–472). Chicago, University of Chicago Press.

Boyer, R. (1996). 'State and Market: a New Engagement for the Twenty-First Century?' In R. Boyer & D. Drache (Eds.), *States against Markets: The Limits of Globalization* (pp. 62–85). London, Routledge.

Boyer, R. & Drache, D. (2005). 'Introduction'. In *States against Markets: The Limits of Globalization* (pp. 1–30). London, Routledge.

Brownlie, I. (2003). *Principles of Public International Law* (Vol. Sixth edition). Oxford, Oxford University Press.

Buchheit, L. C. (1995). 'The Sovereign Client'. *Journal of International Affairs*, 48(2), 527–40.

Buchheit, L. C., Gulati, G. M. & Thompson, R. B. (2007). 'The Dilemma of Odious Debts'. *Duke Law Journal*, 56(5), 1201–62.

Callon, M. (1998). 'The Embededdness of Economic Markets in Economics'. In M. Callon (Ed.), *The Laws of the Markets* (pp. 1–57). Oxford, Wiley-Blackwell.

Carruthers, B. (2013). 'From Uncertainty Toward Risk: The Case of Credit Ratings'. *Socio-Economic Review*, 11(3), 1–27.

Clavel, D. (2020). 'What's in a Fraud? The Many Worlds of Gregor MacGregor, 1817–1824'. *Enterprise & Society*, 1–40. doi:10.1017/eso.2020.25

Clift, B. (2018). *The IMF and the Politics of Austerity in the Wake of the Global Financial Crisis*. Oxford, Oxford University Press.

Conklin, A. L. (1997). *A mission to civilize: the republican idea of empire in France and West Africa, 1895–1930*. Stanford, Stanford University Press.

Cooper, F. & Stoler, A. L. (1997). *Tensions of Empire: Colonial Cultures in a Bourgeois World*. Berkeley, University of California Press.

Davis, K., Fisher, A., Kingsbury, B. & Merry, S. E. (Eds.). (2012). *Governance by Indicators: Global Power Through Classification and Rankings*. Oxford, Oxford University Press.

De Sousa Santos, B. & Rodríguez-Garavito, C. (2005). *Law and Globalization from Below. Towards a Cosmopolitan Legality*. New York, Cambridge University Press.

Dyson, K. (2014). *States, Debt, and Power: 'Saints' and 'Sinners' in European History and Integration*. New York, Oxford University Press.

Eaton, J. & Gersovitz, M. (1981). 'Debt with Potential Repudiation: Theoretical and Empirical Analysis'. *The Review of Economic Studies*, 48(2), 289–309.

Eaton, J., Gersovitz, M. & Stiglitz, J. E. (1986). 'The Pure Theory of Country Risk'. *European Economic Review*, 30(3), 481–513.

Edwards, S. (2018). *American Default: The Untold Story of FDR, the Supreme Court, and the Battle over Gold*. Princeton, Princeton University Press.

Eichengreen, B. (1991). 'Historical Research on International Lending and Debt'. *Journal of Economic Perspectives*, 5(2), 149–69.

Eichengreen, B. & Portes, R. (1989). 'After the Deluge: Default, Negotiation, and Readjustment During the Interwar Years'. In B. Eichengreen & P. Lindert (Eds.), *The International Debt Crisis in Historical Perspective* (pp. 12–37). Cambridge, MA: MIT Press.

Esteves, R. (2013). 'The Bondholder, The Sovereign, and The Banker: Sovereign Debt and Bondholders' Protection Before 1914'. *European Review of Economic History*, 17 (4), 389–407.

Evans, P. (1997). 'The Eclipse of the State? Reflections on Stateness in an Era of Globalization'. *World Politics*, 50(1), 62–87.

Flandreau, M. (2013). 'Sovereign States, Bondholders Committees, and the London Stock Exchange in the Nineteenth Century (1827–68): New Facts and Old Fictions'. *Oxford Review of Economic Policy*, 29(4), 668–96.

Flandreau, M. & Flores, J. H. (2012). 'Bondholders Versus Bond-sellers? Investment Banks and Conditionality Lending in The London Market for Foreign Government Debt, 1815–1913'. *European Review of Economic History*, 16(4), 356–83.

Flandreau, M. & Flores, J. H. (2009). 'Bonds and Brands: Foundations of Sovereign Debt Markets, 1820–1830'. *The Journal of Economic History*, 69(03), 646–84.

Flandreau, M. & Zumer, F. (2004). *The Making of Global Finance 1880–1913*. Paris, OECD Publishing.

Flores, J. H. (2012). 'Crying on Lombard Street: Fixing Sovereign Defaults in the 1890s'. *European Review of History: Revue européenne d'histoire*, 19(6), 979–97.

Flores Zendejas, J. H. (2016). 'Financial Markets, International Organizations and Conditional Lending: A Long-term Perspective'. In G. Mallard & J. Sgard (Eds.), *Contractual Knowledge: One Hundred Years of Legal Experimentation in Global Markets* (pp. 61–91). Cambridge, Cambridge University Press.

Flores Zendejas, J. H. & Decorzant, Y. (2016). 'Going Multilateral? Financial Markets' access and the League of Nations Loans, 1923–8'. *The Economic History Review*, 69(2), 653–78.

Gaillard, N. (2012). *A Century of Sovereign Ratings*. Springer.

Gelpern, A. (2011). 'Bankruptcy, Backwards: The Problem of Quasi-Sovereign Debt'. *Yale Law Journal*, 121, 888–942.

Giddens, A. (2001). 'The Second Globalization Debate'. *A talk with Antony Giddens. EDGE: The Third Culture*. www.edge.org/3rd_culture/giddens/giddens_p4.html (Accessed 2 March 2020).

Gleditsch, K. S. (2004). 'A Revised List of Wars Between and Within Independent States, 1816-2002', *International Interactions*, 30(3), 231–62.

Hautcoeur, P. C. & Riva, A. (2012). 'The Paris Financial Market in the Nineteenth Century: Complementarities and Competition in Microstructures'. *The Economic History Review*, 65(4), 1326–53.

Helleiner, E. (1996). *States and the reemergence of global finance: from Bretton Woods to the 1990s*. Ithaca, Cornell University Press.

Hopkins, A. (1994). 'Informal Empire in Argentina: An Alternative View'. *Journal of Latin American Studies*, 26(2), 469–84.

Howland, C. P. (1928). *Survey of American Foreign Relations*. New Haven, Yale University Press.

Jaffe, J. (2015). *Ironies of Colonial Governance*. Cambridge, Cambridge University Press.

James, H. & James, H. (2009). *The End of Globalization: Lessons from the Great Depression*. Cambridge, MA, Harvard University Press.

Jorgensen, E. & Sachs, J. D. (1988). 'Default and Renegotiation of Latin American'. *National Bureau of Economic Research, Working Paper No. 2636*.

Kelber, A. & Monnet, E. (2014). 'Macroprudential Policy and Quantitative Instruments: A European Historical Perspective'. *Financial Stability Review*, 18, 151–160.

Kentikelenis, A. E. & Seabrooke, L. (2017). 'The Politics of World Polity: Script-Writing in International Organizations'. *American Sociological Review*, 82(5), 1065–1092.

Kindleberger, C. P. (1986). *The World in Depression, 1929–1939*: Berkeley and Los Angeles, University of California Press.

King, J. (2016). *The Doctrine of Odious Debt in International Law: A Restatement.* Cambridge, Cambridge University Press.

Knight, A. (2008). 'Rethinking British Informal Empire in Latin America (Especially Argentina)'. *Bulletin of Latin American Research*, 27(s1), 23–48.

Knill, C., Bayerlein, L., Enkler, J. & Grohs, S. (2018). 'Bureaucratic Influence and Administrative Styles in international Organizations'. *The Review of International Organizations*, 1–24.

Krippner, G. R. (2011). *Capitalizing on Crisis.* Cambridge, MA, Harvard University Press.

Krueger, A. O. (2002). *A New Approach to Sovereign Debt Restructuring.* Washington, DC: International Monetary Fund.

Lemoine, B. (2016). *L'ordre de la dette: Enquête sur les infortunes de l'État et la prospérité du marché.* La Découverte.

Lienau, O. (2014). *Rethinking Sovereign Debt: Debt and Reputation in the Twentieth Century.* Cambridge, Mass.: Harvard University Press.

Lipson, C. (1985). *Standing Guard: Protecting Foreign Capital in the Nineteenth and Twentieth Centuries* (Vol. 11). Berkeley, University of California Press.

Loriaux, M. (1997). 'The End of Credit Activism in Interventionist States'. In C. U. Press (Ed.), *Capital Ungoverned: Liberalizing Finance in Interventionist States* (pp. 1–16). Ithaca and London, Cornell University Press.

MacKenzie, D. (2006). *An Engine, Not a Camera: How Financial Models Shape Markets.* Cambridge, Mass.: MIT Press.

Mallard, G. (2019). *Gift Exchange. The Transnational History of a Political Idea.* Cambridge and New York, Cambridge University Press.

Mauro, P. & Yafeh, Y. (2003). 'The Corporation of Foreign Bondholders'. *Working Paper 03/107.*

Mauro, P., Sussman, N. & Yafeh Y. (2006). *Emerging Markets and Financial Globalization: Sovereign Bond Spreads in 1870–1913 and Today.* New York, Oxford University Press.

Mitchener, K. J. & Weidenmier, M. D. (2005). 'Supersanctions and Sovereign Debt Repayment'. *NBER working paper 11472.*

Moore, J. B. & Wharton, F. (1906). *A Digest of International Law* (Vol. 2). Washington DC, US Government Printing Office.

Nehru, V. & Thomas, M. (2009). 'The Concept of Odious Debt: Some Considerations'. *World Bank Policy Research Working Paper, 4676* (July 2008).

Nelson, S. C. (2017). *The Currency of Confidence: How Economic Beliefs Shape the IMF's Relationship with Its Borrowers.* Ithaca, Cornell University Press.

Pauly, L. W. & Ferran, J. (1997). *Who Elected the Bankers?: Surveillance and Control in the World Economy.* Ithaca and London, Cornell University Press.

Pénet, P. (2014). *Calculating and Governing Risk in Times of Crisis. The Role of Credit Ratings in Regulatory Reasoning and Legal Change (1930s—2010s).* Sociology PhD dissertation, Northwestern University & SciencesPo Paris. Retrieved from www.theses.fr/2014IEPP0053 (Accessed 23 November 2020).

Pénet, P. (2018a). 'The IMF Failure that wasn't: Risk Ignorance During the European Debt Crisis'. *British journal of sociology*, 69(4), 1031–1055.

Pénet, P. (2018b). 'Rethinking Odious Debt in the Age of Predatory Lending'. *Books and Ideas*, 19 March 2018. Retrieved from www.booksandideas.net/Rethinking-Odious-Debt.html (Accessed 23 November 2020).

Pénet, P. (2019). 'Rhetorical Metrics: Building Securities Regulation in America's Era of Booms and Busts, 1890–1940'. *European Journal of Sociology/Archives Européennes de Sociologie, 60(1), 69–107.*

Pénet, P. & Mallard, G. (2014). 'From Risk Models to Risk Contracts: Austerity as the Continuation of Calculation by Other Means'. *Journal of Critical Globalisation Studies, 7*, 4–47.

Platt, D. C. M. (1968). *Finance, Trade, and Politics in British Foreign Policy, 1815–1914.* London: Clarendon.

Polanyi, K. ([1944] 2001). *The Great Transformation: The Political and Economic Origins of Our Time.* Boston, Beacon Press.

Pooley, S. (1991). 'The State Rules, OK? The continuing political economy of nation-states'. *Capital & Class*, 15(1), 65–82.

Ralph, M. (2015). *Forensics of Capital.* Chicago, University of Chicago Press.

Sack, A. N. (1927). *Les effets des transformations des états sur leurs dettes publiques et autres obligations financières. Traité juridique et financier.* Paris, Recueil Sirey.

Sinclair, T. (2005). *The New Masters of Capital: American Bond Rating Agencies and the Politics of Creditworthiness.* Ithaca, Cornell University Press.

Skocpol, T. & Finegold, K. (1982). 'State Capacity and Economic Intervention in the Early New Deal'. *Political Science Quarterly*, 97(2), 255–78.

Snyder, F. (1999). 'Governing Economic Globalisation: Global Legal Pluralism and European Law'. *European Law Journal*, 5(4), 334–74.

Spivak, G. C. (1988). 'Can the Subaltern Speak?', in R. C. Morris (Ed.) *Can the Subaltern Speak? Reflections on the History of an Idea* (pp. 21–78). New York, Columbia University Press.

Stiglitz, J. E. (2000). 'The Contributions of the Economics of information to Twentieth Century Economics'. *The quarterly journal of economics*, 115(4), 1441–78.

Stiglitz, J. E. (2002). *Globalization and Its Discontents.* New York: Norton.

Stone, R. W. (2002). *Lending Credibility: The International Monetary Fund and the Post-Communist Transition.* Princeton, Princeton University Press.

Strange, S. (1987). 'The Persistent Myth of Lost Hegemony'. *International organization*, 41(4), 551–74.

Strange, S. (1996). *The Retreat of the State: The Diffusion of Power in the World Economy*. Cambridge, Cambridge University Press.

Suter, C. (1990). *Schuldenzyklen in der Dritten Welt: Kreditaufnahme, Zahlungskrisen und Schuldenregelungen peripherer Länder im Weltsystem von 1820 bis 1986* (Vol. 32). Meisenheim and Glan, Anton Hain.

Tomz, M. (2006). *Reputation and International Cooperation. Sovereign Debt across Three Centuries*. Princeton, NJ, Princeton University Press.

Toussaint, E. (1999). *Your Money or Your Life. The Tyranny of Global Finance!*. London, Pluto Press.

Toussaint, E. (2017). *Le système dette: histoire des dettes souveraines et de leur répudiation*. Paris, Les Liens qui libèrent.

Trebesch, C. (2008). *Delays in Sovereign Debt Restructurings. Should we really blame the creditors?* Paper presented at the Proceedings of the German Development Economics Conference, Zurich.

Waibel, M. (2007). 'Opening Pandora's Box: Sovereign Bonds in International Arbitration'. *American Journal of International Law*, 101(4), 711–59.

Waibel, M. (2011). *Sovereign Defaults before International Courts and Tribunals* (Vol. 81). Cambridge, Cambridge University Press.

Weidemaier, M. C. (2010). 'Contracting for State Intervention: the Origins of Sovereign Debt Arbitration', *Law and Contemporary Problems*, 73(4), 335–55.

Weidemaier, M. C., Gulati, M. & Gelpern, A. (2016). 'When Governments Write Contracts: Policy and Expertise in Sovereign Debt Markets'. In G. Mallard & J. Sgard (Eds.), *Contractual Knowledge: One Hundred Years of Legal Experimentation in Global Markets* (pp. 92–117). Cambridge, Cambridge University Press.

Williams, J. F. (1924). *International Law and International Financial Obligations Arising from Contract. Including a Short Discussion of the Drago Doctrine and of the Hague Convention of 1907 on the Recovery of Contract Debts; Being Three Lectures Given in August 1923 at the Hague Academy for International Law*. Leiden, E. J. Brill.

Williamson, J. (1990). 'What Washington Means by Policy Reform'. In J. Williamson (Ed.), *Latin American Adjustment: How Much Has Happened* (Vol. 7, pp. 7–20). Washington DC: Peterson Institute for International Economics.

Yeates, N. (2002). 'Globalization and Social Policy: From Global Neoliberal Hegemony To Global Political Pluralism'. *Global Social Policy*, 2(1), 69–91.

SECTION 1
IMPERIAL SOLUTIONS TO SOVEREIGN DEBT CRISES (1820–1933)

2
Sovereignty and Debt in Nineteenth-Century Latin America

Juan Flores Zendejas and Felipe Ford Cole

2.1 Introduction

The nineteenth century witnessed a high number of episodes in which a government's failure to repay its debt led to the erosion of the country's sovereignty. In the most extreme cases, such disputes would trigger the intervention of European powers—mostly Britain and France—and the establishment of colonial regimes. In a somewhat less extreme version, such disputes were followed by the creation of systems of international foreign control. These intermediate solutions implied the creation of commissions and autonomous bodies formed by representatives of bondholders (private), governments (public), or both (mixed) that could, in their most invasive form, have a direct role on public policies.[1] Though foreign control episodes could vary in their forms and practices, they were responses to problems in which the resolution of debt disputes was defined under a case-by-case praxis, involving a very diverse group of actors that could include companies' promoters, banks, bondholders, and creditor states (Deville, 1912; Pamuk, 1987; Tunçer, 2015).

Interestingly, the colonial wars and foreign control commissions that could be observed in Southern Europe, North Africa, and the Middle East (see Coşkun Tunçer in this volume) were seldom seen in Latin America. This is odd given that Latin American governments frequently defaulted on their external debts during this period. This observation does not mean, however, that debt defaults and the use of military coercion were entirely unconnected. In certain cases, conflicts over unpaid government loans prompted an active intervention from European states and increasingly also from the US. For instance, the French invasion in Mexico in 1862 and the naval blockade against Venezuela imposed by Britain, Italy, and Germany in 1902 were both triggered by a debt dispute. In Mexico, the military intervention led to the establishment of a new political regime run by Maximilian I from the House of Habsburg and supported by the French government. This

[1] On a classification see Megliani (2014).

Juan Flores Zendejas and Felipe Ford Cole, *Sovereignty and Debt in Nineteenth-Century Latin America* In: *Sovereign Debt Diplomacies: Rethinking Sovereign Debt from Colonial Empires to Hegemony.* Edited by: Pierre Pénet and Juan Flores Zendejas, Oxford University Press (2021). DOI: 10.1093/oso/9780198866350.003.0003

experience involved the formation of a Commission in Paris responsible for the management of several aspects of the Mexican fiscal policies. In Venezuela, discussions were held by creditor governments regarding the establishment of a similar Commission (Gille, 1998). Other cases in which foreign control instances were established include the customs receiverships installed by the US in countries of the Caribbean and Central America in the early twentieth century.[2]

However, the absence of military interventionism did not imply that Latin American countries escaped the consequences of European and US imperialism. Historians have frequently evoked other mechanisms of control, resulting in the loss of economic and political autonomy by the prerogatives of European and US imperialism. For some scholars, the nations of Latin America could preserve their political autonomy while remaining firmly planted in the orbit of either British or US influence. This line of argumentation emphasizes the economic component of power relationships in the region and identifies trade and credit as specific variables that strongly influenced Latin America's public policies. Nevertheless, scholars have not yet provided a precise analysis of sovereign debt in this context. Sovereign debt is an important variable because it played a key role in the formation of Latin American nation states, in their relations with other governments, and in the region's interaction with the world economy. The difficulties faced by governments in repaying their debts had different short- and long-term consequences, including the limitation of sovereignty and the imposition of certain economic policies.

Furthermore, military confrontations and the persistent threat of foreign interventions interacted with the development of international law, which first attempted to provide diplomatic and legal means to justify foreign interventions. The above-mentioned case of Venezuela became relevant because it triggered different reactions from Latin American governments. One such reaction was to advance the construction of a legal framework that would impede, rather than justify, the use of military means to force repayment. Latin American lawyers attempted to utilize international law to regulate imperial competition and to bring legal and diplomatic mechanisms to the fore as resolution devices for debt disputes. By intersecting with political rivalries and economic interests, international law could provide a systematic venue to prevent imperial powers to justify the use of military force. As a result, the changes introduced in the early twentieth century also laid the foundations for the development of international law thereafter.

In this chapter, we analyse how public debt was used as a device for external control. We describe both the economic and legal tools that relate episodes of defaults with the limits on Latin America's sovereignty. Our focus on sovereign

[2] See for instance Rosenberg (1999) or Maurer & Arroyo Abad (2017).

debt complements but also qualifies previous claims over the external influence on Latin American governments during the nineteenth century. As we show below, the foreign governments and foreign, private agents that participated in the market for sovereign debt were in a position to impose certain limits on the sovereignty of Latin American countries. This chapter is divided into four sections. In the first section we provide a brief literature review on the debates over informal empire and dependency theory. Sections 2.2 and 2.3 analyse sovereign debt disputes as an important cause of foreign intervention and assess the range of mechanisms restricting the sovereignty of Latin America countries following a debt dispute. Section 2.4 surveys the evolution of the legal framework within which such interventions were justified. After reviewing different episodes of foreign control, we show how each experience led to the perception by Latin American policymakers that international law was the sole 'exit option' that remained to prevent foreign interventions. Ultimately, we suggest that these perceptions had a lasting influence on the development of international law thereafter. Section 2.5 concludes.

2.2 Sovereign Debt and Theoretical Debates on Dependency and Informal Empire

During the early independent years of Latin America, 'sovereignty' was only vaguely defined, as territorial limits were still unknown and stable governments needed some time to emerge. The new Latin American republics were slow to acquire these essential characteristics of sovereign nation states (Burr, 1955). Latin America's governments turned to external loans as a means to support their fiscal needs, given the disintegration of the fiscal basis built by the Spanish crown during the colonial period (Grafe & Irigoin, 2006). The loans issued in the London Stock Exchange were also strongly intertwined with the need, as perceived by these new governments, for diplomatic recognition and for the recovery of trade and investment (Dawson, 1990). Even then, some of these loans were issued before formal recognition was granted by the British government. These financial transactions reflected an economic reality in which British merchants and investors developed strong interests in the region even before its independence (Dawson, 1990; Ford Cole, 2017).

Sovereign debt contracts fell into disarray after the first wave of defaults, beginning in 1825. One of the effects from non-payment was the exclusion of Latin American governments from European financial markets. However, the continuous tensions with bondholders did not deter bilateral trade between Europe and Latin America, which expanded in this period, albeit at a slow pace. Furthermore, many Latin American countries witnessed an increased presence of British firms, banks, and investors, surpassing the presence of their respective counterparts from any other European country. This presence was more visible in the Southern Cone, where British economic activity was consolidated by 1870.[3] French and German investment and trade with Latin American also intensified during the same period, while the US also began its economic expansion in Mexico and Central America.

Since the mid-nineteenth century, foreign loans formed an essential part of the diplomatic relations between European governments and their Latin American counterparts, triggering occasional conflicts between the new republics and (mainly) Britain. Historical evidence shows that European governments were actively supporting the different associations of bondholders in Peru, Mexico, Argentina, and Colombia, and this support was further consolidated after 1868 with the formation of formal associations of bondholders, among which, the British Corporation of Foreign Bondholders (CFB) was foremost.[4] Even if the success of bondholders in forcing Latin American governments to resume debt service was rather limited, the CFB and its counterparts on the European continent managed to obtain more political weight, raising more effectively their claims to the British government.[5]

The extent of diplomatic support from the British and French governments to their bondholders rarely led to military interventions in Latin America. This lack of European military interventionism has motivated a copious literature that analyses the reasons for this relative passivity, which is striking when compared with the more active stance adopted in other regions (see Coşkun Tunçer in this volume). While there is an overall consensus on the lack of geopolitical interest in the region, at least on behalf of France and Britain, the debate concentrates on alternative mechanisms of control employed by the major powers over Latin America, and how did this control affected the long-term development of Latin America.

Three different bodies of literature have extensively analysed the relations between European and US imperialism and Latin America. A first, major strand in the literature has used the concept of informal empire to analyse the expansion of British interests in the world beyond the territories in which Britain held formal political control. One of the basic premises of this literature suggests that bilateral relations between Britain and Latin American countries were based on an asymmetry of power, in which the dominant power exerted a significant amount of control over the other. This interpretation contradicts the alternative view in which the bilateral relations were based on the premise of mutual advantage. In their seminal paper, Gallagher and Robinson (1953) argued that there was a

[3] See McLean (1995).

[4] The activities of the CFB in different countries has been reported in Costeloe (2003), Mauro & Yafeh (2003), Esteves (2013).

[5] On the debate of the relative success of the CFB see Flandreau & Flores (2012) and Flandreau (2013).

willingness and a preconceived strategy by the British government to favour British interests over other countries in foreign trade and investment. To achieve its goals, the British government was ready to provide direct and indirect assistance, and intervene militarily if deemed necessary. The use of credit was one among other mechanisms of control, and served to open and retain Latin American markets to British products and to secure the collaboration of governments to favour British interests.[6] The British state would stand behind British private agents (traders, merchant houses, banks, firms), allowing them to influence the political decisions of Latin American governments. As a result, policymakers in the region maintained their commitment to free trade despite the negative consequences that such an arrangement would have on their respective economic development.

Other historians have investigated the relations between the US and Latin America. The US presence in Latin America has been deemed imperialist, particularly in Caribbean and Central American countries. US expansionism has had different motives. According to Pletcher (1998), US post–Civil War foreign relations experienced a shift from territorial to commercial expansionism. As US investment and trade with Latin America surged during the nineteenth century, the government's interest for enlarged control also increased. However, the US government sought alternative approaches to colonialism that would swap supervision for fiscal and social reform (Rosenberg, 1999). While there were some parallels to the British model regarding the different methods to secure political and economic control, the US model shows several differences from its British counterpart.

In the case of British imperialism, there was a close connection between public and private interests (Cain & Hopkins, 2014). These common interests stemmed from the fact that bankers, bondholders, and members of parliament developed personal relations as they were linked by a common social network (Feis, 1931; Rosenberg, 1999; Cain & Hopkins, 2014). On the contrary, US politicians and State Department officials did not necessarily share the same interests with bankers or firm promoters. Furthermore, the US government sought to increase the country's sphere of influence as declared in the Roosevelt Corollary to the Monroe doctrine. The resulting dollar diplomacy would later involve investment bankers and technicians ('money doctors'), but this was part of a foreign policy led by the US government having a civilizing target (Rosenberg, 1999). British interventionism and establishment of foreign control instances would rather protect financial interests—through an overlap of public and private interests—which would then encompass other targets if those were considered necessary.

[6] A precise definition can be found in (Osterhammel, 1986).

A final strand of literature, based on dependency theories, focuses on the long-term consequences of the world's trade and production division. Dependency theorists have looked at how the dynamics of the nineteenth-century capitalist system weakened the long-term potential for economic development in the region (Frank, 1967). In a seminal study, Prebisch (1950) has shown that business cycles affecting core countries could be exported to the periphery, resulting in a fall in demand for imports and a decline in capital exports. Ford (1956) called the Baring crisis affecting Argentina in 1890 a 'development crisis', as the benefits from investments in the form of railway construction and land improvement needed several years to trigger an increase in exports, while the loans granted to Argentina's government had to be repaid continuously, for which a continuous flow of external capital was needed. The sudden stop of these inflows generated the type of shocks that generally affected borrowing countries. Marichal (1989) also used investment business cycles to classify the history of sovereign debt crises in Latin America based on the successive waves of sovereign debt lending since the early nineteenth century until the 1930s.

Today, studies on informal empire and dependency theory are abundant. Nevertheless, there is no consensus on the long-term economic consequences of colonialism in Latin America or on the existence and the long-term repercussions of the so-called informal empire. Quite the contrary, the need to redefine this term has re-emerged (Brown, 2008). Moreover, the general trend in this scholarship is to renege on the idea that Britain exerted any kind of control in the region (for reasons either of willingness or incapacity on behalf of the British government). Among the many scholars that first rejected Gallagher and Robinson's claims, Platt (1968) has most eloquently raised the major criticisms that have been revisited in the literature. In a nutshell, he argued that there is no historical evidence supporting the claim that the British government willingly intervened on behalf of British bondholders and merchants. For Platt, the most the British government would ask for was equal treatment and for the free operation of international trade. Regarding sovereign debt disputes, Platt quoted Palmerston's famous circular of 1848 that announced that the British government would only intervene diplomatically if it so chose (a question of 'discretion' and not of 'international right').[7] His narrative on the different fronts on which the British government was called upon for support suggests that the British government most often refrained from intervening, while other scholars have also emphasized the geographical and financial factors to explain why Britain provided limited support to bondholders.

[7] 'Foreign Loans. Circular Addressed by Viscount Palmerston to Her Majesty's Representatives in Foreign States, Respecting the Debts Due by Foreign States to British Subjects'.

2.3 Sovereign Debt as a Control Mechanism

Not all scholars support this hands-off perspective. For different reasons, many unrelated to debt disputes, European and US governments could also justify particular interventions. France and Britain intervened on a number of occasions, such as the Anglo-French Blockade of Rio de la Plata in 1845, mainly for commercial interests; the US invasion in Mexico in 1846 was motivated by territorial annexation, as was Spain's occupation of the Dominican Republic in 1861. In the case of Panama, geopolitical rivalries between Great Britain and the US were motivated by the region's strategic geographic situation since the 1840s.[8] Here again, geopolitics and trade were the most relevant elements that explain the perceived necessity, particularly from the US perspective, to pursue a proactive foreign policy, falling short of military interventionism (Lafeber, 1989). As we shall see, in Mexico (1862) and Venezuela (1902) debt was used as a justifying motive for military intervention. In both cases, this proactive stance was also motivated by territorial concerns. Britain feared US annexation of Mexico after the Mexican–American War of 1848, while Napoleon III in France engaged in a policy of territorial expansionism, sending troops to various countries in the world including New Caledonia, Senegal, Lebanon, and China.[9] In Venezuela, the threat of military confrontation with Britain was years in the making because of the border dispute between Venezuela with British Guyana.

Debt disputes were therefore far from the sole or even the main factor that may have triggered foreign interventions. By the 1840s, and following the fall in the number and volume of Latin American government loans in the London Stock Exchange, sovereign debt may have been considered a minor issue for British policymakers. However, for British merchant banks, sovereign debt remained an important vehicle for building economic ties with foreign governments and communities at the local level (Chapman, 1984). Furthermore, given the fragile position of public finances in Latin America and the continuous state of wars, credit was instrumental to the states' own survival. In certain cases, governments could resort to short-term and expensive loans, though very often defaulting on them. This was also the case of loans granted by foreign investors or foreign banks operating in the region. Because of this pattern of defaults, a convention emerged in which diplomatic actors from creditor states (e.g., Britain, France) stepped in to force the borrowing governments to repay its debt (Bazant, 1981, see section 2.4).

[8] Drawing on Gleditsch's (2004) database on wars between and within independent states, and focusing only on the period 1825–1913 in Latin America, we computed sixteen episodes of interstate wars. Among them, three prompted the military intervention of colonial powers. Extra-systemic wars, defined in Gleditsch (2004) as either imperial or colonial wars, were virtually absent in Latin America, the exception being the First Buenos Aires war of 1859 and the Spanish–Cuban War 1895–98.

[9] On the British rationale to invade Mexico, see George Bentinck's address in House of Commons, Sitting of Monday, 24 August 1846 (source: British Parliamentary Papers, Third Series, Volume 88). On the French rationale, see Topik (2000).

Gradually, the holders of foreign debts developed the expectation that their representative government would intervene to protect their claims against a recalcitrant debtor. We explore this kind of legal mechanisms justifying foreign intervention in section 2.4.

Latin America's historiography has also linked sovereign debt to economic development. External government loans were not only used as a means to cover the recurrent public deficits. They also served also as a tool to finance public infrastructure, such as railroads. The construction of new railroad lines served to integrate more regions and territories to the global economy. Economic historians have referred to railways as a main driver of the expansion of British and European imperialism and—relatedly—of the deindustrialization of the periphery (whether colonies, such as Egypt or India, or independent countries, such as the Ottoman Empire or Latin American nations). Yet very often, governments would favour foreign investment in this sector through the entitlement of a minimum dividend to shareholders, thereby placing more pressure on the fiscal balance. Therefore, a default would affect investment rates on railroad construction, affecting the export's potential of the country (Bignon, Esteves, & Herranz-Loncán, 2015). In the case of Brazil, Leff (1997) attributes the delay of Brazil in the construction of railroads to the lack of foreign investment, given that 'British investment was directed away from Brazil by such non-market considerations as imperial policy' (Leff, 1997, p. 45). The reform of public finances after the establishment of the new constitution in 1889 allowed for an increased fiscal capacity, leading both regional and federal states to provide the guarantees necessary to boost investment in this sector.

The capacity of governments to have access to external funds became therefore essential for the survival of the states and for the financing of public investment. A default could generate costs that most governments were willing to avoid. This dependence upon external credit also implied that even without the threat of the use of gunboat diplomacy, control through the conditions attached to public credit could be effective. Investors and merchant banks had the means to exclude governments from financial markets, and very often these investors could coordinate so as to encompass other stock exchanges in these boycotts. Furthermore, even when governments were able to issue new bonds, most of the proceeds were kept in the hands of the underwriting banks, which meant that any deviation from the norm of repayment would allow these banks to keep the proceeds from the issue.

Individual cases of external control in Latin America have been analysed in diverse national historiographies. Two of the most debated cases were Peru and Argentina. In the case of Peru, there is a long-standing debate on the role of British and French governments supporting their bondholders against the defaults of

Peru's government.[10] An interesting feature regarding Peru was the prominence of merchant banks in the fiscal management of the country, in which Peru's government basically delegated the management of the proceeds from guano exports (the main exported commodity) to Gibbs & Sons, a firm that would also hold the commercial monopoly over this particular export. This loss of sovereignty over the management of fiscal revenues was a major condition that allowed Peru's government to access London's capital market.

Peru is not unique. Other Latin American cases suggest that public borrowing was a major bone of contention with foreign agents and governments. Argentina is an interesting case because it has been the country that has been most studied in the literature of informal empire, given the active interest that British and French governments and traders very soon showed in the country.[11] Knight (2008) evoked the role of non-coercive imperialism (or hegemony), in which force was one element of declining importance compared to other type of pressures and influences used by the British government. Knight (2008) has also argued that Argentina enjoyed a different status than most other countries in Latin America, given its political stability and mature institutions, that bore resemblance to British Dominions, allowing for a more intensive development of commercial relations.

Thus, while Argentina was not a target for the use of force, other elements need to be analysed in this context. The Baring crisis has been illustrative of how British actors could impose their conditions on Argentina. By the time of the crisis, Jones (1980) described Argentina's economy as one in which British groups were largely dominant. Hopkins (1994) adds that Britain's main priority in Argentina was centred on finance, and that the political authority of Argentina's elites depended on the power of the City. For our present purposes, the question that we may ask is whether merchant banks could impose a certain control over Argentina's government and how much did sovereign debt play a role. The historical narrative shows that since the 1880s, Baring tried to acquire the formal monopoly over the federal government's issues in London (and Europe) and to grant the loans issued by Baring a prior claim over the revenues stemming from the customs duties (Ferns, 1992). Baring failed to impose such conditions over Argentina's government, partly due to competition from other banks in Britain, France, and Germany, as argued by (Thompson, 1992). However, this picture changed due to a currency crisis in Argentina in 1885, and the resulting need for fresh funds on behalf of the government. The loan issued in 1886 and 1887, for which most of the competing

[10] For contrasting views on the threats perceived by Peru's governments on British interventions see Mathew (1968) and Tantaleán Arbulú (1991). Peru's default of 1876 involved more than 24 million pound sterling, while Egypt's defaulted debt amounted to 11 million. Egypt's debt settlement prompted intervention from Britain and France and eventually led to full colonization. Debt figures are from Stone (2003).

[11] See for instance Ferns (1960) and McLean (1995).

banks jointly participated, was granted with the customs duties guarantee. In fact, this loan was the sole loan on which Argentina's government did not default in 1890.

The negotiations for the funding loan that was organized in 1891 were undertaken by a group of banks led by the bank Rothschild (Marichal, 1989). The resulting agreement imposed certain restrictions on the fiscal balance, on the collection of customs duties (that were supposed to be levied in gold), and on the monetary issues, which targeted Argentina's return to the gold standard and paved the way for the *Caja de Conversión*, an autonomous institution that would restrict the monetary issues to secure the convertibility of the paper peso (Rapoport, 2006). Finally, while the Romero Arrangement gave some breathing space to Argentina's government, Argentina was unable to borrow until the turn of the century, when Baring effectively held again the monopoly over the federal government's external financing.

This monopoly situation of a bank over a government's public finances was not restricted to Argentina. To a large extent, this was also the situation of Brazil during most of the nineteenth century. The Rothschild bank, which effectively held the monopoly over Brazil's external loans since the mid-nineteenth century, could impose certain limits on the government's indebtedness, and on its fiscal and monetary policies (Flandreau & Flores, 2012).[12] These restrictions met with certain resistance during the 1890s. However, when in 1898 Brazil defaulted, Rothschild imposed the same type of restrictions as those imposed in Argentina seven years before within the same framework of a funding loan.

2.4 Legal Tools and Foreign Interventions

This section revisits three foreign interventions in Mexico (1861), Peru (1890), and Venezuela (1902), each triggered by sovereign debt defaults and each indicative of the growing importance of law in sovereign debt disputes in late-nineteenth-century Latin America. We draw on the examples of diplomatic conventions in Mexico and direct contracting in Peru. We then show that during the Venezuela Crisis (1902), US and Latin American jurists focused on the use of these legal techniques and the use of force in debt collection in crafting two separate understandings of the status of debt disputes under international law: the former claiming that sovereignty was contingent on fulfilment of obligations like debts, the latter arguing for non-intervention rooted in absolute sovereignty. Despite these differences of interpretation, the Latin American context reveals the

[12] This monopoly was somewhat relieved, as the Brazilian states could also borrow, which they increasingly did in Paris.

growing centrality of legal discourses in sovereign debt disputes and can be seen as a harbinger of future debt debates in the twentieth century.

Diplomatic Conventions: Mexico, 1861

The French, British, and Spanish intervention in Mexico (1861) represented the culmination of decades of difficult sovereign debt diplomacy between Mexico and its foreign creditors. Since the default on its independence-era debt in 1827, Mexican state finance suffered tremendously under the stress of repeated coups d'état and palace wars. In this period, foreign investors, under the diplomatic protection of their home governments, solicited and received indemnity payments in compensation for property and personal damage. But as early as the Pastry War of 1838—named after the particularly strong representation by the French for the losses of a French pastry chef based in Mexico City—European powers had also contemplated military intervention to enforce property rights in cases where compensation was not forthcoming. Alongside these damage and injury claims, the debt claims of foreign (mostly British) bondholders weighed heavy on the Mexican state in the early nineteenth century (Salvucci, 2009). In the 1840s a novel legal form, the diplomatic convention debt, emerged from the combination of injury and debt claims into a single debt. The defaults on these convention debts served as the immediate trigger for the bombardment and seizure of the customs houses of the Mexican ports of Veracruz and Tampico by the allied fleet in 1861 (Robertson, 1940; Rippy, 1940).

What did a diplomatic convention debt look like? The key but understudied Doyle Convention (also known as the English Convention Debt) that encompassed three separate earlier conventions. The first, signed in 1842, consisted of bundled injury claims amounting to 306,931 pesos at 12 per cent. Second was a defaulted 2-million-peso loan arranged by an English firm and Mexican *agiotistas* over which the British government exercised diplomatic protection and repackaged into a 12-per-cent convention debt. Third was another repackaged debt, in the form of defaulted tobacco bonds held by a Mexican firm operated by two naturalized Britons who successfully obtained diplomatic protection and worth 3.6 million pesos (Borchard & Wynne, 1951, p. 16). The latter two conventions were secured with the support of the British minister in Mexico, Francis Pakenham, who learned in Mexico that securing the diplomatic protection of a foreign government was a tactic of domestic creditors.[13] More diverse still were the Spanish conventions valued at 6.6 million pesos, which between 1851 and 1853 combined the debts incurred in the expropriation of Spanish missionaries

[13] As early as 1847, the liberal president Mariano Arista attempted to outlaw diplomatic conventions altogether. See Lieher (1998).

during the 1820s and debts belonging to the colonial vice-regal government in Mexico. The French for their part bundled 1.7 million pesos worth of over thirty different claims, including the unpaid advances made to the Mexican government by the infamous Swiss Juan Jecker and his firm (Borchard & Wynne, 1951, pp. 17–18).[14]

The conventions converted claims of many kinds into contract debts, working much in the same way as a contemporary bundled asset, combining debts of varying quality and significance into one robust instrument. On the surface, the conventions were almost indistinguishable from a debt contract, containing schedules, rates, and remedies for non-repayment (Payno, 1862, pp. 62, 85, 90, 139–41). Successive Mexican governments in the 1850s understood their importance, endeavouring to pay them at whatever cost. In May 1861, Benito Juarez, after only two only months as the President of Mexico and less than a year after defeating the conservatives in the Reform War, announced the immediate suspension of service on foreign debts, but specifically not the convention debts, which were serviced until July 1861, when the state's finances reached their breaking point (Borchard & Wynne, 1951, p. 23).

There was no better observer of the convention debts than Manuel Payno, the Mexican statesman who served as Finance Minister for a substantial portion of the era. In 1862, Payno authored an extensive report of the convention debts in English, Spanish, and French (Payno, 1862). Throughout his remarkable report, Payno painstakingly detailed every claim bundled into the conventions, taking care to detail which convention debts had been engineered by Mexicans rather than foreign nationals and which had been issued in furtherance of the conservative faction during the Reform War (Payno, 1862, pp. 71, 75, 121, 132, 161, 253). Payno recognized that the intervention of states in the 'singular and disgraceful operations' that saw domestic debts owed to Mexicans become convention debts owed to foreign governments (Payno, 1862, p. 183). In this he echoed the observation of a US traveller in Mexico who wrote that 'he that can buy a foreign ambassador [for the purposes of securing a diplomatic convention] at Mexico has made a fortune' (Tenenbaum, 1979, p. 336).

Direct Contracting: Peru, 1890

Another legal tool for debt resolution involved direct contracting between bondholders and Latin American governments. This drew on two key features of international law in the late nineteenth century. First was Latin America's unique

[14] Jecker bet handsomely on Miguel Miramón and the conservatives during the Reform War. When Benito Juarez and the liberals emerged victorious in 1861, he repudiated the usurious loan, drawing a furious response from the French, who would soon join the allied fleet.

place in international law, then understood as the product of and rules applicable to relations between 'civilized' nations in Europe. Latin American states, despite their long-standing independence and treaties of recognition with European states dating to the 1820s, were situated in the semi-periphery, between civilized Europe and the colonial world (Anghie, 2007). Standing outside of the 'family' of civilized nations made Latin American states and the rest of the semi-peripheral states subjects rather than objects of law—treaties could be applied to them by European states, but they could not reliably enforce European obligations of the same treaties (Lorca, 2015). A European investor's claim clothed in the diplomatic protection of their home government became an obligation under international law, regardless of the investor's conduct. Second was the long record of direct contracting and negotiation between foreign bondholders and Latin American states. The mere availability of direct contracting and negotiation reflected the extensive experience with foreign borrowing and deep permeation of foreign direct investment in the region and the outsized importance of both in a context of limited availability of capital, capital goods, and expertise. Even a small group of shareholders of a strategic railway or buyers of a large bond offering could hold in their hands the fortunes of an entire nation. Cases of debt resolution via direct contracting in nineteenth-century Latin America vary in size but not in terms of relevance to the local political economy.[15]

The most important example in this genre is by far the Grace Contract, an agreement undertaken between Peru and its creditors in 1890. Named after its broker, the merchant Michael Grace, the contract settled £33 million in default since 1876. How did the Grace Contract come into existence? Discussions began within days of the 1876 default, at which point bondholders were blissfully unaware of the complexity of the Peruvian debts. By year's end, as many as 5,550 bondholders subscribed to twelve different loans were represented across four committees based in London, Paris, and Amsterdam.[16] At the outset the British Foreign Office—the bulk of bondholders were British—remained indifferent until the Pacific War (1879–84) further complicated matters by introducing a new class of French bondholders and Chile, now in possession of the territory on which some loans had been secured. Participation from British diplomats increased especially after an 1883 draft treaty between Peru and Chile in which Chile absolved itself of these loans and drew an acrimonious joint protest from

[15] Consider the Soto-Keith Contract (1884), which as Stephen Palmer (1993) shows, swapped Costa Rica's debt for ownership in the small nation's sole railway that served as the main connection to the Caribbean. In this case, the sole bondholder was Minor Keith, the future proprietor of United Fruit Company. Warren (1985) describes the creation of the Anglo-Paraguay Land and Cattle Company in 1873 from a settlement with foreign bondholders—in which each bond entitled the holder to 145 acres of Paraguayan land for a total of 3.8 million acres.

[16] The figure of 5,500 is a conservative figure calculated in 1890, see Box A-2/07-17-1890/'Report of Statutory Meeting of Shareholders', 1; 04-02-1890/'Circular of Committee', 2, Peruvian Corporation Archives, Special Collections of the University College London.

five European nations of the kind that preceded intervention in Mexico in 1861. Armed with an opinion from the Law Officers of the Crown that told the Foreign Office that they could continue to materially assist the bondholders without exercising full diplomatic protection, they pressed on until 1884, at which point the negotiations between bondholders and the Peruvian government fell into the hands of envoys.[17]

In 1885, Michael Grace of the prominent merchant house Grace & Co. purchased the construction contracts for Henry Meiggs's unfinished railways and found himself unable to raise money for the projects in the City of London due to Peru's state of default (Miller, 1976, pp. 80–1). Grace insinuated himself in the dispute, with the substantial interests he acquired at stake, and refocused bondholders' efforts on the railways and other concessions on which the original loans had been secured as compensation rather than liquidation in cash or state revenue. Grace's first tentative agreement reached in 1887 introduced sweeping concessions: the transfer of railways to the bondholders for a period of sixty-six years, the right to discover, own, and operate up to one hundred mines, 1.8 million hectares of land, annual payments of £120,000, a concession of 75 per cent of all remaining guano revenue and the right to exploit and export new guano sources, and the right to operate a bank with the exclusive power to directly collect customs revenue and issue banknotes for twenty-five years. In return the bondholders would undertake comparatively weak obligations to extend the main railway lines and obtain the government's consent before undertaking new lines.[18] Grace's 'gigantic enterprise', became a subject of praise in the London and New York financial press. Peruvian governments 'having made a mess of that poverty-stricken country', were to be replaced by a 'Anglo-American syndicate of capitalists [who have] undertaken the job'.[19] The initial agreement fell through in 1888, but the final version signed in 1890 retained many of its terms, including the railway and land concessions, reduced payments of £80,000 for thirty-three years, the rights to guano deposits and revenue, 2 million hectares of productive land, and the right to build and operate in perpetuity two railways connecting the rail network to Bolivia and to the navigable rivers of the Amazon, all to be managed by the Peruvian Corporation, to formed in a debt for shares swap.

In Peru, those for and against the Grace Contract recognized that the concessions implied surrendering sovereignty. Moreover, there was for many the uncomfortable fact that the counterparty in such a significant cession of sovereignty was entirely private, bound only by their own honour to their obligations in the contract (Basadre, 2014, pp. 90–2; Ramos Núñez, 2003, pp. 284–5; El Señor

[17] Foreign Office/420/40/74/88, Paunceforte to the Law Officers of the Crown, 01/22/1884; Foreign Office/420/40/93/100, Granville to Ampthill, 02/15/1884.

[18] Box A-2/'Translation of Contract', 1–20. Peruvian Corporation Archives, Special Collections of the University College London.

[19] 'A Gigantic Enterprise', *Panama Star*, 8 August 1887.

J. M. Q. y el contrato Grace, 1887, p. 37). On a more fundamental level, this was the spectre of the control of an entire nation—'Grace's Hold on Peru' gleamed the *New York Herald Tribune*—by a small group of foreign financiers.[20] Like the convention debts, the legal form of the agreement—a private contract—simplified the chaotic prospects for resolution of the debt. Whatever misfeasance in the issuance of the debts or their inclusion in the final arrangement were washed clean by the new loan. Grace, for his part, came away with an astounding £150,000 in fees and commissions, and 3 per cent of the proposed corporation's stock (Miller, 1976, p. 100).

Sovereign Debt Enters International Law: Venezuela, 1902

In the closing decades of the nineteenth century, the maturation of international law as a discipline and body of law coincided with the emergence of the United States as a creditor nation and regional hegemon (Coates, 2016; Rosenberg, (1999); Veeser, 2002). Law until this point had played an instrumental role in foreign policy and the collection of sovereign debts, as seen in the cases of the convention debts in Mexico and direct contracting in Peru. From this point forward, however, international law would become central to the practical and geopolitical aspects of collecting sovereign debts in the region. European foreign offices, foreign bondholders, and assorted agents of informal empire would give way to US jurists who sought to redefine the definition of sovereignty to facilitate debt collection in Latin America.

The debt default that sparked the crisis in 1902 was decades in the making. Unlike Peru or Mexico, Venezuela's debts were directly traceable to its inheritance, as a successor state, of Gran Colombia's debts. Loan service was irregular or suspended until 1880, when arrears and the outstanding capital was refinanced into a new £2.75 million loan, the loan that Venezuela would default on in 1892 and 1902. As early as 1869, the strident protests of Venezuela's foreign bondholders attracted the interest of the US State Department, which sought to dissuade potential European designs on intervention pursuant to the Monroe Doctrine, particularly after French Intervention in Mexico. By the time of the 1892 default, the US had sharpened its resolve against European encroachment in the hemisphere after several years mediating the acrimonious Essequibo boundary dispute between Venezuela and the United Kingdom. By 1895, the Essequibo dispute unravelled into a crisis that would see the US and UK openly exchange threats of force. Added to this were foreign policy setbacks in the failure to broker a peace treaty between Peru and Chile in 1883, the defeat of several US projects at the First

[20] 'Grace's Hold on Peru', *New York Herald*, 18 July 1889, 7.

International Conference of American States in 1889, and growing fears of German designs on the Caribbean. It was into this powder keg of geopolitical contention and the Monroe Doctrine—hardly settled by the US victory against Spain in 1898—that the 1902 default would be cast (Mitchell, 1996).

Cipriano Castro announced the default on his nation's debts in 1902, following an ill-fated coup against his government and a sharp decline in the price of coffee, then Venezuela's chief export. Castro, a blustering, recalcitrant strongman, immediately refused to arbitrate the claims and ordered the capture of an island off the coast of Venezuela claimed by the UK. An allied force of the British, German, and Italian navies was dispatched soon thereafter, arriving in December of the same year (Coates, 2015). The US government initially approved of the action, distinguishing between limited intervention—'if any South American country misbehaves toward any European country, let the European country spank it', wrote the equally blustering Theodore Roosevelt at the outset—and the kind of territorial ambition precluded by the Monroe Doctrine (Maass, 2009).

After the initial blockade gave way to the bombardment of Venezuelan naval installations, fears of further escalation led the US to assume a more active role in mediation, brokering an agreement to submit the claims to the Permanent Court of Arbitration in the Hague in May 1903. Eight months later in February 1904, the panel returned their decision on the issue of whether the blockading powers enjoyed seniority in the order of payments. The *Venezuela Preferential* decision confirmed that the blockading powers had indeed enjoyed preferential status, by virtue of their original loan contracts. In Washington the decision was seen as a vindication of intervention itself rather than a narrow reading of contracts, that could potentially serve as precedent for future European infringement of the Monroe Doctrine under the guise of debt collection.

Roosevelt's response came in his December 1904 State of the Union message to the US Congress, where he announced the Roosevelt Corollary to the Monroe Doctrine. The Corollary refocused the reach of the Monroe Doctrine to the Caribbean, where the US would have the exclusive right of intervention to prevent the 'chronic wrongdoing and impotence' of nations from loosening the 'ties of civilized society'. Those nations that kept order and 'pa[id] their obligations' would have nothing to fear, but all else would be made to realize that independence—sovereignty—could not 'be separated from the responsibility of making good use of it'. Non-repayment of debts could lessen a nation's claim to sovereignty, which would in turn authorize only the US to intervene to demand settlement (US Department of State, 1905). In the decades of dollar diplomacy that followed the Roosevelt Corollary's pronouncement, the argument that sovereignty could be diminished by actions like non-repayment of debts would re-emerge repeatedly and become embodied in international law. One of the key agents in this transformation was John Bassett Moore, a scholar of international law at Columbia and advisor to the State Department. Moore previewed the

Roosevelt Corollary's view of debt and sovereignty in his role as counsel to a group of US bondholders in an arbitration with the Dominican Republic between 1903 and 1904. Moore's briefs—filed four days before the *Venezuela Preferential Decision*—in support of the bondholders, organized as the San Domingo Improvement Company (SDIC), argued that the Dominican Republic's general mismanagement of state finance specifically harmed foreign bondholders (Moore, 1904a, 1904b; United Nations, 1904a, 1904b). The nation's natural resources and revenue were enough to ensure its prosperity—Roosevelt made the same observation in the Corollary—but their management by Dominicans was locked in a self-propagating mode of 'improvident' and 'wrongful acts' that would prevent it from ever being able to repay its creditors (Moore, 1904a, p. 115). Moore's proposed solution, an expansive control of the Dominican Republic including full budgetary and administrative discretion, reflected his belief that sovereignty, weighed down by financial misfeasance that harmed bondholders, was no longer valid (Moore 1904a, p. 113). Further research is necessary to understand the extent to which Moore's arguments influenced the drafting of the Roosevelt Corollary, but the affinities are unavoidable.

Moore's work as counsel to US investors did not on its own bring the Roosevelt Corollary's view of debt and closer to international law. Among Moore's academic credentials was his editorship of the *Digest of International Law*, one of the leading international law treatises of the late nineteenth and early twentieth centuries. Along with his appointment at Columbia, the editorship put Moore in a lofty category of jurists whose interpretations of international law could by the treatises they authored—available as authoritative sources in arbitration proceedings—become law (Koskenniemi, 2001, p. 51, 361; d'Aspremont, 2017, pp. 87–92). Like many in his milieu, Moore subscribed to the idea that international law was in large part composed of principles derived from the record of interstate relations, or customs, of civilized nations (Coates, 2016). In the 1906 edition of the *Digest*, Moore applied the Venezuela Crisis, the Roosevelt Corollary, and his representation of the SDIC under the sections on the Monroe Doctrine, claims, intervention (Moore, 1906).

The connection of debt and sovereignty in the Roosevelt Corollary was not without its critics. As early as 1902, the idea that debt non-repayment could form the basis for intervention came under criticism by the Argentine jurist Luis Maria Drago. Then serving as Minister of Foreign Relations, Drago expressed the Argentine position on the Venezuela Crisis in a note to Washington, stating that the use of force to collect sovereign debt was unlawful (Drago, 1907). This kind of intervention contravened the Monroe Doctrine, wrote Drago, and would unavoidably result in territorial occupation. The Drago Doctrine, as it would come to be known, was adopted in a watered-down version—prohibiting the use of force without first acceding to arbitration—as the Drago-Porter Convention at the Second Hague Peace Conference in 1907.

In 1903 the prominent Argentine jurist Carlos Calvo circulated the Drago note to his colleagues at the elite Institut de Droit International in Paris. The responses from Frederic Passy, John Westlake, Ludwig von Bar, and Pasquale Fiore did not converge on a single position regarding the lawfulness of the use of force to collect debts. The jurists did, however, agree that there was no separate right to the use of force in debt collection (Heimbeck, 2014). Over time the debate surrounding the Drago Doctrine would fall into the larger debate on sovereignty doctrine in international law (Lorca, 2015). Despite the ambiguity of the linkage of debt and sovereignty made in the Roosevelt Corollary at international law, the US would begin from this point forward to rely largely on its own sense of the legality involved, particularly during the era of dollar diplomacy.

2.5 Conclusion: The Law and Economics of Foreign Interventions in the Aftermath of Debt Defaults

The history of Latin America is strongly intertwined with the successive waves of public indebtedness in the region. Very often, these cycles ended with debt defaults whose settlement turned out to be problematic. The economic costs of defaults could lead to the fall of foreign investment, the erosion of trade finance, and the exclusion of Latin American governments from capital markets. Most importantly, different episodes of sovereign defaults also witnessed the rise of merchant banks and other, private agents as actors with the capacity to alter the economic policies of a country, or to exert different types of control over public revenues, expenditures, and monetary policy. Therefore, and given Latin America's strong dependence upon external funds, governments averted defaulting whenever possible.

But this does not mean that more heavy-handed options to force repayment were absent. As shown in the Mexican, Venezuelan, or Central American cases, the threat of external interventions existed as the region also fell into the field of imperial competition. The remarkable extent to which sovereign debt collection in Latin America was legalized from the outset was therefore a product of the region's peculiar position in the nineteenth-century legal and economic world order. Recognition between Latin American nations and European powers that came with independence in the 1820s meant that they enjoyed the right to non-intervention. But because Latin American nations were considered throughout the nineteenth century as part of a semi-periphery, neither colonized nor within the family of 'civilized' nations, they could not enforce this right against the same European powers when they sought to enforce debt claims. Had European states opted to ignore their obligations to engage Latin American states as sovereign, in favour of direct diplomacy or force, difficulties of geographic distance, the looming presence of the Monroe Doctrine, and in the context of competition for new markets, the risk of playing into the hands of a rival. Law smoothed over otherwise complex or politically sensitive exchanges.

In the Mexican case surveyed above, a morass of debt and injury claims under diplomatic protection could be streamlined into a single convention debt, and rival English and French navies could sail as allies. The availability and extent of direct contracting in Latin America was another product of the region's unique place in the world. Direct contracting allowed bondholders to escape the legal obligations of their home states while still counting, in the classic example of informal empire, on the support or 'good offices' of their foreign ministries. Consider the scope of the Grace Contract, a private settlement between Peru and its foreign bondholders, and the international financial controls imposed by creditor states on debtor states along the Eastern Mediterranean that Ali Coşkun Tunçer examines in this volume. Had Britain and not British citizens obtained the concessions, the cases would have looked even more similar.

Latin American jurists and governments perceived their position within international law as an opportunity as much as a burden. Governments for their part were enthusiastic promoters of international conferences and multilateralism more generally, understanding that they could punch above their geopolitical weight through the promotion of international law. Geopolitics also provided governments with rare room for manoeuvre, much as Gustavo del Angel and Lorena Pérez show for the Mexican debt negotiators in the 1942 settlement with US creditors. Jurists were more concerned with moving international law away from its reliance on the standard of civilization and toward a positive notion of absolute sovereignty. Contesting intervention premised on debt thus offered a crucial opportunity for jurists like Luis Maria Drago to achieve both ends.

References

Anghie, A. (2007). *Imperialism, Sovereignty and the Making of International Law*. Cambridge: Cambridge University Press.

Basadre, J. (2014). *Historia De La República Del Perú* (Vol. 10). Lima: Producciones Cantabria, S.A.C.

Bazant, J. (1981). *Historia de la deuda exterior de México, 1823–1946*. El Colegio de México.

Bignon, V., Esteves, R. & Herranz-Loncán, A. (2015). 'Big Push or Big Grab? Railways, government activism, and export growth in Latin America, 1865–1913'. *Economic History Review*, 68(4), 1277–1305.

Borchard, E. M. & Wynne, W. H. (1951). *State Insolvency and Foreign Bondholders*. New Haven: Yale University Press.

Brown, M. ed. (2008). *Informal Empire in Latin America: Culture, Commerce and Capital.* Bulletin of Latin American research book series. Oxford: Blackwell Publications

Burr, R. N. (1955). 'The Balance of Power in Nineteenth-Century South America: An Exploratory Essay'. *The Hispanic American Historical Review*, 35(1), 37–60.

Cain, P. J. & Hopkins, A. G. (2014). *British Imperialism: 1688–2000.* London: Routledge.

Chapman, S. D. (1984). *The Rise of Merchant Banking.* London: G. Allen and Unwin.

Coates, B. (2015). 'Securing Hegemony through Law: Venezuela, the US Asphalt Trust, and the Uses of International Law, 1904–1909'. *The Journal of American History*, 102(2), 380–405.

Coates, B. A. (2016). *Legalist Empire: International Law and American Foreign Relations in the Early Twentieth Century.* Oxford: Oxford University Press.

Costeloe, M. P. (2003). *Bonds and Bondholders: British Investors and Mexico's Foreign Debt, 1824–1888.* Westport: Praeger.

D'Aspremont, J. (2017). *International Law as a Belief System.* Cambridge: Cambridge University Press.

Dawson, Frank Griffith (1990). *The First Latin American Debt Crisis: The City of London and the 1822–25 Loan Bubble/Frank Griffith Dawson.* New Haven: Yale University Press.

Deville, F. (1912). 'Les Contrôles Financiers Internationaux Et La Souveraineté De l'état'. Saint-Nicolas: Saint-Nicolas.

Drago, L. M. (1907). 'Argentine Republic: Ministry of Foreign Relations and Worship'. *The American Journal of International Law*, 1(1), 1–6.

El Señor J. M. Q. y el contrato Grace. (1887). Lima: Imprenta Bacigalupi.

Esteves, R. P. (2013). 'The Bondholder, the Sovereign, and the Banker: Sovereign Debt and Bondholders' protection before 1914'. *European Review of Economic History*, 17(4), 389–407.

Feis, H. (1931). *Europe, the World's Banker, 1870–1914: An Account of European Foreign Investment and the Connection of World Finance with Diplomacy before the War.* 2nd print. Publications of the Council on foreign relations. New Haven: Yale University Press.

Ferns, H. S. (1992). 'The Baring Crisis Revisited'. *Journal of Latin American Studies*, 24(02), 241–273.

Ferns, H. S. (1960). *Britain and Argentina in the Nineteenth Century.* Oxford: Clarendon Press.

Flandreau, M. (2013). 'Sovereign States, Bondholders Committees, and the London Stock Exchange in the Nineteenth Century (1827–68): new facts and old fictions'. *Oxford Review of Economic Policy*, 29(4), 668–96.

Flandreau, M. & Flores, Juan H. (2012). 'Bondholders versus Bond-Sellers? Investment Banks and Conditionality Lending in the London Market for Foreign Government Debt, 1815–1913'. *European Review of Economic History*, 16(4), 356–83.

Ford Cole, F. (2018). 'Debt, Bondholders, and the Peruvian Corporation, 1820–1955,' Conference paper, Business History Conference, Baltimore, April 5–7, 2018.

Ford, A. G. (1956). 'Argentina and the Baring Crisis of 1890'. *Oxford Economic Papers*, New Series, 8(2), 127–50.

Frank, André Gunder (1967). *Capitalism and Underdevelopment in Latin America: Historical Studies of Chile and Brazil.* New York: Monthly Review Press.

Gallagher, John & Robinson, Ronald (1953). 'The Imperialism of Free Trade'. *The Economic History Review*, 6(1), 1–15.

Gille, Geneviève (1998). 'Los Capitales Franceses Y La Expedición a México', in *Un siglo de deuda pública en México.* México D.F.: Instituto Mora; Colegio de Michoacán; Colegio de México; Instituto de Investigaciones Históricas-UNAM.

Gleditsch, K. S. (2004). 'A Revised List of Wars Between and Within Independent States, 1816–2002'. *International Interactions*, 30(3), 231–62.

Grafe, Regina, & Alejandra Irigoin, Maria (2006). 'The Spanish Empire and Its Legacy: Fiscal Redistribution and Political Conflict in Colonial and Post-Colonial Spanish America'. *Journal of Global History*, 1(02), 241–67.

Great Britain. Parliament. House of Commons (1849). 'Foreign Loans. Circular Addressed by Viscount Palmerston to Her Majesty's Representatives in Foreign States, Respecting the Debts Due by Foreign States to British Subjects'.

Hopkins, A. (1994). 'Informal Empire in Argentina: An Alternative View'. *Journal of Latin American Studies*, 26, 469.

Heimbeck, L. (2014). 'Discovering Legal Silence: Global Legal History and the Liquidation of State Bankruptcies (1854–1907)', in T. Duve (Ed.), *Entanglements in Legal History: Conceptual Approaches.* Frankfurt: Max Planck Institute for European Legal History.

Jones, Charles (1980). "Business Imperialism" and Argentina, 1875–1900: A Theoretical Note'. *Journal of Latin American Studies*, 12(2), 437–44.

Knight, Alan. (2008). 'Rethinking British Informal Empire in Latin America (Especially Argentina)'. *Bulletin of Latin American Research*, 27(s1), 23–48.

Koskenniemi, M. (2001). *The Gentle Civilizer of Nations: The Rise and Fall of International Law 1870–1960.* Cambridge: Cambridge University Press.

Lafeber, W. (1989). *The Panama Canal: the Ccrisis in Historical Perspective.*Oxford: Oxford University Press.

Leff, N. H. (1997). 'Economic Development in Brazil, 1822–1913', in S. Haber (ed.), *How Latin America Fell Behind.* Stanford, Stanford University Press.

Liehr, R. (1998). 'La Deuda Exterior De México Y Los Merchant Bankers Británicos', in L. Ludlow & C. Marichal (Eds.), *Un siglo de deuda pública en México.* México D.F.:

Instituto Mora; Colegio de Michoacán; Colegio de México; Instituto de Investigaciones Históricas-UNAM.

Lorca, A. B. (2015). *Mestizo International Law: A Global Intellectual History 1842–1933*. Cambridge: Cambridge University Press.

Maass, M. (2009). 'Catalyst for the Roosevelt Corollary: Arbitrating the 1902–1903 Venezuela Crisis and Its Impact on the Development of the Roosevelt Corollary to the Monroe Doctrine'. *Diplomacy & Statecraft*, 20(3), 383–402.

Marichal, C. (1989). *A Century of Debt Crises in Latin America: From Independence to the Great Depression, 1820–1930*. Princeton: Princeton University Press.

Mathew, W. M. (1968). 'The Imperialism of Free Trade: Peru, 1820–70'. *Economic History Review*, 21(3), 562–579.

Maurer, N. & Arroyo Abad, L. (2017). 'Can Europe Run Greece? Lessons from US Fiscal Receiverships in Latin America, 1904-31'. SSRN Scholarly Paper ID 3026330. Rochester, NY: Social Science Research Network.

Mauro, P. & Yafeh, Y. (2003). 'The Corporation of Foreign Bondholders'. IMF Working Paper 03/107. International Monetary Fund.

McLean, D. (1995). *War, Diplomacy and Informal Empire: Britain and the Republics of La Plata, 1836–1853*. New York: British Academic Press.

Megliani, M. (2014). *Sovereign Debt: Genesis—Restructuring—Litigation*. London: Springer.

Miller, R. (1976). 'The Making of the Grace Contract: British Bondholders and the Peruvian Government, 1885–1890'. *Journal of Latin American Studies*, 8(1), 73–100.

Mitchell, N. (1996). 'The Height of the German Challenge: The Venezuela Blockade, 1902–3'. *Diplomatic History*, 20(2), 185–209.

Moore, J. B. (1904a). *Argument of the United States*. Before the Commission of Arbitration under the provisions of the protocol of January 31, 1903, between the United States of America and the Dominican Republic, for the settlement of the claims of the San Domingo Improvement Company of New York and its allied companies.

Moore, J. B. (1904b). *Case of the United States*. Before the Commission of Arbitration under the provisions of the protocol of January 31, 1903, between the United States of America and the Dominican Republic, for the settlement of the claims of the San Domingo Improvement Company of New York and its allied companies.

Moore, J. B. (1906). *A Digest of International Law*. Washington: Government Printing Office.

Osterhammel, J. (1986). 'Semi-Colonialism and Informal Empire in Twentieth-Century China: Towards a Framework of Analysis', in W. J. Mommsen (Ed.), *Imperialism and After: Continuities and Discontinuities*, (pp. 290–314). London: Allen & Unwin.

Palmer, S. (1993). 'Getting to Know the Unknown Soldier: Official Nationalism in Liberal Costa Rica, 1880–1900'. *Journal of Latin American Studies*, 25(1), 45–72.

Pamuk, Ş. (1987). *The Ottoman Empire and European Capitalism, 1820–1913: Trade, Investment and Production*. Cambridge Middle East library 12. Cambridge: Cambridge University Press.

Payno, M. (1862). *Mexico and Her Financial Questions with England, Spain and France*. Mexico City: Ignacio Cumplido.

Pletcher, David M. (1998). *The Diplomacy of Trade and Investment: American Economic Expansion in the Hemisphere, 1865–1900*. Columbia: University of Missouri Press.

Prebisch, R. (1950). The economic development of Latin America and its principal problems (UN Document No.E/CN.12/89/Rev.1). Lake Success: United Nations Department of Economic Affairs.

Platt, D. C. M. (1968). *Finance, Trade, and Politics in British Foreign Policy: 1815–1914*. Oxford: Clarendon Press.

Ramos Núñez, C. (2003). *Historia Del Derecho Civil Peruano* (Vol. 4). Lima: Fondo Editorial PUCP.

Rapoport, M. (2006). *Historia económica, política y social de la Argentina (1880–2003)*. Buenos Aires: Ariel.

Rosenberg, E. S. (1999). *Financial missionaries to the world: the politics and culture of dollar diplomacy, 1900–1930*. Cambridge, MA: Harvard University Press.

Rippy, J. F. (1940). 'Antecedents of the Roosevelt Corollary of the Monroe Doctrine'. *Pacific Historical Review*, 9(3), 267–79.

Robertson, W. S. (1940). 'The Tripartite Treaty of London'. *The Hispanic American Historical Review*, 20(2), 167–89.

Salvucci, R. J. (2009). *Politics, Markets, and Mexico's' London Debt', 1823–1887*. Cambridge: Cambridge University Press.

State, U. S. D. o. (1905). *Papers Relating to the Foreign Relations of the United States, with the Annual Message of the President Transmitted to Congress, December 6, 1904*. Washington: Government Printing Office.

Stone, I. (1999). The Global Export of Capital from Great Britain, 1865–1914: A Statistical Survey. New York: St. Martin's Press.

Tantaleán Arbulú, J. (1991). 'La Deuda Externa Peruana Y El Imperio Inglés En El Siglo XIX'. *Cuadernos//Instituto para la Deuda Externa Latinoamericana*, 1(2), 29–93.

Thompson, A. (1992). 'Informal Empire? An Exploration in the History of Anglo-Argentine Relations, 1810–1914 1'. *Journal of Latin American Studies*, 24(2), 419–36.

Topik, S. C. (2000). 'When Mexico Had the Blues: A Transatlantic Tale of Bonds, Bankers, and Nationalists, 1862–1910.' *The American Historical Review*, 105(3), 714–38.

Tunçer, A. (2015). *Sovereign Debt and International Financial Control: The Middle East and the Balkans, 1870–1914*. Palgrave Studies in the History of Finance. London: Palgrave Macmillan..

Tenenbaum, B. A. (1979). 'Merchants, Money, and Mischief, The British in Mexico, 1821–1862'. *The Americas*, 35(3), 317–339.

United Nations (1904a). San Domingo Improvement Company Claims. *Reports of International Arbitral Awards*: UN.

United Nations (1904b). The Venezuelan Preferential Case. *Reports of International Arbitral Awards*: UN.

Veeser, C. (2002). *A World Safe for Capitalism: Dollar Diplomacy and America's Rise to Global Power*. New York: Columbia University Press.

Warren, H. G. (1985). *Rebirth of the Paraguayan Republic: The First Colorado Era, 1878–1904*. Pittsburgh: University of Pittsburgh Press.

3

Foreign Debt and Colonization in Egypt and Tunisia (1862–82)

Ali Coşkun Tunçer

3.1 Introduction

This chapter explores two interlinked questions: why Tunisia and Egypt were faced with international financial control after their default in 1868 and 1876, and why international financial control eventually led to the colonization of these two polities by France and Britain in 1881 and 1882. Since not all late-nineteenth-century defaults resulted in international financial control and not all cases of international financial control eventually turned into formal colonies of European powers, these questions aim to contextualize Egyptian and Tunisian experiences and contribute to our understanding of the governance of capital flows at the eve of the first financial globalization. Secondarily and more indirectly, answering these broad questions can shed light on European colonial expansion in the Middle East.[1]

Tunisia and Egypt were semi-autonomous provinces of the Ottoman Empire from their conquest in the sixteenth century to the First World War. In practice, however, both countries transferred their political sovereignty to France and Britain, following their occupation by these two major European powers in 1881 and 1882, respectively. The annexation of these two Eastern Mediterranean polities to Western European empires had significant similarities: before direct military takeover, both Tunisia and Egypt experienced a rapid increase in their foreign debt contracted with the intermediation of banking houses in London and Paris, they defaulted on their foreign obligations within almost a decade, they had to consent to the establishment of international financial commissions managed by foreign bondholder and diplomatic representatives, and brief experience of international financial control in each case led to the military intervention of the dominant European power—French in Tunisia and British in Egypt.

[1] There is a long line of literature on drivers of the nineteenth-century imperialism and colonialism. Some of the seminal contributions are Gallagher & Robinson (1953), Feis (1974), Platt (1968), Landes (1969), Cole (1999), Dumett (1999), Cain & Hopkins (2016). This chapter is engaging with this literature only at a very basic level. For a discussion of debt and imperialism in the context of Latin America see Flores Zendejas and Cole in this volume.

Ali Coşkun Tunçer, *Foreign debt and colonisation in Egypt and Tunisia, 1862–82* In: *Sovereign Debt Diplomacies: Rethinking Sovereign Debt from Colonial Empires to Hegemony.* Edited by: Pierre Pénet and Juan Flores Zendejas, Oxford University Press (2021). © Oxford University Press. DOI: 10.1093/oso/9780198866350.003.0004

During this period, the rapid increase in capital flows in the form of sovereign debt was punctuated by defaults on foreign obligations in many debtor countries including Tunisia (1868), the Ottoman Empire (1875), Egypt (1876), Spain (1877), Argentina (1890), Portugal (1892), Greece (1893), Serbia (1895) and Brazil (1898).[2] Response to these defaults varied from case to case and evolved as the century progressed. Sanctions included seizing assets of debtor countries through military intervention, trade restrictions, preventing access to future credit, and finally putting debtor nations under 'international financial control' or 'fiscal house arrest' by imposing foreign administrators, who were authorized to collect revenues of debtor states. The method of establishing foreign control over state finances following defaults first started with Tunisia. Later, this form intervention became the dominant form of dealing with defaults in the Middle East and the Balkans from the 1870s to 1914, including Egypt, the Ottoman Empire, Serbia, Bulgaria, and Greece.[3]

Traditional historiography on the late-nineteenth-century international financial control organizations approaches them in the context of the imperialism debate since one of the consequences of this kind of European intervention was the loss of fiscal and/or political sovereignty of debtor states. More recent views, however, emphasize their function of restoring creditworthiness of debtor governments, and their contribution to the modernization of state finances.[4] Given that in two cases, Tunisia and Egypt, the process of foreign borrowing, default, and European intervention eventually gave way to the colonization of these countries, it is not possible to completely disregard the traditional conceptualization of international financial control as instruments of imperialism.

In this context, this chapter focuses on the Tunisian and Egyptian cases to review the historical and historiographical nexus between international law and finance and imperial history in the nineteenth century. More specifically, it aims to reassess how foreign bondholders at the time viewed the key turning points in the political and financial history of these two sovereign borrowers in the region. The rest of the chapter is organized chronologically. Section 3.2 gives a historical context and outlines the origins of foreign debt in Tunisia and Egypt. Section 3.3 provides the history of defaults and the process of establishing international financial commissions in these two polities. Section 3.4 focuses on the transition from international financial control to the colonization. The conclusion maintains

[2] Dates of default are in parentheses.

[3] For a comparative study of international financial control in the Ottoman Empire, Egypt, Greece, and Serbia see Tunçer (2015). For Bulgaria see Avramov (2003) and Tooze and Ivanov (2011). The Egyptian case outlined in this chapter is primarily based on Tunçer (2015).

[4] Most of these traditional views extend back to contemporary nationalist interpretations of European control. These views were echoed in later studies such as Blaisdell (1966) for the Ottoman Empire and Zouari (1998) for Tunisia. The revisionist views expressed in Suter (1992), Esteves (2013), Mitchener and Weidenmier (2010), and Tunçer (2015) put more emphasis on their creditworthiness restoring function.

that, in Egypt and Tunisia, international financial control organizations were unable to successfully address the conflicting interests among bondholders. This failure contributed to the colonization process, which replaced international financial control organizations with direct foreign control by the dominant imperial power in each country.

3.2 First International Borrowing

From the date of their conquest in 1517 and 1574 to the First World War in 1914, Egypt and Tunisia remained *de jure* part of the Ottoman Empire. Up until the nineteenth century, the Ottoman rule was never deeply rooted, and the pashas appointed by the Porte effectively governed these provinces. Despite this lack of integration with the Ottoman centre, the Ottoman government was satisfied with this arrangement as long as local ruling elites formally recognized the sultan's sovereignty by accepting the governor and other Ottoman representatives appointed by the centre, sending the annual tribute, and supplying soldiers to fight in military campaigns in Asia, Europe, or the Mediterranean (Daly, 1998; Fage & Oliver, 1982).

In Tunisia, a rule of succession by seniority of birth had emerged by the mid-eighteenth century, whereas in Egypt this sort of hereditary rule was only secured in the early nineteenth century following the French occupation, which gave rise to one of the most influential figures in the nineteenth century in the Middle Eastern history, Muhammed Ali, who started ruling Egypt from 1805 onwards. His period was characterized by a wide range of social, economic, and financial reforms, which contributed to the economic expansion and the modernization of the state and the army. By 1838, Muhammed Ali began to lobby with European consuls for an independent Egypt free from the Ottoman rule. This caused a military confrontation with the Ottoman centre, resulting in the defeat of the latter. Consequently, a conference was assembled in London in July 1840 leading to the 'Convention for the Pacification of the Levant'. This arrangement gave Muhammed Ali an ultimatum to withdraw from Syria, Adana, Crete, and Arabia. When he refused to comply, a British force landed at Beirut in September 1840, defeated Muhammad Ali's army, and forced him to withdraw to Egypt. However, despite his defeat, Muhammad Ali managed to secure the title of 'governor of Egypt for life' and his male descendants, known as 'Khedives', were granted hereditary rights to the office (Fahmy, 1998; Aharoni, 2007).[5]

[5] This episode referred in the imperial history literature as the 'crisis of 1839–41', which marks Lord Palmerston's policy of keeping the territorial integrity of the Ottoman Empire and siding with the Ottoman sultan against the Egyptian Khedive (Rodkey, 1929, 1930; Bailey, 1942).

Tunisia in the early nineteenth century was also ruled by ambitious governors who aimed at modernizing the economy and the army. Despite princely quarrels and assassinations, on the accession of Muhammad al-Sadiq in 1859, the Tunisian dynasty possessed both the strength built up over 150 years' hereditary transmission of power and the tradition of independence which gave the 'Beys' the authority of sovereign princes and even more extensive prerogatives than the Egyptian Khedives. They had the autonomy of legislation, their army and navy, the freedom to mint their coins and maintain diplomatic relations, declare war and sign treaties. Although they had neither legations nor consulates abroad, they could, in Tunis, discuss political matters with the consuls of the major European powers. Finally, similar to the British interests in Egypt, the privileged situation of France in Tunisia was reinforced after the French conquest of Algeria in 1830, which transformed the Tunisian regency almost into a de facto protectorate, yet the Porte still asserted its suzerainty both over the Bey and the Khedive (Daly, 1998; Fage & Oliver, 1982).

Ambitious modernization projects in Egypt and Tunisia in the first half of the nineteenth century increased the pressure over their budgets. The 1840 Treaty and following decrees did not grant any privileges to the governor of Egypt to issue a state loan, but it neither excluded him from this right. Because the first Ottoman foreign loan was issued in 1854, this was not an issue to consider yet for the Porte. Yet, the 1841 decree issued by the Sultan underlined that all the taxes and revenues in Egypt would be levied and collected in the Ottoman Sultan's name, thus implying that the Egyptian Khedive would not be able to issue a foreign loan as an independent sovereign without first getting the permission of the Porte (Tunçer, 2015). In 1858, to finance the construction of Suez Canal, the Egyptian Khedive Said Pasha found a way to get over this borrowing restriction by resorting to the issue of treasury bonds. The next two years saw a large increase in their volume, and soon the Khedive had to turn to other forms of borrowing.

In 1860, to fulfil his obligations to the Suez Canal, the Khedive borrowed 28 million francs from a French banking house on his *personal* account. Eventually, in 1862, for the first time in Egypt's history, the Khedive negotiated a state loan to the amount of £3.3 million with the permission of the Ottoman Sultan. This was followed by several others, and during the period 1862–67, the Egyptian government issued five other bonds in London and Paris amounting to £18 million with the support of several British and French banking houses including Frühling & Goschen and Anglo-Egyptian Bank. These loans were secured on the revenues of the provinces of the Delta, Dekahlieh, Charkieh, and Behera and general revenues of the Egyptian state. Moreover, some bonds, for instance, the 7 per cent loan of 1866, were secured on the Dairas or large *personal* estates of the Egyptian Khedive and his family and not on the revenues of the *state*. In 1868, the Khedive managed to contract another loan for £11.9 million with an effective interest rate of 8.86 per cent with the syndicate of the Imperial Ottoman Bank, Société Générale, and

Oppenheim. Although this loan came with the condition of not issuing another loan for five years 'either on the Bourses of Europe, or in Alexandria, or elsewhere' (Fenn, 1885, p. 422), in 1872 the Egyptian government managed to issue another loan, this time with the help of Franco-Egyptian Bank and the support of the Porte.

Finally, in 1873, the Egyptian government contracted the largest external loan in its history, amounting to £32 million, with the Imperial Ottoman Bank, Bischoffsheim, Société Générale, and other banking houses in Alexandria, Istanbul, and Amsterdam. This loan was secured by the revenues of the railways of Lower Egypt, the proceeds of the personal and indirect taxes, the salt tax, and other several taxes. Taken together with previous ones, overall guarantees corresponded to almost all general revenues of the Egyptian government. Acquiring this loan was seen as a success by the government, however, with the financial crisis of 1873, surplus capital started to deplete in the international financial markets (Suter, 1992). Moreover, the partial default of the Ottoman government on its outstanding debt in October 1875 had an immediate effect on Egyptian credit, and the government could not borrow further (Tunçer, 2015). In need of money, the Khedive sold to the British government 45 per cent of the shares of the Suez Canal, for around £4 million, with the intermediation of Rothschild in November 1875 (Crouchley, 1938, p. 122; Wynne, 1951, p. 582). In the meantime, in September 1875, as a result of an agreement between the Khedive and the Great Powers, a system of 'mixed courts' was introduced. Based on the Ottoman capitulations, the mixed courts gave way to legal pluralism and extraterritoriality for European nationals. Under this scheme, foreigners were empowered to bring cases in the mixed courts against the government, the administration, and the estates of the Khedive and the members of his family, if an established private right was violated by an administrative act. Thus, the Khedive's loans were brought within the jurisdiction of the mixed courts (Hoyle, 1986; Cannon, 1972). A similar scheme also existed in Tunisia as early as the 1860s, as briefly outlined below. It is important to note that the mixed courts not only undermined the sovereignty of the Khedive and the Bey, but in certain cases it also challenged the interests of Britain and France, respectively in Egypt and Tunisia, as they enabled the other European powers to bring their financial claims against the government on an equal footing.

In Tunisia, the timeline of borrowing was quite similar to Egypt, although the scale of operations was significantly small given the size of Tunisian regency's economy.[6] Growing European (especially French and British) interest in Tunisia affected the course of political reform: an outbreak of Muslim–Jewish tension in

[6] In 1881, Tunis occupied an area of 45,779 square miles with a population of 1.5 million; Egypt was almost ten times larger with an area of 400,000 square miles and *c.*10 million population. *Statesmen Yearbook: Statistical and Historical Annual of the States*, London, 1913.

Tunis led the European powers to demand that the Tunisian Bey adopt some of the reforms recently promulgated in the Ottoman Empire.[7] Influential consuls of Britain and France, Richard Wood and Léon Roches exerted significant pressure on the Bey and as a result, in September 1857, the Tunisian Bey announced a reform programme guaranteeing the rights of all its subjects regardless of their religion, promising protection of persons and property; regularization of taxation, military service, and justice; and concessions to non-Muslims in the settlement of disputes. Other reforms included the authorization to establish a British-Tunisian bank and similar concessions were granted to the French consul to attract French capital. Shortly after, at the beginning of the 1860s, a constitution was introduced together with a series of reforms aimed at modernizing the government and the army. As a result, the foreigners were also granted equal footing in the right to possess immovable properties, as well as litigation right to their respective consuls, namely by the mixed courts (Brown, 2002; Harber, 1970, pp. 29–32).[8]

During these years, the cost of reforms was covered by the regency's treasury funds. The domestic floating debt of the regency in 1861 was only around half a million pounds, and this sum doubled in 1862. In 1863, the Bey signed its first foreign loan contract with the Parisian banking house d'Erlanger to repay its floating domestic debt and fund the reforms.[9] The loan had a face value of 35 million francs (£1.4 million) with 7 per cent interest rate, 96 issue price and fifteen years maturity, and secured by the revenue of the *majba* tax (poll tax). Although this seemed to be a reasonable deal compared to local costs of borrowing, which was around 12 per cent at the time, the Bey ultimately received only around 30 million francs. The terms of the bond issue involved a controversy around the banking house d'Erlanger, which held 14.5 per cent of the total loan as the subscription fee and other bank charges. As a result of these allegedly onerous terms, the Bey agreed to repay to d'Erlanger in total 65 million francs for receiving less than half of this sum (Zouari, 1998, pp. 181–6). From the beginning, the servicing of this loan would become a problem. The short-term solution put forward by the Tunisian Bey was to double the rate of the poll tax and extend its scope beyond the countryside, making it a countrywide obligation. This led to a

[7] The *Tanzimat* reforms in the Ottoman Empire were marked by two reformation decrees of 1839 and 1856, which helped to accelerate the centralization and bureaucratization of the Ottoman Empire. They offered guarantees to all subjects of security of property and a regular system of assessing taxes, regardless of ethnicity or religion, with strict observance of annual budgets (Karpat, 1972; Quataert, 1994).

[8] *Convention between the governments of Great Britain and of Tunis, Relative to the holding of real property by British Subjects in Tunis.* London, 1864. Other powers received similar rights following Britain: Austria in 1866, Italy in 1868, and France in 1871 (Harber, 1970, p. 44).

[9] Although Rothschild was also involved in the negotiations of this loan promoted by the British consul of Tunisia, Richard Wood, their offer of a loan of 25 million francs at 8 per cent was rejected by the Tunisian Bey under the French influence (Harber, 1970, p. 54).

nationalist rebellion in 1864, which initially united the long-separated rural tribes and rapidly spread to the urban areas. Britain, France, and Italy sent naval detachments to Tunisian ports to protect their subjects and to bring pressure on the Bey. The French consul was particularly active in mediating between the rebels and the government and in persuading the Bey to abolish the 1860 Constitution and to abandon reforms. The rebellion was eventually violently suppressed by the government with the use of military force and the Ottoman support, and it marked a shift in government policies towards a more authoritarian rule (Piquet, 1914; McKay, 1945).

There were several parallels between Egypt and Tunisia in their first encounters with the international financial markets. First, given their *de jure* links to the Ottoman Empire and imperial interest of Britain and France in the region, the great power rivalry became a defining context for their ability to borrow. Second, both Egypt and Tunisia had ambitious and costly Western-style reform programmes in the first half of the nineteenth century which increased their demand for foreign funding and European influence. Third, both the Bey and the Khedive hypothecated revenues from several tax sources as well as their private sources of wealth in order to secure borrowing. Together with the Ottoman capitulations, which recognized legal pluralism and extraterritoriality for European powers, the guarantees offered in bond contracts would later turn into a justification for the creation of international financial commissions, as outlined in section 3.3.

3.3 Default and International Financial Commissions

The default of the Tunisian Bey arrived sooner than the Egyptian Khedive. After the suppression of the 1864 revolt, the financial difficulties of the Tunisian regency were not over, as substantial funds were needed to make the repayments of 1863 loan, and the events of 1864 had undermined the economy of the regency. In 1865, the Bey signed another Parisian loan with d'Erlanger with a face value of 25.9 million francs with similar conditions to the previous one. In 1867, the outstanding debt of the regency had reached £6.7 million, and it required the service of around £1 million exceeding the total tax revenues of the government. In August 1867, the regency missed the deadline for coupon payments on its consolidated debt, and this led to the collapse of Tunisian bond prices in Paris stock exchange (see Figure 3.1).

The first response to the default came from the French government by putting pressure on the Bey to grant guarantees to the French creditors and to accept a financial commission for the payment of the debt. The proposal of founding an international financial commission was also supported by Britain and Italy, as it was seen as a way to 'secure greater regularity both in the collection and disposal

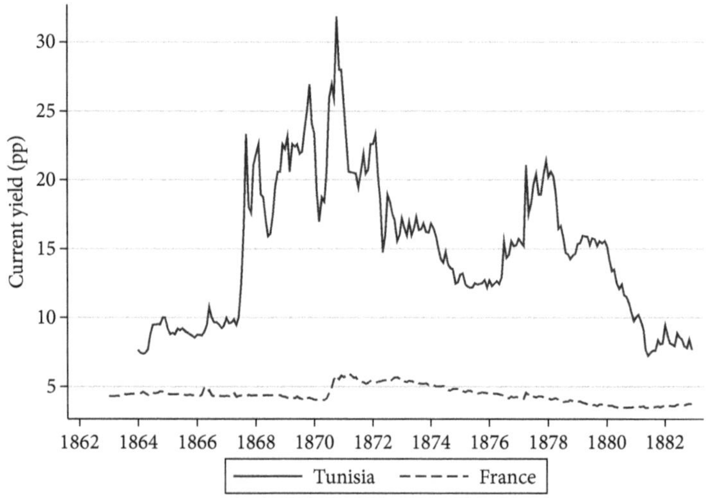

Figure 3.1. Current yield: Tunisia 1862–82

Source and notes: *Cours authentique*, Bourse de Paris, Compagnie des agents de change (1862–1882). Current yield is calculated by using the end of month prices of the 7 per cent loan of 1863, the 7 per cent loan of 1865, and the 5 per cent general debt of 1872. French *rentes* is based on *Global Financial Database* as reported in Tunçer (2015).

of revenues, and thereby increase the chances of a final payment'.[10] The main difficulty, however, was the French demands to fully control the commission, and a solution excluding Italian and British representation was not acceptable by either of them. Hence, the intervention of the French government, followed soon after by Britain and Italy, resulted in a compromise between the three powers, which imposed a tripartite control over the Tunisian finances. On the recommendation of these three powers, the Tunisian Bey consented in April 1868 to the establishment of a nine-member international financial commission (*Commission Financière Internationale*) and entrusted it with the task of reviewing and settling its liabilities (Ganiage, 1959; Comte & Sabatini, 2018, p. 17). The director of the commission was the prime minister of the regency, Hayreddin Pasha, who was assisted by the French Treasury inspector, Victor Villet. The commission consisted of two subcommittees: the executive committee and the control committee. The former composed of two Tunisian officials and one French inspector, and was responsible for the debts and revenues of the regency. The control committee had two French, two English, and two Italian members, and it was given the task of verifying the operations of the executive committee and giving them the executive approval (Zouari, 1998; Berger, 1896).

[10] 'State of Tunis', *The Times*, 26 March 1869, p. 5; Issue 26395.

The arrangement also unified the outstanding debt and reduced its value and annual interest charges. The outstanding debt of the Tunisian government in December 1869 was estimated at 121,640,500 francs, and the commission proposed to reduce this to 56,028,490 francs with a gradual decline in interest payments. However, the proposed debt and interest reduction faced opposition from local bankers and Tunisian bondholders who demanded guarantees for the repayment of the debt. Following negotiations, in March 1870, the Bey agreed on the new proposal of the commission, which put forward a new unified and reduced debt with 5 per cent interest. In exchange, the Bey agreed to transfer revenues from customs, land tax of several provinces, stamp duty, tobacco monopoly, and olive trees to the international financial commission for the repayment of the debt. The total sum of these twenty-six revenue items was close to 6,500,000 francs per year, and they were placed under the control of a council of five appointed members, a Tunisian delegate, appointed by the executive committee, and four creditors' representatives, one French, one English, one Italian, and one European of any nationality, appointed by the entire commission. This commission would be responsible for collecting and centralizing the proceeds of the conceded revenues, under the exclusive control of the executive committee, to which they would have to give a detailed account of their management each quarter.

The arrangement officially sanctioned by the Bey of Tunisia in March 1870 did not lead to immediate recovery of Tunisian bond prices in Paris, as the commission could not start its operations until March 1872 due to several conflicts between the parties (see Figure 3.1). The initial reason behind this lack of recovery was the concern of European bondholders to recoup the outstanding coupon payments as well as the actual principal on the bonds. This situation was also complicated due to contradicting estimates about the actual size of the Tunisian debt by British, French, and Italian diplomatic representatives (Zouari, 1998, p. 261; Ganiage, 1959). The second reason related to the prospects of the Tunisian finances under the international financial commission. As a financial body, the commission gave the European powers the supreme control over the finances, the economy, and the internal administration of the regency. Administratively, it was a mixed control mechanism and it combined the interests of foreign bondholders and diplomatic representatives. Although representation from different countries was seen as an advantage to encourage further capital inflows to the country, it was also likely to cause conflicts of interests. Moreover, as agents of the Tunisian government, the members of the commission were bound to come into conflict with the creditors who composed the controlling section. In other words, the international financial control ended up having a multilateral character due to the great power rivalry, but it did not provide a framework to settle the conflicts of interests between rival groups (Raymond, 1954; Fage & Oliver, 1982; Megliani, 2015).

The Egyptian path from default to the establishment of the international financial commission was quite similar, however, the process started relatively later. London banking houses were keener to supply Egypt with funds due to its rich resources as well as the promising Suez Canal operation. Since the crisis of 1839–41, Britain and Egypt were much more closely connected in diplomatic, commercial, and financial terms compared to France and Tunisia (Landes, 1969). Nonetheless, in December 1875, when the Ottoman Empire defaulted on its foreign debt, the Egyptian credit abroad was directly affected, and it was no longer possible to obtain new loans from the international financial markets. First, in April 1876, the payment of Egypt's treasury bonds was suspended. This failure led to the establishment of an institution named the *Caisse de la Dette Publique* (Caisse) in May 1876, under the direction of foreign commissioners nominated by their respective governments; these commissioners were authorized to receive the revenues intended to service the debt directly from the local authorities. Taxes from several Egyptian provinces, Cairo, and Alexandria; salt and tobacco taxes; and customs revenues were assigned to the Caisse to service various public loans. The Egyptian government committed itself not to modify these revenues or to contract any new loans without the consent of the commission. In return, the arrangement foresaw the unification of the entire debt of the country, which at the time amounted to £91 million. French, Italian, and Austrian creditors agreed to the establishment of the Caisse to have control on the collection and disbursement of the public revenues and therefore nominated their respective commissioners. However, the British government was at this stage unwilling to commit itself to any course of action that might interfere with the internal affairs of Egypt (Wynne, 1951, p. 587–8).

Similar to the Tunisian case, the establishment of international financial control in Egypt did not bring about an immediate recovery of its bond yields in London (see Figure 3.2). Upon the dissatisfaction among various groups of creditors, in July 1876, the British Corporation of Foreign Bondholders applied to G.J. Goschen—head of a major banking house, which acted as an intermediary for most of the Egyptian loans—to represent the bondholders' interests in Egypt. Goschen proceeded to Egypt together with M. Joubert, the representative of a French syndicate and the director of the Banque de Paris et des Pays-Bas. Within a few weeks, Goschen and Joubert had developed a plan of settlement, known as 'Dual Control' which was accepted by the Khedive in November 1876. The decree established a special administration of the railways and the port of Alexandria under the direct control of a special commission of five members: two English, one French, and two Egyptians. Moreover, two controllers-general would be appointed: a controller-general of receipts and a controller-general of audit and public debt—one of whom would be British and the other French, nominated by their respective governments and chosen by the Egyptian government. The *Caisse de la Dette Publique* was to be permanent until the entire debt was redeemed.

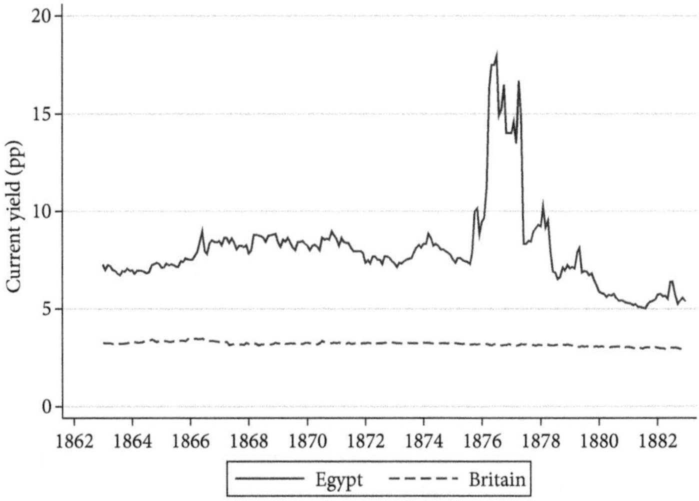

Figure 3.2. Current yield: Egypt 1862–82

Sources and notes: Tunçer (2015) and *Investors Monthly Manual*, London (1862–82). Egyptian bond yields calculated by using end of month prices of based on the 7 per cent loan of 1862 and the 5 per cent preferred loan of 1877. British consols are from *Global Financial Database* as reported in Tunçer (2015).

All revenues assigned to the service of the debt were to be paid by the collection officials directly into the Caisse agents, and not through the treasury. The government without the consent of the Caisse could not change the taxes nor raise a loan. The decisions of the Caisse were taken by the majority of four commissioners; but any single member could sue the government, of his initiative, before the mixed courts. Finally, the capital of the unified debt was reduced to £59 million. The rate of interest was fixed at 6 per cent, to which a sinking fund of 1 per cent was added. From the international law perspective, perhaps the most controversial issue in all these arrangements was to differentiate the personal debt of the Khedive from the public debt of the Egyptian state. Having relied on the mixed courts, the decrees of 1876 implied a unification of the two areas of debt, and this resulted in the hypothecation of the revenues of the Egyptian state and the personal wealth of the Khedive to compensate the creditors for their losses (Tunçer 2015).

In both Egypt and Tunisia, the emergence of international financial commissions was a solution to the range of private financial claims against their governments. Although France had strong political influence in Tunisia, and Britain enjoyed a politically more advantageous situation in Egypt; the existence of foreign bondholders from different European powers acted as a check over the concentration of the power in the hands of a single European country. As section 3.4 elaborates, this fact made the international financial commissions short-lived, as their structure did not sufficiently address the conflicts of interests among different creditor groups, hence undermining the confidence of bondholders to these organizations. Finally, as far as the debt consolidation was concerned, although the capital of the debt was unified and reduced in both cases, this did not mean an immediate end of the fiscal difficulties in Egypt and Tunisia. Now, the new (Anglo-French) administrations had to confront this challenge.

3.4 From International Financial Control to Colonization

Several international factors in the 1870s contributed to the timing of military occupations in Egypt and Tunisia by Britain and France. The defeat of France in the Franco-Prussian War of 1870 was a severe blow to French influence throughout North Africa. At the same time, British interests in the Mediterranean were shifting eastward as the Suez Canal had opened in 1869. These changes in regional geopolitics in the 1870s led the Tunisian Bey to follow a middle-way policy and brought him closer to the Ottoman sultan. The British press at the time viewed this move as a positive development. Commenting on the formal visit of the Tunisian Bey's representative Hayreddin Pasha to London, *The Times* reported that "de facto independence of Tunis has hitherto possessed has neither been of advantage to its inhabitants nor served the purposes of its rulers". Renewing the old ties with the Ottoman centre could serve as a check over "the tyranny and vexations" of the Tunisian Bey towards his subjects, and improve his relations with foreign powers.[11] The only major opposing party to the closer relationship between the Tunisian Bey and the Ottoman Sultan was France due to its African possessions, as this renewed alliance could potentially change the status quo in the region. Following the official visit of Hayreddin Pasha, in 1871 the Ottoman government issued a decree recognizing the autonomy and hereditary rule of the Tunisian Bey in domestic political and economic matters as well as its relations with foreign powers as long as it observed the Sultan's rights over the province.[12] In other words, the decree did not make a significant change of the status quo of Tunisia, yet slowed down the colonization process by reinstating the Ottoman government's rights in the province.

In the meantime, the finances of the Tunisian regency were improving, and from the issue of consolidated debt in 1872 until 1876 the bond yields gradually recovered (Figure 3.1). During these years, there were large capital inflows to the regency mainly from Britain investing in several railways and infrastructure companies. The British consul also managed to secure a concession to create a private bank with the right to issue paper money. This bank was founded in

[11] 'Turkey And Tunis' *The Times*, 31 October 1871, p. 5; Issue 27208.
[12] 'Turkey And Tunis', *The Times*, 8 November 1871, p. 7; Issue 27215.

London in August 1873 under the name of the London Bank of Tunis, and secured the support of key banking houses in the city such as the Baring Bank and the Glyn Mills. Eventually, however, none of these initiatives were successful, and by 1876 most of them were bankrupt or in the hands of French capital groups. In 1873, Hayreddin Pasha, who was supportive of a European style reform programme and worked in harmony with the French consul, became the Prime Minister. His extensive reform programme increased the government revenue for the first time since 1870 and the demands of creditors were met on time (Ganiage, 1959, pp. 240–90).

From 1875 onwards, however, the system started showing its first signs of weakness. First, the Ottoman government defaulted on its outstanding debt shaking major final financial centres in Europe in October 1875. Despite the default of the Ottoman government, The Tunisian correspondent of the Times was still optimistic:

> our finances are in good condition, and unlike, the gentlemen at Constantinople, we pay our coupons regularly. Our international finance commission has proved an excellent institution, and it is a great pity the foreign governments have not persuaded the Turks to follow our example. It would have saved the creditors and saved the Porte from the disgraceful necessity of repudiation, with all the political disadvantages accruing from it.[13]

The commentary continued with a suggestion to induce the Egyptian Khedive to adopt a similar system of administration. The press viewed the effectiveness of the system on two grounds: the Tunisian government was unable to raise new loans without the approval of the international financial control, and all tax revenues were used for the payment of interest on the existing debt.[14] These comments indeed accurately prophesied how the events would unfold in the Ottoman Empire and Egypt in the next few years. First Egypt in 1876, then the Ottoman Empire in 1881 had to agree with their foreign creditors to establish international financial control organizations similar to the one that was in operation in Tunisia for several years, but only in the Ottoman Empire, the operation would turn out to be a financial success without the formal colonization (Tunçer, 2015).

A turning point in the diplomatic history of the region was the defeat of the Ottoman Empire in the Russo-Turkish Wars of 1877–78, which resulted in the convening of the Congress of Berlin and determined the fate of Tunisia (Langer, 1925, 1926). The Congress recognized Britain's acquisition of Cyprus in 1878, driven by its need to safeguard the approaches to the Suez Canal. This shift led Britain to dissociate itself more or less entirely from Tunisian affairs and

[13] 'Finances of Tunis', *The Times*, 25 January 1876, p. 11; Issue 28534.
[14] 'Finances of Tunis', *The Times*, 16 February 1876, p. 7; Issue 28553.

contributed to international recognition of French dominance in the Tunisian regency, determining the outcome of the ongoing great power rivalry in the region. From this point onwards, the French military takeover of Tunisia was simply a matter of time. Only in the spring of 1881, France decided to send a military expedition to Tunisia as a response to raids over the Algerian border by the desert tribes. Despite opposition by Italy, this process eventually gave way to the establishment of the French protectorate over Tunisia in May 1881 when the Tunisian and French governments signed the Treaty of Bardo (McKay, 1945; Perkins, 2005).

Initially, the British government expressed its concerns at this move of France, given that the invasion contradicted its stated position to maintain the integrity of the Ottoman Empire to counter Russian ambitions in the region (Lewis, 2013, p. 19). Yet, gradually the British view towards the French intervention became more neutral given its interests in Egypt. In April 1881, right after the French expedition, *The Economist* noted that:

> so long as Egypt is let alone, it is of no consequence to this country who rules on the southern shore of the Mediterranean, or rather, it is advantageous that a half-civilized ruler should be replaced by a civilized one. Her trade will not be diminished, or her influence lowered, while her direct power over France, which consists in her power of separating France from her colonies, will be materially increased.[15]

Overall, the British press did not see supporting Italy or protecting the Ottoman Empire as valid arguments to interfere with French interests in Tunisia. Moreover, as seen from Figure 3.3, holders of Egyptian and Tunisian bonds in London and Paris also viewed this major diplomatic turning point as a sign of the settlement of the debt problem, as both Egyptian and Tunisian bond spreads declined significantly.

It took several years for France to negotiate a settlement with the European powers to bring their subjects under French legal institutions and eliminate legal pluralism. All European powers in the Ottoman Empire enjoyed extraterritoriality thanks to the capitulations granted by the Ottoman government recognizing the mixed courts. In Egypt, since 1876 the mixed courts under the oversight of fourteen European powers concluded civil and commercial disputes. Although initially this system was not supported by France, by the time it came up for renewal in 1881, the French government viewed it as a way of checking British influence over Egypt and perpetuating capitulations. Similarly, following the Treaty of Bardo, the French government proposed a judicial reform to establish

[15] 'France And England In Tunis', *The Economist*, 9 April 1881, p. 441; Issue 1963.

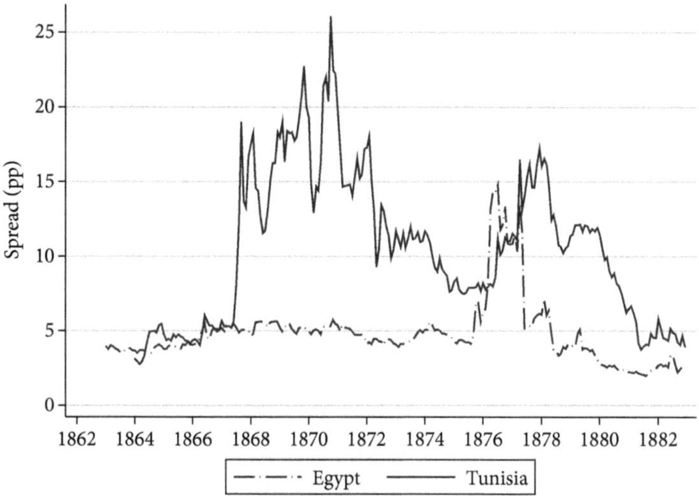

Figure 3.3. Bond spreads: Egypt and Tunisia, 1862–82

Sources and notes: See Figure 3.1 and 3.2. Bond spreads are difference between current yields of Egyptian bonds and British consols for Egypt, and Tunisian bonds and French *rentes* for Tunisia.

French tribunals as a replacement for the mixed courts in Tunisia, in a move similar to that of the British in Cyprus and the Austrians in Bosnia. Eventually, this was also agreed by Britain and later by other European powers.[16] Effective from 1884, the British government closed its consular court in Tunis and Italy signed a similar protocol suspending the capitulations (Lewis, 2013, pp. 28–39; Fahmy, 1998).

As a result of this agreement between the Bey and the French government, France also agreed to guarantee the Tunisian debt, thus rendering the international financial commission irrelevant. Moreover, the Bey of Tunis accepted not to contract any future loans unless approved by the French government. The handover of the functions of the international financial commission to the newly created Ministry of Finance under French control took place in 1884. As the initial deal for guaranteeing the debt, France insisted on placing key agencies, beginning with the Ministry of Finance, under the leadership of French specialists accountable to the resident general. Besides modernizing the tax collection, reducing tariffs and poll tax, and supervising government expenditure, the new Ministry of Finance also reformed the monetary system and undertook three successive debt conversions in 1884, 1889, and 1892 which led to additional inflow of funds to the treasury, replacement of the old non-guaranteed debts with guaranteed

[16] *Correspondence respecting the Establishment of French Tribunals and the abrogation of foreign consular jurisdiction in Tunis: 1882–83*. House of Commons Parliamentary Papers. London, 1884.

ones, and further reductions in the outstanding debt and interest payments (Berger, 1896; Viner, 1928).

As for Egypt, while the debt conversions and new dual-control were being implemented, an exceptionally bad harvest and the Russo-Turkish Wars 1877–78 aggravated the financial situation. In March 1878, a new commission of inquiry was assembled to reassess the whole financial situation of Egypt. The commission reported that among the important causes of Egypt's difficulties were an arbitrary tax system, the lack of a proper budget system, the unequal distribution of lands and water for irrigation, and forced labour used in the Khedive's estates. Implicitly, the fiscal reform was linked to a reform of the state. The Khedive accepted the report of the committee and therefore agreed to establish a constitutional government, which included a British-headed Ministry of Finance and a French-headed Ministry of Public Works. This was an extension of the controller system established in 1876, and soon after its establishment, the new government attempted to raise a new loan. In 1878, Egypt was enabled to borrow the sum of £8.5 million with the intermediation of Rothschild, and the loan was secured again with the Khedive's personal property. However, according to the terms of the agreement, the Khedive's estates were no longer under his administration. They were to be transferred to the state, and accordingly, an international commission of three members, consisting of one English, one French, and one Egyptian national, would be responsible for administering this property and revenue (Feis, 1974, p. 386; Wynne, 1951, p. 596).

The political consequence of all these new regulations was to exclude the Khedive from the administration of Egyptian finances and a transition from the personal government of the Khedive to the government by an executive council whose leading members were foreigners. This situation led to violent protests, which the Khedive and rich landowners supported, to undermine the new administration. The outcome was a *coup d'état.* The initial attempt to govern Egypt without the Khedive had failed and a new government was formed consisting entirely of Egyptians. The new government ruled out the possibility of pursuing the fundamental reforms suggested by the commission of inquiry and therefore the debt settlement process was suspended (Wynne, 1951, p. 600; Feis, 1974, pp. 386–7; Cromer, 1908, p. 46–110).

As noted above, the mixed courts of Egypt were a special arrangement for foreign creditors, through which they could sue the Khedive for unpaid debt. Although many foreign creditors succeeded in obtaining judgments in their favour, the Egyptian government, as a rule, refused to implement these decisions based on the claim that the government lacked enough money to pay off the claims. As far as the creditors were concerned, the existence of mixed courts was seen as an obstacle to reaching a general arrangement, which would benefit all the creditors, because it encouraged individual action for the sake of collective one. Therefore, the Great Powers suggested a new system, which would be binding on all groups of creditors and would exempt the mixed courts from accepting suits by those who did not agree with the general arrangement. The new government formed by the Khedive in 1878 refused any kind of arrangement involving foreign intervention, and the negotiations came to a dead end. To overcome the crisis, the six Great Powers pressed the Porte to replace the Khedive, who was forced to abdicate in favour of his son, Prince Tewfik (Tunçer, 2015).

The new Khedive expressed his willingness to re-establish the system of two controllers-general introduced in 1876. By a decree issued on 10 November 1879, it was once again agreed that the entire administration of the country would be supervised by England and France through the controllers-general. Under this decree, E. Baring and M. de Blignières were appointed as British and French controllers-general, respectively. The controllers-general, who represented not only the foreign bondholders but also their respective governments, reinstated some of the suspended reforms, yet within a few months, the controllers-general reported that Egypt was not in a position to fulfil its engagements and suggested the appointment of a Commission of Liquidation. This led to the Law of Liquidation, which consolidated the floating debt and reduced the interest rate on the unified debt. The revenues of the state were divided into 'assigned' and 'unassigned' revenues. The former would be used for meeting the charges of the debt and would be under the control of the Caisse; the latter was left to the government for administrative expenses. The members of the commission were recognized as legal representatives of the foreign bondholders and had the right to sue the government before the mixed courts (Cromer, 1908, p. 173).

However, because of the political implications of the Law of Liquidation, there were signs of nationalist opposition to European control. This movement consisted of a coalition of different interest groups. Landowners were concerned about the increases of taxes and the amount of land which was being seized for non-payment of debt following the Mortgage Law of 1876. The bureaucrats were concerned with the extensive employment of Europeans in the civil service. Military officers were laid off because of attempts of the financial control to reduce military expenditure. Finally, religious notables, or ulama, were concerned by the Christian rule and consequent changes in the law. These groups turned into an effective force only in 1881 when they allied with the nationalist army officers led by Colonel Arabi (Owen, 2011).

French and British governments were in agreement to keep Khedive Tewfik in power against the nationalist movement to protect the interests of the bondholders. However, once the violent attacks on Europeans in Alexandria started taking place, this led to the fear that the bondholders' agreement could be suspended once again. As a result, in 1882 English forces launched a military campaign—in which France, the Ottoman Empire, and other powers did not participate. Following the military intervention, the Great Powers assembled a conference in Istanbul in June 1882 and a few months later, in September 1882, British forces defeated the Egyptian army.[17] Within a few months after the British took charge, the Anglo-French Dual Control was abolished. The British Consul-General was given overall authority and English advisers were placed in the Egyptian ministries. From 1883 until 1907, Lord Cromer held the position of Consul-General, and under the Egyptian Constitution of 1883, he was the real governing power of Egypt. However, the power of the British consuls to modify Egyptian financial affairs was restricted by previous agreement with the bondholders and by the powers of the Caisse. The French government and bondholders refused to permit any reduction in the authority of the Caisse. Moreover, the separate administration of railways, the Daira, and the domains, on all of which France was represented, was maintained (Feis, 1974, p. 391; Wynne, 1951, pp. 616–17).

3.5 Conclusion

This chapter revisits two decades of the financial history of Egypt and Tunisia from 1862 to 1882 to explore the links between sovereign debt and the colonization experience of these two polities. The comparison reveals several parallels between Egypt and Tunisia in their involvement of borrowing from international financial markets, default, and international financial control. The great power rivalry, especially between Britain and France, became a defining context for their ability to borrow in London and Paris. Combined with ambitious and costly Western-style reform programmes initiated by Egyptian and Tunisian rulers in the first half of the nineteenth century, this process gave way to an increase in their demand for foreign funding and made them vulnerable to European influence. To convince their creditworthiness to British and French bondholders and secure foreign funds, both the Tunisian Bey and the Egyptian Khedive hypothecated revenues from several tax sources as well as their private sources of wealth. Together with the Ottoman capitulations which recognized legal pluralism and extraterritoriality for European powers, the guarantees offered in bond contracts later turned into a justification for the creation of international financial commissions.

The emergence of international financial commissions was a multilateral solution to a range of private financial claims against the Egyptian and Tunisian governments. Although France had strong political influence in Tunisia, and Britain enjoyed a politically more advantageous situation in Egypt; the existence of foreign bondholders from different European powers acted as a check over the concentration of the power in the hands of a single European country. This was

[17] Cromer (1908, pp. 175–375) documents in detail the events, which led to the British intervention, and the negotiations, which took place between the powers. Moreover, see Cain (2006), Hopkins (1986), Cameron (1898, pp. 259–69), and Milner (1892).

one of the reasons why these international financial commissions did not give confidence to the bondholders, as evidenced by Egyptian and Tunisian bond spreads in London and Paris. In other words, administratively they did not turn out to be sustainable, as their structure did not sufficiently address the conflicts of interests among different creditor groups. Only following the establishment of the formal French protectorate of Tunisia in 1881 and the *veiled* British protectorate of Egypt in 1882, the legal pluralism and multilateral nature of the financial control organizations came to an end, and the creditworthiness of Egypt and Tunisia started to recover in international financial markets.

These two cases are at odds with other cases of international financial control in the region such as the Ottoman Empire, where the multilateral representation of foreign bondholders was, in fact, a contributing factor to its success. This chapter shows that the success of multilateral international financial control organizations in the first age of financial globalization to address the conflicting private interests of different groups of bondholders and restore creditworthiness was not unconditional. Although other cases of international financial control before 1914 offered a solution to competing imperial and bondholder interests, in the case of Egypt and Tunisia, international financial control organizations became obstacles to the ongoing colonization process by Britain and France, rather than instruments.

References

Aharoni, R. (2007). *The Pasha's Bedouin—Tribes and States in the Egypt of Mehmet Ali, 1805-1848.* New York: Routledge.

Avramov, R. (2003). 'Advising, Conditionality, Culture: Money Doctors in Bulgaria, 1900–2000', in Mark Flandreau (Ed.), *Money Doctors: The Experience of International Financial Advising 1850–2000* (pp. 190–215). London: Routledge.

Bailey, F. E. (1942). *British Policy and the Turkish Reform Movement: Study in Anglo-Turkish Relations, 1826–1853.* Cambridge: Harvard University Press.

Berger L. (1896). *La Tunisie: histoire et description.* Paris: Association française pour l'avancement des sciences.

Blaisdell, D. C. (1966). *European Financial Control in the Ottoman Empire.* New York: AMS Press, Inc.

Brown, N. J. (2002). *Constitutions in a Nonconstitutionalist World: Arab Basic Laws and the Prospects for Accountable Government.* Albany: State University of New York Press.

Cain, P. J. (2006). 'Character and Imperialism: the British Financial Administration of Egypt, 1878–1914'. *Journal of Imperial and Commonwealth History*, 34(2), 177–200.

Cain, P. J. & Hopkins, A. G. (2016). *British Imperialism: 1688–2015.* New York: Routledge.

Cannon, B. D. (1972). 'A Reassessment of Judicial Reform in Egypt, 1876–1891'. *International Journal of African Historical Studies*, 5(1), 51–74.

Cole, J. R. (1999). *Colonialism and Revolution in the Middle East: Social and Cultural Origins of Egypt's 'Urabi Movement*. Cairo: The American University in Cairo.

Comte, G. & Sabatini, G. (2018). 'Debt and Imperialism in Pre-Protectorate Tunisia, 1867–1870: A Political and Economic Analysis'. *Journal of European Economic History*, 1, 9–32.

Cromer, E. B. (1908). *Modern Egypt, Vol. 1*. London: Macmillan.

Crouchley, A. E. (1938). *The Economic Development of Modern Egypt*. London: Longmans, Green and Co.

Daly, M. W. (ed.) (1998). *Cambridge History of Modern Egypt—Volume 2*. Cambridge: Cambridge University Press.

Dumett, R. E. (1999). *Gentlemanly Capitalism and British Imperialism: The New Debate on Empire*. London: Longman.

Esteves, R. P. (2013). 'The Bondholder, the Sovereign, and the Banker: Sovereign Debt and Bondholders' Protection Before 1914'. *European Review of Economic History*, 17 (4), 389–407.

Fage, J. D. & Oliver, R. A. (1982). *The Cambridge history of Africa*. Cambridge: Cambridge University Press.

Fahmy, K. (1998). 'The Era of Muhammad Ali Pasha', in Martin W. Daly (ed.) *Cambridge History of Modern Egypt—Volume 2*, Cambridge University Press, 139–179.

Feis, H. (1974). *Europe, the World's Banker 1870–1914*. New York: Kelley.

Fenn, C. (1885). *A Compendium of the English and Foreign Funds*. London.

Gallagher, J. & Robinson, R. (1953). 'The Imperialism of Free Trade'. *The Economic History Review*, 6(1), 1–15.

Ganiage, J. (1959). *Les origines du Protectorat français en Tunisie (1861–1881)*. Paris: PUF.

Harber, C. C. (1970). *Reforms in Tunisia, 1855–1878*. Unpublished PhD Thesis, The Ohio State University.

Hopkins, A. G. (1986). 'The Victorians and Africa: a Reconsideration of the Occupation of Egypt, 1882'. *Journal of African History*, 27(2), 363–91.

Hoyle, M. S. W. (1986). 'The Mixed Courts of Egypt 1875–1885'. *Arab Law Quarterly*, 1(4), 436–51.

Karpat, K. (1972). 'The Transformation of the Ottoman State, 1789–1908'. *International Journal of Middle East Studies*, 3, 243–81.

Landes, D. S. (1969). *Bankers and Pashas: International Finance and Economic Imperialism in Egypt*. New York: Harper.

Langer, W. L. (1925). 'The European Powers and the French Occupation of Tunis, 1878–1881, I'. *The American Historical Review*, 31(1), 55–78.

Langer, W. L. (1926). 'The European Powers and the French Occupation of Tunis, 1878-1881, II'. *The American Historical Review*, 31(2), 251–65.

Lewis, M. D. (2013). *Divided Rule: Sovereignty and Empire in French Tunisia, 1880s—1930s*. Berkeley, CA: University of California Press.

Mckay, D. (1945). 'The French in Tunisia'. *Geographical Review*, 35(3), 368–90.

Megliani, M. (2015). *Sovereign Debt: Genesis—Restructuring—Litigation*. London: Springer, Cham.

Milner, A. (1892). *England in Egypt*. London: Edward Arnold.

Mitchener, K. J. & Weidenmier, M. D. (2010). 'Supersanctions and Sovereign Debt Repayment', *Journal of International Money and Finance*, *29* (1), 19–36.

Owen, R. (2011). *The Middle East in the World Economy, 1800–1914*. London: I.B. Tauris.

Piquet, V. (1914). *La colonisation française dans l'Afrique du Nord: Algérie-Tunis-Maroc*. Paris: Colin.

Platt, D. C. M. (1968). *Finance, Trade, and Politics in British Foreign Policy 1815–1914*. Oxford: Clarendon Press.

Quataert, D. (1994). 'The Age of Reforms'. Part 4 of H. Inalcik et al. (Eds.) *An Economic and Social History of the Ottoman Empire 1600–1914*, Vol. 2. Cambridge: Cambridge University Press.

Perkins, K. J. (2005). *A History of Modern Tunisia*. New York: Cambridge University Press.

Raymond, A. (1954). *British Policy towards Tunis (1830–1881)*. Unpublished PhD thesis, University of Oxford.

Rodkey, F. S. (1929). 'Lord Palmerston's Policy for The Rejuvenation of Turkey, 1830–41: Part I, 1830–39'. *The Journal of Modern History*, 1(4), 570–93.

Rodkey, F. S. (1930). 'Lord Palmerston and the Rejuvenation of Turkey, 1830–41: Part II, 1839–41'. *The Journal of Modern History*, 2(2), 193–225.

Suter, C. (1992). *Debt Cycles in the World Economy: Foreign Loans, Financial Crises and Debt Settlements, 1820–1990*. Boulder, Colorado: Westview Press.

Tooze, A. & Ivanov, M. (2011). 'Disciplining the "Black Sheep of the Balkans": Financial Supervision and Sovereignty in Bulgaria, 1902–38'. *The Economic History Review*, 64, 30–51.

Tunçer, A. C. (2015). *Sovereign Debt and International Financial Control: The Middle East and the Balkans, 1870–1914*. Basingstoke: Palgrave Macmillan.

Viner, J. (1928). 'Political Aspects of International Finance'. *The Journal of Business of the University of Chicago*, *1* (2), 141–173.

Wynne, W. (1951). *State Insolvency and Foreign Bondholders—Volume II—Selected Case Histories of Governmental Foreign Defaults and Debt Readjustments*. New Haven, Connecticut: Yale University Press.

Zouari, A.-J. (1998). *European Capitalist Penetration of Tunisia, 1860–1881*. Unpublished PhD thesis, University of Washington.

4

Independence and the Effect of Empire

The Case of 'Sovereign Debts' Issued by British Colonies

Nicolas Degive and Kim Oosterlinck

4.1 Introduction

A large literature has attempted to determine whether belonging to an empire could reduce borrowing costs. A recurring theme in this literature is the role of borrowing and borrowing costs on development but also the relationship between core and periphery or colonial power and colonies. Gunder Frank (1966) has argued that contemporary economic underdevelopment was partially due to the development of the capitalist system. By contrast, Ferguson and Schularick (2006, p. 308) claim that colonies could benefit from 'the importation (or imposition) of less dysfunctional economic, legal, and political Institutions'. The scope of this chapter is more limited. It does not attempt to determine whether the proceeds of loans were used for constructive purposes but rather it aims at understanding to which extent colonial guarantees were viewed as credible by market participants.

The positive impact of colonial status on borrowing costs has been suggested for a long time (Cairncross 1953; Davis & Huttenback 1986). The literature has mostly focused its attention on the period covering the end of the nineteenth century to the First World War. Obstfeld and Taylor (2003) measure this impact by including a colonial dummy capturing the 'Empire Effect' in their analysis. They conclude that membership in the British Empire during the gold standard period was 'neither a necessary nor a sufficient condition to get a preferential access on the London Stock Exchange'. More precisely, they find no statistically significant link between colonial status and borrowing cost for the gold standard period and for 1926–31. On the other hand, and using a similar approach, Ferguson and Schularick (2006) find a substantial reduction in risk premium for colonies. Accominotti et al. (2011) attribute these contradictory results to a misspecification of the models. According to them, being a colony would not have a marginal impact but a structural one: as long as a country remained part of the empire, its default risk was the same as the one of the colonial power. Pooling all

Nicolas Degive and Kim Oosterlinck, *Independence and the Effect of Empire: The Case of 'Sovereign Debts' Issued by British Colonies* In: *Sovereign Debt Diplomacies: Rethinking Sovereign Debt from Colonial Empires to Hegemony.* Edited by: Pierre Pénet and Juan Flores Zendejas, Oxford University Press (2021). © Oxford University Press.
DOI: 10.1093/oso/9780198866350.003.0005

countries (independent and colonies) in a unique regression would then lead to biased estimates.

If colonies benefited from an implicit guarantee from the colonizing powers, then colonial default risk should be negligible. Colonial powers had much larger resources than the colonies. If the colonial power had a credible commitment to bail out troubled colonies, then yields on colonial bonds should have been close to yields on the colonial power's bonds. Furthermore changes in colonial yields should have been driven mostly by factors affecting the guarantor's capacity to repay not by the colonies' standard determinants of default risk (Accominotti et al., 2011). During the gold standard, colonial rule was well established and hardly questioned. After the First World War however, some colonies started asking for more autonomy or even independence. In this framework, were investors still expecting the imperial guarantee to apply or did they envision a world in which some colonies would gradually become independent and thus lose part of this guarantee? Figure 4.1, which tracks the spread between the yield to maturity of colonial bonds and British consols between 1900 and 1936, provides insights in this respect. Our data covers both colonies which at some point had a dominion status (Australia, Canada, New Zealand, and South Africa) and colonies which never did (Ceylon and India). Whereas before the First World War the spreads were experiencing a slow declining trend, after the war, they became much more volatile and reached levels never observed before.

During the interwar period, two series stand out: Australia and India with spreads exceeding 200 basis points. By contrast, for other colonial bonds (Canadian and Ceylonese) the spreads remained in the same range as during the end of the gold standard. Figure 4.1 is thus interesting because of the contrast existing before and after the war but also across countries. Before the war, the spreads across countries were relatively similar. Chavaz and Flandreau (2017) have argued that these spreads mainly reflected liquidity risk. But the difference

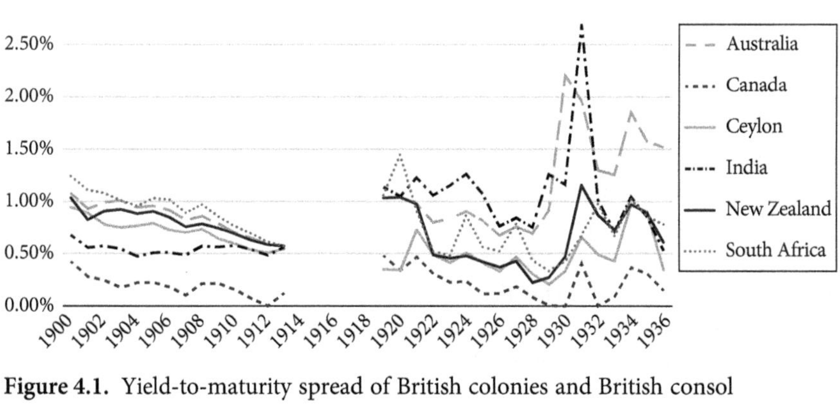

Figure 4.1. Yield-to-maturity spread of British colonies and British consol

observed after the war can hardly be linked to liquidity as Indian bonds were one of the most liquid assets on the British markets (and certainly more liquid than bonds issued by Ceylon).

This chapter investigates whether the difference across colonies may be attributed to a different market perception regarding the informal guarantee provided by the British government to colonial bonds In other words, this chapter tests the Accominotti et al. (2011) hypothesis in two ways. In a first pass, the role of colonial variables on colonial borrowing costs is assessed. If the guarantee was perceived as credible then one would expect economic variables to play no (in case of full commitment), or a limited, role as long as the colony's independence seemed unlikely. In a second phase we analyse colonies' bond price reactions when investors may have wondered if the British guarantee would last. This question became more important during the interwar period with the rise of nationalism in some British colonies. We also assess whether markets believed Britain would honour its guarantees when it was forced to abandon the gold standard. In view of the spreads presented in Figure 4.1, Australia and India may be viewed as two cases where the default-free feature of British colonies was questioned.

In order to develop our points, the balance of the chapter is organized as follows. Section 4.2 presents the mechanism of the empire guarantee on the colonies. Section 4.3 provides an in-depth description of the data and the methodology. Results are discussed in section 4.4 and section 4.5 concludes.

4.2 Implicit Guarantee Mechanism

The literature has highlighted the role played by Britain as guarantor of the debts issued by its colonies (Ferguson and Schularick, 2006; Accominotti et al., 2011). According to Davis and Huttenback (1988, p. 139), 'Indian government bonds, for example, were backed by the full faith and credit of the British government.' Even though part of the public was probably convinced that investing in colonial bonds was as safe as investing in consols, there is, to the best of our knowledge, no legal text mentioning a direct British responsibility for these debts. Britain sent however many signals regarding the quality of colonial bonds which may have been interpreted as an implicit guarantee. The Trustee Act, but also the treatment of colonial bonds by the financial press played an important role in this respect.

In 1893 the British Empire passed the *Trustee Act* (1893). This Act compelled trustees to invest in a limited list of authorized investments to avoid personal liability in case of losses. This list of securities stamped as 'Trustee investment status' included, among others, funds and government securities of the United Kingdom and Indian sterling bonds. Later, the *Colonial Stock Act* (1900) added bonds issued by all British colonies to the Trustees List. The Act provided that any litigation regarding the bonds would be dealt with in an English court. This point warrants a particular mention since a large part of the sovereign debt literature has stressed the difficulty to designate a court responsible for dealing with sovereign defaults. The low-risk nature of the authorized assets was explained by one or more of the following reasons: the British government's preceding right to examine the new issues of those assets, its ability to take action in case of troubles with the borrower, and the existence of an explicit guarantee or satisfactory collaterals such as railways. The fact that the Bank of England was a 'regular underwriter of colonial securities' (Accominotti et al., 2011) was probably also important for the investing public who could interpret this as an additional proof of the low level of risk of colonial securities.

An investor at the time would have been convinced that those securities enjoyed an implicit guarantee first because they were pooled for prudential measures with other securities that were explicitly guaranteed. This had been argued in 1933 by Neville Chamberlain at the House of Commons during the debates concerning the default of Newfoundland. He stated that 'default [...] would at once begin to tarnish the name of those trustee securities which are trustee securities under the Colonial Stock Acts.'[1] Second, because it would have been unlikely that the British Empire would allow any of the securities of the trustee list to fail since British Institutions were considered as trustees and were compelled to invest only in this list. However, the British government never officially stated that it would bail out the securities included in the trustee list. This discordance was pointed out by the legal scholar Ellissen (1904)[2] in his interpretation of the Trustee (1893) and Colonial Stock Acts (1900). He warned readers that 'although the securities mentioned in [his] work comply with the requirements of the Act, it does not necessarily follow that all of them are securities in which it is safe for trustees to invest trust fund.' In 1908, Under-Secretary of States for the Colonies, Winston Churchill, was challenged on this issue during the Questions in the House at the Commons Sitting. Parliamentarians asked whether the 'words trustee stock [...] imply that the trustee stock is guaranteed by the Government'. Churchill's answer was anything but ambiguous. He stated they were not guaranteed, 'but [he] should like to have notice of these Questions.'[3] This discordance was confirmed in 1930 when the Indian Office reacted to the possibility of the repudiation of the Indian debt: the Permanent Under-Secretary of State for India, Sir Hirtzel declared that

> India Sterling securities, while issued by the authority of Act of Parliament and charged on the revenue of India, are not guaranteed by the British Government. Like many other stocks [...] they are by law constituted stock in which British

[1] HC Deb 07 December 1933 vol. 283 cc1845–913.

[2] Barrister-at-law from the Inner Temple.

[3] HC Deb 09 March 1908 vol. 185 cc1105–6.

> trustees are authorised to invest; but that is a separate question'. He added that '[The] Government have no intention of allowing a state of things to arise in India in which repudiation of debt could become a practical possibility and that it is inconceivable that [...] the Parliament could fail to provide safeguards [...] against a breach of the conditions under which these loans were issued.
>
> (Hirtzel, 1930)

During the interwar period, colonies and dominions still benefited from a privileged status. In 1920, and as a consequence of the First World War, the London capital market suffered from congestion, as many firms had been willing to tap the market but had not been authorized to. To address this issue, the British government limited the number of overseas issues. Between 1921 and 1924, colonies and dominions were however allowed to issue bonds whereas foreign governments suffered from an embargo (Atkin, 1970). A few years later, the trustee status was changed. By 1934 the right of disallowance had been agreed upon by all Dominion governments but South Africa. The *Colonial Stock Act* of 1934 changed the rules of the game and replaced the right of disallowance by a mere duty for the dominion to honour the contracts.

The press also played a role in signalling an implicit guarantee. Indian Government Loans were listed in the column 'British Government Stocks' or British Funds in most publications (the official chronicle of the London Stock Exchange, T*he Economist*, the *Investor Newspaper* or the *London Daily Stock and Share List* to give just some examples). This was, however, not the case for other colonial bonds, which were listed under the label 'Dominion and Colonial Governments'. The distinction made between colonies is taken into account in our sample which will be described in section 4.3.

The guarantee provided by the Trustee Status remained credible as long as the British government had enough economic and military power. The credibility of the guarantee provided by the Trustee Status was however jeopardized during the interwar period as Britain faced rising economic difficulties and an increasing demand for more autonomy from the Dominions and India. Early signs of demand for more autonomy appeared at the 1919 Paris Peace Conference where Dominions and India requested separate representation (MacMillan, 2002). Accepting this request marked a first step towards more freedom for dominions and India in the conduct of their foreign policy which remained nonetheless managed by the British government until 1931 Statute of Westminster.

The First World War had dramatic consequences for British public finances: Britain accumulated debt during the war at high interest rates resulting in an increase of the debt-to-GDP ratio from 25.3 per cent in 1914 to 135.2 per cent in 1919 (Reinhart & Rogoff, 2011). The economy was also affected: Greasley and Oxley (1996) have shown that the macroeconomic shocks surrounding the First World War exerted a powerfully depressing influence on British industry throughout the interwar period. Crafts and Fearon (2010) have shed light on the development of the great depression and the fall of sterling: the return to the gold standard in 1925 at the pre-war parity induced an overvaluation of sterling and further depressed British export industries. The 1929 Depression in the US was transmitted internationally: the reduction of imports and international lending forced countries to use restrictive monetary and fiscal policies to deflate their economies. At the end of the 1920s, British exports were declining, real interest rose, and the budget was balanced through the imposition of public expenditures cuts. Britain faced withdrawal of foreign deposits as holders of sterling feared a loss from devaluation. On 21 September 1931, Britain was forced to leave the gold standard and devalue sterling, the pound losing 25 per cent of its value against the US dollar.

4.3 Data and Methodology

The sample includes six British Empire dependencies: four self-governing colonies[4] (Australia,[5] Canada, New Zealand, South Africa), one Crown Colony[6] (Ceylon), and India.[7] The period of analysis is divided into two parts: the first starts in 1900 and ends in 1913; the second starts in 1919 and ends in 1936. The First World War years are excluded from the sample because of the trading restrictions placed by the government to limit the collapse in the prices of securities.[8] The yields-to-maturity are extracted from the Global Finance Database created by Accominotti et al. (2010) for the first period. For the second period, yields-to-maturity are obtained using hand-collected prices from the Stock Exchange Daily Official List (SEDOL). Every country yield is an average of the yields-to-maturity of a sample of debt instruments listed by the country at the end of the year. The sample includes Registered and Inscribed stocks, and rejects debentures and bonds because those specific instruments were not issued by all the countries of our sample.[9] The size of the loan issues and the stock of debt

[4] Those dependencies were granted the self-governing status at different time: Australia in 1901, Canada in 1867, New Zealand in 1907, and South Africa in 1911.

[5] Australia had a gold clause embedded in its bonds issued in New York. This clause was not respected, an element which might be considered as a technical default. The amount of the debt including such clause was small relatively to the total Australian debt. Furthermore, the countries which left the gold standard did de facto not respect the gold clauses of their bonds Kuhn, 1934). As a result, this technical default is unlikely to affect much our results.

[6] Ceylon had the Crown Colony Status for the full analysis period.

[7] Other dependencies have been rejected from our analysis because their sovereign bond prices were not available for the whole period of the analysis.

[8] See Michie (1999).

[9] Debentures were only issued by Australia, Ceylon, New Zealand, and South Africa; bonds were only issued by Canada.

varied considerably with Indian loans dwarfing the others. For the period ranging from 1883 to 1912, Sunderland (2004) estimates a mean size of publicly issued Indian loans of £3.68 million, compared to £1.9 million for 'responsible' government colonies and £0.76 million for Crown colonies. The large size of Indian borrowing should however not be interpreted as a sign that India was free to run its loan issues as it wanted. The Bank of England was indeed central in the loan issues and even blamed for an unsuccessful issue in 1922 (Sunderland, 2013, pp. 36–7).

The literature has mostly focused on the difference in yields between sovereign and colonial bonds. As a result, regressions usually take into account these two types of bonds. By contrast this chapter focuses solely on colonial bonds. The methodology used in the chapter is therefore slightly different from the one existing in Obstfeld and Taylor (2003), Ferguson and Schularick (2006) or Accominotti et al. (2011). Since the chapter is dedicated to colonial bonds only, there is no colonial dummy in our regression. Furthermore, since none of the colonies included in our sample defaulted before our sample period, we do not include a previous default variable. As a result, in our baseline model, and following Accominotti et al. (2011) we assess whether colonies benefited from an implicit guarantee by regressing the spread on a series of fundamentals. In the absence of guarantee the spread should be influenced by macroeconomic fundamentals but not otherwise. More precisely we estimate the following equation (equation 1)

$$Yield_{c,\triangle t} - Yield_{UK,\triangle t} = FE_c + \beta_1 CreditRisk_{c,\triangle t} + \beta_2 Budget_{c,\triangle t} + \beta_3 TradeOpenness_{c,\triangle t} + \varepsilon_{c,t}$$

Where $Yield_{c,t}$ represents the yield to maturity of colony c at time t, $Yield_{UK,t}$ the yield to maturity of British consols at time t, the left hand-side of the equation is thus the spread between colonial bonds and British consols. $CreditRisk_{c,t}$ is measured using the debt service ratio of colony c at time t. $Budget_{c,t}$ is the budget surplus of colony c at time t divided by its revenues. Trade $Openness_{c,t}$ is the export per head of colony c at time t divided by United Kingdom export per head for the same year. Augmented Dickey-Fuller and Kwiatkowski-Philips-Schmidt-Shin tests suggest that variables are non-stationary. Regressions are therefore run using variables' first difference.

Chavaz and Flandreau (2017) have recently expanded this model to take a potential liquidity premium into account: Since our main focus is on the interwar period our liquidity variables are limited to this period, we therefore compare baseline results with the pre-war period without taking liquidity into account but we include it in all subsequent analyses on the interwar period. Liquidity is defined as in Alquist (2010) as the relative bid-ask spread:

$$Bid - Ask_{i,t} = \frac{(UpperPrice_{i,t} - LowerPrice_{i,t})}{1/2(UpperPrice_{i,t} + LowerPrice_{i,t})}$$

The guarantee of the British Empire on colonial debts is expected to hold during the first period when the dependence status of the colonies was unquestioned and Great Britain's economy stable. In the presence of a full guarantee the risk borne by colonial debt should be the same as the guarantor plus a liquidity premium and the economic variables are expected to be non-significant. The interwar period was characterized by two types of events which may have jeopardized the guarantee: the economic turmoil in Great Britain and the emergence of independence movements. We should highlight from the onset that both events should not be viewed as mutually exclusive. Investors could simultaneously fear that a given colony would become independent and that the implicit guarantee extended by Britain would not be honoured because of local financial trouble. One element distinguishes, however, both types of event. The likelihood that a colony would become independent is colony-specific. For the period under study, independence was highly unlikely for the African colonies. By contrast, countries with a dominion status already enjoyed a large autonomy. On the other hand, the likelihood that Britain would be unable to honour its implicit guarantee was similar for all colonies (except if one believes that Britain would have selectively saved some colonies and not others).

Great Britain was forced to leave the gold standard in 1931. This may have prompted investors to revise their opinion regarding the British guarantee. If the guarantor experiences economic difficulties, the guarantee might become unaffordable. Arghyrou and Tsoulakas (2011) have highlighted this phenomenon for the recent Greek crisis: once the cost of bailout exceeds a certain threshold, investors realize that the government expected to bailout the debt cannot afford it, leading to a sharp decline in the debt's price. In other words, in times of trouble, even if Britain had been willing to bail out colonies, it might have been unable to. Changes in the perceived guarantee may affect the yields in many ways. If the consol was believed to be safer than colonial bonds, then investors may have sold the later to buy consols. This 'flight to quality' would have increased the spread between colonial debts and consols. Investors may also have concluded that all British bonds were risky. In this case all yields would have increased, but as long as some investors felt the consol to be safer than the colonial debt, the spread should have increased too.

In the event of independence, colonial debts could have faced different fates. If the former colonizer was expected to reimburse the colonial debt, there should be no difference in the spread. By contrast, if the former colony was expected to become responsible for the reimbursement of the colonial debt then the spread should reflect its reimbursement capacity and the former colony's economic variable should become significant. But of course, in the case of independence, investors may also have expected the debt would be repudiated. In this case its yields should be very high and not connected to economic fundamentals. In other words, if investors expected repudiation,[10] the spread should increase in proportion to the probability of repudiation and colonial economic variables should be non-significant.

4.4 Results and Discussion

Baseline Results

Table 4.1 reports the results for our baseline regression (equation 1) for the pre-war (1901–13) and interwar (1920–36) periods with and without the liquidity variable. Results are in line with Accominotti et al. (2011) since none of the fundamental variable is statistically significant at the conventional levels, and this goes for both for the pre-war and the interwar period. The liquidity variable has the expected sign as in Chavaz and Flandreau (2017).

As mentioned previously, the value of a British guarantee depended on the economic conditions in Great Britain. As long as the British economy seemed in good shape, investors had little reason to question the guarantee. But in 1931, Great Britain had to leave the gold standard; a move which strongly affected investors' perception of British stability. In this context, investors may have expected the British government to exploit the ambiguity regarding its guarantee to refuse to bail out a colony should it be in financial trouble. If this was the case, then one would expect the year 1931 to be exceptional. To test this hypothesis, we also run equation 1, to which we add dummy variables for 1931 and 1932 (taking a value of 1 for the year in question and 0 otherwise). Results are reported in column 4 of Table 4.1.

Both dummy variables are statistically significant, reflecting the fact that the spread increased in 1931. Yields on colonial bonds thus increased more than yields on consols in 1931. This is consistent with the hypothesis that investors valued the guarantee differently during the crisis. The negative sign observed for the 1932 dummy could then reflect expectations of a return to a more normal situation. It might also be explained by the fact that, in 1932, Britain had honoured the guarantee it had given on Irish land bonds and on bonds issued by

[10] For bondholders at the time, repudiation was probably perceived as a mob rule and the recent example of the repudiation by the Soviets of their debts was certainly present in their mind as many people in Britain had been holders of Russian bonds (Oosterlinck, 2016). Nowadays, two opposing views exist regarding the obligation to take over debts issued before independence: the clean slate approach suggests newly independent countries should not have to take over these debts, whereas proponents of universal succession argue they should (for an in-depth discussion see chapters 8 and 9 by Mallard and Waibel in this volume).

Table 4.1 Results of baseline regression

Model	Period 1 Panel without liquidity variable	Period 2 Panel without liquidity variable	Period 2 Panel with liquidity variable	Period 2 Panel with liquidity variable and dummy for 1931 and 1932
Country Fixed-Effects	Incl[†]	Incl[‡]	Incl[‡]	Incl[‡]
Time Fixed-Effects	Incl	Incl	Incl	
Debt Service	0.00100	0.00952	0.00188	0.00086
Budget Surplus	−0.00020	0.00120	0.00110	−0.00059
Export per head	0.00030	0.00071	−0.00001	−0.00041
Liquidity			0.11809**	0.12701***
1931 Dummy				0.00366***
1932 Dummy				−0.00392***
# of observ.	72	96	96	96
Adjusted R-square	53.59%	32.65%	37.63%	33.94%

Note: Pre- and interwar periods. All models are estimated using a panel data with a country-fixed effect. The dependent variable is the spread between colonial yields and the yields on British consols. Period 1: 1901–13; Period 2: 1920–36; Incl stands for included.

[†] All statistically significant.

[‡] None significant at the conventional levels. ** $p < 0.05$, *** $p < 0.01$.

Newfoundland (Foley-Fisher & McLaughlin, 2016). Results from Table 4.1 would thus suggest that even during the interwar period investors believed all British colonies benefitted from the imperial guarantee. As a result, colonies enjoyed a lower borrowing cost. This came however at a political cost which should of course not be forgotten. When in 1915 the Indian Office rejected the Treasury's' proposal to tap the Indian market to fund the war effort, the Treasury's officials limited access to the London market (Sunderland 2013, pp. 82–3). As a result, the Indian government eventually reluctantly agreed to contribute financially to the war effort. Our results also show that the perceived value of the guarantee was, however, affected by the economic situation of the guarantor. Figure 4.1 indicates, however, that both Australia and India experienced an idiosyncratic yield trajectory. Observing high yields for colonial bonds is hard to reconcile with the concept of guarantee unless one considered that exceptional conditions were jeopardizing the guarantee. These two cases will therefore receive specific attention in the next sections.

The results for other dominions and colonies are consistent with their different economic and political dynamics. Accominotti et al. (2010) highlighted the different ways the British government managed its possessions in the pre–First World War period: the so-called self-governing dominions (Australia, Canada, New Zealand, and South Africa) were monitored by subjecting their governments to the rule of law, imperial courts, and deepening of democracy because exit was a credible strategy. On the other hand, dependent colonies such as India and Ceylon were monitored by the direct transfer of decision-making to London. During the interwar period, the self-governing dominions obtained gradually more autonomy without any political unrest making unlikely the event where complete independence would be reached unilaterally. The guarantee would be at risk in those dominions only under domestic financial pressures. The Great Depression was spread internationally but affected the dominions differently. Haubrich (1990) showed that financial distress had few macro-economic consequences in Canada during the Great Depression. Calomiris (1993) attributed the smaller impact of the depression to the concentration of lending and the reliance on banks for loan in Canada. South Africa was the only member of the British Empire which did not devalue because of its 'strong external position and exceptional attachment to a stable gold price,[11] attributable to its position as a gold producer' (Eichengreen & Sachs, 1985). New Zealand had a similar economy to that of Australia depending mainly on exports and suffered from the contraction of demand during the Great Depression. However, New Zealand kept a reasonable debt level. The dependent colonies were also affected by the Great Depression since they were also depending on exports. In the case of India, the risk for investors came rather from the rise of nationalism as discussed in the next sections. In Ceylon, the amount of debt was very low and a loss of guarantee was not a credible risk.

Australian Debt Crisis

Results from the baseline regression indicate that markets viewed the 1931 crisis as a potential threat to the imperial guarantee. The dummy variable captures an overall effect, but it seems reasonable to conjecture that the disappearance of the guarantee would have been more harmful for bonds issued by colonies which were themselves experiencing financial troubles. This was the case of Australia, which saw the progressive deterioration of its economy over the course of the 1920s, avoiding default on a portion of its external debt only thanks to its ties with Great Britain (Eichengreen & Portes, 1990).

[11] All countries were off the gold standard by 1931, while South Africa remained under the gold standard until 1933.

In the years following the end of the First World War, the Australian government expenditures and debt reached worrying levels. During the First World War, gross Australian government debt increased from 2 per cent to 50 per cent of GDP, with around one third of this increase met through loans issued in London (Di Marco et al., 2009). The high level of debt was due to the financing of the war but also to the large investments required to develop transportation in the country. The latter resulted in an increase in borrowings of 43 per cent between 1918 and 1926. In 1926, the situation was exposed in a pamphlet by Cooke and Davenport (1926) and relayed by *The Economist*.[12] That year, total expenditures increased by 14 per cent, the government debt by 35 per cent, while revenues increased by only 8 per cent. In the case of Australian states, 27 per cent of expenditures went to pay interests on public debt and 30 per cent in the working of the railways that were in deficit.

At the time, the alarming situation of Australian finances was attributed to the deterioration of the global economy and the poor governance of the Federal Government of Australia. During the 1920s, the world prices of primary commodities decreased sharply, hurting significantly Australian exports. In 1928, Andrew Williamson,[13] in the presence of the Australian Prime Minister, reminded an audience that 'all our dominions should ever bear in mind that extravagance and wasteful expenditure inevitably injure credit.' He added that 'the valuable privilege accorded by the Colonial Stock Act to our Dominions imposes on them a corresponding responsibility in their borrowings to ensure that their loans shall always be worthy of the high position of a British Trustee Stock.'[14] Despite Williamson's warning, other instances of bad governance emerged. In 1930 the British Economic Mission reported that

> Loan moneys raised overseas can only come to Australia in the form of goods. These goods are subject to the Custom Duties [. . .] and are in this way taxed to an extent estimated at 15 to 20 per cent. of their value. The result is that this proportion of moneys borrowed abroad for capital purposes comes to the Commonwealth as revenue and is spent accordingly. This diversion of capital funds to revenue is obviously bad finance.

The crisis worsened to the point that Australia resorted to borrow money in London to pay interests on its overseas debt.

In 1930, a committee consisting of the Under-Treasurers of the Commonwealth and the various states and of four economists was appointed to define the Premier

[12] 'Australian Finance', *The Economist*, 6 October 1926, p. 625; issue 4338.
[13] Andrew Williamson was the chairman of the annual meeting of the English, Scottish, and Australian bank.
[14] 'Australia Finance', *The Economist*, 20 November 1926, p. 862; Issue 4343.

Rehabilitation Plan to restore financial equilibrium. The plan consisted in tax increase and expenditure reduction including the reduction in interest payable on the whole of internal loan debt[15] of the Commonwealth and all the states. The case of New South Wales default revealed the risk faced by investor holding trustee securities. On 29 January 1932, New South Wales failed to meet interest payments on the 6.5 per cent 1930–40 sterling loan. Under the terms of the Financial Agreement Validation Act of 1929, default of New South Wales would thrust the responsibility of meeting the debt service of the loans upon the Federal Government. However, the Australian Commonwealth first ensured it would have legal tools in order to seize financial assets of the defaulting state. This was guaranteed on 12 March 1932 by the Financial Agreement Enforcement Act. The uncertainty regarding the existence of a guarantee and the length of the delay of the hypothetical repayment can be observed in the bond prices.

To test whether Australia was perceived as different during the crisis, we add to regression 1 interaction terms between the Australia dummy and its economic fundamentals. If indeed the bad economic condition of Australia only mattered when the guarantee was threatened, then one would expect at least some of the interaction terms to be statistically significant. Results are reported in Table 4.2.

Table 4.2 shows that the interaction term between the Australia dummy and interest payment is statistically significant. Australia had not only an idiosyncratic yield evolution, but that part of this evolution was driven by its fundamentals.

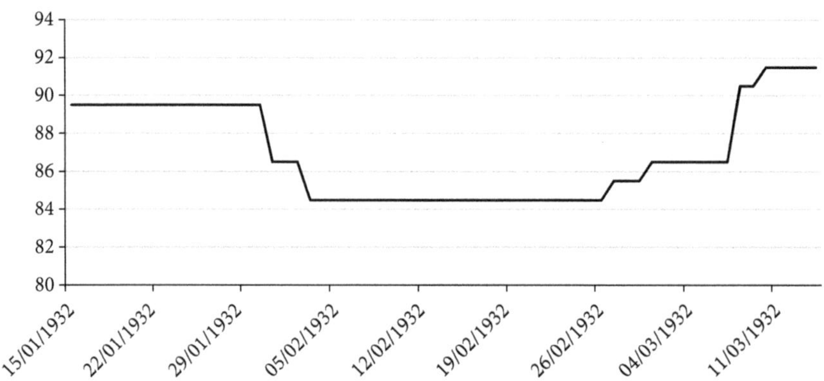

Figure 4.2. Daily prices (in British pounds) of New South Wales 6.5 per cent (1930–40) bond

[15] This was achieved by 'the Great Conversion' in 1931. The public was asked to convert £558,000,000 into new loans bearing lower interest rates and this to balance the budget. The conversion rate was a staggering 97 per cent rate. The remaining 3 per cent were forced to convert later in the year (Roberts, 1932). Conversions were a common practice, and if authorized in the loan agreement or by law they should not be considered as a default.

Table 4.2. Results for Australia

Model	Panel	Panel	Pooled
Country Fixed-Effects	Incl[†]	Incl[‡]	–
Time Fixed-Effects	Incl	–	–
Debt Service	−0.00714	−0.00784	−0.00782
Budget Surplus	0.00035	−0.00069	−0.00078
Export per head	−0.00200	−0.00144	−0.00153
Aus x Debt Service	0.12039***	0.10132**	0.10117**
Aus x Budget Surplus	0.00131	0.00047	0.00139
Aus x Export per Head	0.00142	0.00055	0.00062
Liquidity	0.04985	0.09491**	0.09647**
1931 Dummy		0.00504***	0.00502***
1932 Dummy		−0.00400***	−0.00402***
# of observ.	96	96	96
Adjusted R-square	42.43%	32.99%	36.64%

Note: The dependent variable is the spread between colonial yields and the yields on British consols. Period: 1920–36; Incl stands for included.

† Significant for Australia.

‡ None significant at the conventional levels.

During the interwar period, colonies facing extreme financial trouble were no longer considered safe, and in these circumstances bondholders doubted the implicit guarantee would protect them.

Indian Independence Pressures

In India, independence movements gradually emerged at the end of the nineteenth century. The Indian National Congress was created in 1885, followed twenty-one years later by the Muslim League. Despite these creations, many nationalists still envisioned India's future within the British Empire. For instance, in *Hind Swaraj*, Gandhi (1909) first presents the Indian National Congress as a body wishing to perpetuate British rule. When the war broke out, India proved loyal to the Empire, hoping to gain responsible government status as reward for its efforts. This hope was fuelled by a declaration of the imperial government suggesting such was its goal for India (Huttenback, 1966).

In view of the hopes entertained by Indians, the publication in January 1919 of a draft of what would eventually become the Rowlatt Act led to a general outcry (Huttenback, 1966). The Act was meant to limit revolutionary movements in India. Any holder of a document advocating opposition to the king, the government, or public servants risked a jail sentence. The Act was felt as utterly unjust. Building on his experiences in South Africa, Gandhi published in March 1919 an appeal to observe on 6 April 1919 a day of fasting, public meetings, and suspension of labour (Dalton, 1993). Four days later, Gandhi was arrested, leading to protests and the killing of several Indians and five European in Amritsar (Punjab). The Brigadier-General Reginald Dyer and his troops were sent to restore order. Interpreting a gathering in the Jallianwala Bagh public garden as a challenge to his authority, Reginald Dyer ordered its troops to open fire on the crowd, killing 379 and wounding more than 1,000. Following the massacre, martial law was imposed and as a result the news of the incident took months to reach other parts of India (Herman, 2009). The Amritsar Massacre represented a watershed in Indo-British relations (Huttenback, 1966). As stressed by Herman (2009), 'more than any other events, Amritsar and its aftermath solidified national support for independence.' The Amritsar Massacre also changed Gandhi's view on the Empire and transformed him from supporter to staunch opponent (Dalton, 1993).

The absence of real sanctions following the Amritsar Massacre outraged the Indian population and prompted action from the independence movements. Gandhi gradually took a leading position in many respects. On 4 September 1920 a special session of the Indian Congress adopted a 'Resolution on Non-cooperation' (Dalton, 1993). To the surprise of many, the issue at stake chosen by Gandhi was the fate of the Constantinople Caliphate. Herman (2009) argues that this choice, a clear sign for the Muslim community, allowed Gandhi to get a first nationwide coalition. The non-cooperation campaign was to follow several stages. After having resigned British honorary titles and positions, Indians were to boycott the future elections. Following this, Indians were expected to resign from their positions within British courts before adopting a 'buy-Indian' policy. Once these stages would have been completed, members of the police and the Army were to resign and everybody should stop paying taxes.

The non-cooperation movement proved particularly successful for the lower and middle classes but only produced a short-lived enthusiasm amongst educated ones. The boycott of British goods led to a drop in British exports to India but not of large enough proportions to prompt action on the British side (Herman, 2009). A proclamation by Muslim leaders, the Ali brothers, in July 1921 changed the British position. The leaders were indeed pushing forward a resolution stating that serving in the British Army was equivalent to an act against the Muslim faith. This statement was taken seriously by Great Britain since most Englishmen believed that Hindus were poor fighters compared to Muslims (Herman, 2009). In October 1921, and following four months of violence, the Ali brothers were arrested. A month later a resolution in the Indian Congress declared that serving in the British Army was contrary to national dignity. At the end of November 1921 riots broke out in Bombay. In December 1921 and January 1922 the government took energetic measures against the non-cooperation movement leading to the jailing of close to 30,000 opponents to the British rule (Dalton, 1993). In February a mass civil disobedience campaign was launched in the district of Bardoli. On 5 February

1922 a nationalist demonstration degenerated in Chauri Chaura, leading to the deaths of twenty-two police officers who were attempting to stop the movement. Following Chauri Chaura, the use of civil disobedience was momentarily stopped, only to resume on a large scale during the Salt March (Dalton, 1993). In view of his implication in the non-cooperation campaign, Gandhi was sentenced to six years of jail in March 1922 but was released in February 1924 on health grounds.

The failure of the non-cooperation campaign and Gandhi's imprisonment had taken away his credibility as leader. He would remain in the shadows until 1927. Following the 1919 Government of India Act, the Secretary of State for India, Earl Birkenhead, created in November 1927 a commission (later named the Simon Commission) to decide whether to grant self-rule to India. Convinced that India should remain under British rule, he made sure that the commission did not count any Indian. This event led the Indian National Congress to state that it would not accept anything but complete independence. As for the Simon Commission, it met fierce resistance within India. The year 1928 ended in a political impasse. In this context, Gandhi appeared as a trustworthy figure to many Indians. He pleaded for a dominion status and threatened to launch a mass non-cooperation campaign should Great Britain reject this demand. In October 1929 the Viceroy of India, Lord Irwin announced that India would gain a dominion status without, however, specifying any schedule. This declaration provoked the anger of part of the British political world, amongst others that of Winston Churchill (Herman, 2009). On the Indian side, Irwin's declaration was met with some scepticism. Despite internal divisions a joint declaration (the Delhi Declaration) demanded immediate release of political prisoners and full Dominion status before any roundtable conference was to be held. Eventually, the Indian National Congress agreed in December 1929 on the following ultimatum: if India did not receive dominion status by New Year's Eve then the Congress would undertake all necessary action to gain full independence.

The British government refused the Indian National Congress conditions. For a few weeks, this decision seemed to have no effect as life continued as usual. This moment of hesitation may be attributed to diverging views regarding the actions to undertake. The decision to launch a campaign against the salt tax was taken only a few days before the Salt March began (Dalton, 1993). Gandhi had attacked the salt tax in earlier texts (Gandhi, 1909) stressing that its burden also fell on the shoulders of the very poor as salt was vital. In an open letter dated 2 March 1930 and addressed to Lord Irwin, Gandhi explained the motivations behind his decision to begin his civil disobedience movement. This letter proved to be crucial, since it was widely publicized and drew much media attention to Gandhi's campaign. The aim of the march was to put into question the state monopoly on salt. On 12 March 1930 the group led by Gandhi started a march to the sea to collect salt from the seashore, thus without paying the required tax. The choice of the salt tax proved to be extremely shrewd. Indeed, it led many Indian women to support the cause and attracted a large popular support. The publicity around the march was guaranteed by the media eager to follow Gandhi's odyssey. On 6 April 1930 the salt was collected; the government had not dared interrupt the march and Gandhi would not be arrested before 5 May. Gandhi's example was swiftly followed and would lead to more than 60,000 imprisonments (Dalton, 1993). Eventually, Lord Irwin was left with little choice but to convene a roundtable between Indian and British representatives. In view of the impasse in which they found themselves, Lord Irwin released Gandhi in January 1931. An agreement was reached in March 1931. The Gandhi–Irwin pact exchanged suspension of civil disobedience for freedom of political prisoners; the salt tax, however, remained, and for many Indians the concessions from the British Raj were far from their expectations.

In September 1931 Gandhi arrived in London to present the Indian requests. At the same moment, religious riots were taking place in India and Great Britain was experiencing a rapid turnover in governments. The roundtable conference ended without any agreement between the parties. Meanwhile in India, Lord Willingdon had replaced Lord Irwin as viceroy and terror attacks began to take place frequently. Lord Willingdon acted quickly and declared emergency rules: a clear attack on the Indian National Congress. In reaction, a new civil disobedience campaign was launched, but the arrest of Gandhi in early 1932 deprived the movement of its leader and the campaign ground to a halt by mid-1932 (Herman, 2009). The British government then produced a document to deal with the issue of religious representation. The following years saw the expression of diverging views among Indian leaders. In January 1935, however, a bill devolving more power to India was presented in Parliament. It was fiercely opposed by Churchill and many amendments were added. Eventually however the Government of India Act passed on 4 June 1935 without having seen fundamental changes in its spirit (Herman, 2009). Despite the fact that the new act granted new prerogatives to Indians it still met with serious criticisms in India (Shah, 1937).

In view of the momentum gained by independence movements after the First World War, investors may have believed that the guarantee would disappear should India become independent. In the case of independence, two scenarios could be considered. On one hand, in the case of a negotiated independence, bondholders would probably have assessed the value of their bonds on the basis of Indian fundamentals. On the other hand, in the case of a hard independence, bondholders may have feared that the new Indian government would decide to repudiate the Indian bonds. Several precedents of state succession which had led to the repudiation of foreign bonds existed. For example, the United States refused to take over the Cuban bonds issued by Spain after the annexation of Cuba following the Spanish-American war. Collet (2013) has shown that markets had been strongly affected by this move. This option was certainly viewed as credible since several Indian movements fighting for independence had pledged to repudiate these bonds should they come to power. During the 1920 Special Session of the Indian Congress held in Calcutta, a majority of the delegates carried the resolution of non-cooperation sponsored by Gandhi. The resolutions supported a disengagement of Indians from the British political, economic, and social structures. More specifically, point d) of the resolution challenged the legitimacy of British judiciary for Indian matters. The resolution advised a 'gradual boycott of British Courts by lawyers and litigants, and the establishment of private arbitration courts [...]'. The subject of debt repudiation was explicitly addressed at the 1922 Congress in Gaya.

> Whereas by reason of unjustifiable military expenditures and other extravagances, the Government has brought the national indebtedness to a limit beyond recovery. [...] The people of India, though holding themselves liable for all debts [...] incurred hitherto by the Government, will not hold themselves bound to repay any loans or discharge any liabilities incurred on and after this date on the authority or sanction of the so-called legislature.

The 1929 Lahore Congress went even further, passing the resolution that 'every obligation, every concession, no matter how incurred or given, would be repudiated, if it is not found by [an independent] tribunal to be just and justifiable.' The arguments advanced by the Indian independence movement are very close to those evoked by the proponents of the odious debt doctrine. The debts which had been issued against the interest of the Indian population should not be repaid once independence would be achieved. Previous studies (Collet, 2013; Collet & Oosterlinck, 2019; Gulati & Panizza, this volume) have shown that markets react when debts are denounced as odious. An increase in the perception that India might repudiate the debt could thus translate into higher yields.

To test an independence effect, we rely on a variable that counts the number of articles in *The Economist* that mention 'Gandhi' for every year between 1919 and 1936. The word 'Gandhi' was preferred to other independence-related terms because of its higher frequency of occurrence ('Gandhi' was mentioned in *The Economist* in 154 articles, against forty-three articles talking about either 'independence', 'autonomy', 'swaraj[16]', 'unrest', or 'Nerhu').

Results in Table 4.3 show that the spread was influenced by independence movements in India. The Gandhi variable is indeed statistically significant. Its inclusion, however, changes the significance of the 1931 and 1932 dummies. This is hardly surprising, as some of the most visible actions were taken by Gandhi in 1931 and 1932. We interpret this result as the sign that bondholders did not believe the guarantee would last in case of independence. The nature of the

[16] Hindi term referring to the self-governance, used by Indian Independentist to refer to India independence.

Table 4.3. Results for India

Model	Panel	Panel	Pooled
Country Fixed-Effects	Incl†	Incl†	–
Time Fixed-Effects	Incl	–	–
Int	0.00387	–0.00132	–0.00127
Bud	0.00177	–0.00027	–0.00018
Xpt	0.00021	–0.00036	–0.00038
Ind x Int	0.02849	0.02040	0.01845
Ind x Bud	0.00747	0.00762	0.00620
Ind x Xpt	–0.01887	0.01030	0.01305
Liquidity	0.21586	0.17339***	0.17268***
1931 Dummy		0.00198	0.00202
1932 Dummy		–0.00143	–0.00143
Gandhi	0.00038***	0.00034***	0.00033***
# of observ.	96	96	96
Adjusted R-square	59.27%	48.07%	49.71%

Note: The dependent variable is the spread between colonial yields and the yields on British consols. Period: 1920–36; Incl stands for included.

† None are significant at conventional levels.

bondholders may have strengthened this effect. States may decide not to default on their debt if they fear that this would have strong consequences on their own economy. In line with this idea, empirical studies show that sovereigns are more likely to default on external than domestic debts (Van Rijckeghem & Weder, 2009; Erce & Malluci, 2018). Oosterlinck (2003) argues that holders of bonds issued under the Vichy regime considered a government ruled by Charles de Gaulle as a relatively good outcome. Indeed, he was perceived as less likely to repudiate these debts in order to protect the French banks which were holding them. The Indian case offers a stark contrast. For the debts issued between 1923 and 1933 and for which the information regarding ownership is available, only 8.5 per cent of the debts were bought by Indians, even though for some issues the proportion could be significantly higher (Sunderland 2013, 26). Selectively defaulting on the debts held by non-Indian would thus have been an easy way to force foreigners (mostly British) to bear the brunt of debt repudiation.

4.5 Conclusion

The literature has attempted to determine to which extent being part of an empire benefited the colonies. Lower borrowing costs are usually presented as one of the benefits colonies reaped from their subjection. These lower borrowing costs would result from market participants' belief that colonial bonds were guaranteed by the colonial power. Despite the central role played by this guarantee, its specific workings have received little attention in the literature. This chapter overcomes this shortcoming. It does not attempt to determine whether the proceeds of loans were used for constructive purposes[17] but rather it aims at understanding to which extent colonial guarantees were viewed as credible by market participants.

To understand whether colonies' borrowing costs were reduced because of their colonial status, the yields on colonial bonds are compared to the yields from a panel of sovereign bonds. In general, results tend to show that yields on colonial bonds are relatively low; an observation attributed to the implicit guarantee of the colonial power. Noteworthy, some authors find no impact of the colonial status on borrowing costs. This chapter attempts to reconcile the differences observed in the literature. To do so, we rely on a novel approach to assess the importance of the colonial guarantee. More precisely, we focus on the interwar period, a period for which we argue investors may have doubted the willingness or the ability of the colonial power to bail out troubled colonies. The interwar period was indeed characterized by financial instability. The United Kingdom was forced to leave the gold standard in 1931. In parallel, independence movements were gaining ground in some colonies, most notably in India.

To test whether investors still viewed colonial bonds as guaranteed by the colonial power, we construct a database tracking the yields of six British colonies between 1919 and 1936. We then regress the spread between these yields and British consols on a series of economic indicators. As in Accominotti et al. (2011), we find that when colonies are pooled together, none of the variables linked to economic fundamentals are statistically significant. Yields of Australian and Indian bonds, however, follow an idiosyncratic path. We test whether this might reflect the fact that bondholders distinguished the value of the guarantee in function of the fundamentals of the colonies. For colonies with sound finances, the value of a guarantee should not be expected to be high. By contrast, the guarantee may be valuable for countries for which economic fundamentals are less rosy or which may become independent.

To test this hypothesis, we first focus on Australia. Australia is a good candidate to assess to which extent bondholders valued the guarantee more for countries experiencing financial troubles. Indeed, recklessness in management of public finances in conjunction to a deterioration of the country's export seriously reduced the country's ability to repay its debts. The default of New South Wales in 1932 only aggravated the situation. Our results indicate that bondholders perceived Australia differently. Once interaction terms between fundamentals and Australia are included, we find them to be statistically significant.

The Indian case is somehow different. Here bondholders were less concerned about the colony's ability to pay than about its independence. Several

[17] An inherently difficult task, as in some instances the intended uses of the funds mentioned in prospectus were known *ex ante* to be fake (Sunderland, 2013).

independence movements had pledged to repudiate the debts should they come to power. In this case, fundamentals of India would not have mattered since the new Indian government would have refused to pay the debts on political grounds rather than on economic ones. In parallel, independence would have removed the implicit imperial guarantee. Results indicate indeed that fundamentals were not significant but that our proxy to capture the strength of independence movement is statistically significant.

Our analysis shows that bonds issued by colonies benefited indeed from an implicit guarantee. But the implicit nature of the guarantee led investors to expect that in case of extreme financial distress the guarantor would not be willing to honour the guarantee. Furthermore, the guarantee was conditional on the colonies not becoming independent. The implicit guarantee shaped the relationship between the Empire and its colonies. The effect of the guarantee was twofold. On the one hand, it allowed colonies to have access to the capital markets and to borrow at a relatively cheap rate. Investors believed that lending to the colonies was not risky since the British Empire would intervene in case of default. In the case of India, bond prices dropped at the moment investors realized that an independent India might repudiate Indian bonds. On the other hand, the control of the British Empire may have forced colonies to finance their own subjection. The guarantor–obligee relationship was a tool of subjection, as it increased the cost of independence. The implicit guarantee thus provided direct benefits to Britain. However, these benefits came at a cost: the British Empire had to avoid the default of colonial bonds. Those were issued under the British treasury authority and were stamped as sufficiently safe to be part of the list in which trustees are authorized to invest. The default of any of those top-rated assets might have created a systemic crisis. This historical example offers a striking parallel with market perceptions of Greek debts before the Eurozone crisis. Before the crisis, investors rationally considered that the EMU countries had an interest in Greece's continued participation in the EMU (Arghyrou & Tsoukalas, 2011). Bonds were therefore priced as if they were guaranteed. The withdrawal of this implicit guarantee on Greek debts negatively affected the price of Greek bonds. More generally, our research suggests that implicit guarantees are only credible for minor crisis but that markets question these as soon as the amounts at stake become large.

References

Accominotti, O., Flandreau, M. & Rezzik, R. (2011). 'The Spread of Empire: Clio and the Measurement of Colonial Borrowing Costs'. *The Economic History Review* 64(2), 385–407.

Accominotti, O., Flandreau, M., Rezzik, R. & Zumer, F. (2010). 'Black Man's Burden, White Man's Welfare: Control, Devolution and Development in the British Empire, 1880–1914'. *European Review of Economic History* 14(1), 47–70.

Alquist, R. (2010). 'How Important is Liquidity Risk for Sovereign Bond Risk Premia? Evidence from the London Stock Exchange'. *Journal of International Economics*, 82(2), 219–29.

Arghyrou, M.G. & Tsoukalas, J.D. (2011). 'The Greek Debt Crisis: Likely Causes, Mechanics and Outcomes'. *The World Economy*, 34(2), 173–91.

Atkin, J. (1970). 'Official Regulation of British Overseas Investment, 1914–1931'. The Economic History Review, 23(2), 324–35.

Cairncross, A.K. (1953). *Home and Foreign Investment, 1870–1913*. London: Cambridge University Press.

Calomiris, C.W. (1993). 'Financial Factors in the Great Depression'. *Journal of Economic Perspectives*, 7(2), 61–85.

Chavaz, M. & Flandreau, M. (2017). "High & Dry': The Liquidity and Credit of Foreign Government Debt in the First Age of Globalization (1880–1910)'. *The Journal of Economic History*, 77(3), 653–91.

Collet, S. (2013). 'The Financial Penalty for 'unfair' Debt: The Case of Cuban Bonds at the Time of Independence'. *European Review of Economic History*, 17(3), 364–87.

Collet, S. & Oosterlinck, K. (2019). 'Denouncing Odious Debts'. *Journal of Business Ethics*, 160(1), 205–23.

Colonial Stock Act (1900). Parliament of the United Kingdom.

Cooke, S.R. & Davenport, E.H. (1926). *Australian Finance*. London: Pelican Press.

Crafts, N. & Fearon, P. (2010). 'Lessons From the 1930s Great Depression'. *Oxford Review of Economic Policy*, 26(3), 285–317.

Dalton, D. (1993). *Mahatma Gandhi*. New York: Columbia University Press.

Davis, L.E. & Huttenback, R. (1986). *Mammon and the Pursuit of Empire, The Political Economy of British Imperialism, 1860–1912*. London: Cambridge University Press.

Di Marco, K., Pirie, M. & Au-Yeung, W. (2009). 'A History of Public Debt in Australia'. *Economic Round-Up*, 1(1), 1–16.

Eichengreen, B. & Portes, R. (1990). 'The Interwar Debt Crisis and its Aftermath'. *World Bank Research Observer*, 5(1), 69–94.

Eichengreen, B. & Sachs, J. (1985). 'Exchange Rates and Economic Recovery in the 1930s'. *The Journal of Economic History*, 45(4), 925–46.

Ellissen, H. (1904). *Trust Investments: An Annotated and Classified List of Securities Authorised for the Investment of Trust Fund Under Section I of the Trustee Act, 1893, and the Colonial Stock Act, 1900*. London: William Clowes and Sons.

Erce, A. & Malluci, E. (2018). 'Selective Sovereign Defaults'. *FRB International Finance Discussion Paper 1239*.

Ferguson, N. & Schularick, M. (2006). 'The Empire Effect: The Determinants of Country Risk in the First Age of Globalization'. *The Journal of Economic History*, 66(2), 283–312.

Frank, A.G. (1966). 'The Development of Underdevelopment'. *Monthly Review*, 18(4), 17–31.

Foley-Fisher, N. & McLaughlin, E. (2016). 'Sovereign Debt Guarantees and Default: Lessons from the UK and Ireland, 1920–1938'. *European Economic Review*, 87, 272–86.

Gandhi, M.K. (1909). *Hind Swaraj or Indian home rule*. Ahmedabad: Navjeevan Trust.

Gandhi, M.K. (1921). *Hind Swaraj or Indian home rule*. Madras: GA Natesan and Company.

Greasley, D. & Oxley, L. (1996). 'Discontinuities in Competitiveness: the Impact of the First World War on British industry'. *The Economic History Review*, 49(1), 82–100.

Haubrich, J.G. (1990). 'Nonmonetary Effects of Financial Crises: Lessons from the Great Depression in Canada'. *Journal of Monetary Economics*, 25(2), 223–52.

Herman, A. (2009). *Gandhi and Churchill. The Epic Rivalry That Destroyed an Empire and Forged Our Age*. New York: Bantam.

Hirtzel, A. (1930). *The Stock Exchange Official Intelligence for 1930; India Sterling Securities*.

Huttenback, R.A. (1966). 'Indians in South Africa, 1860–1914: The British Imperial Philosophy on Trial'. The English Historical Review, 81(319), 273–91.

Kuhn, A.K. (1934). 'The Gold Clause in International Loans'. The American Journal of International Law, 28(2), 312–15.

MacMillan, M. (2002). *The Peacemakers. The Paris Peace Conference and Its Attempts to End War*. London: John Murray.

Michie, R. (1999). *The London Stock Exchange: A History*. Oxford: Oxford University Press.

Obstfeld, M. & Taylor, A. (2003). 'Sovereign Risk, Credibility and the Gold Standard: 1870–13 versus 1925–31'. *The Economic Journal*, 113(487), 241–75.

Oosterlinck, K. (2003). 'The Bond Market and the Legitimacy of Vichy France'. *Explorations in Economic History*, 40(3), 326–44.

Oosterlinck, K. (2016). *Hope Springs Eternal. French Bondholders and the Repudiation of Russian Sovereign Debt*. New Haven: Yale University Press.

Reinhart, C.M. & Rogoff, K.S. (2011). 'From Financial Crash to Debt Crisis'. *American Economic Review*, 101(5), 1676–706.

Roberts, S.H. (1932). 'The Crisis in Australia: September, 1930-January, 1932'. *Pacific Affairs 5* (4), 319–32.

Shah, K.T. (1937). *Indian Constitution. Vol. I: Provincial autonomy (under the Government of India Act, 1935)*. Bombay: Vora and Company.

Sunderland, D. (2004). *Managing the British Empire: The Crown Agents for the Colonies 1833-1914*. Suffolk: Boydell Press.

Sunderland, D. (2013). *Financing the Raj: The City of London and Colonial India, 1858–1940*. Suffolk: Boydell Press.

Trustee Act (1893). Parliament of the United Kingdom.

Van Rijckeghem, C. & Weder, B. (2009). 'Political Institutions and Debt Crises'. *Public Choice*, 138(3–4), 387–408.

Appendix

Commonwealth of Australia	**India 5.5% Stock, 1936–38**
Australia (Commw. of) 5.25% Registered Stock (1920–22)	India 4%, 1948–53
Australia (Commw. of) 5.5% Registered Stock (1922–27)	India 5%, 1942–47
Australia (Commw. of) 6% Registered Stock (1931–41)	India 3.5%, 1954–59
Australia (Commw. of) 6% Registered Stock (1935–45)	
Australia (Commw. of) 4.75% Registered Stock (1940–60)	New Zealand
Australia (Commw. of) 5% Registered Stock (1945–75)	New Zealand 4% Consolidated Stock, Inscribed (1929)
	New Zealand 3% Inscribed (1945)
Dominion of Canada	New Zealand 4% Inscribed Stock (1943–63)
Canada (Dominion of) 3.5% Stock, Registered (1909–34)	New Zealand 6% Inscribed Stock (1936–51)
Canada (Dominion of) 3% Stock, Registered (1938)	New Zealand 5% Inscribed Stock (1935–45)
Canada (Dominion of) 2.5% Inscribed Stock (1947)	New Zealand 4% Inscribed Stock (1933–43)
Canada (Dominion of) 3.5% Registered Stock (1930–50)	New Zealand 4.5% Inscribed Stock (1944)
Canada (Dominion of) 4% Stock (1940–60)	New Zealand 4.5% Inscribed Stock (1945)
Canada (Dominion of) 4 % Registered Stock (1953–58)	New Zealand 5% Inscribed Stock (1946)
Canada (Dominion of) 3.5% Registered Stock (1950–55)	New Zealand 4.5% Inscribed Stock (1947)
	New Zealand 4.5% Inscribed Stock (1948–58)
Ceylon	New Zealand 5% Inscribed Stock (1949)
Ceylon 4% Inscribed Stock (1934)	New Zealand 5% Inscribed Stock (1956–71)
Ceylon 3% Inscribed Stock (1940)	New Zealand 3.5% Inscribed Stock (1949–54)
Ceylon 3.5% Inscribed Stock (1934–59)	New Zealand 3.5% Inscribed Stock (1955–60)
Ceylon 4% Inscribed Stock (1939–59)	New Zealand 3% Inscribed Stock (1952–55)
Ceylon 6% Inscribed Stock (1936–51)	

Commonwealth of Australia	**India 5.5% Stock, 1936–38**
Ceylon 5% Inscribed Stock (1960–70)	Union of South Africa
Ceylon 4.5% Inscribed Stock (1965)	South Africa (Union of) Consolidated 4% Stock, Inscribed (1943–63)
Ceylon 3.25% Inscribed Stock (1959)	South Africa (Union of) 4.5% Inscribed Stock (1920–25)
	South Africa (Union of) Consolidated 6% Stock (1930–40)
India	South Africa (Union of) 5% Inscribed Stock (1933–43)
India 3.5% Stock, Redemption on or after 5 January 1948	South Africa (Union of) 5% Inscribed Stock (1940–60)
India 5.5% Loan, 1932	South Africa (Union of) 5% Inscribed Stock (1945–75)
India 4.5% Loan, 1950–55	South Africa (Union of) 4.5% Inscribed Stock (1955–75)
India 4.5% Stock, 1958–68	South Africa (Union of) 5% Inscribed Stock (1950–70)
India 6% Stock, 1932–33	South Africa (Union of) 3.5% Inscribed Stock (1953–73)
India 6% Stock, 1933–34	South Africa (Union of) 3.5% Inscribed Stock (1955–65)
India 6% Stock, 1933–35	South Africa (Union of) 3% Inscribed Stock (1954–64)
India 6% Stock, 1935–37	

SECTION 2

DEBT DISPUTES IN THE AGE OF FINANCIAL REPRESSION: WHEN REPAYMENT TAKES A BACKSEAT (1933–70s)

5

The Fortune of Geopolitical Conditions in Debt Diplomacy

Mexico's Long Road to the 1942 Foreign Debt Settlement

Gustavo Del Angel and Lorena Pérez-Hernández

5.1 Introduction

In November 1942, the Mexican government reached an agreement with international creditors for payment of its foreign debt. This came after a period of more than twenty-five years with recurrent problems meeting its financial obligations and twenty years of failed negotiations. The settlement ruled that the Mexican government would pay approximately 10 per cent of its total foreign debt, relief that was unprecedented in the history of Mexico and unusual in the global history of foreign debt (only Bolivia in 1950 reached a similar deal). This was extraordinary, given that by that time the government was managing to clean up its finances and had better fiscal tools at its disposal to meet its financial needs. In this chapter, we aim to show that this was the result of two factors: first, a change in the geopolitical situation, in light of the United States entering the Second World War; second, Mexico's governments having taken a proactive stance in debt negotiations with its international counterparts.

We believe that this case is relevant because literature in economics typically associates the chances of debt resolution with the debtor's capacity to pay (Sachs, 1989; Reinhart & Rogoff, 2014), its interest in maintaining a reputation in foreign markets (Eaton & Gersovitz, 1981; Eaton, 1990; Cole, Dow & English, 1995; Reinhart & Rogoff, 2014), and the capacity of lenders to gain rights on the borrower's assets (Bulow & Rogoff, 1989). The notion that a debtor country is interested in its standing in debt markets might explain part of the story in this chapter.

However, we aim to explain a story in which the geopolitical context is what explains that particular settlement. We also aim to show how debt diplomacy explains the course of the negotiations, this in terms of how individual actors negotiate and hence, influence the outcomes. With this, we bring together purely

Gustavo Del Angel and Lorena Pérez-Hernández, *The Fortune of Geopolitical Conditions in Debt Diplomacy: Mexico's Long Road to the 1942 Foreign Debt Settlement* In: *Sovereign Debt Diplomacies: Rethinking Sovereign Debt from Colonial Empires to Hegemony.* Edited by: Pierre Pénet and Juan Flores Zendejas, Oxford University Press (2021). © Oxford University Press.
DOI: 10.1093/oso/9780198866350.003.0006

economic elements, such as the fiscal capacity of a debtor country, with other elements like political stability, the political stances of creditor countries, the ability of the debtor country to take a proactive stance and the agency of individual actors.

At the turn of the twentieth century, Mexico was in excellent condition in the international financial markets. It had moderate foreign debt, combined with relatively healthy public finances. However, when the Revolution of 1910 broke out, both the armed struggle and the political instability affected the economy as a whole, and particularly the financial system and public finances. The Mexican government entered into a spiral where it needed financial resources from abroad but wasn't in a position to ensure repayment. Even so, the various groups of warlords who had seized power obtained loans from international bankers. At the same time, the government faced international investors who sought compensation for losses incurred due to the Mexican Civil War. By 1921, when it is considered that the most difficult and unstable part of that Civil War was over, the government restarted negotiations with international bankers.

To study the process of public debt negotiations during the period from 1921 to 1942, this study is divided into two stages that reflect the state of the most important agreements reached between those years. In the first, from 1921 to 1934, several agreements took shape, but Mexico was unable to comply with them. In addition to the conditions of the agreements being relatively astringent, Mexico's negotiating strategy was erratic. In the second stage, from 1934 to 1942, Mexico had a more proactive strategy in the negotiations, as it initiated buybacks of debt bonds in the market. It also coincided with a historic moment in which the United States gave a central weight to Mexico's strategic situation in geopolitics.

In international negotiations, the agency of a key player is key to explain the outcome reached. Eduardo Suárez, who was the Minister of Finance (*Secretario de Hacienda*) between 1935 and 1946, had participated in debt negotiations since 1926. From 1934, he achieved an important shift in Mexico's position before its international creditors, represented on the International Committee of Bankers on Mexico (*Comité Internacional de Banqueros*). Suárez took advantage of the crisis among creditor countries, and in particular the growing weakness of the United Kingdom and France, the impartiality of American courts, as well as the precarious situation of Mexican debt bonds in the international markets.

In turn, the government of the United States considered Mexico an important geopolitical ally even before entering the Second World War. The North American governments always stressed their concern that Mexico should maintain a clear and unwavering position alongside the Allied Nations and be emphatic in its rejection of the Axis Nations. This was crucial in light of the proximity of the countries and the sympathy that some Latin American countries showed toward the Axis Nations. In that context, the Mexican government did not hesitate to join the Allied Nations and collaborate with the United States during the War. As part of the negotiating package to reach an agreement, resolution of Mexico's foreign debt became an important concession by the North American government.

This chapter is based on contemporary reports by the Ministry of Finance and Bank of Mexico, the central bank, press information from the archives of the Ministry of Finance, the memoirs of the Ministers of Finance—Eduardo Suárez and Alberto J. Pani—and secondary literature.

The next section discusses possible conceptual frameworks for the story. Section 5.3 explains, as a point of departure, the events after the 1910 Revolution and the reopening of the debt negotiations. Sections 5.4 and 5.5 describe the first series of negotiations, which were unsuccessful and ended in suspension of payments in 1934. Section 5.6 explains the shift in the relationship with the United States. Sections 5.7 and 5.8 bring perspective to the 1942 settlements.

5.2 An Attempt to Frame the Story

Jorgensen and Sachs (1989, p. 71) assert that: 'It is interesting to note that the longer a debtor held out, the better it fared in the conditions of settlement.' Table 5.1 shows the arrangements of other Latin American countries. Compared to those nations, Mexico's 'present value ratio post-default' was 0.10 in 1942. However, as explained in this chapter, the strategy was far from intended. Historical evidence shows that the Mexican government was interested in recovering reputation in the international financial markets rather than delaying the negotiations, but the conditions for achieving a good arrangement were far from optimal.

Proposing a conceptual frame for the events under study is a task yet to be developed. Our task is two-fold. First, we seek to have a rationale that explains why the Mexican government, as a debtor, was not able to honour its foreign debt and to reach an agreement over a period of almost two decades. Second, we need a rationale that explains that unique and unprecedented settlement.

The spiral of war and political instability that Mexico experienced after 1911 led, among other consequences, to a deterioration of its financial system and public finances and consequently, the inability to pay its external public debt.

Table 5.1. Latin American debt settlements

	Year of settlement	Present valueratio post-default
Bolivia	1950	0.08
Chile	1948	0.31
Colombia	1940	0.63
Peru	1947	0.39

Source: Jorgensen and Sachs (1989).

The Mexican government had learned how to build a good reputation, after foreign debt defaults, repudiation and re-entrance to the international debt markets during the nineteenth century. Apparently, the government of that country 'learned from its mistakes', in the way portrayed by Reinhart and Rogoff (2008). However, civil war and political instability is an unexpected cause of disruption in public finances; these also create uncertainty about who (what administration/government) would take care of the government's debt; mostly if that debt was acquired by an enemy faction.[1]

In the economics literature on sovereign debt, an accepted explanation of why governments repay their foreign debt relies in the notion that they need to maintain a good reputation, as borrowers, to be able to access lending in the future (Eaton & Gersovitz, 1981; Eaton, 1990; Cole, Dow & English, 1995; Reinhart & Rogoff, 2014). This argument has been contested, but it still is intuitively valid and is a consensus among practitioners. However, this idea assumes that governments are stable. In the case of the Mexican government, this concern about its standing in foreign debt markets is found in several sources.

For Bulow and Rogoff (1989), international lending to a less developed country cannot be based on the debtor's reputation for making repayments. Less developed (or any) countries always have an incentive to default. They argue that loans to developing countries depend on the legal and political rights of lenders. Their argument obviates that a precondition for this is that institutions (legal and political) are relatively stable and relatively functional; this also implicitly assumes that governments are stable enough to maintain commitments. The argument of Bulow and Rogoff can explain the position of some of the creditors, however, does not fully apply to the story.

A model that might provide insights for a rationale for the case under study is Amador (2004). The author explains that when international financial markets are complete, political considerations restrain a country from implementing the saving sequence that the Bulow and Rogoff argument requires. The model is built on the insight that politicians are not continuously in power. The incumbent politicians have a bias towards the present, due to the uncertainty on who will be in power in the future. They know however, that when tomorrow arrives, whoever is in power will be impatient in the short term as well. This time inconsistency can generate strong inefficiencies in the savings done by governments. However, even under a situation of shifting governments, foreign debt obligations can be maintained. Lienau (2014) emphasizes the importance of debt continuity when a political regime changes.

A different frame is needed to explain the rationale of how and why creditors can forgive the foreign debt of a borrower that has continuously defaulted. This

[1] Sachs (1989) explains as the main origins of debt crisis bank lending behaviour, global shocks, debtor's policies, and trade regime.

study bases its argument in two empirical facts of this story: a form of debt diplomacy, and more important, how geopolitical circumstances contributed to establish a debt settlement.

5.3 The Point of Departure in the Mexican Story

At the beginning of 1911, Mexico's foreign public debt was £441,453 (Bazant 1968, p. 174). Porfirio Díaz's regime, from 1876 to 1911, led to a situation of relative order in the country's foreign public debt and prestige in international markets.[2] But the Mexican Revolution, which broke out in 1911, initiated a new cycle of public credit. The Civil War and political instability, ever-growing throughout the decade, altered the country's economic conditions.[3] This is the starting point to explain our story.

After Porfirio Díaz left Mexico, the government received three international loans. The first was brokered in 1911 by the provisional president, Francisco León de la Barra, and the second by President Francisco I. Madero in 1912; each was for £10 million and both had an annual interest rate of 4.5 per cent. The last loan was taken out in June 1913 by Victoriano Huerta, a warlord who deposed Madero. This was for £16 million with a 6 per cent nominal annual interest rate. Foreign public debt grew to almost 500 million pesos. This amount including the so-called railroad debt bonds, for the railroad company, which were guaranteed by the government.[4] It was hoped that these loans would help control the instability facing the country.[5]

However, the continuing civil war suspended all possibility of payment. On 17 December 1913, Victoriano Huerta presented Congress with an initiative to declare the suspension of debt payments, which was approved in January 1914. The suspension would last six months. But it was not possible to resume payment of the debt. The period between 1914 and 1918 was the most violent of this episode. Consequently, for the Mexican government, international sources of credit disappeared between 1914 and 1921, as did markets for any new issuance of bonds. Moreover, bonds circulating in the world stock exchanges had decreased in value (Secretaría de Hacienda y Crédito Público, 1960, p. 53). Mexico was the only Latin American country that suspended payments completely at that time

[2] There is a strand of literature studying the external debt of the Mexican government from the first loans in 1824 to 1911. See Ludlow and Marichal (1998) for a chronology of relevant events during that period.

[3] See Haber, Maurer and Razo (2003) for general economic conditions and Anaya Merchant (2001) for the financial outcomes of the Revolution.

[4] See Bazant ([1968] 1995, pp. 179–83), Secretaría de Hacienda and Crédito Público (1960, pp. 40–1) and Meyer (1991, pp. 118–28).

[5] See Weller (2018) for the capacity of Mexico to access loans in that context, understood as a problem of asymmetric information.

(Ludlow & Marichal, 1998, p. 22). It was only at the beginning of the 1920s, seven years later, that the government renewed efforts to resume negotiations surrounding public debt.

Moreover, the global environment changed significantly in those years. The First World War dramatically changed international diplomatic and economic relations, because it altered the financial positions of Great Britain, France, Germany, and the United States as creditor and debtor countries. After financing the Allies in that War, the latter became the main creditor worldwide. Under these new circumstances, Mexico was definitely within the American sphere of influence (Riguzzi, 2010, p. 402).

A special concern for the US government was the status of the economic interests of US citizens in Mexico—particularly oil and agricultural companies—and payment of claims for losses caused to its citizens and properties by the Revolution (Meyer, 2000, p. 846). This was no coincidence—the Mexican Constitution, passed in 1917, gave the State power over private property, weakening private property rights. Additionally, Article 27 of the Constitution affected foreign investors because it declared State ownership of natural resources underground (Del Angel & Martinelli, 2009; Medina, 1995, p. 88).

The end of the First World War created the conditions needed for foreigners with investments in Mexico to resolve their outstanding issues. To begin with, in 1919 the so-called International Committee of Bankers on Mexico was created by a group of banks from the United States, England, and France (Germany, which was also a creditor, was not represented). Despite the fact that 80 per cent of bonds were held by Europeans, the Committee was controlled by the New York company J. P. Morgan and Co. One of its partners, Thomas W. Lamont, presided over the Committee from October 1921 to November 1942. A timely reflection of this new situation was the relocation of the Mexican Finance Agency (*Agencia Financiera Mexicana*), a financial representation of the Mexican government, from London to New York (Bazant, 1968, pp. 190–1, 221; Meyer, 1991, p. 393; Riguzzi, 2010, p. 402).

However, the outlook of the Mexican financial system was bleak. As a result of the Revolution, the banking system had collapsed, damage had also been caused to the transport infrastructure, and markets had been disarticulated by the War (Haber, Maurer & Razo, 2003; Medina, 1995, p. 85; Suárez Dávila, 1988, pp. 350–3). Furthermore, payment was pending of compensation for loss of life of foreign citizens and damage to their property. But of all the problems, the one the government gave most immediate attention was public debt. A key aspect for governments that followed after 1920 was recovering foreign credit, but regaining international financial confidence first required an agreement to be reached regarding recommencement of payment of the debt (Medina, 1995, pp. 87–8).

Before explaining the negotiations, the data is eloquent about the evolution of the government debt and finances. Figures 5.1, 5.2a, and 5.2b show the evolution of the public debt, total and foreign, in value and as a ratio of fiscal revenues, for the period 1922–46. Figures 5.3 and 5.4 show the evolution of the public finances. The behaviour of the data series reflects the events explained in the following sections of this chapter, for instance, the different agreements and the repurchase of bonds by the government after 1932.

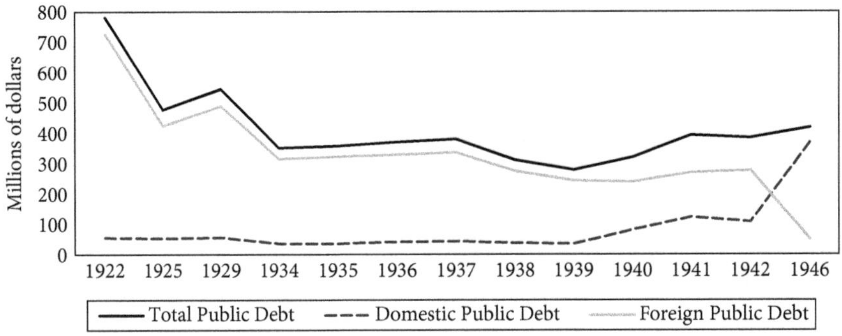

Figure 5.1. Public Debt 1922–1946 (Millions of Dollars).
Source: Estadísticas Históricas de México, INEGI.

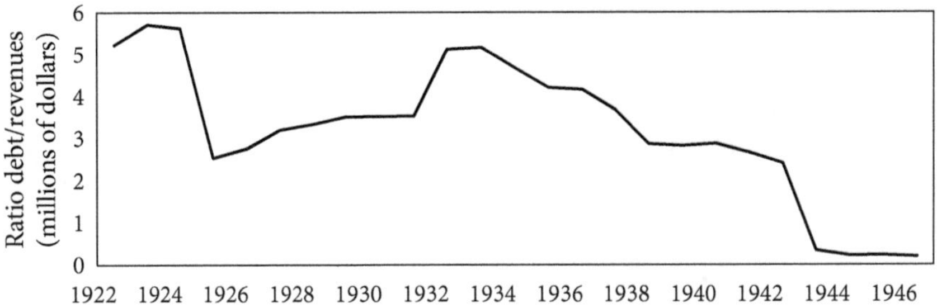

Figure 5.2a. Ratio Foreign Public Debt / Fiscal Revenues 1922–1946.
Source: Estadísticas Históricas de México, INEGI.

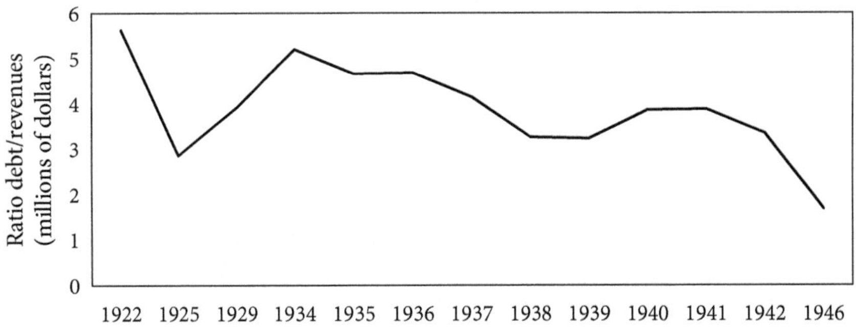

Figure 5.2b. Ratio Total Public Debt / Fiscal Revenues 1922–1946.
Source: Estadísticas Históricas de México, INEGI.

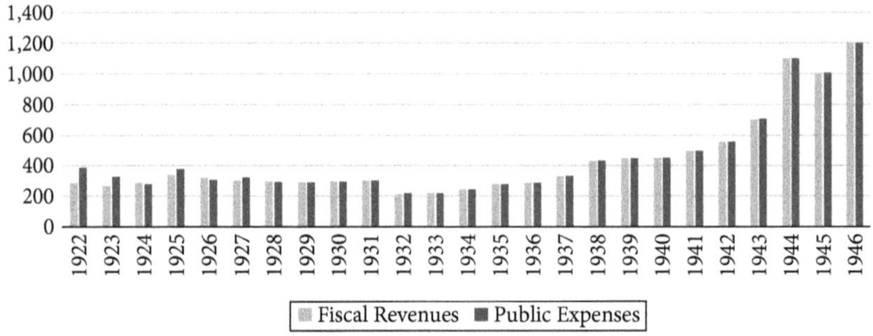

Figure 5.3. Budget balance of the federal government (Millions Pesos MX).
Source: Estadísticas Históricas de México, INEGI.

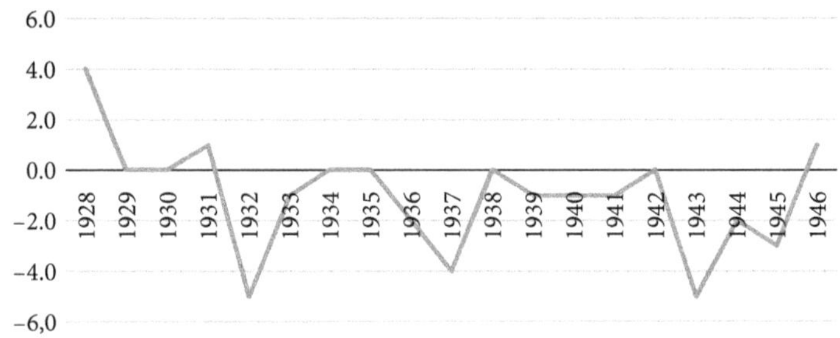

Figure 5.4. Primary Deficit (Millions of Pesos MX).
Source: Estadísticas Históricas de México, INEGI.

5.4 The Beginning of a Difficult Path for Negotiations

In 1921, the government of Álvaro Obregón, a warlord, began a new phase of negotiations with foreign creditors. Mexico needed access to new loans to finance a reconstruction process. It was therefore urgent for Obregón that his government be recognized by European countries, and particularly by the United States. This was not easy; on the contrary, it was complicated by the decisions his administration took on tax matters (Medina, 1995, pp. 89; Pani, 1949).

Furthermore, the US governments took a hard line during most of the 1920s. This started with the Democrat President Woodrow Wilson, and was continued and toughened even further by the Republican administrations of Warren G. Harding and Calvin Coolidge. The first step that Washington took to pressure the Mexican government and satisfy US citizens' claims in Mexico was to condition diplomatic recognition on first reaching a formal agreement regarding each of the outstanding debt issues (Meyer, 1981b, pp. 154–5; Meyer, 1991, pp. 318–19; Hans Werner Tobler, 1997, pp. 463–81). These problems became the central themes of the binational agenda. The British, for their part, had strong economic interests in Mexico. Although they adopted a tougher stance than the Americans in terms of their claims, they let the United States representatives to lead their position with Mexico.

When Obregón's government took office, the situation of public funds was precarious. To gather resources, the government created two taxes in order to ensure payment for future debt maturities (Pani, 1926, pp. 99–100). The first was a tax on the sale of rural properties (Medina, 1995, p. 89). The second was a tax on oil: on 7 June 1921, the government issued a decree that established a special tax on exports of oil and its derivatives, which worsened relations with oil companies (Meyer, 1981b, p. 176). The oil companies protested but yielded to the government. The companies thus held an agreement, at which it was settled that the tax would be covered by foreign debt bonds.[6] However, Lamont the head of the banker's committee, managed to get Mexico to cancel this agreement with the oil companies in February 1922.[7]

The Minister of Finance, Adolfo de la Huerta, initiated new negotiations with bankers that culminated in the De la Huerta–Lamont agreement, signed on 16 June 1922. With this agreement, the Mexican government pledged that, as of 1 January 1923, it would set up a fund for payment of interest over a period not to exceed five years. An initial instalment of 30 million gold pesos (*pesos oro*) was set up for the first year, increasing by five million pesos annually. The payment of overdue capital would be covered after 1928.

All the oil export taxes would be set aside to put together this sinking fund.[8] In addition, a new levy of 10 per cent would be charged on the gross income of railroad companies and all their profits. Besides, the old debt remained intact. With this agreement, all the foreign public debt was converted from sterling pounds to US dollars (Secretaría de Hacienda y Crédito Público, 1960, pp. 54–5).

In that agreement, the total public debt was increased by the addition of the railroad debt (known as *Deuda Ferrocarrilera*, 367,648,219 pesos) and the railroad bonds that had previously been guaranteed (137,929,122 pesos). That gave a total railroad debt of 505,577,441 pesos (equivalent to $246.62 million)—almost half of Mexican foreign debt. In addition to incorporating the liabilities of the National Railroads (*Ferrocarriles Nacionales*) into the public debt, the Mexican government was obliged to return the railroads seized in 1914, during the Civil War, to the private companies (Secretaría de Hacienda y Crédito Público, 1960, p. 55). The agreement also included bonds from the Loan Fund for Irrigation and Agricultural Development Works (*Caja de Préstamos para Obras de Irrigación y*

[6] Bonds 'se aceptarían al 100% de su valor nominal mientras las compañías los adquirirían en el mercado de Nueva York al 50% o 40% de ese valor'. See Meyer (1981b, p. 177).

[7] Decree of 21 February 1922. See Bazant ([1968] 1995, p. 193).

[8] Decree of 7 June 1921.

Fomento de la Agricultura), which were unconditionally guaranteed by the federal government.[9]

Therefore, public debt increased from 667,467,826 pesos to 1,037,116,145 pesos (plus 414,621,442 pesos that corresponded to the payment of interest). In summary, the total debt was 1,451,737,587 pesos (equivalent to $708.16 million). In addition, Lamont secured the representation of bondholders, reaching 90 per cent of bank bonds and 98 per cent of railroad bonds (Bazant, 1968, pp. 194–9).

The Mexican Congress opposed the agreement for two reasons. First, because it surpassed the country's capacity to pay. And second, because they considered it inconvenient to incorporate railroad debt. However, the agreement was approved by decree on 29 September 1922 (Secretaría de Hacienda y Crédito Público, 1960, pp. 55–6).

Obregón's government was recognized by Washington as a result of the signing of a binational agreement, known as the *Bucareli Agreements*, in August 1923. These agreements limited the government's ability to affect oil companies, as well as protected American landowners. The agreements also set up two claims conventions: a special commission to review complaints proceeding from the Revolution (between 1910 and 1920), and another general one to examine mutual claims since 1868 (Meyer, 1998, p. 237).[10] With this agreement, the Mexican government managed to normalize diplomatic relations with the United States, France, Italy, and Belgium. Britain refused to recognize Obregón, a position that changed in September 1925 when it agreed to resume diplomatic relations with Mexico (Meyer, 1991, pp. 33, 344, 375, 398ss, and 412).

The 1924 presidential succession pitted the warlords who had risen from the Revolution against each other. It was a military rebellion that cost the public purse 43.2 million pesos (Medina, 1995, pp. 91–2; Bazant, 1968, pp. 199–200; Garciadiego, 1999, pp. 29–30). This economic bloodletting and the refusal of the Committee of Bankers to grant the government an advance of 30 million pesos guaranteed by the oil production tax obliged President Obregón to suspend payment of the debt by means of a decree on 30 June 1924 (Bazant, 1968, p. 200). With this decision, Obregón handed down the problem to his successor.

5.5 The Pani–Lamont Amendment

The new President, Plutarco Elías Calles, and his Minister of Finance, Alberto J. Pani, sought to restore public finances and reduce administrative expenditure. The plan reduced the fiscal deficit from 58 million pesos in 1923 to 23 million in

[9] This fund was established to resolve problems with creditors in agricultural activities, and it was nationalized on 2 June 1917. See Pani (1926, pp. 106–7).

[10] See also Pani (1936, pp. 279–85).

1924 and it almost balanced out the following year. This situation made possible the establishment of a central bank, the *Banco de México*, in 1925. Likewise, government development banks were established, like the National Bank for Agricultural Credit (*Banco Nacional de Crédito Agrícola*) and the National Program for Roads and Irrigation Works (*Programa Nacional de Caminos y Obras de Irrigación*), both in 1926. That same year, payment of foreign debt resumed (Suárez Dávila, 1988, p. 363).

The last suspension of debt payments allowed the Mexican Treasury to clean up its finances and balance its budgets. This enabled the government to set out negotiations regarding foreign debt between Pani and Lamont. Both parties agreed to accept some amendments and additions to the 1922 agreement. On 25 October 1925, the Mexican government and the bankers reached a new agreement, known as the 'Pani–Lamont Amendment', based on which Mexico restarted debt payments in 1926 (Pani, 1926, pp. 103–4).

On that occasion, the Mexican government gained several advantages through the negotiations, reducing the amount of the debt and increasing the government's financial power through the separation of the *Deuda Ferrocarrilera* from the public debt and exchange of bonds for the Loan Fund for Irrigation for public debt bonds (Secretaría de Hacienda y Crédito Público, 1960, p. 58).[11]

Another concession obtained by the Mexican government was the rearrangement of the 1924 and 1925 loans, which came to 75 million pesos. These loans would be paid from 1928 and liquidated in deferred payments over eight years, a period 'during which they will be liquidated according to a progressive scale of repayments and with an annual interest rate of 3% on outstanding amounts, incurred from the date upon which payment is due' (Pani, 1926, p. 104). The government also pledged to return the railroads to the companies, which would take over management and payment of the debt (Secretaría de Hacienda y Crédito Público, 1960, p. 59). Regarding the Loan Fund for Irrigation, which was in the process of liquidation due to default of payment by plantation owners of what they had been lent, 'the government would assume the debts, and in exchange the Fund would relinquish its rights to land, mortgages and property to the former' (Bazant, 1968, p. 203). This turned out to be to the government's advantage, because it could dispose of assets that were subject to various levies (Secretaría de Hacienda y Crédito Público, 1960, p. 59).

As such, Mexican public debt reduced from 1,562,838,348 pesos to 998,217,794 pesos by 31 December 1925 (from $769.88 to $491.73 million) (Bazant, 1968 1995, p. 204). Moreover, Mexico retained the collateral of the oil export tax. This was

[11] It managed to separate railroad debt from the public debt, except for interest corresponding to the period from 1923 to 1925 (an amount of 63,964,674 pesos). According to Pani (1926, p. 105), this agreement relieved Mexico of 'toda responsabilidad sobre las obligaciones ferrocarrileras no garantizadas por el [gobierno] originalmente y estas obligaciones importaban, por capital e intereses atrasados, nada menos que $671 236 456.11'.

strategic by the Mexican government, because it divided the bankers and the oil companies and pitted them against each other (Bazant, 1968, p. 203).

In 1926, debt service payments resumed. However, once again the government was unable to meet its financial obligations due to a significant drop in trade and oil extraction, which had a negative impact on taxes on production and export (Suárez Dávila, 1988, p. 366). In light of this economic situation, Mexico was just able to pay the debt service but was forced to suspend payments temporarily in 1928. But in that year, the government was able resume debt service, which rose to 77 million pesos. Other payments derived from the national debt—approximately 100 million pesos and a third of the government's regular income—were added to this (Bazant, 1968, pp. 204–5). This again hindered the government's capacity to pay.

5.6 The Montes de Oca–Lamont Agreement

By 1 July 1929, public debt rose to 1,089 million pesos ($523.6 million), of which 656.6 million corresponded to capital and 443.3 million to outstanding interest.[12] In light of the delays of payment by the government, the parties entered into negotiations once again. On 25 July 1930, the Minister of Finance Luis Montes de Oca signed the Montes de Oca–Lamont Agreement. In that agreement, they approved a single emission of bonds for $267,493,240, divided into two series of similar amounts payable over a term of forty-five years, which would be set aside to exchange the government's debt bonds (Secretaría de Hacienda y Crédito Público, 1960, p. 60).

However, the monetary problems that affected the gold standard worldwide, as well as the persistent economic crisis that erupted since 1929, prevented Mexico from complying with the agreement. For this reason, the President at the time, Pascual Ortiz Rubio, decided not to submit the agreement to the Mexican Congress (Secretaría de Hacienda y Crédito Público, 1960, p. 62).

In 1931, Ortiz Rubio authorized his Finance Minister, Montes de Oca, to sign a supplementary agreement with the International Committee of Bankers, modifying the previous one. The agreement was signed on January 29, 1931. It was agreed that the new issuance and payment to bondholders would be postponed for two years, and it also stipulated that during this period the government would deposit in Mexico, in silver pesos, the approximate value of the debt service in gold that had been pledged the previous year.

On 1 January 1933, whatever the exchange rate, the funds would be converted into dollars and the Mexican government would cover the difference, if needed

[12] This amount excludes payments made between 1923 and 1927. See Bazant (1968, p. 210).

(Bazant, 1968, p. 216). But nor was the Mexican government able to comply with this commitment once more, due to the global economic crisis which affected the balance of payments. Once again, Mexico was forced to suspend payment of the debt through the Decree of 21 January 1932, cancelling the 1931 agreement (Secretaría de Hacienda y Crédito Público, 1960, pp. 62–3).

By 1933, Mexico, the Soviet Union and Great Britain were part of a list of countries that had suspended payment of their foreign debt. In part, this was a result of the Great Depression. Toward the end of that same year, British holders of Mexican bonds had not lost hope of recovering their investment, just they lost their patience. They opted to negotiate independently of the International Committee of Bankers, controlled by US interests. To this end they formed The British Committee of Mexican Bondholders, a group of 500 bondholders whose investment totalled £6 million. The British Committee established contact with the Mexican authorities. There is no evidence that they succeeded.

The enactment of the Johnson Act in April 1934 might have added stress to the Bankers Committee.[13] And indeed, after tensions during the negotiations, the Mexican government broke off relations with the International Committee of Bankers on 21 May 1934.

5.7 Second Stage: From the *Impasse* to the Beginning of Bilateral Agreements

In December 1934, Lázaro Cárdenas began his Presidency of Mexico. He was undoubtedly one of the most influential leaders this country has ever had. Cárdenas brought stability to the Presidency and consolidated a system of authoritarian government based on one dominant party supported by corporatist organizations. On the one hand, Cárdenas handled mass politics with a popular and anti-business discourse, supported trade unions and operated an unprecedented land redistribution policy. For the latter, he confiscated property from Mexican and foreign landowners. In March 1938, after several confrontations, he expropriated the (mainly English and American) oil companies operating in Mexico, which was a severe blow to the interests of international corporations in the country.

On the other hand, the Cárdenas government maintained a close relationship with large business groups and particularly some Mexican bankers, who provided him with support organizing the country's finances. Cárdenas himself, like his government team, also sought to maintain a harmonious relationship with the

[13] The Johnson Act prohibited foreign nations in default from marketing their bond issues in the United States.

United States throughout his term in office. Under Cárdenas regime, public finances improved. The ratio debt/revenues of the government began to drop. Fiscal revenues and expenses increased, and the public deficit was maintained relatively stable (as shown in Figure 5.3 and 5.4).

The outbreak of the Second World War was a crucial event, as it opened a door of opportunity for the government. President Lázaro Cárdenas himself openly took a stance in support of the Allies and against the Axis countries. Similarly, in the later years of his administration, his government actively promoted a new shaping of Mexican trade relations with the United States. But there were still many outstanding issues to resolve with the United States and other countries, and more problems had accumulated with this administration's policies. Debt was one of many issues.

For example, the following negotiating groups all had outstanding historical claims: the American-Mexican Claims Commission (*Comisión General de Reclamaciones México-Estados Unidos*), which operated from 1924 to 1934; the British-Mexican Claims Commission (*Comisión General de Reclamaciones México-Gran Bretaña*), 1928–32; and the French-Mexican Claims Commission (*Comisión General de Reclamaciones México-Francia*). In addition, there was railroad debt (*Deuda Ferrocarrilera*). This is without even mentioning government debt—the subject of this research. Solutions to all of them progressed slowly.

While compensation for Americans affected by the Civil War had still not been resolved, mass confiscation of land between 1935 and 1938 made the problem with regard to the United States even worse, as it impacted nearly three hundred US landowners. This affected the US government's expectations as to the negotiations (Dwyer, 2008; Riguzzi & de los Rios, 2014, pp. 284–5).

Another factor that played a part in negotiations was the international silver market, in which both countries were important players. Negotiations between the US Treasury Department and the Mexican Ministry of Finance started in 1936, to establish agreements to purchase silver from Mexico. These agreements in 1936 and 1937 were revealing, because they evidenced the concern of the Secretary of the Treasury, Henry Morgenthau, about potential infiltration of the Axis powers in Latin America, both in trade and military terms (Riguzzi & de los Rios, 2014, p. 286; Suárez Aranzolo, 1977).

The bilateral relationship was changing drastically. For example, two decades beforehand, during the First World War, tensions between Mexico and the United States were exacerbated; at its worst point in 1914, American troops occupied the port of Veracruz. But with the emergence of the Second World War, the relationship was redefined. This was partly a result of Roosevelt's government's concern for the southern flank—principally California and the Pacific area—as well as concern about Fascist interference in Latin American countries. Another factor was the Mexican government's recognition that such opportunities were important for the country (Cramer & Prutsch, 2014; Riguzzi & de los Rios, 2014, p. 312).[14]

After Lázaro Cárdenas finished his term in office in 1940, President Manuel Ávila Camacho continued his politics. In diplomatic matters, Ávila Camacho took a more aggressive stance towards the Axis powers. The rest of the political establishment, including powerful leftist labour leaders, also endorsed the alliance with the United States. In this context, as a signalling that everything was under control, the then ex-President Cárdenas became head of the Pacific Military Region and subsequently the Minister of National Defense (*Secretario de la Defensa Nacional*).

From 1941, cooperation mechanisms were activated with greater intensity between the two countries, including on issues relating to trade, the military and international law. Just before the Japanese attack on Pearl Harbor in December 1941, the two governments reached a settlement to form an alliance between their countries and to normalize the relations and outstanding problems from years beforehand.

In light of the attack on Pearl Harbor, the Latin American countries (except Argentina and Chile) reached a consensus at the Rio de Janeiro Conference in January 1942 to break off diplomatic relations with the Axis Nations. Mexico declared war on the Axis in May 1942 (Riguzzi & De los Rios, 2014, p. 314). In this context, Roosevelt visited Mexico in 1943—the first visit by a US President.[15]

On November 19, 1941, Mexico and the United States signed the *Good Neighbor Agreement* (Suárez Dávila, 1988, p. 381). With this agreement, the Mexican government pledged to pay $40 million to settle the general and special claims, and claims for damages and agricultural expropriation in particular. For its part, the United States agreed to grant Mexico two loans: one for $40 million to create an exchange rate stabilization fund for the peso (against the dollar), and the other for $20 million to straighten out the transport system. Finally, it committed to resume monthly purchases of silver from Mexico. In the case of the oil dispute from the 1938 expropriation, they agreed to set up a commission to assess the confiscated property and determine the terms of compensation. A commitment to negotiate a trade agreement was also agreed (Meyer, 1981b, pp. 388–9; Meyer, 2000, p. 879; Riguzzi & de los Ríos, 2014).

An interesting anecdote is that Eduardo Suárez, the Minister of Finance, appointed Salvador Ugarte to begin negotiations for the trade agreement in 1941. Ugarte was a renowned banker in Mexico, close to Suárez. His American counterpart was Nelson Rockefeller, who was then a young civil officer in the Department of State (Suárez Aranzolo, 1977, pp. 265–6). Rockefeller was the

[14] The literature on diplomatic events revolving around these developments is abundant, Riguzzi and de los Rios (2014) summarize some of the relevant works.

[15] The visit was to Monterrey, near the US border, as a cross-border exchange with his Mexican counterpart.

Coordinator of Inter-American Affairs.[16] In his memoirs, Suárez notes that the deep friendship that formed between the two men streamlined negotiations. But President Roosevelt's decisiveness was instrumental for official approval.

The trade agreement, signed in December 1942, was important as it turned Mexico into a US supplier of raw materials during the war. The treaty not only formalized the trading partnership between the two countries, but it was also a trigger for future trade agreements in the bilateral relationship. Likewise, and hand in hand with the negotiations for this agreement, the Bracero Program was signed in August 1942 to transfer labour from one country to the other. This programme would initiate a completely unexpected, nevertheless significant, cycle in the future bilateral relationship.

An important actor in the negotiations was Eduardo Suárez, the Minister of Finance under Presidents Lázaro Cárdenas and Manuel Ávila Camacho. Suárez was appointed Minister of Finance on 18 June 1935. Suárez had gained experience of international negotiations throughout his career. He had participated in the British-Mexican Claims Commission since 1928 and the French-Mexican Claims Commission in 1930, and he was head of the Mexican Delegation to the League of Nations in 1932. Another important experience was negotiating the debt with the International Committee of Bankers. That path would help him to finally resolve the government's debt.

5.8 Debt Diplomacy: Negotiation of the Debt for the 1942 and 1946 Agreements

During his stay in New York in 1932, for the trial of a $6.5-million fund held by the International Committee of Bankers, Eduardo Suárez realized that it was easy 'to purchase Mexican bonds on the New York Stock Exchange for ridiculous prices, completely discredited by virtue of the several suspensions in payment' (Suárez Aranzolo, 1977, p. 267). To that end, he asked his US lawyers on the case to advise him on how to purchase the bonds. He also received support from his friend Gustave Galopin, a Swiss man who trained him on the mechanics of the Stock Exchange and put him in contact with brokers. He then ran an experiment and purchased 'some Mexican bonds at the price of one-dollar cent per bond with a face value of $100, with coupons for overdue interest that were worth the same' (Suárez Aranzolo, 1977, p. 267). In 1934, convinced of the feasibility of this transaction, Suárez advised Marte R. Gómez (then Minister of Finance) that the Ministry and the central bank, *Banco de México* should purchase these bonds. But he warned that the deal should be done with complete discretion to avoid

[16] Rockefeller headed the Office of Inter-American Affairs for most of its existence. See Cramer and Prutsch (2014).

speculators beginning to invest in these bonds and drive up their price (Suárez Aranzolo, 1977, p. 266).

Once appointed Minister of Finance in 1935, Suárez continued to purchase bonds through the *Banco de México* and employed several brokers from the New York Stock Exchange for this purpose. Suárez subsequently made the *Banco de México*, through the *Chase National Bank* (its correspondent in New York), propose to bondholders that the bank would pay ten-dollar cents per hundred-dollar bond with all its coupons. Plenty of bondholders accepted the proposal (Suárez Aranzolo, 1977, p. 267).

After draining the market of bonds that were held by investors as well as speculators, Suárez decided to resume relations with the International Committee of Bankers. For this, it also helped that the Court of Appeals of the State of New York overturned a judgment in Mexico's favour relating to $6.5 million that the International Committee of Bankers had retained. The Court instructed the Committee to distribute the funds among bondholders (Suárez Aranzolo, 1977 and Bazant, [1968] 1995, p. 217).

When talks resumed between the Ministry of Finance and the International Committee of Bankers in 1942, Suárez set out two proposals for a new agreement to Thomas Lamont. First, he requested that the bonds the Committee had retained be used to help Mexico pay its foreign debt commitments, and that only bondholders who abided by this rule would be eligible to enter the agreement. Second, he suggested that the agreement exclude 'bondholders who were in Central Europe, dominated by the Axis countries [. . .], in accordance with the recommendation of the 1942 International American Conference on systems of economic and financial control' (Suárez Aranzolo, 1977, pp. 250–2).[17] In this way, Mexico rid itself of 'payment of bonds with a nominal value of several million dollars'. The government estimated that there were Mexican bonds with a nominal value of $50–60 million in continental Europe dominated by the Axis countries. That's why it was 'necessary to avoid that any adjustment and payment agreement benefit the aggressor nations' (Bazant, 1968, p. 222).

Moreover, Suárez reminded Lamont that, since the 1932 Montes de Oca–Lamont Agreement, the then US ambassador, Dwight Morrow, had declared to him 'that it was completely unfair and inappropriate, both for the Mexican government and for bondholders, to enter into an agreement that would be beyond Mexico's capabilities to comply with'. As a result, Mexico was able to pay the foreign debt with the following conditions: full write-off of interest up to the date of signing, and conversion of the principal of the bonds to pay one peso for every one US dollar. Moreover, it made it a requirement for holders to present their bonds for registration (Secretaría de Hacienda y Crédito Público, 1960, p. 65).

[17] The amount was $29.7 million.

In his memoirs, Suárez said that it was very hard work to convince Lamont, but he eventually agreed because the United States had already entered the World War. Lamont undertook to persuade US and English bondholders, but not the French. In order to persuade the French, he recommended that Suárez ask Agustín Legorreta, the CEO of the Banco Nacional de Mexico, then the largest bank, to go to Paris and use 'the great influence he had at the Banque de Paris et des Pays-Bas' to get them to accept the Mexican government's proposal. Suárez spoke with Legorreta, who agreed to meet with the French. The mission was successful, because Lamont told Suárez that French bondholders approved the agreement as proposed by the Minister of Finance (Suárez Aranzolo, 1977, pp. 268–9).

The Agreement was finally signed on 5 November 1942, and 'established the basis for the adjustment and payment of "direct foreign debts"'. For the 1922 Convention, the Committee was composed of American, English, French, Swiss, Dutch, and German representatives. However, due to the wartime context, only the American, English, and Swiss divisions attended this convention (Secretaría de Hacienda y Crédito Público, 1960, p. 64). This convention proposed that Mexico pay one peso for every dollar, which represented a write-off of capital. In this way, the government's direct liabilities reduced from $230,631,974 to 230,631,974 pesos, with the caveat that it would be paid at the holders' discretion in dollars or pesos at the exchange rate of 4.85 pesos per dollar (Secretaría de Hacienda y Crédito Público, 1960, p. 65).

In short, the 1942 agreement reduced Mexico's foreign debt from $509,516,220 in capital and interest to $49,560,750, i.e., less than 10 per cent of the original amount. The bonds purchased by Mexico in the market should be deducted from this figure (Suárez Aranzolo, 1977, p. 270). The debt was reduced further by subtracting the so-called enemy bonds. In the end, Mexico's actual debt decreased from $49.5 million to $43 million (Bazant, 1968, p. 227).[18] Finally, the government pledged to submit a proposal for settling the consolidated railroad debt (Secretaría de Hacienda y Crédito Público, 1960, p.66). However, the agreement to settle the debt would not be signed until 1946.

Unlike the US bondholders, who accepted the agreement, the British considered the settlement too advantageous for Mexico.[19] This disagreement was clearly reflected by the British press. In the midst of this disagreement, Eduardo Villaseñor, head of the Banco de México, travelled to London to ensure fulfilment of the debt settlement, which the Mexican Senate approved on 24 December.[20]

[18] The enemy bonds were estimated to be originally equivalent to $29,760,000.

[19] *El Nacional*, 20 de octubre de 1943, DO9081 (1941–1949), Deuda Exterior: México, Archivos Económicos, Fondo Biblioteca Miguel Lerdo de Tejada, SHCP.

[20] *El Nacional*, 20 de octubre de 1943, El Nacional, 24 de diciembre de 1943, DO9081 (1941–1949), Deuda Exterior: México, Archivos Económicos, Fondo Biblioteca Miguel Lerdo de Tejada, SHCP.

In an editorial in 1943, the newspaper *Financial News* stated that 'Mexico's position is stronger today than it was decades ago [which is why] there may be a case for the country paying more to bondholders abroad.' The editorial revealed that demands had already been made in the House of Commons, but that the Chancellor of the Exchequer was waiting for a formal offer to bondholders to proceed. The English government's attitude acknowledged the 'fact that Mexico is an ally of England against the Nazis, coupled with the Committee of Bankers in New York having already accepted the offers of settlement and liquidation'.[21]

For the liquidation of capital, the agreement set out that the 'secured' debts should be repaid no later than 1 January 1963, and the 'unsecured' debts by 1 January 1968. It is worth mentioning that the agreement would only be implemented a year after it was signed. To this end, they drew on the services of banks in Mexico, New York, and London. However, the war prevented solving existing obligations in continental Europe. After the conflict ended, there was interest in extending the agreement's offer to bondholders residing in that area (Secretaría de Hacienda y Crédito Público, 1960, pp. 66–7).

On 20 February 1946, the government made an offer to railroad company bondholders, via the International Committee of Bankers, for their adjustment and payment. There was a similar reduction in that agreement to the 1942 one. The debt was reduced to 233,112,385 pesos, which was equivalent to $48,064,409.28. The interest owed between 1914 and 1946 was minimized and the maximum term for the government to repay the bonds in full ended on 1 January 1975 (Secretaría de Hacienda y Crédito Público, 1960, pp. 67–9). In 1960, the Mexican government announced the early repayment of all those bonds, bringing this chapter in Mexico's history to a close.

After the end of that episode, from 1946 to 1967, Mexico had little involvement in international debt markets, with occasional lending from multilateral banks for specific developmental purposes. Most public debt was domestic. However, in the early seventies, Mexico began again to embark as a major borrower in international markets.

References

Anaya Merchant, L. (2001). 'De Convenios Y Deudas en la Revolución Mexicana', *Boletín Fideicomiso Archivos Plutarco Elías Calles y Fernando Torreblanca*, 36, enero-abril.

Amador, M. (2004). 'A Political Model Sovereign Debt Repayment'. 2004 Meeting Papers 762, Society for Economic Dynamics.

[21] Novedades, 12 de agosto de 1943, *El Nacional*, 20 de octubre de 1943, DO9081 (1941–1949), Deuda Exterior: México, Archivos Económicos, Fondo Biblioteca Miguel Lerdo de Tejada, SHCP.

Bazant, J. (1968). *Historia de la deuda exterior de México, 1823-1946*. México: El Colegio de México.

Bulow, J. & Rogoff, K. (1989). 'LDC Debt: Is to Forive to Forget?' *American Economic Review*, 79, 43–50.

Cramer, G. & Prutsch, U. (2014). *¡Américas unidas!: Nelson A. Rockefeller's Office of Inter-American Affairs* (1940–46). Madrid & Frankfurt: Iberoamericana Vervuert.

Cole, H., Dow, J., & English, W. (1995). 'Default, Settlement and Signalling: Lending Resumption in a Reputational Model of Sovereign Debt'. *International Economic Review*, 36(2), 365–85.

Del Angel, G. A. & Martinelli, C. (2009). *La expropiación bancaria de 1982 en México. Un enfoque de economía política*. México: Centro de Estudios Espinosa Yglesias.

Dwyer, J. J. (2008). The Agrarian Dispute. The Expropriation of American owned Land in Postrevolutionary Mexico. Duke University Press.

Eaton, J. (1990). 'Debt Relief and International Enforcement of Loan Contracts'. *Journal of Economic Perspectives*, 4, 43–56.

Eaton, J. & Gersovitz, M. (1981). 'Debt with Potential Repudiation; Theoretical and Empirical Analysis'. *Review of Economic Studies*, 48(2), 289–309.

Garciadiego, J. (1999). 'Del Antiguo Régimen Al Nuevo Régimen', in Archivo General de la Nación, *México en el siglo XX*, Tomo 1 (pp. 18–41). México: Secretaría de Gobernación.

Haber, S., Razo, A., & Maurer, N. (2003). *The politics of property rights: Political instability, credible commitments, and economic growth in Mexico, 1876–1929* (Political economy of institutions and decisions), Cambridge: Cambridge University Press.

Lienau, O. (2014). *Rethinking Sovereign Debt Politics, Reputation, and Legitimacy in Modern Finance*. Cambridge, MA: Harvard University Press.

Ludlow, L. & Marichal, C. (Eds.) (1998). *Un siglo de deuda pública en México*, México: Instituto Mora.

Medina, L. (1995). *Hacia el nuevo Estado. México, 1920–1994*, México: Fondo de Cultura Económica.

Meyer, L. (1981b). *México y los Estados Unidos en el conflicto petrolero, 1917–1942*. México: El Colegio de México.

Meyer, L. (1991). *Su Majestad Británica contra la Revolución Mexicana, 1900–1950*. México: El Colegio de México.

Meyer, L. (1998). 'Charles B. Warren', in A.R. Suárez Arguello (Ed.), *En el nombre del Destino Manifiesto. Guía de ministros y embajadores de los Estados Unidos en México, 1825–1993* (pp. 233–40). México: Instituto Mora-Secretaría de Relaciones Exteriores.

Meyer, L. (2000). 'La Institucionalización Del Nuevo Régimen', in *Historia General de México*. México: El Colegio de México.

Pani, A. J. (1926). *La Política Hacendaria y la Revolución Mexicana*. México: Editorial Cvltvra.

Pani, A. J. (1936). *Mi Contribución Al Nuevo Régimen (1910–1933)*. México: Editorial Cvltvra.

Pani, A. J. (1949). *La Cuestión Internacional Mexicano-Americana durante el Gobierno del general don Álvaro Obregón*. México: Editorial Cultura.

Secretaría de Hacienda y Crédito Público (1960). *La vieja deuda exterior titulada de México*. México: SHCP.

Reinhart, C. M. & Rogoff, K. (2008). "This Time is Different: A Panoramic View of Eight Centuries of Financial Crises," NBER Working Papers 13882, National Bureau of Economic Research, Inc.

Reinhart, C. M. & Rogoff, K. (2014). "This Time is Different: A Panoramic View of Eight Centuries of Financial Crises," *Annals of Economics and Finance*, vol. 15(2), pages 215–268, November.

Riguzzi, P. (2010). 'México y la Economía Internacional, 1860–1930', in *Historia Económica General de México*. México: El Colegio de México.

Riguzzi, P. & de los Rios, P. (2014). *Las relaciones México-Estados Unidos 1756–2010. Tomo II ¿Destino no manifiesto?*. México, UNAM: Secretaría de Relaciones Exteriores.

Sachs, J. (Ed.) (1989). *Developing Country Debt and Economic Performance*. Chicago, Il: University of Chicago Press.

Suárez Aranzolo, E. (1977). *Comentarios y recuerdos (1926–1942)*. México: Editorial Porrúa.

Suárez Dávila, F. (1977). Bosquejo Biográfico, in E. Suárez Aranzolo (Ed.), *Comentarios y recuerdos (1926–1942)* (pp. LIII–CXXIV). México: Editorial Porrúa.

Suárez Dávila, F. (1988). 'Política Hacendaria y Economía Política en el México Posrevolucionario', in *México. Setenta y cinco años de Revolución*. Tomo I. México: Fondo de Cultura Económica.

Tobler, H. W. (1997). *La Revolución Mexicana. Transformación social y cambio político (1876–1940)*. México: Alianza.

Weller, L. (2018). 'Loans of the Revolution: How Mexico Borrowed as the State Collapsed in 1912–13'. *The Economic History Review*, 72, 3.

6
The Multilateral Principle-Based Approach to the Restructuring of German Debts in 1953

Laura de la Villa

6.1 Introduction

Germany was the biggest defaulter of the interwar period. After the First World War, the German Reich accumulated an enormous mass of foreign debts and claims: the war reparations imposed by the Treaty of Versailles and the private loans to German public and private borrowers that had boomed between 1924 and 1930, including the Dawes and the Young bonds.[1] During the 1930s, Germany defaulted on its foreign obligations but continued to accumulate debts through the deficits in clearing accounts imposed by the Nazi regime to its satellites. After the Second World War, Germany continued to accumulate claims from Allied post-war relief programs and, significantly, from Marshall Plan funding. However, in February 1953, twenty-one countries, together with the Federal Republic of Germany,[2] signed an international treaty, the London Debt Agreement on German Debts (LDA), which settled more than twenty years of default on Germany's foreign debts. All external debt of Germany, sovereign and private (owed to both official and private creditors) was settled in one unified operation led by the three Allied governments (France, the UK, and the US) following a multilateral principle-based negotiation. The LDA consisted of two separate, but interrelated, deals. Firstly, the Intergovernmental Agreement for the settlement of pre–Second World War German Debts which was negotiated in an international

[1] The German Reich borrowed $200 million through the Dawes Plan Loan issued in 1924 in several markets and currencies as part of a deal to resume reparations payments and help stimulate the German economy. The Dawes bonds had priority claim on Germany's foreign exchange and were secured by certain revenues. The Dawes Plan soon proved to be both politically and economically untenable. It was replaced in 1930 by the Young Plan, which rescheduled reparations payments and provided for the withdrawal of French troops from German territory. It also included a new international bond issue. The Young Plan Loan raised approximately $300 million, with bonds denominated in nine different currencies. The Young Loan bonds had no priority on foreign exchange transfers; however, all its tranches were indexed to gold at their value on the date of issue.

[2] For the sake of simplification, I use Germany or West Germany indistinctly to refer to the Federal Republic of Germany (FRG).

Laura de la Villa, *The Multilateral Principle-Based Approach to the Restructuring of German Debts in 1953* In: *Sovereign Debt Diplomacies: Rethinking Sovereign Debt from Colonial Empires to Hegemony.* Edited by: Pierre Pénet and Juan Flores Zendejas, Oxford University Press (2021). © Oxford University Press. DOI: 10.1093/oso/9780198866350.003.0007

conference with more than 300 participants representing both government and creditors (private and public) from sixty-five countries.[3] Secondly, the bilateral agreements that settled the debts arising out of the economic assistance furnished to Germany after the end of the Second World War by the Allied governments. Altogether, both agreements led to a major reduction of German external debt: in total, the LDA dealt with DM29.8 billion of external debt and reduced it to DM14.2 billion. Further significant relief on those debts was granted through significant interest reductions, extension of maturities, and postponement of amortizations. Moreover, article 5(2) of the agreement deferred all claims arising from the Second World War, such as the clearing debts, until a future reunification: virtually a cancellation, since it was not expected to be soon.[4]

The LDA contributed to Germany's post–Second World War economic performance and development, as it allowed her reintegration into world finance and trade networks and a balanced path to recovery.[5] Economic historians have rediscovered the experience of the German debt relief provided after the Second World War: the LDA was at the core of the financial reconstruction of Germany and the Marshall Plan (Ritschl, 2012b),[6] allowing the normalization of West Germany's international financial relationships (Guinnane, 2015). Some re-revisionist contributions emphasized that the Marshall Plan was a US far-reaching recovery programme based on the integration of Europe in which German reconstruction was central. In this vein, the economic and financial basis of the Marshall Plan in Germany was not just about American transfers in the form of loans and deliveries which promoted exports and helped to eliminate bottlenecks to industry and created announcement effects in output (Borchardt and Buchheim, 1991) but the financial and economic reforms that underpinned its subsequent growth model. Those reforms included, firstly, the currency reform which eased the burden of domestic public and private debts (Lutz, 1949; Buchheim, 1994; Kindleberger & Ostrander, 2003), and secondly, the creation of the European Payments Union (EPU) that allowed the reintegration of Germany in European trade. As a result, Germany, was able once again to specialize in importing raw materials and exporting capital goods, pushing the rest of Europe towards trade liberalization (Bordo, 1993; Eichengreen, 1993). The final reform

[3] The original signatory countries were: Belgium, Canada, Ceylon, Denmark, French Republic, Greece, Iran, Ireland, Italy, Liechtenstein, Luxembourg, Norway, Pakistan, Spain, Sweden, Switzerland, the Union of South Africa, the United Kingdom of Great Britain and Northern Ireland, the United States of America, and Yugoslavia. Until 1963, twenty-six more countries signed the agreement.

[4] Other claims arising out of both world wars were settled during the conference and embedded in parallel agreements, but they are not included in the common statistical summaries of the LDA since they were not strictly part of the agreement (nor pre-war debts). See, for example, Kaiser (2013) and Kampffmeyer (1987).

[5] For a review of the literature on the impact of the LDA and a quantitative investigation see Galofré-Vilà et al. (2016).

[6] See the discussion between Ritschl (2011, 2012a) and Sinn (2012) about the scope of the Marshall Plan aid and debt relief.

was the LDA that settled and reduced the burden of Germany's foreign debts. The LDA was key to Germany's reconstruction because reopening its economic borders required the reactivation of international trade finance. Without the LDA, new credits would have ranked in the bottom of the seniority queue and, therefore, would have been valueless given the debt and claims still in default. The creation of a parallel trade and payment system guaranteed by the dollar allowed for the problems of trade and German debts (Berger & Ritschl, 1995) to be dealt with separately, and once this proved successful, the problem of external debts was settled.

However, as I argue in this chapter, the LDA was significant and exceptional not only from the point of view of post–Second World War reconstruction, but also from the perspective of sovereign debt resolution procedures. As I document in this chapter, the concerns of the different actors involved and methods and tactics available to each of them shaped the resolution of German debts from the end of Second World War until 1953. The LDA was not only the result of creditors' governments diplomatic intervention: the collective pressure of private creditors was also an important contributing force in the discussions. As I argue, this led to the design of a multilateral resolution procedure based on the principles of equity of treatment and ability to pay that settled in one unified and orderly operation the question of German debts that had remained at the core of international economic and political disputes since the end of the First World War.

The previous chapter in this volume showed how the American government negotiated bilaterally with the Mexican government during the war, agreeing to a massive debt reduction. The 1953 German debt settlement was also the result of creditor governments' intervention and the influence of diplomacy in the resolution of sovereign debt disputes. Indeed, the LDA appears in the literature mostly as a debt relief operation resulting from the prevailing political considerations of Allied governments after the Second World War. Demands for Germany to service an enormous debt was incompatible with strengthening the German economy and therefore creditor concessions were the price to pay for a higher purpose: maintaining a central political and economic ally in Europe (Guinnane, 2015). Indeed, once the debts entered the diplomatic agenda, the goal of debt recovery was balanced against other national economic interests, a transatlantic cooperation agenda, and global security concerns. In this sense, creditors' governments conceived the LDA against the background of several pressing economic and political difficulties. Firstly, the three most important creditors' governments (the US, the UK, and France) were ruling over most of the policy areas of West Germany under the Occupation Statute and were negotiating with the Federal Republic of Germany the transition to full sovereignty. Secondly, the LDA was conceived as a last step to ensure the self-sustainability of West Germany, in particular, and Europe, in general. Marshall Aid was about to finish and the Americans were determined to avoid the 1920s growth model that was dependent on continued American transfers, since this was highly unstable: the priority this time was the reactivation of direct investment and trade finance, not debt repayment. Last, but not least, the resolution of debt claims occurred alongside the negotiation of Second World War Peace Treaties and the question of reparations and restitution (especially the claims of the Jewish community) as well as the complication of Cold War politics, given the parallel negotiation of the FRG's contribution to Western defence (Buxbaum, 2005; Rombeck-Jaschinski, 2005).

In any case, private creditors were also an important contributing force in the settlement. The emphasis on government intervention to ensure the enforcement of the principle of capacity to pay in order to underpin the Allied policy of restoring Germany's economic strength has overshadowed its *raison d'être*: the reconstruction of German credit. The normalization of financial relations was a prerequisite to reintegrate Germany to the Western economic system. Indeed, the reconstruction of German credit was the central concern in the debates about the prospects of financing investment and trade once Marshall aid would evaporate. Consequently, it was precisely the problem of new money that resurfaced the questions about pending claims in the Allies' policy agenda. Conceptions of the LDA as an imposed scaling down of private creditors' claims obscured creditors' expectations, the tools they had available to enforce their claims, and lead to a misguided understanding of the LDA resolution procedure. Indeed, given the big concessions agreed on the settlement, it is puzzling that bondholders' organizations were sufficiently content with the settlement to endorse it and that public opinion regarded it as a step forward in the restoration of the sanctity of contracts and the foundation stone for the restoration of German public credit.[7] As I document in this chapter, pre-war creditors of the German government and private debtors had seen their prospects for recovery, if any, prevented since the end of the war by Allied policy on reparations and reconstruction. The allied governments blocked any transfer as regards foreign claims. Private creditors' organizations (representing the claims against public and private German debtors from main creditor countries), acted in a coordinated manner in order to influence inter-state negotiations since the end of the war. Whereas their attempts were unsuccessful for many years, they found ways to participate and orient the discussions to their advantage when the Allied governments started considering the need to reactivate private channels of international financing for the German economy and to dismantle the reserved powers and, as a result, gained a privileged seat in the negotiation table. Indeed, private creditors claims were prioritized over

[7] 'Germans Uphold Faith With Bond', *The New York Times*, 2 May 1955; ProQuest Historical Newspapers: *The New York Times*, p. 29; 'Sanctity Of Bond Restored In 1952: German And Japanese Pacts Call For Payments', *The New York Times*, 5 January 1953; ProQuest Historical Newspapers, *The New York Times*, p. 64; See also, Foreign Bondholders Protective Council (FBPC), Report 1951–1953, p.v.

the huge amount of other restitution, reparation, and wartime claims that were deferred until reunification.

Finally, in contrast to the 1930s experience with Germany's debt default, the 1953 debt agreement was a unified and orderly workout. The LDA was negotiated in an international conference with more than 300 participants, closely supervised and controlled by the three Allied governments. It was bound to a procedure and principles that consolidated the creditor front but also allowed for the balancing of all interests, reaching a compromise solution for a complex problem that was not only about providing debt relief but also reconstructing Germany's creditworthiness. As I show in the following section, the Allied governments deferred the settlement of any claims until it was possible to negotiate the question of past foreign debts altogether. The primary concern was to ensure a permanent macroeconomic equilibrium in which the overall amount that Germany would be required to pay for debt service would be in accordance with her ability to pay. Nevertheless, the principle of equity of treatment was also of paramount importance. It responded to the need to protect creditors who had comparatively fewer remedies available (bondholders) and to the need of overcoming past accusations of discriminatory treatment. In the mid-1930s, the Nazi government negotiated separate settlements with various creditor countries linked to trade concessions that led to discriminatory treatment between European and American bondholders. This generated frustration and accusations of bad faith, especially in the US, but also put pressure on the American government because whereas the European governments actively used its advantage to obtain the protection of certain foreign investments, the US state department maintained its hands-off policy and only intervened to register complaints about the discriminatory treatment.[8]

By reconstructing the pre-history of the LDA, focusing on the interplay of the Allied governments with bondholders' organizations through archival investigation, I show how creditors' modified their expectations and tactics of debt collection when the preferred mechanisms of repayment were no longer available and how creditors' governments adapted to their role balancing multiple interests and their own economic and foreign policy agenda. The LDA sheds some light on how a principles-based (or integrated approach) can provide for an effective resolution of debt disputes and balance the many different interests involved in debt disputes. Moreover, this chapter documents an important fact about the norm of repayment too: far from being stable and inevitable, the debt continuity norm is inherently political and historically variable. To do so, I rely on US and UK governmental and bondholders' organizations archival sources and press records. After this introduction, in section 6.2, I show how interactions between creditors' organizations and their respective governments led to the recognition of

[8] See for example, Accominotti et al. (2017); Clement (2004); Schuker (1988); Securities Exchange Commission 1937; Ritschl (2012b).

pre-war debts by Germany. In section 6.3, I analyse all the concerns and interests that Allied governments tried to reconcile with the procedure and principles that framed the negotiations. In section 6.4, I describe the multilateral principles-based approach to German debts at work and its outcomes. In section 6.5, I conclude.

6.2 The Road to Official Recognition of Pre–Second World War Debts

The bondholders' committees were naturally inactive during the Second World War, but when there was reason to believe that the war was approaching its end, they organized and coordinated their efforts to force on Germany their governments' policies regarding the protection and enforcement of their claims. During the immediate years after the armistice, private creditor organizations initially struggled to gain an official acknowledgement for their role in resolving pre–Second World War debts. It was not until the Potsdam Conference in 1945, when the Allied governments would discuss reparations, that creditors saw an opportunity to gain some official recognition. But granting priority to the repayment of debt over reparations was a controversial subject.[9]

Potsdam was disappointing for private creditors' interests. Firstly, the Economic Principles undermined the prospect that Germany could generate sufficient foreign resources to pay creditors back.[10] Secondly, the Potsdam agreement failed to grant priority of old debt claims *vis-à-vis* reparations. Finally, Potsdam protected Germany from creditors' retaliation. During the conference, the American delegation insisted on the first charge of imports over exports proceeds (ranking before reparations)[11] and the establishment of the dollar as the currency of payment of foreign trade, which helped Germany to avoid creditor retaliation (Berger & Ritschl, 1995). What motivated this clause was the long battle over indirect reparations and the reaffirmation of the principle of self-sustainability that Americans pursued immediately after the war. As Gimbel (1976, p. 54) explains, besides all disagreements between the different US departments and agencies, there was consensus on one thing from the very first discussions at Yalta: the US should avoid the mistakes it had made after the First World War and among them, the advancement of American dollars and credits to Germany to facilitate its debts and reparations repayments.[12] This

[9] Note of a discussion between the British Treasury and Mr Rogers, May 1945. CLC/B/060/MS34691/20, London Metropolitan Archives (Henceforth: LMA).

[10] 'In an article at the 26 April 1946 Investors' Chronicle, the effect of this program on creditors was clearly stated: "it should be faced that the prospects of an export surplus from Germany are, so far as the visible future is concerned, dim and remote". Germans loans and reparations, something must be done.' 27 April 1946; Investors Chronicle, OV34/212, Bank of England Archives.

[11] Clause 19, Potsdam Protocol.

[12] For an excellent review of the history of reparations, see Schuker (1988) and Ritschl (2012b).

implied not only a refusal to keep the German economy alive through the extension of loans but also through indirect payment of reparations, i.e., assuming at its own expense the burden of supplying essential goods or equipment to Germany. The other side of the first charge policy was the dollar clause imposed on all trade (Wallich, 1955, pp. 230–5; Schwartz, 1991, p. 174). This clause was criticized for having reduced Germany's capacity to trade with her neighbours due to the generalized lack of dollars and non-convertibility (Abelshauser, 1991; Hogan, 1991), but it did mean that German exports proceeds would not be seized by creditors as retaliation for wartime debt and reparation claims.

Realizing that their prospects were not good, French, British, and American creditor organizations gathered in London in August 1945. They agreed that Germany should grant formal recognition to their claims, regardless of Germany's transfer capacity.[13] Although their claims were not officially recognized, the pressure on Allied governments produced some results. The British government, which maintained close contacts with different creditors' organizations, pushed Allied policy towards the protection of creditors' interests. When Potsdam was carried one stage further at the Paris Conference on Reparations in January 1946, pre-war claims were protected through article 2c.

During the first years of the Marshall Plan, the attitude of creditors' organizations became even more defensive, since it was not only Allied policy that stood in the way of their efforts to recover part of their investments for the foreseeable future, but also the legal status of their claims was threatened by the legislative action discussed and enacted in the occupation zones.[14] While private creditors expressed several times that they held a realistic view of the situation and that nothing could be expected until Germany's position ameliorated, they were desperate to secure any governmental declaration reaffirming the legal position of their claims. Uncertainty prevailed over the future of their claims, and there were even rumours that the US government planned to suspend pre–Second World War debts.[15]

The debate over pre-war debts became a source of contention between the UK and the US (Rombeck-Jaschinski, 2005, pp. 76–7). General McCloy, the US High Commissioner for Germany, was pressuring the Allied High Commission to give transfer priority to new investment over the payment of pre-war debts.[16] Meanwhile, private creditors' organizations were complaining to their

[13] Clip international conference bondholders August 1945. CLC/B/060/MS34691/21, LMA.

[14] The Allied High Commission abrogated the gold clauses in 1947 eroding the value foreign claims and the currency reform affected all claims in Rm, some of them also held by foreigners. Moreover, foreign creditors were pushing for the restoration of the legal status of their claims which was undermined by wartime Nazi discriminatory taxation and debts discharge system (the *Konversionskasse*).

[15] 'M'Cloy for delay on German debts to spur investing', *The New York Times*, 23 January 1950; ProQuest Historical Newspapers, *The New York Times*, p. 1.

[16] Letter Foreign Office to the Council 28/3/1949 in CLC/B060/MS34691/22, LMA.

governments that encouraging new investment would dilute their debts claims. Both the US and the UK wanted Germany to become self-sufficient as soon as possible, and both agreed that this would require capital inflow.[17] However, whereas the US investment potential in Germany was not dependent on pre-war debt, the UK's precarious financial position would limit its investment activity in Germany. Henceforth, the US government saw the problem of new foreign investment as distinct from old debts, while the British government saw the repayment of old debt as a precondition to secure new investment opportunities in Germany. Furthermore, the UK government opposed the US position in supporting the repayment of old debts (particularly short-term debts) between German debtors and foreign creditors in DM rather than dollars. The negotiation on future investments reached a deadlock and the question of currency redenomination was deferred.[18]

The intensification of the Cold War accelerated the return of this reconstituted state into the Community of Western nations and the debate over its contribution to Western defence. In this context, Germany pushed for a considerable revision of the Occupation Statute and the Allied Powers discussed this transition in the ensuing Foreign Ministers' meetings between 1950 and 1951. The Allied Powers established the Intergovernmental Study Group (ISG) early in 1950, which was in charge of doing all the preliminary work relating to the new legal and political status and, consequently, take steps to ensure its return to full international economic status. Among all the questions, the ISG was in charge of making recommendations to the Foreign Ministers on debt claims against Germany.

The coordination between private creditors' organizations in 1950 was high. The president of the British Committee warned that 'there is a danger that if the creditors do not reach agreement amongst themselves and make their common views appreciated by their governments and by the Germans, they may be overtaken by events and be confronted with decisions which they will regret.'[19] In a meeting between American, British, and French bondholders' organizations in mid-February 1950, creditors emphasized again the need that Germany recognized its liability for government claims and recognize the transfer liability of non-Reich debts. They claimed that the full rehabilitation of Germany's sovereignty required the recognition of her creditors in order to restore normal commercial relations and a good credit standing.

In its report to the New York meeting of Foreign Ministers in September 1950, the ISG recommended 'the Federal Republic to undertake responsibility for the German pre-war external debt and in respect of the post-war economic assistance

[17] Minutes of a meeting of the Committee for Long and Medium Term Creditors of Germany, 4/4/1949 in CLC/B060/MS34691/22, LMA.

[18] Memorandum Lever talk with Treasury 12/8/1949 CLC/B060/MS34691/23, LMA.

[19] Letter from Lever to Rogers, 16/12/1949. CLC/B060/MS34691/24, LMA.

to the Western Zones, as well as to give an assurance of co-operation in the working out and implementation of a settlement plan'.[20] The Allied Powers considered the Federal government as the only German government, entitled to assume the rights and fulfil the obligations of the former German Reich, pending a final peace settlement. At the same time, the Allies conceded that the debt arrangements should account for the limitations on its territorial jurisdiction and would therefore be provisional and subject to revision in a final peace settlement. In a letter sent on 23 October 1950, the Allied High Commission informed the German Federal Chancellor, Konrad Adenauer, that in return for debts acknowledgement and a commitment to work out a settlement plan, the Allied High Commission would proceed with the modification of the controls in the Occupation Statute on the lines agreed in New York.[21]

After the governments made the debt settlement a precondition for the revision of the Occupation Statute, the US Foreign Bondholders Protective Council (FBPC) and the British Corporation of Foreign Bondholders (CFB) were optimistic. The representative of the CFB expressed to his American counterpart that even if they could not be entirely satisfied, real progress was on course and that the outlook for the creditors had improved beyond what he had privately dared to hope.[22] However, more contentious was the issue of the priority of post-war aid over old claims because of the securities clauses of the Dawes and Young Loans. The trustees of those loans claimed that the special rights granted to those debts should be duly respected. Allied governments countered that if Germany had any capacity at all to make payments, it was due to the external economic support received, and that they would not modify the priority unless the settlement was such that it did not jeopardize the economic recovery in which they had invested large sums.[23]

It took almost five months until Germany accepted pre-war and post-war debt responsibility. The Bundestag was reluctant to recognize debt claims without having a much more precise knowledge of what would likely emerge from tripartite discussions. These talks were happening at a time when Germany would have to shoulder compensation to persecuted subjects in Israel and other possible future reparation obligations to other Allied countries, as well as to contribute to Western defence in the so-called 'contractual arrangements' (Buxbaum, 2005, p. 6). In the end, and after considerable pressure, the German government confirmed its liability for pre-war external debt of the German Reich,

[20] FRUS, 1950 vol. III, p.1292 ff.

[21] Letter to the German Federal Chancellor from the Allied High Commission. 23rd October 1950. Published in Enclosure1, Appendix 1, Conference on German External Debts, Memorandum prepared by the Tripartite Commission, December 1951. FO371/100079, National Archives (Henceforth: NA).

[22] Letter Mr Butler (CFB) to Mr Rogers (FBPC), 26/10/1950. CLC/B/060//MS34691/27, LMA.

[23] Principles relating to the settlement of German external debts, 8/5/1951. IGG/P(51)101, FO371/93903, NA.

declaring them liabilities of the FRG, recognized liability as regards transfer for private debts as well as for interest and other charges on securities of the government of Austria during the period of the Anschluss. It also acknowledged the debt arising from post-war economic assistance and its priority over all other claims against Germany or German nationals. In the letter, they expressed their desire to resume payments in accordance with a plan to be worked out with all parties.[24]

Once the Federal government accepted the priority of post-war assistance over all other claims against Germany, the Allied governments stated that they intended to modify this priority to the extent necessary to permit the fulfilment of the agreed plan to settle pre-war debts. It was a recognition that a settlement plan of the scope envisaged could not work out if post-war assistance was to keep its priority because the ability of Germany to pay and transfer would be mobilized to pay the post-war government creditors and nothing would be left for the pre-war private creditors. However, this modification of the priority was not just designed as a way to ensure that private creditors would receive some return on their old investments. The modification of priority was crucially qualified: it was conditional on the three governments' acceptance of the agreements reached on private credits. Henceforth, it was a device to ensure that the process would comply with their view of what was an acceptable arrangement. In the following section, I turn to examining the set of principles and procedures guiding the negotiations of pre-war claims into an acceptable agreement.

6.3 Principles and Procedure of the LDA

The bondholders associations' proposal to negotiate pre-war debts was to undertake a comprehensive rehabilitation of German credit by fixing all debt outstanding on an international basis and with a supervisory body, such as a committee of the Allied High Commission, which could track the negotiations' effect on Germany's exchange position.[25] The CFB, the FBPC, and their French counterpart had targeted most of the concerns that would later become the cornerstone of the procedure and principles that the Intergovernmental Study Group (ISG) developed in 1950 and 1951 in order to frame the settlement of German debts.

One of the first procedural issues that the ISG discussed was the participation of private sector claimants. Whereas the US delegation agreed on consulting private creditors' representatives, they refused to allow them direct involvement and

[24] Letter to the Allied High Commission from the German Federal Chancellor. 6 March 1951. Published in Enclosure1, Appendix 1, Conference on German External Debts, Memorandum prepared by the Tripartite Commission, December 1951. FO371/100079, NA.

[25] Letter Roger to Mc Cloy 23/9/1949 CLC/B060/MS34691/23, LMA.

preferred an intergovernmental conference. However, the British delegation was absolutely against it and favoured private creditors' direct participation (Buxbaum, 2005, p. 60). The procedure that the ISG agreed in early 1951 was a compromise between the US and UK positions. On the one hand, decisions affecting creditors' contractual rights should be taken with the general agreement of representatives of the parties. At the same time, they also empowered the Tripartite Commission on German Debts (an organism representing Allied governments) to keep a close control over the procedure at each stage of the international negotiations. Specifically, the multilateral approach designed would allow creditors' committees to negotiate an agreement on concrete proposals and then the Tripartite Commission would evaluate it at the Steering Committee. That committee was a mediator in charge to ensure that the concrete settlement proposals negotiated between creditors and debtors were acceptable to the three Allied governments.

This procedural set-up gave some leeway to creditors while allowing the three Allied governments to retain full control over the outcome of the negotiations through their position as main creditors and occupying powers. The US, the UK, and France reserved their rights as priority creditors (especially the US, through its government claims) and their powers under the Occupation Statute to block any settlement proposal that would not conform to their policy goals. However, when the Brussels Foreign Ministers meeting in December 1950 agreed to give up the reserved powers in order to ensure German contribution to Western defence, the ISG decided to revise the procedure. Indeed, the existence of reserved powers put the Allied governments in a much stronger position since operating through the Allied High Commission, allowed them to act on behalf of the government of Germany and hence to control all the steps towards settlement. The ISG then agreed to an alternative that elevated the disputes to a diplomatic level: an International Treaty should incorporate the arrangements negotiated between private creditors and Germany. Henceforth, the Allied governments would not sign their own bilateral agreements with Germany in respect of post-war debts until Germany was fully committed to the pre-war debt settlement by an intergovernmental agreement.[26]

The Allied governments justified their role in the negotiations as protectors of well-recognized principles in sovereign debt practices: the principles of capacity to pay and of equality of treatment. If any of those principles were not satisfied, Allied governments were prepared to leave private creditors without possibilities to recover their claims. So, how did the actors conceive those principles and what role did they play in framing and guiding the negotiations?

[26] IGG/P(51) 11 (5 February 1951) Report by Claims Committee to the Steering Committee of the IGG—Claims against Germany. FO371/93901, NA.

Principles (I): Capacity to Pay

In the letter written to Chancellor Adenauer in October 1950, the Allied Powers recognized that the determination of the manner and the extent to which Germany was to fulfil those obligations had to account for 'the general situation of the Federal Republic, including, in particular, the effect of the limitations on its territorial jurisdiction'. The Allied Powers also made clear that the settlement 'should not dislocate the German economy through undesirable effects on the internal financial situation, nor unduly drain existing or potential German foreign exchange resources' and that 'it should also avoid adding appreciably to the financial burden of any Occupying Powers.'[27]

Private creditors were in absolute disagreement. They opposed any capital reduction in their claims owing to Germany's territorial limitation or any other reason. They sought to keep government intervention at bay and enforce contractual terms in full. Since the FRG was the sole successor of the Reich state, creditors believed there was no legal reason to partition the debts. In a much more practical stance, they told their governments that there was no doubt that Germany had the capacity to discharge the liabilities and that it was important that no assumption should be made as regards the apportion of Reich debts due to territorial changes. In exchange, they made clear that they were ready to make concessions on current debt service.[28]

For the ISG as well as the creditors themselves, the main restriction of Germany's ability to repay was the capacity to transfer foreign exchange. The ISG warned, 'it will be necessary to take suitable action to prevent the representatives of the creditors at the negotiation cherishing unjustifiable hopes about the scale of foreign currency payments that may be possible in the years during which Germany is receiving foreign aid.' At the same time, the ISG considered it reasonable to assume that in the long term the German external payments could be balanced without any need for exceptional assistance and that Germany would be able pay a tolerable percentage of her foreign exchange expenditure to the service of debts.[29] The ISG refrained from imposing any scaling-down on creditors, considering that it was 'extremely difficult to reach conclusions [. . .] as to the capacity of any country to pay since such judgments must take into account

[27] Letter to the German Federal Chancellor from the Allied High Commission. 23 October 1950. Published in Enclosure1, Appendix 1, Conference on German External Debts, Memorandum prepared by the Tripartite Commission, December 1951. FO371/100079, NA.

[28] Note of three meetings on the 15th, 16th, and 17th February 1950 between Rogers, Fournier and Martin, Lever, Niemeyer and Butler, and Memorandum Settlement of pre-war claims against Germany expressed in non-German currency, Prudential to Foreign Office 28/4/1951 CLC/B060/MS34691/24, LMA.

[29] IGG/P(51)101 (8 May 1951) IGG Principles relating to the settlement of German external debts. FO371/93903, NA.

many complex economic and political factors both of an internal and external nature'.[30]

At the first stages of the conference, the German delegation made an effort to assess Germany's capacity to repay. The Germans presented in December 1951 two memorandums separating the issue of capacity to pay from the problem of capacity to transfer (a distinction that would disappear afterwards). The memorandums emphasized as general determinants of capacity to repay the reduction of the territory suffered as a result of the division, war damage, and extraordinary burdens on the economy such as the huge inflow of refugees, the increase on social expenditure, and the bearing of occupation costs and aid to the city of West Berlin. Altogether, they argued this would justify a reduction of debts of about 50 per cent. Creditors and their governments took note of the limitations of Germany's transfer capacity due to the non-convertibility of currencies, an unsurmountable trade deficit with the dollar area, and the instability of the surpluses in the European Payment Union,[31] to conclude that the prospects for repayment of loans as expressed in these reports to be far from encouraging.

In the end, as Dernburg (1953) stated, even if Germany's capacity to pay received a great deal of attention during the first phase of the negotiations, the final sums agreed to transfer were more the outcome of bargaining and diplomacy than the result of scientific balance-of-payment analysis. As Kaiser (2013) describes, the capacity to pay principle was embedded in the agreement emphasizing the link between debt transfer and exports, a link on which the German delegation put much emphasis at the later stages of the conference. The section 21 of the Report on the Conference made clear that neither international reserves nor capital inflow should be employed for debt service purposes. Instead, the transfer of payments under the settlement plan 'implie[d] the development and maintenance of a balance of payments situation in which those payments (debt service), like other payments for current transactions, can be financed by foreign exchange receipts from visible and invisible transactions'.[32] Furthermore, recognizing that currency convertibility was not yet re-established, the Report recognized that the only solution to the problem of transfer was the extension and liberalization of trade and that austerity was not a possibility (Abs, 1959).

[30] Ibid.

[31] See Conference on German External Debts—Memorandum prepared by the Tripartite Commission on German Debts (Dec 1951), FO371_100079, NA; and Memorandum on the German Capacity to Pay in DM (20/11/1951), Memorandum on the German Capacity to transfer (10/11/1951) FO371_100077, NA.

[32] Report of the Conference on German External Debts. London, February-August 1952. FO371/100086, NA.

Principles (II): Equality of Treatment

The concern about equality of treatment was central to the elaboration of the proposal to settle German debts. The decision to approach the problem of German debts on an international basis was to 'prevent a series of separate negotiations based on trade influence and prestige positions which threaten to produce charges of discrimination'.[33] A plan for the settlement of German debts should assure fair and equitable treatment of all interests affected, regardless of the currency of denomination and the type of claim.

Firstly, German pre-war debts were denominated in twenty-two currencies (mainly dollar and sterling) and there was a general concern that the lack of convertibility could lead to different possibilities of transfer according to currency denomination. Specifically, European currencies would be easier to transfer than the dollar because Germany maintained a trade deficit with the US and, on the contrary, a surplus position with the European countries. Moreover, there was the concern that some countries, specifically Switzerland, could take advantage of their trade deficit and use this position to make separate satisfactory transfer arrangements by means of bilateral agreements rather than by participating in an international settlement.[34] Indeed, Swiss creditors tried unsuccessfully to include the resumption of old debt payments in the recently discussed Trade and Payments Agreements negotiated between Germany and the Swiss government.[35]

The second and central questions about equity concerned the treatment of different kinds of debts: the set of pre-war debts included public and private debtors (56.8 and 43.2 per cent respectively), bonded and non-bonded debts, and both short-term and long-term debts. However, the market incentives for Germany to settle certain classes of debts were limited. Indeed, Germans preferred to settle short-term debts over long-term debts, and within the latter, industrial debts over debts incurred by the Reich and other public bodies. The CFB and the FBPC were concerned that a step-by-step approach to the settlement of German debts would leave long-term governmental bondholders in a very poor position.

Mr Rogers, president of the US FBPC, pressured the US State Department to ensure that the debt settlement should simultaneously resolve all Germany's external obligations. He argued that if this commitment was not undertaken, Germany's foreign exchange obligations would remain uncertain, her currency

[33] Report of the Conference on German External Debts. London, February-August 1952. FO371/100086, NA.

[34] Letter from Mr Rogers to Mr Butler 6/11/1949 and Letter from Mr Butler to Mr Rogers 15/11/1949; CLC/B/060/MS34691/23, LMA.

[35] Report of visit to Germany September/October 1949 (by Mr Legget and Dr Dalberg). CLC/B/060/MS34691/23, LMA.

devalued, and diplomatic and trade relations harmed. The Dawes and Young Loans were considered by some to be the most important German debts, in terms of prestige, wide distribution, amount outstanding, and the degree to which the whole system of international finance was implicated. On many occasions, bondholder organizations, trustees, and underwriters suggested that it was good policy and good politics to include those debts if Germany ever wanted to regain its status among nations and show itself worthy of confidence, describing its treatment as 'the principal criterion in the minds of the investing public'.[36]

Indeed, as the UK Foreign Office delegate at the Tripartite Commission made clear, the real difficulty in negotiations was likely to centre around public debts since 'the restoration of German credit in this field is not likely to have immediate short-term benefits whatever advantages it may bring for Germany as a whole in the long term.'[37] This concern was at the root of government intervention in questions of equity, as the US treasury delegate at the Tripartite Commission confirmed: 'leaving decisions of equity to the process of debtor-creditors bargaining could only lead to an unbalanced settlement under which the long-term creditors would come out very badly' and that 'creditors would be very well advised not to try to arrange things independently of their governments.'[38] He made clear that the US governments 'could not possibly accept a solution which would result in the virtual liquidation of the short-term debt over a small number of years whereas providing virtually no return for long-term creditors'. In early 1951, the German government had tried to include a specific mention that the settlement plan should be directed towards debts which could help Germany normalize her commercial and financial relations and that 'it should therefore provide for the possibility of a direct settlement of private commercial debts.' The US delegation at the ISG considered this condition unacceptable and inconsistent with the principle of equitable treatment and a 'complete surrender to pressures from New York and British and Swiss Banks'.[39] When the French and British bondholders' representatives discussed this eventuality, they were relieved to learn that the allied governments were pressing for comprehensive debt negotiations on an international basis, embracing all forms of German indebtedness and that meanwhile no transfer facilities would be given to anybody.

[36] Note of French, UK, and US creditors pre-war Reich debt—territory limitation 21/2/1950, CLC/B/060//MS34691/24, LMA.

[37] Minutes meeting Foreign Office UK 22/4/1952, Mr Crawford Comments on Reuter's economic commentary on Germany FO371_100066, NA.

[38] Conversation with Mr. Lowell Pumphrey (US delegation Tripartite Commission—Treasury) FO371/9390412, NA.

[39] FRUS 1951 vol III, 1419 ff.

6.4 The Multilateral Principles-Based Approach to German Debts at Work

The three Allied governments had declared in the 1951 exchange of letters that they were going to make important concessions—with respect to the priority of their claims for post-war economic assistance over all other foreign claims against Germany and with respect to the total amount of these claims—on condition that Germany's pre-war external debts were settled satisfactorily. The principles of ability to pay and equity of treatment were the basis of any satisfactory agreement reached at the multilateral negotiation. The Allied governments announced their concessions before the start of the international conference that was held to address pre-war debts, but it was only formalized after the signature of the pre-war debts agreement in 1953 so their own concessions could be leveraged to guide the negotiations. The US reduced its $3.266 million claim (DM13.716 million) to $1.2 million (DM5.04 million) (in thirty-five annuities bearing 2.5 per cent interest); the UK reduced its £201 million claim (DM2.365 million) to £150 million (DM1.764 million) (no interest and repayment over twenty years); and France reduced its $15.7 million claim (DM65.94 million) to $11.84 million (DM49.73 million) (no interest and repayment over twenty years).

In the first stage of the conference to settle pre-war debts (from 28 February to mid-May 1952), the talks were divided under different committees according to four broad classes of claims: a) Reich debts and other debts of public authorities; b) industrial bonded debts; c) standstill debts; and d) commercial and miscellaneous debts. During this first stage, the negotiations did not progress towards concrete proposals: creditors presented their cases and Germany defended her limited capacity to pay and to transfer. The major tension was that standstill and commercial creditors were ready to settle in DM immediately to resume business, but the Tripartite Commission vetoed it: as explained in the previous section, the agreement had to be comprehensive, and settling the most pressing claims for Germany would undermine the rest of creditors. On their side, the standstill creditors knew that without their governments' agreement, their settlement could not come into force (US Senate Committee on Foreign Relations, 1953).

On 19 May 1952, the Conference initiated its second stage, after several weeks of recess, with a German proposal to assume a debt service burden of 500 million DM per annum. In the German proposal, only 170 million were devoted to the settlement of pre-war debts; this implied not only an interest rate reduction, the abrogation of gold clauses, and the almost complete annulment of over twenty years of arrears but also a 40 per cent reduction of outstanding capital. The strong negative reaction of the creditors and the support they received from the Tripartite Commission brought about the rejection of the proposal. After the first offer, the negotiations entered into a different procedure: negotiation of concrete and

Total pre-war debts	13.493.00	
Public	**8.071.40**	
I. German Federal Republic	7.609.10	56%
a) External loans of the Reich	5.572.60	41%
Dawes Loan	1.158.32	9%
Young Loan	3.518.48	26%
b) Other claims	2.036.50	15%
II. Laender	313.40	2%
III. Municipalities	148.90	1%
Private	**5.421.60**	
I. Long-term loans	1.369.40	10%
II. Standstill debts	618.60	5%
III. Fixed interest bearing bonds	112.00	1%
IV. Private restitution claims	700.00	5%
V. Other liabilities	2.461.60	18%

Figure 6.1. Pre-war debts negotiated in the LDA.

Note: Amount outstanding including partial account of interest arrears. Amounts are in millions of DM and percentage over the total.

Source: Own Calculations. Report on claims. Statistical Committee. NA FO371/100084

acceptable agreements for each class of debts, beginning with Reich debts, especially the Dawes and Young loans, which would establish a pattern for other debts. As shown in Figure 6.1, those debts represented almost 35 per cent of all pre-war debts and due to their contractual securities it was recognized that an acceptable agreement in the Young and Dawes Loans was needed in order to assure a comprehensive agreement on pre-war debts. This was pursued not under the committee's framework but under informal negotiations between the creditors' representatives and the German delegation.

The negotiations between the German delegation, the FBPC and the CFB led to an agreement concerning the Dawes and Young Loans that would reduce interest rates by 28.56 per cent and 18.18 per cent respectively (at 5 and 4.5 per cent rather than at 7 and 5 per cent respectively). Interest arrears were calculated at those reduced rates, but seven years of accrued interest were deferred until reunification: henceforth, the capitalization of interest arrears was 21 per cent for the Dawes Loan and 15 per cent for the Young Loan.

However, the discussions about the treatment of gold clauses in the Young Loan brought the conference to a deadlock that threatened to derail the whole agreement. In contrast to the Dawes Loan in which only the American tranche contained a gold clause, all the tranches of the Young Loan (dollar, sterling, Swiss franc, French franc, Belgian franc, Italian lira, Dutch guilder, Swedish kronor, and Reich mark) had been protected from currency devaluations by a gold clause. Indeed, whereas all debts issued in the US since the Civil War customarily included gold clauses, in European contracts they were only incorporated as a result of negotiations to facilitate the origination of those loans and therefore were a specific protection that only some loans featured.[40] After the statutory abrogation of the gold clauses in the US in April 1933 by the Roosevelt Administration, the US holders of foreign bonds had never insisted on enforcing those clauses and both the US government delegates and the FBPC had the intention to continue this policy in Germany. For European creditors, the question was more controversial, and the stance of the various European countries varied widely. For example, when the European countries negotiated bilateral arrangements during 1933 and 1939 with the Nazi government, they ignored gold clauses (Clement, 2004). On the contrary, the French government intervened on many occasions in the 1930s to protect the enforcement of gold clauses in foreign debt contracts held by its nationals.[41]

Taking into account the huge devaluations that occurred since the 1930s, the application of gold clauses would impose an unsurmountable annual burden. To offer some perspective on its magnitude of the debt, the concessions agreed by the three Allied Powers would amount to DM309 million per annum, while including gold clauses in the Young Loan would amount to more than DM150 million in the servicing the interest alone (no amortization). The European delegations recognized that enforcing such conditions was not compatible with the payment of other debts, arguing instead that for them to omit gold clauses would represent a very significant sacrifice on their part, and claimed compensation. As it is shown in the Figure 6.2, the differences in currency depreciation against gold implied very different sacrifices: an Italian creditor would face a 98.2 per cent devaluation of his claim, whereas a Swiss creditor would face devaluation of only 28.6 per cent.

	Against gold	Against dollar
US dollar	40.9	--
Pound Sterling	66	42.5
Swiss Franc	28.6	(20.8)
French Franc	95.7	92.7
Belgian Franc	57.6	28.2
Italian Lira	98.2	97
Dutch Guilder	61.3	34.5
Swedish Kroner	57.4	27.9
German Reichmark	41	0.2

Figure 6.2. Percentage of currency depreciation in August 1952 as against 1930.
Source: Dernburg (1953)

[40] For a review on the question of US abrogation of gold clauses and its impact over foreign bonds, see Kroszner (1999).

[41] See for example Waibel (2011, ch. 4).

In November 1951, the Tripartite Commission agreed to substitute the gold clause for the dollar clause as a compromise solution.[42] For the Europeans, its substitution meant a sacrifice of 40 per cent of the value of their claims. However, the FBPC held an opposing viewpoint: the substitution of a dollar clause for the gold clause implied a revaluation of all the claims except for the dollar and the Swiss Franc claims. The British delegation regarded this as entirely unfounded unilateral action by the FBPC's president, but it ended up being a successful holdout strategy that mobilized several diplomatic layers and demonstrated the domestic political risks of governments' involvement in debt issues. When Rogers walked out on the discussions in London on 24 June 1952, bringing the conference near to collapse, he claimed he would inform Congress that the proposed agreement with the Germans discriminated against US bondholders and was unacceptable to them. The US State Department was concerned that an emotional symbol such as discrimination would be dangerous during the electoral campaign.[43] The message sent to the British and French diplomats from the US executive, particularly from Undersecretary of State Acheson, was that some compensation should be offered to the American bondholders in order to bring them back to negotiations.[44] While recognizing that it was not possible to assure payments by arranging an alternative agreement on European pre-war claims without the American government on board, the British and French agreed to concede an increase of 0.5 per cent in the American tranches of both the Dawes and Young loans. This compensation was justified afterwards as a compensation for the discrimination that occurred against dollar bondholders in the 1930s.

After reaching agreement on Reich debts, the rest of the committees proceeded with their own claims. Although many disagreements arose, a final settlement on each class of debt was agreed by the end of the conference. On 27 February 1953, the Allied governments and Germany signed the London Debt Agreement on German Debts. As Figure 6.3 shows, the LDA lead to a major reduction of German external debt: in total, the LDA dealt with DM29.8 billion of external debt and reduced it to DM14.2 billion.[45] Public debts were reduced from DM23.85 million to DM10.85 million, hence by 54.5 per cent. Among those public debts, DM7.7 million were pre-war debts held by private creditors who assumed a 48 per cent reduction and agreed to substantial interest reductions, maturity extensions, and deferral of interest arrears up to the reunification. Only accounting partially,

[42] Minutes of the 46th meeting of the Tripartite Commission, treatment of gold clauses in foreign exchange obligations 13/11/51, FO371/100103, NA.

[43] Discussion between TC and US Bondholders, 13/6/52. FO371/100103, NA.

[44] Crawford's Minute 14/6/52. FO371/100103, NA.

[45] Some other specific claims arising out of both world wars were settled during the conference and embedded in parallel agreements, but they are not included in the common statistical summaries of the LDA since they were not strictly part of the agreement (nor pre-war debts). See for example: Kaiser (2013); Kampffmeyer (1987).

		Old claim	New claim	Debt relief
		Billions of DM		
Official creditors	US	13.72	5.04	63.3%
	UK	2.36	1.76	25.4%
	France	0.07	0.05	24.6%
	Total	16.15	6.85	57.6%
Private creditors	Public debtors	7.70	4.00	48.1%
	Private debtors	5.80	3.50	39.7%
	Total	13.50	7.50	44.4%
TOTAL		29.65	14.35	51.6%

Figure 6.3. 1953 London Debt Agreement on German debts. Face value haircut.

this part of the operation represented an external debt relief of about 22 per cent of GDP in 1952 (Sinn, 2012).

More importantly, during the later stages of negotiations, the German delegation succeeded in incorporating article 5(2) of the agreement in which all claims arising from the Second World War were lumped with reparations, deferring its settlement until a future reunification. In other words, virtually a cancellation, since the reunification was not expected any time in the near future. This clause implied, too, a major reduction of Germany's foreign claims.

6.5 Conclusion

After the Second World War, Germany's private creditors faced a common problem in that period. After the collapse of the capital market during the Great Depression and the establishment of capital controls in the immediate years after the Second World War, holders of public foreign bonds lacked their traditional enforcement mechanisms and consequently sought to enlist their governments to sponsor their private claims. In this chapter, I showed that the exceptional geopolitical circumstances regarding the reconstruction of Germany in the post-war era are key to understand the equally extraordinary and innovative outcome that was the London Debt Agreement. The German case stands out from the rest of dispute settlements of that time because the whole external debt of Germany was settled in one unified operation.

The procedures of debt dispute adjudication designed by the three Allied governments brought Germany under strong incentives to recognize and settle all her privately held pre-war debts in a comprehensive manner. These procedures also facilitated a reconciliation of the multiple interests involved. The principles of capacity to pay and equality of treatment were instrumental in achieving an orderly debt restructuring. These principles were flexible enough to enable creditors to negotiate directly with Germany. This was possible because of the involvement of Allied Governments in the question of German debts and, specifically, their position both as occupying powers and major creditors themselves. Although their involvement allowed for conciliating debt relief with respect to a certain seniority structure, there were difficulties, as the Young Loan gold clauses affair illustrates.

Reading the LDA through the lens of the inter-state regime of sovereign debt disputes offers a more nuanced perspective on private creditors' relations with their governments at the time. The LDA sheds some light on how a principle-based (or integrated approach) can provide for an effective resolution of debt disputes that can balance all stakeholder interests. Moreover, it is interesting in itself that public opinion and creditors themselves considered the agreement a watershed for the restoration of the sanctity of international investment, as well as Germany's creditworthiness. That both creditworthiness and sanctity of contracts, keystones of our understanding of international financial relations, were compatible with important creditors' concessions highlights that both concepts perhaps can be more flexible and encompassing than we might otherwise assume.

References

Abelshauser, W. (1991). 'Assessing the Economic Achievement: American Aid and West German Economic Recovery: A Macroeconomic Perspective', in C.S. Maier & G. Bischof (Eds.), *The Marshall Plan and Germany: West German development within the framework of the European Recovery Program*. New York: Berg.

Abs, H. (1959). 'Das Londoner Schuldenabkommen. Zusammenfassende Darstellung aus Vorträgen, Gehalten in der Zeit vom 11. September bis 26. November 1952'. Frankfurt: Zeitfragen der Geld- und Wirtschaftspolitik.

Accominotti, O., Kessler, P. & Oosterlinck, K. (2017). 'The Dawes Bonds: Selective Default and International Trade'. Available at: http://cepr.org/sites/default/files/Oosterlinck%2C Kim.pdf (Accessed 11 November 2017).

Berger, H. & Ritschl, A. (1995). 'Germany and the Political Economy of the Marshall Plan, 1947–52: A Re-revisionist View', in B. Eichengreen (Ed.), *Europe's Post-war Recovery* (pp. 199–245). Cambridge: Cambridge University Press.

Bordo, M. (1993). *The Gold Standard, Bretton Woods and other Monetary Regimes: An Historical Appraisal*. NBER Working Paper Series, WP n.4310. Cambridge, MA.

Borchardt, K. & Buchheim, C. (1991). 'The Marshall Plan and Economic Key Sectors: A Microeconomic Perspective', in C.S. Maier & G. Bischof (Eds.), *The Marshall Plan and Germany: West German development within the framework of the European Recovery Program*. New York: Berg.

Buchheim, C. (1994). 'Marshall Plan and Currency Reform', in J.M. Diefendorf, A. Frohn & H.J. Rupieper (Eds.), *American Policy and the Reconstruction of West Germany, 1945–1955*. Cambridge: Cambridge University Press.

Buxbaum, Richard M. (2005). 'The London Debt Agrement and Its Consequences', in H. Rasmussen-Bonne (Ed.), *Balancing of Interests: Liber Amicorum Peter Hay Zum 70. Geburtstag*. Frankfurt am Main: Verlag Recht und Wirtschaft GmbH.

Clement, P. (2004). '"The Touchstone of German Credit": Nazi Germany and the Service of the Dawes and Young Loans'. *Financial History Review*, 11(1), 33–50.

Dernburg, H. J. (1953). 'Some Basic Aspects of the German Debt Settlement'. *The Journal of Finance*, 8(3), 298–318.

Eichengreen, B. J. (1993). *Reconstructing Europe's Trade and Payments: the European Payments Union*. Ann Arbor: University of Michigan Press.

Galofré-Vilà, G., McKee, M., Meissner, C.M., & Stuckler, D. (2016). 'The Economic Consequences of the 1953 London Debt Agreement'. NBER Working Paper Series, No. 2257, August 2016.

Gimbel, J. (1976). *The Origins of the Marshall Plan*. Stanford: Stanford University Press.

Guinnane, Timothy W. (2015). 'Financial Vergangenheitsbewältigung: The 1953 London Debt Agreement'. Economic Growth Center Discussion Paper, Yale University.

Hogan, M. J. (1991). 'European Integration and German Reintegration: Marshall Planners and the search for Recovery and Security in Western Europe', in C. S. Maier & G. Bischof (Eds.), *The Marshall Plan and Germany: West German Development within the Framework of the European Recovery Program*. New York: Berg.

Kaiser, J. (2013). One Made It out of the Debt Trap: Lessons from the London Debt Agreement of 1953 for Current Debt Crises. Berlin: Friedrich-Ebert-Stiftung.

Kampffmeyer, T. (1987). *Towards a Solution of the Debt Crisis. Applying the Concept of Corporate Compositions with Creditors*. Berlin: German Development Institute.

Kindleberger, C. P. & Ostrander, F. T. (2003). 'The 1948 Monetary Reform in Western Germany', in M. Flandreau, C.L. Holtfrerich & H. James (Eds.), *International Financial History in the Twentieth Century*. Cambridge: Cambridge University Press.

Kroszner, R. (1999). 'Is it Better to Forgive than to Receive?: Repudiation of the Gold Indexation Clause in Long-Term Debt During the Great Depression'. Center for Research in Security Prices, Graduate School of Business. University of Chicago.

Lutz, F. A. (1949). 'The German Currency Reform and the Revival of the German Economy', *Economica*, 16(62), 122.

Ritschl, A. (2011). 'Germany Owes Greece a Debt', *The Guardian*, 21 June. Available at: https://www.theguardian.com/commentisfree/2011/jun/21/germany-greece-greek-debt-crisis (Accessed 2 March 2020).

Ritschl, A. (2012a). 'Germany, Greece and the Marshall Plan', *The Economist*, 15 June. Available at: https://www.economist.com/blogs/freeexchange/2012/06/economic-history (Accessed 2 March 2020).

Ritschl, A. (2012b). 'The German Transfer Problem, 1920–33: a Sovereign-debt Perspective', *European Review of History: Revue européenne d'histoire*, 19(6), 943–64.

Rombeck-Jaschinski, U. (2005). *Das Londoner Schuldenabkommen: die Regelung der deutschen Auslandsschulden nach dem Zweiten Weltkrieg*. London: German Historical Institute.

Schuker, S. (1988). 'American "Reparations" to Germany 1919.33: Implications for the Third-World Debt Crisis.' *Princeton Studies in International Finance*, 61, 72–81.

Schwartz, T. (1991). 'European Integration and the "Special Relationship": Implementing the Marshall Plan in the Federal Republic', in C.S. Maier & G. Bischof (Eds.), *The Marshall Plan and Germany: West German development within the framework of the European Recovery Program*. New York: Berg.

Securities and Exchange Commission (1937). 'Securities and Exchange Commission Report on the Study and Investigation of the Work, Activities, Personnel and Functions of Protective and Reorganization Committees'. Washington: U.S. Government Printing Office, 419–34.

Sinn, Hans-Werner (2012). 'Germany, Greece and the Marshall Plan, a Final Riposte'. Free exchange blog, *The Economist*, 29 June 2012. Available at: https://www.economist.com/blogs/freeexchange/2012/06/economic-history-3 (Accessed 2 March 2020).

Waibel, Michael. (2011). *Sovereign Defaults Before International Courts and Tribunals*. New York: Cambridge University Press.

Wallich, H. C. (1955). *Mainsprings of the German Revival*. New Haven: Yale University Press.

US Senate Committee on Foreign Relations (1953). Hearings before the US Senate Committee on Foreign Relations, 38th Congress, 1st session, on June 17–18, 1953, p. 143.

Archives

Corporation of Foreign Bondholders. London: London Metropolitan Archives
Foreign Bondholders Protective Council. Stanford: Stanford Library.
Foreign Office Records. UK National Archives.
Foreign Relations of the United States (FRUS).

7

The Revenge of Defaulters

Sovereign Defaults and Interstate Negotiations in the Post-War Financial Order, 1940–65

Juan Flores Zendejas, Pierre Pénet, and Christian Suter

7.1 Introduction

The post-war era holds a special and important place in the long history of sovereign debt disputes. The majority of states suspended interest payments on their foreign obligations after 1931. In 1945, nearly half of all countries representing 40 per cent of the world income were in default (Reinhart & Rogoff, 2009, p. 73; Suter, 1992). Never before had creditors faced a wave of defaults of this magnitude. Previous scholarship has demonstrated that the economic consequences of the Great Depression were the main causes of debt defaults, and the Second World War further delayed the negotiations between borrowers and bondholders in certain cases (Eichengreen, 1991; Eichengreen & Portes, 1989). Less well known, however, are the important changes affecting the actors, tools, and forums governing the settlement of debt disputes. For debtors and creditors, the post-war settlement of debt disputes represented an enormous task not only because of the sheer amount of debt in default but also because old methods of debt settlement no longer applied.

The methods that debtors and creditors use to settle debt disputes have greatly varied over time. Since the mid-nineteenth century, bondholder committees had furnished creditors with their most efficient method to protect their rights against recalcitrant states. Bondholder committees derived their authority from the capacity to sponsor market access to preferred customers and to refuse to list new bonds from a creditor in default through stock exchange regulations (Hautcoeur & Riva, 2012; Flandreau, 2013). Yet, when the question of debt repayment resurfaced in 1945, capital markets were virtually shut down. Having abandoned bond markets, states borrowed domestically or through public lending schemes from Export Promotion Agencies and multilateral organizations. Syndicate bank lending emerged as the main source of private external finance, while sovereign bond issuances would not return to pre-war levels until the post Brady-plan era of financial globalization. This major shift in the structure of debt financing critically

Juan Flores Zendejas, Pierre Pénet, and Christian Suter, *The Revenge of Defaulters: Sovereign Defaults and Interstate Negotiations in the Post-War Financial Order, 1940–65* In: *Sovereign Debt Diplomacies: Rethinking Sovereign Debt from Colonial Empires to Hegemony.* Edited by: Pierre Pénet and Juan Flores Zendejas, Oxford University Press (2021).
 DOI: 10.1093/oso/9780198866350.003.0008

weakened bondholders' bargaining power. After the war, creditors began to seek diplomatic support from their government (i.e. creditor states) to remedy broken agreements.

This chapter examines how bondholders and their governments adapted to this new context. How did states act as the agent of private creditors? To what extent did they accept to turn themselves into protectors of private capital? How did bondholders react when creditor states refused to grant diplomatic recognition to private contracts? How did this new context affect investors' gains and losses as compared to previous periods? The post-war context raises many issues for the economic, sociological, and legal history of sovereign debt disputes, their actors and forums, and, more broadly, the capacity of foreign creditors to protect their rights in times of radical uncertainty.

This chapter offers three insights. First, the norm of debt repayment is politically and historically variable (Lienau, 2014). Using the post-war context as empirical illustration, we argue that the sanctity of debt contracts varies according to the identity of the agent charged with conducting debt talks. So long as private creditors were the main negotiator agents, debt talks were strictly restricted to one background expectation: repayment. But as states began to assume a more explicit role as enforcer of debt contracts, negotiating on behalf of their domestic bondholders, debt acquired a broader public and diplomatic meaning. Creditor states did not give consideration to debt repayment without considering as well other concerns such as peace, trade, reparation and the building of a new international order. As a result, the sanctity of debt contracts was durably undermined. No longer universal, the value of debt claims became contingent upon creditor states' recognition.

Second, we suggest that the perceived advantages of legal forums grew in relation to the weaknesses of the diplomatic channel as method of debt settlement. For the great majority of creditors, there was no need to elevate the dispute to international legal forums because creditor state mediation operated according to expectations. But in a few cases, creditors grew dissatisfied with the diplomatic channel and began pursuing alternative legal remedies. Although such attempts failed for the most part, they are significant because they foreshadow many aspects and problems in the current debate on legal tools of debt dispute settlements.

Third, we reflect on the posterity of post-war repudiations in current debt talks. The post-war context was remarkable because it challenged the repayment norm. But the forms of diplomatic involvements that prevailed during these years did not translate into new institutions. As a result, the departure from the repayment rule should be characterized as merely a transitional rather than a permanent one. Negotiations were conducted on a case-by-case basis, outside comprehensive schemes. The post-war experience of settling debt defaults was not codified into principles providing a legal basis for non-repayment. This all but guaranteed that the norm of repayment would once again prevail once creditors recovered their bargaining power. The revenge of defaulters would be short-lived.

The chapter proceeds as follows. Section 7.1 analyses the main causes explaining the shift from a bondholder to a creditor state mediation. Section 7.2 builds on several cases of debt disputes to examine how states fulfilled their task to represent creditors' interests. Section 7.3 explains the complicated post-war development of international law. Section 7.4 assesses the efficiency of different methods of debt settlements against selected metrics of performance. Section 7.5 concludes.

7.2 The Political Economy of Debt Dispute Settlement: A Long-Term Perspective

The history of sovereign debt dispute settlements is one of remarkable resilience and adaptation to a changing political and economic landscape. During the first era of bond finance, foreign creditors began to organize themselves into bondholder committees to conduct debt negotiations with recalcitrant states and maximize the repayment of principal and interests. In 1868, the British Corporation of Foreign Bondholders (CFB) was established to represent British bondholders' interests (Mauro, Sussman & Yafeh, 2006). The British CFB was a particularly efficient forum for the resolution of defaults. Thanks to the close ties it maintained with the banking sector and the London capital market,[1] the British CFB had the ability to sponsor market access to preferred customers and to refuse to list new bonds from a defaulter. Its efficiency of the CFB was also enhanced through its collaboration with underwriting banks (Esteves, 2005, 2013; Flandreau & Flores, 2012). Other CFB-type organizations were established elsewhere (cf. Figure 7.1). Eichengreen and Portes (1989) found that the lack of a CFB-type organization in the US during that period resulted in US bondholders obtaining lower returns on their foreign bonds than their British counterparts, though their results were more recently questioned by Kamlani (2008) and Flandreau (2013).[2]

In the pre-1914 period, the concentration of financial exchanges in London and a few other stock exchanges made it unlikely for a defaulter to obtain capital access elsewhere. Cross-national coordination between European bondholder associations allowed creditors to present a united front against defaulters.[3] Mauro and

[1] For instance, the governing council of the CFB included representatives of the British Bankers' Association and the London Chamber of Commerce.

[2] The US Foreign Bondholders Council Protection was only founded in 1934.

[3] Kelly (1998) and Kamlani (2008) evoke Ecuador as an exceptional case of a defaulting government having succeeded in avoiding this global exclusion. After having defaulted on its foreign debt in 1909, a Railway Company with state guarantee issued new bonds in Paris in 1911 and the government issued a short-term loan in the US in 1910 (Corporation of Foreign Bondholders, Annual Report 1911). Kamlani also mentions the case of Guatemala, whose government reportedly obtained credit from the US and Germany while being in default to British bondholders. The original source (CFB Annual

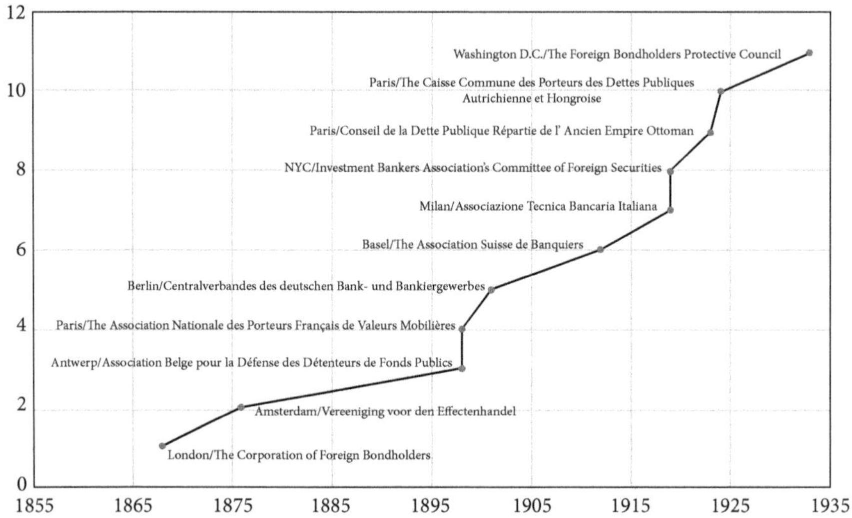

Figure 7.1. Main bondholder committees, 1868–1934 (by year of foundation)
Source: Winkler (1933) and online sources for dates of foundation

Yafeh (2003) report that such coordination efforts convinced the Mexican government to negotiate in 1874 while similar actions were undertaken during default negotiations with the Greek government in the same year. Debtor countries were thus under strong reputational incentives to work out a solution with bondholder committees in order to avoid being cut off from capital markets. In 1873, the CFB in London partnered with Amsterdam to prevent Guatemala from issuing a new bond because of its failure to repay old loans. During the period 1870–1914, bondholder committees reached their gold age, making the cost of defaulting on its foreign obligations a prohibitive one (Mauro & Yafeh, 2003).

The coordination function of CFBs weakened considerably during the 1930s. For instance, the correspondence held by the British Corporation of Foreign Bondholders shows that it actively sought, but ultimately failed, to establish a close collaboration with the US bondholders committee and the US State Department.[4] Without transatlantic coordination, the British CFB privately recognized that its bargaining position was sluggish. During the negotiations with

reports of 1895 and 1908) is unclear regarding the chronology of the arrangement (1895) and the issue of a new loan in Germany, but the dispute referred to in those documents concerned mainly the security for the new loan (Coffee Warrants) and the respective priority over these assets.

[4] See, for instance, London Metropolitan Archives (LMA), Archives of the Corporation of Foreign Bondholders, files Ms34661/3 and Ms 34661/4. Elliot Butler, Director General of the CFB, pushed the idea of an 'Anglo-American approach to all foreign governmental external debts composed of both dollar and sterling loans', an idea supported by the British Treasury (as expressed by Rowe-Dutton) and by the Bank of England (as expressed by Otto Niemeyer).

Chile's government in 1945, Otto Niemeyer from the Bank of England recognized: 'we are unlikely to get anywhere without US support.'[5] Very often therefore, each committee attempted to obtain a favourable bilateral agreement with defaulting governments. One reason for this, as argued by Eichengreen and Portes (1989), were the original terms of the loan contracts issued in London and New York, which were drafted differently and led to occasional disputes between the British and US CFBs. An illustrative example of these disputes were the guarantees granted to each loan. Contrary to dollar bonds, most sterling loans were secured, and bondholders insisted that such loans received a preferential treatment over the US (non-secured) loans. In many instances, the British CFB also blamed the US Foreign Bondholders Protective Council for settling unilaterally with defaulters, as this obliged British bondholders to accept the same terms (Eichengreen & Portes, 1989, p. 216).

Another contrast between the post-1940 period and the pre–First World War years was the role of creditor states. Bondholder committees had always entertained close relationships with government authorities. Before 1914, government diplomats provided bondholder committees with some degree of cooperation with respect to routine tasks. They also served as liaison in the country where they operated. But states seldom intervened in debt disputes, performing only a passive, subsidiary role (Lipson, 1985). This is reflected in US Secretary of State Bryan's dictum: 'When you go abroad you have to take your chances.' The British Foreign Office operated under a similar frame of mind in accordance with the Palmerson doctrine—'When people choose to lend money to a foreign country, they [do] so at their own risk' (Williams, 1924, p. 18)—that forbade British authorities to provide 'authoritative representation' in support of the bondholders.

As a rule, governments acted as the sword arm of private creditors only when the mediation of bondholder clubs had failed. Episodes of gunboat diplomacy in the aftermath of a sovereign default were rather infrequent (Flores, 2012; Tomz, 2006, pp. 114–57).[6] Far from mechanical, creditor state support required a great deal of persuasion from bondholders. And creditor state–lent military support against recalcitrant countries only when they found political and diplomatic interest to do so. Episodes of gunboat diplomacy were few but rather 'loud' events because of the use of military force and the social and human toll exacted on the invaded territories. In Egypt and North Africa, England and France granted diplomatic protection to their bondholders because doing so intersected with their agenda to expand colonial rule. Geopolitical interests were also relevant in Southern Europe and the Middle East, where creditor governments established Commissions of Foreign Control. In cases such as Greece, Serbia, or the Ottoman

[5] Letter by Otto Niemeyer to Mather-Jackson from the Treasury Chambers, 25 June 1945, LMA, Ms 34661/4.

[6] See also Coskun Tunçer and Flores Zendejas & Cole in this volume.

Empire, bondholder representatives directly participated in the decision-making of fiscal policies.[7] To summarize: debt talks were mostly a private matter that concerned the debtor country and his private creditors. Support from the official sector only provided a dissuasive 'plan B'.

The Great Depression durably undermined the structure of capital flows. Sovereign debt market evaporated after 1931, debt issuances came to a halt along with the fall of capital exports from the US, and bondholder committees lost their most precious bargaining power (Jorgensen & Sachs, 1988). The threat to block a country's future debt issuances was persuasive only in a context of continuous sovereign debt borrowing. With the global retreat of external debt markets, this threat had lost its dissuasive authority on defaulters. The post-war financial order relegated CFBs to the background: few countries issued, domestic and official lending dominated bond financing and the reputational system that bondholder clubs had spent decades to build no longer mattered. The structural dependence link between the repayment of past debt and the issuance of future debt that creditors had long exploited to force debtors to repay their debt no longer existed. The great bargaining power that creditors had enjoyed during the first globalization through their bondholder committees was, after all, fragile and reversible.

Nevertheless, this dull horizon does not show the whole picture. Faced with the declining significance of bondholder committees, creditors increasingly sought the mediation of their governments. The first signs of creditor states' expanding role were manifested in the onset of the Second World War. The US government developed a financial strategy based on geopolitical interests.[8] This involved a direct participation in the negotiations with foreign governments willing to secure US aid and public loans (Adamson, 2002). The final outcome, as perceived by the bondholders, was far from satisfactory (Kamlani, 2008). In the case of Mexico, the US government pressed US creditors to secure a financial settlement (Aggarwal, 1996). Roosevelt insisted in 1941 that the US investors (represented by the so-called International Committee of Bankers on Mexico) acknowledged the Mexican government's programme for debt repudiation. During the 20s and 30s, the inflexible behaviour of US creditors toward Mexico had poisoned Mexican–American relations. But this legalistic approach to repayment increasingly ran up against governmental interests. Anxious to enlist Mexico into the war effort, Roosevelt called to normalize the economic relations between the US and Mexico, persuading JP Morgan, the coordinating force behind US bondholders, to forbear a portion of Mexican debt. For the US government, debt had become a secondary concern to the most pressing issue of bolstering diplomatic and trade

[7] See Pamuk (1987) and Tunçer (2015).

[8] For the case of Latin America and the effects of the 'Good Neighbor' policy of the US government on debt negotiations with Latin American governments, see Wallich (1943).

ties with foreign allies. The sovereign interest of the US government prevailed with the signature of the debt settlement of 1942 providing for the drastic reduction of both the principal and interest (see Del Angel and Pérez-Hernández contribution in this volume).

A similar pattern occurred in Egypt. The relationship between British bondholders and the Foreign Office had long been marked by a spirit of cooperation and mutual interests. After the Egyptian default of 1876, England used military force to oblige Egypt to repay foreign bondholders, and episode that ended in full colonization after 1882. A Public Debt Commission ('Caisse de la dette') was organized to maintain regular debt service and give foreign creditors (British and French for the most part) a direct line of communication with Egyptian officials (Saul, 1997; Wynne, 1951). The British support for its bondholders began to vanish since the early 1930s, when disputes over the interpretation of gold clauses emerged and the British government positioned itself on the Egyptian government side.[9] In 1940, the British government sought to bolster its ties with Egypt, which British officials (quite rightfully) predicted would play an important role during the war. In July 1940, in the midst of the Battle of London, British and French authorities reached an agreement with Egyptian authorities concerning the dissolution of the much-hated Caisse. The revenues payable to the Caisse would be assumed by the National Bank of Egypt and by Egypt's government.[10] Most importantly, the agreement gave Treaty recognition to Egyptian authorities' request to redeem its foreign debt in pounds sterling, something that British creditors adamantly opposed, claiming their rights to receive debt repayment in gold, and this in spite of Great Britain's abandonment of the gold standard in 1931. Taking advantage of this provision, Egypt redeemed at par her outstanding foreign loans in 1943.

It is an understatement to say that creditors did not appreciate states meddling into their affairs. But creditors' defiant attitude towards their own governments began to change after the War. In the face of uncooperative behaviour from defaulting and recalcitrant governments, the threat to block market access was no longer dissuasive because markets were shut down. Creditors were left with no other choice than to seek the mediation of their governments to press their rights. Of course, when debtor states were cooperative, creditors could still rely on the mediation provided by bondholder committees to reach a settlement. In Japan, US and British creditors obtained the resumption of debt service at the full contractual rates. But when state debtors had neither the will nor the capacity to repay,

[9] See Bank of England Archives, File C40/270. A letter addressed to Montagu Norman, governor of the Bank of England, by Frederick Leith Ross, chief economic advisor to the British government, dated 26 July 1932, referred to the importance of the support to the Egyptian Government based on 'political grounds'.

[10] The correspondence and text of the agreement can be found in the Bank of England Archives, file C40/270.

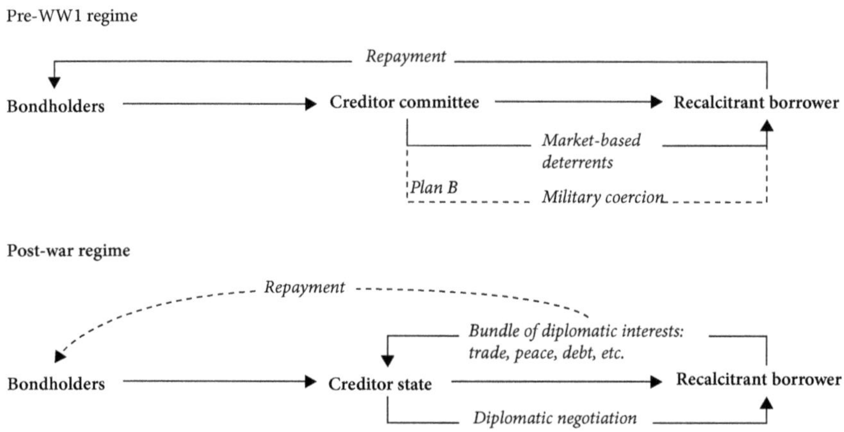

Figure 7.2. The new political economy of debt dispute settlement before and after the Great Depression

foreign creditors depended ultimately on brokerage resources from their representative states.

As a result, the post-war period was marked by the transfer of the functional control over international enforcement of sovereign debt claims from creditor committees to creditor states. In the hands of states as ultimate enforcers, bond contracts lost their universal validity and their value became contingent upon diplomatic recognition. Debt became one layer or tranche of interests in the bundle of interests (peace, commercial interests, etc.) which a state was prepared to defend during interstate negotiations (cf. Figure 7.2).

7.3 When Debt Repayment Takes the 'Backseat'

The much-discussed case of Germany cements the view that political and commercial interests primed over debt repayment. German debts amounted to about 800 billion DM, a sum that no one expected Germany could repay. At the London Agreement on German External Debts of 1953, commercial and trade issues prevailed over the issue of debt repayment (see de la Villa's contribution in this volume). The macroeconomic background mattered considerably when assessing the validity of debt claims. In the next twenty-five years, trade and debt policies became intimately connected.

The emergence of state-sponsored Export-Import banks ('Exim Banks') further affected bondholders' private bargaining power. The first of such banks was created in England in 1919. As shown in Figure 7.3, the development of Exim Banks accelerated during the early 1930s and then after the war until the late

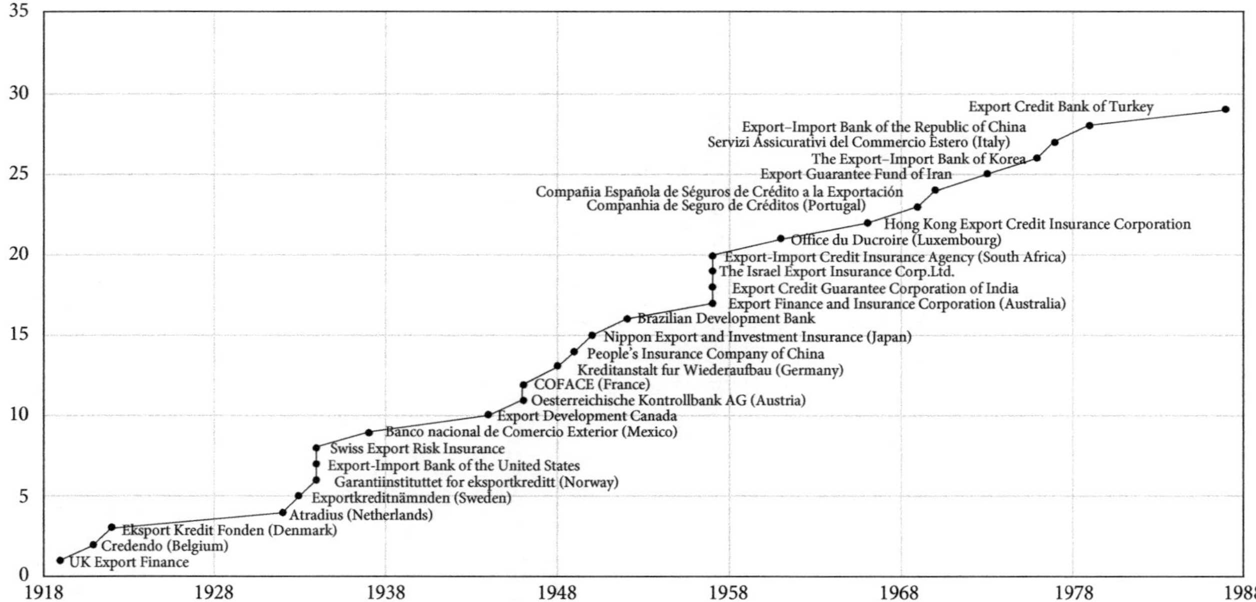

Figure 7.3. Exim banks, 1919–89 (by year of foundation)

Source: OECD (2002)

1950s, precisely when bond financing, which since the nineteenth century had provided states with their main source of external financing, was in disarray. During those years, the market for commercial credit remained open, providing tremendous incentives for countries to stay current on their commercial debts.

In the United States, Exim Banks were a lever that state authorities used to pressure debtor states to service their external debt. But at least in their early years, Exim Banks refused to link trade policies to debt repayment. From the US Export-Import Bank semi-annual reports, we have computed a total of forty loans from the bank granted to countries whose governments were in default regarding their dollar debts between 1945 and 1962. In its report for July–December 1945, the US Exim Bank announced that following a request from Congress, it would remove any prohibition on loans to countries in default. It further insisted that 'the bank has not ordinarily made payment of service on outstanding dollar obligations a condition of its loans to foreign countries' (Export-Import Bank, 1945, p. 29). Disgruntled bondholders criticized the extension of commercial credits to defaulters, and pressed their governments for a change in this policy. That countries in default could access external capital sent strong signals that the reputational cost of default was in fact negligible. This undermined the bargaining power of creditors. Placing defaulters under trade embargoes would have bolstered bondholders' bargaining power. But, in general, state authorities refused to accede to creditors' calls for commercial sanctions against defaulters. This is particularly true to the US government and to a lesser extent Britain. France and Germany, on the other hand, were more prompt to intervene in support of bondholders (Wynne & Borchard, 1933).

The claim that bondholder interests took the backseat seem particularly relevant in the US where the common practice was to not make Exim Bank loans conditional upon the resumption of debt service, though the US government could encourage borrowing governments to show a tangible will to settle its disputes with its creditors. Most often, nevertheless, decisions to extend such loans were premised on politics (Eichengreen, 1991, pp. 163–4). The Mexican debt agreement of 1942 was followed the same year by a trade agreement involving the extension of credits through the US Exim bank to finance highway construction in Mexico (Wynne, 1951, pp. 95–6). In the 1940s and 1950s, the US Exim Bank also granted different loans to Chile, Bolivia (both defaulters), and Argentina to finance infrastructure projects. Official flows also served to finance commercial arrears on imports from the US (Jorgensen & Sachs, 1988).

US-Latin America trade relations experienced a boom under the Roosevelt administration. In a 1939 speech, Roosevelt warned Congress that defaulted Latin American bonds were 'ancient history' (Eichengreen, 1991, p. 164). The President urged creditors to put the national interest above their own. On some occasions, the US administration invoked diplomatic interests to pressure bondholders into accepting important reductions in interest payment. Roosevelt even presented a formal apology to the President of Bolivia, blaming the greed of US bankers as chief causes for the default on a loan contracted in 1927 and claiming that 'the era of financial exploitation in Latin America was over.'[11] It should be noted that the situation was somewhat different in the UK, where debt repayment was construed by state authorities as standing within the public interest.

Switzerland is another illuminating case of our argument of debt repayment taking the 'back seat'. In the 1970s, Swiss banks continuously granted a set of loans to the government of and companies from Rhodesia despite a default in 1965.[12] The Swiss financial market became an attractive alternative to borrowing states that used to obtain their external funds from London or New York. After 1952, South Africa became a recurrent borrower in the Swiss market.[13] Swiss authorities were also pursuing an aggressive policy of exports promotion, and many of these loans were accompanied by promises for purchases of Swiss products. This example also exposed the lack of coordination between investors in the post-war era, as trade raised to a prominent level.[14] As a result, the attitude of the British authorities was to refrain South Africa's government from seeking loans from other countries or from the IBRD and IMF, as this could also prejudice UK exports.[15]

Creditors struggled to adapt to this new context of contingent validity of debt claims. But there was not much that creditors could do if they failed to obtain diplomatic representation of their private debt claims. Additionally, creditor states' reluctance to use military force to help creditors recover their claims also weakened the bargaining power of creditors. Disappointed by the trade-off between commercial interests and debt repayment, creditors began to contemplate alternative tactics to force repayment. Although creditors relied primarily on the extrajudicial enforcement of creditor states, they were also keen on exploring the possibility of having their debt claims adjudicated in international courts when the mediation of their home state proved unsatisfactory or inefficient.

The IBRD assumed a friendlier stance to bondholders' committees. The need by this new body to borrow from private capital markets imposed a policy in which the bank would avoid lending to governments in default (Lienau, 2014). Very often therefore, governments would negotiate with bondholders when the possibility for securing a IBRD loan was imminent. This was the case of the default settlements of Chile (1948), Ecuador (1955) or Peru (1952), which were

[11] 'President Says Old Bolivian Loan Was Exploitation', *The New York Times*, 8 May 1943.

[12] Swiss National Bank Archives, Box 264.252.

[13] Swiss National Bank Archives, Box 2.6/2144, 'Die Schweizerische Kapitalanlagetätigkeit in Ausland seit Kriegsende, 1950–1983'.

[14] The practice known as stock exchange 'shopping' has always been a tactic pursued by defaulters. Recall that, in the nineteenth century, the British CFB was never able to reach a settlement about US states' defaulted debt precisely because the US developed a rival debt market.

[15] Bank of England Archives, file C40/1216, correspondence between the Foreign Office and the Bank of England, 1966.

immediately followed by a loan from the IBRD. But even then, governments in creditor countries would press its bondholder committees to accept the offers from defaulting governments to allow them to benefit from these public loans. This also included unilateral offers from the governments with which the Foreign Bondholder Protective Council (hereafter FBPC) did not necessarily agree.[16] Furthermore, the IBRD granted several loans to Yugoslavia despite the country being in default (FBPC Annual Report, 1953–54). There was the competition with the Exim bank, which was finally settled in 1953 with the announcement of a State of Principles, in which the IBRD would concentrate in loans for development purposes and the Exim bank would confine itself to short- and medium-term commodity loans, though certain exceptions were foreseen and it managed to continue to provide an important tool for export promotion and to achieve foreign policy goals.

7.4 Bumpy Legal Roads Towards Repayment

State mediation posed important problems for creditors, one being the concern over inequality of treatment. Unequal treatment was a manifestation of the way talks were structured: since state mediation was organized along territorial borders, debt talks were fragmented along national borders. In certain cases, a group of bondholders was given preference as compared to others. For instance, in 1954 the government of Ecuador reached an agreement with the US FBPC and British CFB, but it excluded a Railway loan originally issued in Paris (Foreign Bondholder Protective Council Annual Report, 1954). That Ecuador's government was a defaulter (at least in the view of French bondholders) did not prevent the World Bank from granting a loan in 1954. In the case of Costa Rica, the government first reached a deal with the FBPC before having one with the British CFB one year thereafter. A similar case concerned Peru, for which the initial debt agreement of 1951 included only Peruvian's dollar bonds, while British bondholders could only reach an agreement two years thereafter. These cases show debtor countries actively exploiting the competitive dynamics building up between different bondholder clubs. In the face of the costs implied by bilateral debt disputes, national rivalries grew within bondholders. In some cases—as in the cases of Japan and Norway which we present below—creditors sought alternative means to remedy broken contracts.

The Japanese government first reached an agreement with US bondholders in July 1952. Negotiations with the British and French bondholders had to be prolonged because of rival interpretations of currency clauses in the debt

[16] Kamlani (2008) mentions the offers by Colombia, Peru, and Brazil in the 1940s.

contracts. The British succeeded in achieving an agreement in the same year, one that was to have the approval of the US government and the FBPC.[17] After the French government's failed mission to convince the Japanese government to honour the gold clause included in bonds, French bondholders appointed a Conciliator (Mr Black, President of the IBRD) to settle the dispute. The settlement involved a revalorization of bond value to take equitable account of the severe depreciation of the yen but the settlement fell short on recognizing French bondholders' contention that bonds included a gold clause (Waibel, 2011, pp. 80–1).

The dispute between French bondholders and Norway is also interesting along those lines. French bondholders bought Norwegian bonds from 1925 to 1955. The key question was whether debt payment was due in gold or in kroner currency. Norway refused to recognize the gold clause inserted into bond contracts. French creditors attempted to elevate debt claims against Norway to the International Court of Justice. But the court was not receptive to French bondholders' claims (in the meantime, Norway obtained new loans from the Swiss financial market). The Court denied jurisdiction because it deemed the dispute an interstate issue. The lack of reciprocity was another argument cited by the court: since the state of France did not acknowledge the jurisdiction of the court, the Court refused to seize upon the case. This case is not an isolated one: international forums frequently declined jurisdiction (Borchard, 1915, p. 302; Schoo, 1940, pp. 410, 437; Weidemaier, 2010, p. 340).

These examples suggest that law provided a weak remedy against non-repayment. Legal instruments provided little protection for bondholders and did not effectively contribute to hold debtor countries to their contractual obligations. As a rule, debt was negotiated not litigated (Borchard, 1951). The post-war context is instructive of an important change affecting bondholders' expectations regarding international law. The early development of arbitration in late nineteenth century was construed by investors as a method to enlist creditor state support of private claims (Weidemaier, 2010). The reluctance of creditor states to provide diplomatic protection of bondholders' rights led them to reconsider. They developed the idea—and this was a novel idea—that they could themselves elevate their claims to legal forums without the mediation of the creditor state. What creditors could not obtain through the diplomatic channel, they began to pursue through legal methods. As we have suggested this new representation was not immediately consequential. In Japan and Norway, international forums refused to accede to French creditors' claims. Courts extended jurisdiction only to interstates disputes, meaning that states had to have accepted to submit to arbitration, which France hadn't. Sovereign immunity is another cause for the complicated

[17] London Metropolitan Archives—CFB, Ms 34727/4.

development of international law. This is shown in the court's fear of over-extending its jurisdiction. The chance of successful legal action was limited under the principle of sovereign immunity, a principle well institutionalized until the mid-1950s which made it virtually impossible for bondholders to sue sovereign debtors.

7.5 Inter-Period Performance Assessment

As economists and historians have noted, the post-war context did often not generate favourable settlements for creditors and was often quite harmful to their interests. But we still lack precision as to how post-war debt settlements compare to settlements reached during previous periods. This section provides a comparative assessment of the outcome performance of debt dispute resolutions across three periods. Our analysis uses two metrics of performance, namely 1) the duration of debt disputes (measured by the time span between the outbreak of debt-servicing incapacities and the final conclusion of the debt settlement arrangement), and 2) bondholder losses (estimated from three indicators: a) the capitalization rate of arrears in interest, b) reductions in outstanding debts, and c) reductions in interest rates).[18] We applied these metrics to debt settlements from three periods: the pre–First World War period (1868–1914), the interwar (1919–33), and the Second World War and post war years (1940–73). As suggested above, the starting years for each period (1868, 1919, 1940) correspond to a major turning point (the creation of the British CFB, the signature of the Versailles Treaty, and the beginning of the Second World War, respectively) in the history of sovereign debt.[19]

Based on our reasoning developed in the previous sections, our presumption is that these periods are characterized by different degrees of bargaining power (i.e. the capacity of private creditors to act strategically to force the repayment of debt) and conceptions of state responsibility (i.e. broad conceptions that govern states' decisions to intervene into debt disputes). We expect that changes in creditors' bargaining power and conception of state responsibility will translate into more or less favourable terms for creditors. Additionally, we expect to witness substantial variations in debt settlement outcomes within each period, most particularly during the post-1945 period.

During the nineteenth century, bondholder committees had enough bargaining power to coerce recalcitrant borrowers to repay their debt in time and in full. Defaulting countries were blacklisted from Europe's capital markets. Those who

[18] To compute bondholder losses, we updated the database originally compiled by Suter (1990, 1992).

[19] Our analysis does not cover settlements reached between 1933 and 1940 because they were too few. Debt liquidations that included the assignment of state railways to bondholders have also been excluded (El Salvador and Peru). For these two cases, we were not able to compute creditors' losses.

accepted creditors' terms could regain access through a process known as 'white-listing'. Not only creditors possessed bargaining power, but they could also count on the diplomatic mediation of their home state to remedy broken contracts. As explained above, the diplomatic channel was not always available. But when states accepted to intervene, their diplomatic mediation generally worked in favour—not against—creditors. Overall, due to high bargaining power and occasional support granted to them by their home states, we expect that debt settlements from 1868 to 1914 generated favourable terms for creditors, both in terms of duration and bondholder losses.

The interwar period witnessed the emergence of the Reparations Commission and the League of Nations, whose active implication in the settling of debt disputes compromised the uncompromising stance adopted by creditors before 1914. During the Great Depression sovereign debt market evaporated after 1931 and debt issuances came to a halt. As a result, bondholder committees lost their most precious bargaining power.[20] From the 1940s onward, the rising influence of the US State Department and Exim banks further eroded creditors' claims. These new political actors conveyed a radically different conception of state responsibility in which debt was relegated to a secondary concern to the most pressing issue of rebuilding diplomatic and trade ties with foreign allies. This resulted in states adopting a stance of forbearance towards defaulters. Given this combination of lower bargaining power and forbearance, we expect that debt settlements after 1918 began generating less favourable terms for creditors, both in terms of duration of negotiation and creditors' losses as compared to the pre-1914 period. Our assumptions are broadly verified (see Table 7.1). Table 7.1 shows that the duration of negotiations and bondholders' losses were at their lowest during the first period which corresponds to the 'pure' CFB-based regime (1868–1914). The first column of Table 7.1 shows that the CFB participated as main mediators in 86 per cent of the cases reported.[21] Governments' remained at a secondary stage as they directly intervened in 24 per cent of all cases.[22] The duration of debt disputes increased from 6.1 to 9.5 years from the first to the second, interwar period (while losses remaining stable at 18.9 per cent), which suggests a more hostile context in which bondholders had to negotiate harder and longer to obtain comparable settlements. The post-1940 context is markedly different with considerably longer negotiations (18.8 years) and massive private losses (just over 50 per cent), while governments increased their assistance (more than 52 per cent

[20] A good illustration for the loss of this power source and the consequent weakness of the CFB in the post-Great Depression period are the settlements of defaulted pre-war bonds concluded in the 1980s with the Soviet Union and China, where the CFB had to accept quite unfavourable arrangements negotiated by the British government which was interested in opening up the London bond market to these countries.

[21] The prominence of CFB representation in debt settlements is reported in Esteves (2013).

[22] These interventions are broadly defined: military, customs' control, diplomatic participation, and financial support. These interventions also include those from international organizations.

Table 7.1. Yearly duration of debt dispute settlements and degree of bondholders losses

	Bondholder committees as main mediators (in percentages)	Direct government intervention (in percentages)	Average duration of debt dispute settlement (in years)	Average bondholders' losses (in percentages)
1868–1914	86.0(45)	24.4(45)	6.1(47)	18.9(42)
1919–1933	92.9(14)	58.3(12)	9.5(14)	18.9(11)
1940–1973	73.9(23)	52.2(23)	18.8(23)	50.1(23)

Number of agreements in brackets.

Note: The boundary between the periods is, of course, more fluid than suggested by our periodization. Yet we chose this characterization in three periods because it broadly aligns with the conventional representation adopted by financial historians. Our data suggests—although we are unable to present these results within the scope of this chapter—that the content and conditions of settlements also varied within the three financial periods.

Source: Updated data originally from Suter (1990, 1992).

of all cases), albeit assuming a different approach. These findings suggest that CFBs no longer had the upper hand in debt dispute negotiations. The creation of the US Foreign Bondholder Protective Council in 1934 did not contribute to reverse creditors' gradual loss of bargaining power. Several cases in our data show that the US FBPC, unlike the British CFB during its heydays, did not succeed in blacklisting defaulting sovereign borrowers on the New York stock exchange and blocking new lending.

A telling example are the exchange bonds unilaterally offered by Peru in 1949 to buy back bonds that have been defaulted in 1931. This offer came after several years of unsuccessful negotiations between Peru and the FBPC and CFB. FBPC representatives complained bitterly about the offer to the British CFB but acknowledged that they were 'powerless to stop it' (Kamlani, 2008, p. 146). Interestingly, the terms of the final agreement concluded between Peru and the FBPC (which was reached only two years later) have been rather similar to the 1949 unilateral bond offer which creditors had refused.[23] These rather favourable conditions for Peru represented a loss of about 60 per cent for US bondholders (thus slightly above the period's average). The British CFB, finally, concluded a settlement with Peru on the Sterling bonds in 1953. The fact that the terms of this agreement were identical to the FBPC settlement conditions powerfully suggests the erosion of bondholder committees' bargaining power.

[23] The offer included a reduction in interest rates from 6–7 per cent to 2.5 per cent and a full debt release of all arrears of interest, whereas in the final agreement of 1951 interest rates were reduced from 6–7 per cent to 3 per cent and arrears of interest were capitalized at 10 per cent.

We interpret higher levels of creditors' losses after 1940 as the effect of the new forbearing stance adopted by creditor states during and after the Second World War. This is especially true for the US State Department, which intervened in several debt disputes in order to protect the political, economic and strategic interests of the US, with detrimental effects on bondholders' financial interests, which were then subordinated to national US interests. As stated above, such diplomatic interference ran high in several high-profile cases. As already explained (see also Del Angel & Pérez-Hernández in this volume), the extremely favourable settlement obtained by Mexico in 1942 was due in large part to the Roosevelt administration's quest to bolster diplomatic and trade ties with a country it hoped to turn into an ally during the Second World War. Another telling example is the lending into arrears policies of the US government in, for instance, Bolivia (in the 1940s) and Yugoslavia (in the 1950s). Bolivia received loans for infrastructure construction from the US Export-Import Bank, as part of a general effort by the US government to boost its exports to Latin American countries. In additional to US capital, Yugoslavia received loans from the World Bank and IMF at the time when pre-war bonds were still in default. Granting such loans carried strategic meaning in the then particularly tense political context in Eastern Europe (Lampe et al., 1990).

In a great many cases, debt agreements were reached within inter-governmental frameworks, which often involved political or economic aspects such as investment or trade. Switzerland held bilateral trade agreements with Bulgaria, Poland, or Czechoslovakia. In later decades, these agreements would also encompass access to private capital markets. China settled its debt disputes under an intergovernmental agreement with the UK signed in June 1987. This agreement allowed (only) British bondholders to recover about 5 per cent of the value assigned to the bonds that had been in default since 1939 (CFB Annual Report, 1988). China's government regained access to London's capital market, after being barred during several decades (*New York Times*, 8 June 1987). On the contrary, US bondholders did not succeed in excluding China from US capital markets and, as a result, never obtained any compensation for their unpaid bonds.

7.6 Conclusion

Sovereign debt disputes are as old as bond financing itself. During the post-war context, the locus of debt disputes shifted to the interstate level. Dispute resolution became firmly anchored within the ambit of state authority. Government pursued peaceful modes of negotiation and abandoned gunboat diplomacy. But the attitude of creditor states towards bondholders was selective since creditor states' lending of diplomatic support was contingent upon states' interests. In some cases, governments granted diplomatic protection to bondholders and help them recover their debt claims. But in other cases, states emancipated themselves from their domestic creditors and pushed debtor states to forgive a large portion of their external debt in the name of political, diplomatic, and commercial interests. This spirit of forbearance was a defining trait of post-1945 settlements. After the Second World War, states were a far cry from serving as 'protectors of private capital', a role which they began to assume after the 1980s (Abdelal, 2007).

The legacy of the post-war years is hard to assess with precision. As a rule, post-war interstate negotiations unfolded in a disorganized fashion outside any institutional pattern. After the First World War, the World War Foreign Debt Commission successfully restructured the debts of European countries during a single negotiation event (Waibel, 2011, pp. 119–20). The only post–Second World War international event that compares to the WWFDC is the London conference on German debt. The conference was a resounding success: for the first time in history the entire debt of a major industrialized country had been renegotiated in one comprehensive plan (see de la Villa in this volume). But, unfortunately, this ad hoc experience was not codified into hard, legal principles of international debt restructuration. As a result, the forms of diplomatic involvements that prevailed during these years—and the spirit of forbearance often adopted towards defaulters—did not translate into new institutions. This all but guaranteed that the norm of repayment would once again prevail once creditors recovered their bargaining power. The revenge of defaulters would be short-lived after all.

Yet, this chapter suggests that the post-war era fathered new habits and modes of legal reasoning. In particular, this period reflects an important change in creditors' preference towards legal remedies beyond creditor state representation. Until 1914, legal methods of enforcement like arbitration clauses were not meant to open to litigation but served merely to enlist the participation of creditor states in sovereign debt disputes (Weidemaier, 2010). After 1945, creditors developed new modes of legal reasoning which would durably alter future episodes of debt restructuring. In the event states refused to lend creditors their diplomatic support, creditors turned to international courts, expecting that these courts could serve as the prime enforcers of broken contracts. We showed that, in many instances, international courts refused jurisdiction. For instance, the International Court of Justice refused to recognize the claims of French bondholders against Norway because it deemed the dispute an interstate issue. 1950s courts were cognizant that international debt contracts stood outside their competence.

This interpretation of sovereign debt as an interstate matter began to erode following the US legislative decisions to weaken the doctrine of sovereign immunity in the 1950s. The US repeal of sovereign debt immunity provided impetus for debtor litigation and arbitration as means to sanction recalcitrant borrowers (Buchheit, 1995). The post-1970s context has seen an increasing 'legalization' of debt markets. Over the last three decades, international creditors have increasingly resorted to litigation in national courts, though without much success. Studies in law and society have noted that international law is not nearly as triumphant as it is usually felt. Not only litigation delays the resolution process (Trebesch, 2008), it also weakens the prospect of effective resolution (Bi, Chamon & Zettelmeyer, 2011; Krueger, 2002). Another development is arbitration, in particular the initiative to take a defaulting country before the International Centre for Settlement of Investment Disputes (ICSID). This legal option has yet to produce the desired results (Waibel, 2007). The role of international law in the stabilization of creditor–debtor interactions is more wish than reality.

The premise of this chapter—and of this volume as a whole—is that the meaning of debt, the sanctity of contracts, and the extent to which debt can and should be repaid have been controversial subjects and will remain so in the years to come. Debt conflicts are inherent to sovereign indebtedness, rather than anomalies that could be cured. This observation finds substance in the post-1980s context. According to Cruces and Trebesch (2013), the recent decades have been marked by a dual pattern of financial uncertainties. On the one hand, despite the availability of legal recourses, bondholders' losses—as measured by haircuts—have increased, though this increase has been variable across cases. On the other, governments have faced tougher sanctions, being often excluded from debt markets after a default. In the light of the above, reducing the cost of sovereign defaults is a critically important task that should concern both creditors and debtors.

Sources

Bank of England Archives.
Export-Import Bank Semi-annual Reports, various issues.
International Bank for Reconstruction and Development Annual Reports, various issues.
London Metropolitan Archives, Collection of the Corporation of Foreign Bondholders.
Swiss National Bank Archives.

References

Abdelal, R. (2007). *Capital Rules: The Construction of Global Finance*. Cambridge, MA: Harvard University Press.

Adamson, M. R. (2002). 'The Failure of the Foreign Bondholders Protective Council Experiment, 1934–1940'. *Business History Review*, 76(3), 479–514.

Aggarwal, V. K. (1996). *Debt Games: Strategic Interaction in International Debt Rescheduling*. Cambridge; New York: Cambridge University Press.

Bi, R., Chamon, M. & Zettelmeyer, J. (2011). 'The Problem that wasn't: Coordination Failures in Sovereign Debt Restructurings'. *IMF Working Papers*, 1–28.

Borchard, E. (1915). *The Diplomatic Protection of Citizens Abroad, or, the Law of International Claims*. New York: Banks Law Publishing.

Borchard, E. (1951). *State Insolvency and Foreign Bondholders. Volume I. General Principles*. New Haven: Yale University Press.

Buchheit, L. C. (1995). 'The Sovereign Client'. *Journal of International Affairs*, 48(2), 527–40.

Corporation of Foreign Bondholders. Council. (1895). *Annual report of the Council of the Corporation of Foreign Bondholders* 1895, appendix (23rd). London: Council House.

Corporation of Foreign Bondholders. Council. (1908). *Annual report of the Council of the Corporation of Foreign Bondholders* 1908 (35th). London: Council House.

Corporation of Foreign Bondholders. Council. (1911). *Annual report of the Council of the Corporation of Foreign Bondholders* 1911 (38th). London: Council House.

Corporation of Foreign Bondholders. Council. (1988). *Annual report of the Council of the Corporation of Foreign Bondholders* 1908 (115th). London: Council House.

Cruces, Juan J. & Trebesch, C. (2013). 'Sovereign Defaults: The Price of Haircuts'. *American Economic Journal: Macroeconomics*, 5(3), 85–117.

Eichengreen, B. (1991). 'Historical Research on International Lending and Debt'. *Journal of Economic Perspectives*, 5(2), 149–69.

Eichengreen, B. & Portes, R. (1989). 'After the Deluge: Default, Negotiation, and Readjustment During the Interwar Years', in B. Eichengreen & P. Lindert (Eds.), *The International Debt Crisis in Historical Perspective* (pp. 12–37). Cambridge, MA: MIT Press.

Esteves, R. (2005). *Quis custodiet quem? Sovereign Debt and Bondholders' Protection Before 1914*. Paper presented at the Department of Economics Discussion Paper Serie, Oxford University.

Esteves, R. (2013). 'The Bondholder, the Sovereign, and the Banker: Sovereign Debt and Bondholders' Protection Before 1914'. *European Review of Economic History*, 17(4), 389–407.

Export-Import Bank of Washington, (1945). First Semiannual report to Congress—Export-Import Bank of Washington. [Washington].

Flandreau, M. (2013). 'Sovereign States, Bondholders Committees, and the London Stock Exchange in the Nineteenth Century (1827–68): New Facts and Old Fictions'. *Oxford Review of Economic Policy*, 29(4), 668–96.

Flandreau, M. & Flores, J. (2012). 'Bondholders Versus Bond-Sellers? Investment Banks and Conditionality Lending in the London Market for Foreign Government Debt, 1815–1913'. *European Review of Economic History*, 16(4), 356–83.

Flores, J. H. (2012). 'Crying on Lombard Street: Fixing Sovereign Defaults in the 1890s'. *European Review of History: Revue europeenne d'histoire*, 19(6), 979–97.

Foreign Bondholders Protective Council, Inc. (1954). *Report—Foreign Bondholders Protective Council inc.* New York: Foreign Bondholders Protective Council.

Hautcoeur, P. C. & Riva, A. (2012). 'The Paris Financial Market in the Nineteenth Century: Complementarities and Competition in Microstructures'. *The Economic History Review*, 65(4), 1326–53.

Jorgensen, E. & Sachs, J. D. (1988). 'Default and Renegotiation of Latin American Foreign Bonds in the Interwar Period'. *National Bureau of Economic Research, Working Paper No. 2636.*

Kamlani, S. (2008). *Why Bondholder Councils Don't Matter: The Limited Impact of Private Creditor Representative Institutions on Bargaining Outcomes in Sovereign Debt Restructurings. London School of Economics.* Paper presented at the Presented at the International Studies Association Annual Convention, San Francisco, CA.

Kelly, T. (1998). 'Ability and Willingness to Pay in the Age of Pax Britannica, 1890–1914'. *Explorations in Economic History*, 35(1), 31–58.

Krueger, A. O. (2002). *A new approach to sovereign debt restructuring.* Washington, DC.: International Monetary Fund.

Lampe, J. R., Lampe, J. R., Prickett, R. O., Adamovic, L. S., Adamović, L. S. & Adamović, L. S. (1990). *Yugoslav-American Economic Relations Since World War II.* Durham: Duke University Press.

Lienau, O. (2014). *Rethinking Sovereign Debt: Debt and Reputation in the Twentieth Century.* Cambridge, MA: Harvard University Press.

Lipson, C. (1985). *Standing Guard: Protecting Foreign Capital in the Nineteenth and Twentieth Centuries.* Berkeley: University of California Press.

Mauro, P., Sussman, N. & Yafeh, Y. (2006). *Emerging markets and financial globalization: sovereign bond spreads in 1870–1913 and today.* Oxford: Oxford University Press.

Mauro, P. & Yafeh, Y. (2003). 'The Corporation of Foreign Bondholders'. *Working Paper 03/107.*

Merrills, J. G. (2011). *International Dispute Settlement.* Cambridge University Press.

OECD. (2002). *Export Credit Financing Systems in OECD Member Countries and Non-Member Economies. 2002 supplement.* Paris, France: OECD.

Pamuk, S. (1987). *The Ottoman Empire and European Ccapitalism, 1820–1913: Trade, Investment and Production* (Vol. 12). Cambridge [Cambridgeshire]; New York: Cambridge University Press.

Pénet, P. (2018). 'The IMF Failure that wasn't: Risk Ignorance During the European Debt Crisis'. *British Journal of Sociology*, 69(4), 1031–55.

Reinhart, C. M. & Rogoff, K. S. (2009). *This Time is Different: Eight Centuries of Financial Folly.* Princeton, NJ: Princeton University Press.

Saul, S. (1997). *La France et l'Egypte de 1882 à 1914: intérêts économiques et implications politiques.* Paris: Comité pour l'histoire économique et financière de la France.

Schoo, A. D. (1940). *Régimen jurídico de las obligaciones monetarias internacionales*. Buenos Aires: Editorial Guillermo Kraft.

Suter, C. (1990). *Schuldenzyklen in der Dritten Welt: Kreditaufnahme, Zahlungskrisen und Schuldenregelungen peripherer Länder im Weltsystem von 1820 bis 1986* (Vol. 32). Frankfurt am Main: A. Hain.

Suter, C. (1992). *Debt Cycles in the World-Economy: Foreign Loans, Financial Crises, and Debt Settlements, 1820–1990*. Boulder: Westview Press.

Tomz, M. (2006). *Reputation and International Cooperation. Sovereign Debt across Three Centuries*. Princeton, NJ: Princeton University Press.

Trebesch, C. (2008). *Delays in Sovereign Debt Restructurings. Should We Really Blame the Creditors?* Paper presented at the Proceedings of the German Development Economics Conference, Zurich.

Tunçer, A. C. (2015). *Sovereign Debt and International Financial Control: The Middle East and the Balkans, 1870–1914*. London: Palgrave Macmillan.

Waibel, M. (2007). 'Opening Pandora's Box: Sovereign Bonds in International Arbitration'. *American Journal of International Law*, 101(4), 711–59.

Waibel, M. (2010). 'The Diplomatic Channel'. In J. Crawford & A. Pellet (Eds.), *The Law of International Responsibility* (pp. 1085–98). Oxford: Oxford University Press.

Waibel, M. (2011). *Sovereign Defaults Before International Courts and Tribunals* (Vol. 81). Cambridge: Cambridge University Press.

Wallich, H. C. (1943). 'The Future of Latin American Dollar Bonds'. *The American Economic Review*, 33(2), 321–35.

Weidemaier, M. C. (2010). 'Contracting for State Intervention: the Origins of Sovereign Debt Arbitration'. *Law and Contemporary Problems*, 73(4).

Williams, J. F. (1924). *International Law and International Financial Obligations Arising from Contract. Including a Short Discussion of the Drago Doctrine and of the Hague Convention of 1907 on the Recovery of Contract Debts; Being Three Lectures Given in August 1923 at the Hague Academy for International Law*. E. J. Brill.

Winkler, M. (1933). *Foreign Bonds: An Autopsy; a Study of Defaults and Repudiations of Government Obligations*. Philadelphia: Roland Swain Company.

Wynne, W. H. (1951). *State Insolvency and Foreign Bondholders. Volume II. Selected Case Histories of Governmental Foreign Bond Defaults and Debt Readjustments*. New Haven: Yale University Press.

Wynne, W. H. & Borchard, E. M. (1933). 'Foreign Bondholders Protective Organizations'. *The Yale Law Journal*, 43(2), 281–96.

SECTION 3

POSTCOLONIAL TRANSITIONS AND THE HOPES FOR A NEW INTERNATIONAL ECONOMIC ORDER (1960s–80s)

8

We Owe You Nothing

Decolonization and Sovereign Debt Obligations in International Public Law

Grégoire Mallard

8.1 Introduction

In the 1960s and 1970s, as many newly independent states freed themselves from colonial political ties, they tried to change the rules of old international economic order and establish a 'new international economic order' (NIEO) based on principles of justice, sustainability, and equality between states. As Nico Schrijver (1997, p. 116) observes, the promotion of the NIEO in international law pitted the Global South—conceived at the time as encompassing Latin America, Africa, and Asia—in its search of new economic rights, against Western states (the United States and former European empires in particular), who defended the sanctity of contracts securing the economic rights acquired by Western private companies like oil concessions. The push for the NIEO emerged from the non-aligned movement (Anghie 2005). Whereas the non-aligned states whose conference in Bandung in the 1950s articulated classical claims in favour of sovereign equality of states, the right to self-determination and the protection of human rights in the Global South, in the 1970s, the NIEO leaders ventured to prolong the decolonization fight deep into the economic realm (Group of 77, 1967). The proclamation in favour of the NIEO emerged out of the conference of heads of state and government of the non-aligned countries which took place in September 1973 in Algiers (Byrne, 2016): this conference was a key landmark during which the leaders of the Global South concluded with a call to the UN General Assembly (UNGA, 1974) to agree upon a Programme of Action for the establishment of the NIEO.

In this global struggle, the issue of sovereign debt figured prominently. In their statement, the heads of states gathered in Algiers recommended 'debt renegotiation on a case-by-case basis with a view to concluding agreements on debt cancellation, moratorium, rescheduling or interest subsidization' (section II, article 2.g), starting with the 'the least developed, land-locked and island developing countries and the countries most seriously affected by economic crises and natural

Grégoire Mallard, *We Owe You Nothing: Decolonization and Sovereign Debt Obligations in International Public Law* In: *Sovereign Debt Diplomacies: Rethinking Sovereign Debt from Colonial Empires to Hegemony.* Edited by: Pierre Pénet and Juan Flores Zendejas, Oxford University Press (2021).
DOI: 10.1093/oso/9780198866350.003.0009

calamities' (section II, article 2.i). For the new Global South leaders, newly independent countries were suffocated by the debt they inherited from the colonial past and the low prices of raw materials such as oil, which made their economic models unsustainable. As Mohammed Bedjaoui (1970a, p. 51), the Algerian Ambassador sent to Paris to renegotiate the terms of the oil concessionary contracts between France and Algeria, wrote, 'debt service alone, namely annual amortization and interest payments, would exceed the total amount of new loans by 20 percent in Africa and by 30 percent in Latin America', which meant that the level of state indebtedness inherited by newly independent states from metropolitan states left them crippled at birth.

This new international economic order (NIEO) eventually failed to be established. The common historical explanations account for that failure by pointing to the changing political context in the early 1980s (Abi-Saab, 1991; Rajagopal, 2003; Craven, 2007; Pahuja, 2011; Anghie 2015), and the neoliberal counter-revolution sponsored by the British and American governments of Margaret Thatcher and Ronald Reagan in particular (Blyth, 2013). According to this view, it was not the transformative power of the new legal principles expressed by Third World international law scholars that was responsible for this failure, but the political and ideological context in which their calls for international redistributive justice were received (Colson 1972; Anghie et al., 2003).

Still, other commentators point to inner deficiencies in the NIEO programme (Rist, 1996). For instance, critics notice that nine months after the Algiers Conference, the rights of newly independent states that were defined in the Charter of the Economic and Social Rights of States adopted by the UN General Assembly (UNGA) in December 1974 diluted the radical character of their previous claims expressed in Algiers. The Charter no longer attributed to countries from the Global South an absolute right to nationalize multinational concessionary companies (without obligation to impose an immediate and fair indemnization). NIEO diplomats were either too inexperienced or too quick to compromise when confronted to the pressures of the United States and its European allies. More radically, Gilbert Rist (1996, p. 153) argues that, in fact, the NIEO promoters anticipated and even reinforced the dominant development doctrine of the Global North—and the United States in particular, at least since, the 'Truman Doctrine' of 1947—in which economic growth, expanding international trade, and increased foreign aid to the Global South were seen as the three main pillars of economic growth for the newly independent states. This radical criticism of the NIEO fails to pay attention to the legal dimension of the NIEO programme as it reduces the latter to an economic doctrine, albeit one that remains compatible with, rather than opposed to, the dominant liberal ideology.

This chapter comes back on this criticism—and challenges its validity—by focusing on the legal dimension of the debate on the NIEO in the 1970s. Debates about the legal doctrine of sovereign debt cancellation were opposing the Global North and South in various UN assemblies, like the UN General Assembly (UNGA) or the International Law Commission (ILC). Practitioners of international law were also deeply divided (see Waibel in this volume). This chapter focuses on the legal debates inside the ILC, which lead to contradictions, and ultimately failure to bring about transformation through progress in international law itself. Indeed, an important aspect of the NIEO was its strong juridical dimension (Pahuja, 2011). The importance of law in this conflict may be attributed to the fact that newly independent countries bargained from a position of economic weakness, and therefore thought to move the terrain of discussion from the political and economic realm to the legal terrain, where ideas of global justice have a stronger echo than in purely commercial disputes. Or it may be the result of the professional trajectories of leading NIEO figures like Mohammed Bedjaoui (Mallard, 2019, p. 165–171). In any case, this juridical dimension is key to notice that the principled claims of NIEO leaders were assessed according to legal evaluative standards and criteria rather than on purely geopolitical or economic grounds. As a result, controversies about the legality of claims made by NIEO leaders need to be accounted for and described if one wants to understand the rise and fall of the NIEO.

This chapter, which draws on a broader socio-historical analysis of the transnational circuits in which legal ideas about North-South solidarity were formulated, criticized, and reinvented (Ozsu, 2015; Mallard, 2019), identifies three types of legal tensions, which damaged the transformative project of the NIEO from within, and can account for its failure, in the legal realm. First, the ILC members who were put in charge of elaborating the contours of the UN convention proclaiming the NIEO immediately noticed a tension between their role as legal experts in charge of the 'codification' of existing law, and the legislative dimension of their work when tasked to write a new convention. The ILC was indeed supposed to both survey and codify the treaties, conventions, and devolution agreements of the decolonization era and to prepare the groundwork for the signature of the Convention on Succession of States in respect to State Property, Archives and Debts, which was eventually opened for signature in 1983. The empirical work of codification contradicted the other goal 'legislation', which consisted in identifying rules that worked to the advantage of newly independent states and that could be written in such Convention.

Second, as time passed, and political pressures grew more intense as a result of the Arab countries' decision to nationalize Western oil conglomerates in the early 1970s and to subsequently raise oil prices, the opposition between ILC members from the Global North who wanted to exclude from their consideration the legal obligations between newly independent states and private interests, and those ILC members from the Global South who wanted to extend their reflections to oil concessions granted by former colonial states to private companies, quickly dominated the debate. The intensity of these debates showed that there was no agreement within the ILC over the boundary between private and public law, and whether the jurisdiction of the sub-committee extended to both or not.

The third contentious issue related to the framework that ILC members were prepared to accept for the future negotiations of assets and debt recovery. In particular, the ILC, and its Special Rapporteur Mohammed Bedjaoui, blurred the distinction between creditor and debtor state, by arguing that in most cases, if the negotiation took the entirety of the colonial experience as the basis for the future calculation of sovereign debt claims across the Global North and South, newly independent states were not debtor but creditor states, a claim which elicited strong reactions from countries of the Global North.

Throughout all three dimensions of the legal debates at the core of the NIEO, this chapter pays particular attention, and to some extent, homage, to the role of Algeria's chief diplomat in Paris, the ILC Special Rapporteur Mohammed Bedjaoui, whose work on state succession in financial and economic matters has had a strong influence, at least in academia (Mallard, 2019, p. 165). Bedjaoui worked for the ILC while still serving as Algeria's Minister of Justice (from 1964 to 1970), then as Algerian Ambassador to France (from 1970 to 1979), and then to the UN in New York (from 1979 until 1982). The chapter shows how, within the ILC, the Algerian diplomat and statesman scored a few victories on each of these three contentious debates, although unequally so, and why these processes resulting from these tensions can account for the way the work of the ILC unfolded, with the adoption of a convention that was ratified by a handful of countries only. In this narrative, the failure of the NIEO is thus related to the inner dynamics of committee work, and to tensions within the international legal field rather than to purely external factors, like the changing ideologies in Global North countries, or the diplomatic mistakes of Global South leaders.

8.2 A Contradictory Task: Codification in the Age of Decolonization

Following UN General Assembly resolution 1686 of December 1961 recommending that the Commission study the topic of succession of states and governments in view of the phenomenon of decolonization, the ILC formed a sub-committee in 1962, which submitted its first report in 1963. The ILC had initially nominated Manfred Lachs to serve as Special Rapporteur of the sub-committee in charge of reporting on succession of states with respect to matters other than treaties (while Sir Humphrey Waldock was named the Rapporteur on succession in matters of treaties), but after the latter was elected to the ICJ, Mohammed Bedjaoui replaced him (ILC, 1967, p. 368). Bedjaoui's experience as a jurisconsult during the 1962 Evian negotiation between the French government and the provisional Algerian government (Malek, 1995) proved essential for his new role as the Special

Rapporteur (Mallard, 2019, p. 168). Bedjaoui (1968, p. 96) acknowledged that he focused his attention on the legal texts that he had started to compile when he was jurisconsult for the provisional Algerian government, which he had published in a 1961 book on Algeria and international law.

Bedjaoui's (1961) book on Algeria had demonstrated that, according to the principles found in treaties, conventions, and agreements in classical European international law, the Algerian provisional government was clearly entitled to claim the recognition of statehood for the young Algerian nation. His book was written before Algeria's independence, and borrowed from the West its legal justifications, in order to convince the nations that remained neutral in the fight that opposed the French metropolis and the Algerian provisional government—the United States in particular—to side with the party of independence. By the mid-1960s, when Bedjaoui joined the ILC, Algeria had gained its independence, and the next step on Algeria's pathway toward economic independence was to now attack the legitimacy of the old European international law, which unequivocally worked to the detriment of the newly independent states. Bedjaoui was now asked to expand the range of references and to clearly point to new 'progressive developments' found in the emerging law of decolonization as well as in the principles of the UN Charter.

As Bedjaoui (1968, p. 96) noted in his first report to the ILC, the methodology he applied to codify the law was to look at all treaties, conventions, arbitral decisions, bilateral agreements (as an international public law scholar trained in the French tradition would do), in order to capture the topic under investigation: as he wrote, 'by referring to the criterion of sources [treaties], a distinction may be drawn between *conventional* succession and *unconventional* succession, i.e., between succession resulting from treaties and succession resulting from sources other than treaties.' But by adopting strictly that criterion, one would have been led to exclude from the inquiry 'problems relating to private property, debts, public property, acquired rights, etc., when the latter have been regulated by treaty', which would have then artificially left one side of the subject matter to be treated outside the scope of the inquiry.

At the same time, and even if Bedjaoui (1968, pp. 97, 99) acknowledged that it was not the job of the ILC to 'create new law under the guise of progressive development', it was its duty to analyse emerging 'norms known and accepted by most states to a greater extent than traditional law, in whose formulation most existing states [which had come into being through decolonization wars] took no part'. Codifying obsolete rules would be completely useless, so instead of *codification*, Bedjaoui proposed to engage in an effort of harmonization by basing his work 'on legal constructions embodying to the maximum extent possible the present trends of international law, the principles of the Charter, the right to self-determination, sovereign equality, ownership of natural resources, etc.' Bedjaoui (1970a, p. 463) noticed that the term 'succession' was not neutral, but inherently conservative: intrinsic to the idea of 'succession' was the notion that sovereigns had limited powers to change the order of private property;[1] and that, if they did, they should proceed diligently to compensate private victims of property changes with fair indemnities (Bedjaoui, 1970a, p. 483).

This interpretation of his mission conformed to the 1962 mandate defined by the UNGA 'that the question [of state succession] should be approached with appropriate reference to the views of states which have achieved independence since the Second World War', as well as the line already agreed upon by the ILC under the leadership of Manfred Lachs in its 1963 session, when it set the task to produce a convention rather than a code (in which a judge or arbitrator could have found a list of all relevant cases and rules applicable to each case). The future convention was thus to be signed by independent UN member states, which would therefore agree to confirm or reject past rules and adopt new binding rules. Indeed, the development of international law on the topic of state succession was such that no consensus from which to derive a systematic code had yet been arrived at; and besides, as ILC members remarked, diplomatic arrangements found in decolonization cases 'had to be interpreted with caution, since some of them had been imposed by metropolitan states on new and weak states and might lead the Committee astray if taken as typical examples' (Lachs, 1963, p. 265) to form a customary law. Thus, the ILC members decided to prepare 'terse and brief articles of the type usually included in a convention' (cited in Lachs, 1963, p. 286).

The very empirical work of codification thus contradicted another goal, which consisted in identifying rules that worked to the advantage of newly independent states. Not only did existing public international law tend to protect the economic interests of former metropolises in the postcolonial era, but they had been born obsolete, as their rules were ignored, superseded, or rewritten as soon as newly independent states took command of their economic destiny (Bedjaoui 1970b). This gave enough reason to the ILC members to reject the goal of 'codification' and propose instead to write a convention (e.g. a new politically negotiated document that would supersede existing treaties), thereby stepping outside of its jurisdictional boundary.

In doing so, the ILC distinguished itself from precedent interwar efforts to codify the law of state succession, whose conclusions (and methodology) had been necessarily quite conservative (Ludington, Gulati & Brophy, 2010). Indeed, the main effort of codification in the interwar period had been undertaken by Alexander Sack after the Allied victors had dismantled the Three Empires: the

[1] Bedjaoui (1970a, p. 465) associated such limits with an imperial conception at work in the post–First World War treaties and their understanding of 'limited sovereignty' which was advocated by the Committee on New States at the Paris Peace Conference of 1919. In contrast, the UN General Assembly's Resolution (UNGAR) 1514 of December 1960 solemnly repudiated the imperialist legal theory of state accession that put conditions on the ability of new states to claim a right to statehood (Bedjaoui, 1970a, p. 494), even though the latter is ambiguous on the question of acquired rights.

German Second Reich (with the Versailles Treaty, 1919), the Austro-Hungarian Empire (Treaties of St Germain and Trianon, 1920), and the Ottoman Empire (Treaty of Lausanne, 1923). Alexander Sack, a Russian expatriate who left the Soviet Union to relocate in Paris, tried to codify the rules of state succession found in the post–First World War treaties, with no mandate from any international organization (like the League of Nations) and from a purely academic perspective. The 'folk theory' Sack identified in the texts that could matter to the work of the ILC, to the extent that they elaborated a theory of sovereign debt succession in the colonial context, was found in the provisions that the Allied powers imposed on Germany as far as its colonial possessions were concerned. Sack noted that the Allied powers had agreed that the colonies should not bear any portion of the German debt, nor remain under any obligation to refund to Germany the expenses incurred by the Imperial administration of the protectorate. In fact, it would be unjust to burden the natives with expenditure which appears to have been incurred in Germany's own interest, and that it would be no less unjust to make this responsibility rest upon the mandatory powers which, in so far as they may be appointed trustees by the League of Nations, will derive no benefit from such trusteeship (Cited in Sack, 1927, p. 161–2).

In the interwar settlement, this folk theory found its legal concretization in article 254 of the Versailles Treaty, which left to the Reparations Commission the duty to measure the amount of debt that the German and Prussian governments had contracted to help German nationals colonize Polish lands. Likewise, the Versailles Treaty (article 257, 1) did not create any obligations for the German colonies in Africa and elsewhere—or for the mandate powers designated to administer their development—to repay the debts left by the German state and which had been used for their development (Sack, 1927, p. 164), despite the express German demands to the mandate powers (France and the United Kingdom).

Even if Sack explicitly acknowledged that debts left by the predecessor state were 'odious' to the population when they had been contracted for the 'purpose of enslaving indigenous populations or for the purpose of helping its own nationals colonize the lands', (Sack, 1927, p. 158) the difference between Sack and the ILC was great. Sack had criticized the Versailles Treaty for applying a criterion for sovereign debt cancellation that was too loose, as he claimed that it was not clear that these cancelled Polish debts could de jure be called 'odious' according to his own doctrine: the Germans had bought the lands they colonized from Poles at a very high price (according to Sack), and the Germans did not fund these land purchases with loans, but on the Prussian budget, which meant that German taxpayers had already paid for these purchases. For him, the doctrine of 'odious debt' required the existence of three conditions: lack of consent from, and lack of benefit to, the debtor state, and creditor awareness of the two first conditions.

In contrast, Bedjaoui cited the Versailles Treaty and the Reparations Commission as providing a great precedent of his much more radical theory of sovereign debt cancellation applied to decolonized nations (Bedjaoui, 1977, p. 103). Even if Bedjaoui praised Sack's work for his analytical clarity, he was clearly opposed to Sack's attempt to limit the applicability of the concept of 'odious debt'. (Bedjaoui, 1977, p. 57) Indeed, Sack had claimed that debts that had benefited a territory—or the people in the territory—under subjugation should not be regarded 'odious' if they had proved useful investments that were still active at the time of succession. For Bedjaoui (1977, p. 103), 'even in the case of loans granted to the administering power for the development of the dependent territory (criterion of intended use and allocation), the colonial context in which the development of the territory may take place thanks to these loans disqualifies the undertaking.' In these circumstances, it would be 'unjust', Bedjaoui added, 'to make the newly independent state assume the corresponding debt even if that state retained some trace of the investment, in the form, for example, of public works infrastructures'. Thus, for Bedjaoui, the criteria of intended use and allocation (development rather than war or expropriation of natives by colonizers) that Sack had introduced to limit the applicability of the doctrine of 'odious debts' to the most extreme cases (colonial war or expropriation or personal enrichment of the sovereign) were not useful guides to determine which colonial debts contracted by the metropolitan state should pass on to the newly independent states. In principle, all of the state debts should be disregarded, and left for the metropolitan state to reimburse, unless the latter could really prove that the investment, and the associated debt, could be dissociated from the colonial context, and that it had been contracted after the expression of need by the dependent populations. In other terms, 'the general principle of non-transferability of the debts of the administering power, to which exceptions may be allowed,... places the burden of proof on the predecessor state rather than on the newly independent state' (Bedjaoui, 1977, p. 103).

As Bedjaoui (1977, p. 99) wrote, during the eight years of war between France and the Algerian pro-independence fighters, the administering power had for political reasons been 'overgenerous in pledging Algeria's backing for numerous loans' which had the effect of 'seriously compromising the Algerian Treasury' after independence, to the point that one may wonder if such generosity did not hide darker intentions: that of leaving a nation almost bankrupt at the time of its birth. This was just one example of the poisonous gifts which Bedjaoui suspected to have caused the 'increasingly insupportable debt problem' among newly independent states (Bedjaoui, 1977, p. 100). Thus, Bedjaoui's 1977 report to the ILC concluded with a general condemnation of the level of state indebtedness inherited by newly independent states from metropolitan states, which left them crippled at birth, and which, as Algeria's Head of State said at the 4th conference of Non-Aligned Countries, meant that 'the cancellation of the debt' was called for 'in a great number of cases' (cited in Bedjaoui, 1977, p. 101)—a call that the UN General Assembly endorsed in its resolution for a New International Economic Order.

To prove his point, the rapporteur to the ILC Sub-Committee repeatedly cited Algeria as an example to be followed by other newly independent states, as after gaining its independence in 1962, Algeria 'refused to assume debts representing loans contracted by France for the purpose of carrying out economic projects in Algeria during the war of independence' (Bedjaoui, 1977, p. 99). Thus, Algeria's denunciation of French debts contracted for costs related to the Algerian territory was not limited to the 'war debts that France had [initially] charged to Algeria' (e.g. those debts that even Sack would have considered 'odious'), but they also extended to debts which had been contracted to pay for useful developmental projects. As Bedjaoui wrote, the Algerian delegation to the Evian negotiation (of which he was a member)

> argued that the projects had been undertaken in a particular political and military context, in order to advance the interests of the French settlers and of the French presence in general, and that they were part of France's overall economic strategy, since virtually the whole of France's investment in Algeria had been complementary in nature. (Bedjaoui, 1977, p. 99)

In so doing, Bedjaoui acknowledged that the principle of non-transmissibility of state debts to newly independent states that he wanted to enshrine in the future Convention represented less a 'codification' of established practice—as 'the practice of the newly independent states of Asia and Africa is far from uniform'—than a new principle of international public law which conformed with the new international economic order. Even in the case of the financial deal that was reached in December 1966 (after three years of negotiations) between France and Algeria, Bedjaoui implicitly remarked that the principle of non-transmissibility had not been recognized by both sides, even if, to him, 'Algeria does not seem to have succeeded to the state debts of the predecessor state by making the payment of 40 billion old francs (400 million new francs)' (Bedjaoui, 1977, p. 99).

Considering the wide disparity of cases regarding newly independent states and the issue of state succession in respect to state debt, it was thus not a surprise if Bedjaoui's draft article was received with a dose of scepticism when he presented the complete draft convention to the other ILC members (Bedjaoui, 1981, p. 27). Representatives of the Western states in the ILC criticized this principle of non-transmissibility in the context of newly independent states. Even another ILC member who developed the Third World Approach to International Law (TWAIL) remarked that Bedjaoui's analysis appeared to 'deal extensively with French colonial practice', but much less with Dutch or British colonial practice, which to a much larger extent than the French had left the ability to raise taxes or loans to dependent but still 'separate administrative units that were largely fiscally autonomous' (Bedjaoui, 1981, p. 28). Thus, it seemed that for those newly independent states it was difficult to ground the principle of non-transmissibility of debts on established practice, except in extreme circumstances.

After Bedjaoui released the last report on the Law of State Succession to the ILC, the UN General Assembly decided in December 1981 to convene an international conference of plenipotentiaries to consider the draft articles on succession of states in respect to state property, archives, and debts, and to embody the results of its work in an international convention. The Conference assigned to the Committee of the Whole the consideration of the draft articles adopted by the ILC. Mohammed Bedjaoui participated in the debates as the expert consultant in his quality as the Special Rapporteur to the ILC on state succession (UN Conference, 1983a). In the convention, after six introductory articles, seven articles concerned the issue of 'transfers' of *state property*—or rather, the 'substitution of sovereignty' to which 'property' was attached, as the articles talked about the 'extinction' and 'arising' of rights (article 9) in order to stress discontinuity rather than continuity in the process (UN Conference, 1983b, p. 48)—five articles (14 to 18) concerned the issue of territorial swaps, thirteen articles (19 to 31) concerned the issue of the transfer of state archives, ten articles (32 to 41) codified the issue of *state debt* in cases of state succession. The Conference, on 7 April 1983, adopted the 'Vienna Convention on Succession of States in respect of State Property, Archives and Debts' consisting of a preamble, fifty-one articles, and an annex.

The Convention was opened for signature from 7 April until 31 December 1983, but it has not yet entered into force as it is missing the signature of key UN member states. In particular, the articles that concerned the succession of rights on property and debts in the case of 'newly independent states' for which exceptional rules applied (articles 15 and 38, respectively) were the most controversial, as can be seen from a brief survey of the objections of Western states to the Convention. Already during the plenary conference the main lines of division appeared between the Western states, which refused to sign, and the Communist block and Group of seventy-seven states, which were in favour (Mallard, 2019, p. 194).[2] The Algerian delegate, Mr Moncef Benouniche could only regret that Western states' 'negative attitudes to an instrument which was fully in conformity with trends in the international community paralleled the uncooperative approach which had led to difficulties in the negotiations of the new international economic order' (UN Conference 1983a, p. 27).

[2] The delegates in the plenary conference who voted against represented Belgium, Canada, France, Germany, Israel, Italy, Luxembourg, Netherlands, Switzerland, the UK. and the USA (UN Conference, 1983a, p. 3).

The US representative, for instance, justified his opposition due to 'the extent and scale of the special treatment given to newly independent states and the unnecessary vagueness of the formulation of a number of provisions' (UN Conference 1983a, p. 31). The West German representative objected that a 'conference like the present one, which attempted to formulate existing rules of customary international law and to reach agreements about rules of contractual international law [two different tasks] could not be fulfilled if it did not take into consideration the views of a substantial minority of states' (UN Conference 1983a, p. 27). For him, the articles that related to the treatment of debts for newly independent states (article 38)—which affirmed that no 'state debt of the predecessor state shall pass to the newly independent state, unless an agreement between them provides otherwise' (article 38.1), and that the 'agreement referred to in paragraph 1 shall not infringe the principle of permanent sovereignty of every people over its wealth and natural resources, nor shall its implementation endanger the fundamental equilibria of the newly independent state' (article 38.2)—were particularly controversial, a position shared by the representatives of all Western states. For the Canadian delegate, the 'value of a treaty that did not codify customary law but purported to create new rules, as was unquestionably the case with that convention, depended upon the degree of support it could command among states with different interests on the matter', and as the French delegate regretted, the method of work, which had consisted in voting on articles rather than seeking consensus had imperilled the whole work of the Conference (UN Conference 1983a, p. 28).

8.3 Boundary Crossing Between Private and Public International Law

The extent to which ILC members had been asked to strictly codify existing principles of international law as far as the question of transmissibility of debts in the postcolonial context, or whether they were allowed to propose new principles on the matter—and if so, how consensus could be built—was not the only divisive issue within the ILC. A second issue concerned the extent to which its jurisdiction extended far beyond the strict confines of public international law. In 1963, it appeared that the ILC would extend its study to cover how state succession affected the rights of private individuals, especially of 'nationals of foreign states' (Rosenne cited in Lachs, 1963, p. 287), as these issues were at the centre of negotiations in the case of newly independent states—as illustrated by the Franco-Algerian negotiation. Indeed, as Bedjaoui (1970a, p. 528) wrote, until the age of decolonization, the theory of state succession was mostly concerned with the protection of the acquired rights (*droits acquis*) of the foreign nationals who owned possessions in the territory of the new state, and it was never concerned with protection of the 'vital economic interests' of the new state.

But at the same time, the decolonization process had irremediably showed that the *raison d'être* of newly independent states was the protection of the 'vital interests' of the nation, which sometimes necessitated ignoring the sanctity of property rights, especially when there was a manifest 'public utility' (Bedjaoui, 1970a, p. 533) in their violation. In 1969, Mohammed Bedjaoui thus delivered a (second) report to the ILC that extended beyond the strict confines of international *public* law, as it was concerned with the 'economic and financial acquired rights' of both public and private individuals. In parallel, in 1970, in an important *Recueil de Cours* that Bedjaoui delivered at The Hague Academy of International Law, he synthesized many reflections from his work at the ILC commission on the law of state succession and how it affected 'acquired rights'. In both publications, Bedjaoui claimed that newly independent states' ability to violate acquired rights should never be limited by their ability to compensate victims of expropriation. In fact, it was precisely when the newly independent states were incapable of paying 'just' reparations that the state needed to expropriate large private interests. Although a few individuals could receive reparations for the loss of their properties, newly independent states could not accept the principle that all rights of foreign nationals should be compensated for, as the 'lands, the buildings, the transport, the industry, the trade companies, etc., belonged to private interests' during colonial administration, and thus, 'compensating them for the loss of their property in case of nationalization would mean that the new state would have to buy its whole country back' which would be economically impossible. In this case 'the state would indebt itself in perpetuity, and even [if] the debt was distributed over a very long period, no budget could service such a debt'. (Bedjaoui, 1970a, p. 545) The situation would also look very much like the situation of slaves 'buying back their freedom'.

In the 1970s, Bedjaoui (1970a, p. 535) extended these reflections to oil concession contracts, which, he claimed, should be read as contractual obligations with *private* persons—as the ICJ had established in its 1952 ruling on Anglo-Iranian Oil vs Iran—and not as *public* law documents benefiting from the sanctity attributed to treaties. In so doing, Bedjaoui (1970a, p. 469) clearly opposed the Gaullist idea of 'cooperation' in technical cooperation (especially in the oil sector) in which he saw the *public* law version of the private law doctrine of 'acquired rights'. For Bedjaoui, the real goal of postcolonial cooperation between the former Western oil conglomerates and the newly independent states was the prolongation of colonial relations of interstate subordination. Cooperation agreements in the oil sector were just a public law tool invented to maintain the 'trust' that private investors had in the sustained protection of their private interests and concessionary rights in postcolonial eras. Citing the Evian Agreements between France and Algeria (chapter II), 'cooperation' was indeed a guarantee (*contrepartie*) that

Algeria would protect 'the interests of the French state and the acquired rights of the legal persons on Algerian territory', especially those of the French concessionary companies (Bedjaoui, 1970a, p. 500). Technical cooperation offered 'guarantees' similar to the continued presence of metropolitan military forces in the territory of newly independent states: their overall goal was to insure foreign creditors against the threat that private properties might be redistributed (Bedjaoui, 1970a, pp. 498–9; also 1970b).

Bedjaoui's reflections on the superiority of newly independent states' sovereign 'vital interests' over the private rights of foreign investors divided the ILC's Sub-Committee. Realizing in 1970 that 'the topic of acquired rights was extremely controversial and that its study, at a premature stage, could only delay the Commission's work on the topic as a whole, most members were of the opinion that the codification of the rules should not begin with the preparation of draft articles on acquired rights' (ILC, 1970, p. 300). In order to avoid divisive disputes with the ILC Sub-Committee, Bedjaoui then moved to restrict the original mandate to study only issues of transmission of state property—or rather 'public property appertaining to sovereignty' (Bedjaoui, 1971, p. 177)—and exclude the thorny issue of the private acquired rights of foreign nationals and (multi-) national oil companies. Still, the question of state property needed some clarification: in particular, whether the law of the metropolitan state or that of the successor state would serve as the source for the definition of 'state property'. On this issue, Bedjaoui found in the precedents—mostly decisions made by the Reparations Commissions—that no international body had been 'in a position to carry out the task [of defining which properties belonged to the sovereignty of the state] without reference to the municipal law of the predecessor state' (Bedjaoui, 1971, p. 176).

This general rule, which from his intellectual trajectory and past involvements Bedjaoui seemed ready to accept (as he had defended Algeria's position during the Evian negotiations based on references to French administrative law and European international law), suffered only one exception: when the law of the predecessor state differentiated between the 'public' and 'private' property of the state. Indeed, Bedjaoui (1971, p. 179) proposed that the transmission of state property from the metropolis to the newly independent state should be without compensation for all state property according to the predecessor state's legal definition of the 'public' property, except when the predecessor state had had the possibility of manipulating the distinction between the public and private domains of the state—as in that case, the former metropolis could have kept most its past 'property' intact in the postcolonial age just by calling it 'private' (and thus non-transmissible) a few months before independence, or by granting a legal concession to a 'private' (or semi-private) company on public goods or services right before independence (Bedjaoui, 1970b, p. 146).

As Bedjaoui continued to work in 1971 and 1972 on these conflicts of law between predecessor and successor states, he began to endorse a more radical position on the issue of transmissibility of 'private' property to the newly independent state. The article of the future convention he proposed to the ILC in 1972 no longer relied on the internal law of the predecessor state to dictate which debts and which properties were 'necessary for the exercise of sovereignty' and hence 'devolved automatically and without compensation from the predecessor to the successor state'. Bedjaoui (1972, p. 67) remarked that after reviewing the vast body of precedents, he had found 'no precise answers in international contemporary law to the two following key questions: 1) what property is required for the exercise of sovereignty? 2) what authority has the power to determine such property?' In addition, he further weakened the general rule according to which 'public property should be made by reference to the municipal law which governed the territory concerned' by adding the following exception: 'save in the event of a serious conflict with the public policy of the successor state'. This was an important and broad exception, as it was not completely clear who would decide the 'seriousness' of the conflict of law and thus, the ability of the successor state to impose its legal definition.

Bedjaoui (1972, p. 67) tried to limit the scope and ambiguity of such an exception, by adding that while the newly independent states

> were to have a broader concept of the exercise of sovereignty, which required that property formerly regarded as unnecessary for this purpose should pass within its patrimony [like an oil concession], logic would at least appear to require that the predecessor state should not be made to pay the price for the establishment of a different political and ideological regime or a different institutional model [like a socialist economy].

This general exception found its most manifest illustration in the conflict of law regarding the right to grant (oil) concessions. As Bedjaoui (1973, p. 26) noted in his 1973 report to the ILC, 'it is quite inappropriate to consider the successor state as "subrogated" to the rights of the predecessor state, or as "succeeding" the latter regarding the right in respect to the authority to grant concessions.'

As Algeria took the decision to nationalize oil concessions in 1971 and 1972, Bedjaoui analysed this key issue at great length despite the fact that the ILC Sub-Committee had originally decided to leave all matters related to the recognition of the private rights of private individuals and companies outside of its mandate (Bedjaoui, 1973, p. 25). Citing the French jurist Lyon-Caen, for whom a concession is the 'juxtaposition of a contract and an act of sovereignty', Bedjaoui reintroduced the issue by leaving aside the '*contractual* aspect of the concession', in order to 'deal exclusively with *the act of sovereignty*' (Bedjaoui, 1973, p. 25). Thus, as far as the problem of concession could be split into an international private law issue and an international public law issue, Bedjaoui claimed that the ILC could discuss the latter aspect. As far as this public law aspect was concerned he 'considered that the successor state exercises its own rights as a new conceding authority, which replaces the former conceding authority', meaning that it could freely decide to grant or withdraw 'by virtue of its sovereignty, the title of owner of the soil and subsoil of the transferred territory' (Bedjaoui, 1973, pp. 26–7). In other words, he made it clear that 'the fact that the successor state "receives" the internal juridical order of its predecessor state should not automatically imply that the concessionary regime is thereby renewed' (Bedjaoui, 1973, p. 27).

The evolution in Bedjaoui's thinking on this issue was deeply affected by the Arab states' oil policy in general, and Algeria's oil policy in particular (Mallard, 2019, p. 187), as his opinion gave a legal justification for the decision by the Algerian government to nationalize oil production in February 1971—the first of the Arab states to make such a drastic move, quickly followed by Qaddafi's Libya, which nationalized BP's assets in 1971, and then by Saddam Hussein's Iraq and Saudi Arabia, in retaliation against Western support to Israel in the 1973 war. In 1971, the Algerian government's decision to claim 51 per cent of the property rights of French oil companies operating in Algeria (and 100 per cent on the gas sector and the pipelines) was a unilateral cancellation of the 1965 bilateral agreement by which the Algerian government had agreed to respect France's acquired rights regarding the exploration and exploitation of Algerian oil in the Sahara, provided that the French would reinvest half of its oil revenues in Algeria (Grimaud, 1972). When he learnt of Algeria's decision, French Prime Minister Jacques Chaban-Delmas sent a memorandum to the Algerian Ambassador in Paris, who was no one other than Bedjaoui, in which he listed all the French claims against the unilateral nationalization of the oil sector (Grimaud, 1972, p. 1300). In this memo, the Prime Minister recognized 'Algeria's right to nationalize', but not without a preliminary and fair compensation for the nationalized assets, and he threatened to ask French companies to immediately stop production in the Sahara if a committee charged with determining such compensation was not set up—a demand that the Algerian government rejected, first through the voice of Bedjaoui, and then through the voice of Prime Minister Boumedienne, when the latter abolished all the concessions in April 1971.

Through his reports to the ILC, Bedjaoui thus sought a legal justification grounded in international public law for Algeria's 1971 decision that would rebuke the French arguments against Algeria's right to nationalize oil companies without prior compensation. His report to the ILC added a legal argument to the economic claims that Algerian economists had already made in their denunciation of the French application of the 1965 agreement.[3] Thus, we see that Bedjaoui's

[3] The Algerian side claimed that from 1965 to 1970, the French oil companies made 7 billion francs profit from Algerian oil exploitation while the French claimed only 1.4 billion francs, leading to

changing position on the question of the conflict of law between predecessor and successor state, and its radicalization, paralleled the evolving Algerian position on the question of concessions. Already in this first report, Bedjaoui (1969) made it clear that decolonizing states could and should ignore 'devolution agreements' (for instance, those decreed by France for Algeria) and acquired rights: when concessions had been obtained during colonial times, they were inherently tainted by the colonists' lack of respect for the acquired rights of the colonial subjects (as the colonists often used the *terra nullius* doctrine to appropriate natural resources).

But Bedjaoui did not obtain the success he hoped for in the ILC. The discussion among ILC members revealed equally (or even more) divisive issues in the case of the article on transferability of state assets as in the case of the non-transferability of state debts from metropolitan states to newly independent states (article 38). As Bedjaoui remarked before the Committee of the Whole, article 38 was not that extreme, as the articles on state debt only concerned debts that 'were governed by international *public* law and therefore excluded debts owed by the predecessor state to private creditors' (UN Conference, 1983b, p. 193), thus protecting the latter even in the case of newly independent states. As Bedjaoui said, the ILC had long pondered on the 'advisability to cover any other financial obligation chargeable to a state' but had decided to produce a Convention that only concerned financial obligations from state to state (even though the latter represented a small portion of the debts contracted by states, which increasingly turned to private capital markets to fund their operations). This limitation was welcomed by the Western delegates, like the Austrian delegate, which thus agreed that the Convention protected private creditors from being prejudiced by all state successions (UN Conference, 1983b, p. 194). Bedjaoui added that the ILC was of the opinion that 'transnational corporations were not subjects of international law' and were thus not concerned by article 38 on the non-transmission of debts from metropolitan states to newly independent states (UN Conference, 1983b, p. 196). Furthermore, the Convention explicitly recognized that 'a succession of States does not as such affect the rights and obligations of creditors' (article 36). Still, the Convention maintained that any agreement between state parties was limited by the recognition of the 'principle of permanent sovereignty of every people over its wealth and natural resources' (article 38.2).[4]

disputes about the amount that the French should have reinvested in Algeria per the 1965 bilateral deal (Grimaud, 1972, p. 1285).

[4] The Convention also defined how disputes regarding the passing of state debts were to be solved: 'by a process of consultation and negotiation' (article 42) or by the special conciliation procedure specified in the Annex (with conditions for the nationality and qualification of the conciliators) if the dispute was not settled within six months of the date of state succession (article 43); and if both of these procedures had failed, by 'submitting [the case] for a decision to the International Court of Justice' (article 44); or finally, if there was common consent, by a procedure of arbitration (article 45).

Here again, the issue divided the Western Bloc on one side and the Communist Bloc and Group of 77 on the other side, as witnessed by the Algerian and Bulgarian delegates' defence of Bedjaoui's wisdom (UN Conference, 1983b, p. 202). Bedjaoui's arguments did not reassure Western delegates: the US delegate for instance doubted the validity of the argument that the Convention protected private creditors, as by restricting itself to the succession of state-to-state financial obligations, it left private creditors with no other choice than to 'resort to the general rules of customary international law, and those rules were highly intricate, complicated, often ambiguous and unclear' (UN Conference, 1983b, p. 199). Thus, the German, Swiss, and US delegates concluded, by accepting a strict boundary between *public* and *private* international law in a field in which cases often involved the protection of both public and private interests, the Convention artificially limited its scope to purely state-to-state relations and excluded private creditors from its protection. Western delegates thus felt that by recognizing at the same time the principle of transmissibility of all state properties and non-transmissibility of all state debts in the case of newly independent states, as well as the principle of permanent sovereignty over natural resources (Bedjaoui, 1981), the Convention was deeply unbalanced to the detriment of Western interests in general, and oil concessions in particular (UN Conference, 1983b, p. 227). Among the articles of the Convention, it was the reference to the inalienability of natural resources in newly independent states (article 15) and the 'principle of the permanent sovereignty of every people over its wealth and natural resources' (article 15.4) that divided the West and the Group of 77: as the US delegate remarked, he did not believe that article 15 was 'an accurate statement of existing law and that its provisions should be accepted as progressive development of international law'—a position echoed by the Dutch delegate, according to whom the term 'permanent sovereignty' was not a legal but a 'moral' notion (UN Conference, 1983b, pp. 93, 109).

8.4 Reversible Identities between Creditor and Debtor States

Related to the divisive question of how much newly independent states should compensate private and concessionary companies in the extractive business, in case the former should decide to nationalize the latter, a third line of conflict opened between members of the ILC, which focused on the more general question of how one should choose the adequate framework for assessing in the postcolonial age the debit and credit of nations that were formerly intertwined by complex webs of trade and financial circuits.

Already in 1961, the Declaration by the non-aligned states in Belgrade stated quite clearly that the decolonized states were in fact 'creditor states' rather than 'debtor states' toward the old metropolises (Bedjaoui, 1970a, p. 550). As Bedjaoui

(1970a, p. 556) later asserted, building upon this Declaration, colonial economies were largely extractive and exploitative, as the industrial development of the metropolises had depended upon the ability of colonial private interests to funnel profits toward the metropolis and to cut the local colonial populations off from the benefits of growth. For him, the metropolis had 'contracted a debt' with its colonies, such that the nationalization of private interests could be seen as a reparation paid by the metropolis to its colony. If the debtor state was the metropolis, private individuals who sought compensation should turn to their own state rather than to the new independent state. This had been Raymond Aron's (1957) proposal in favour of giving Algeria its independence, which had infuriated and shocked pro-French Algeria advocates—that the French state, rather than the newly independent Algeria, should compensate the Europeans who returned to France as a result of Algeria's independence.

More generally, Bedjaoui (1970a, pp. 552, 559) supported the idea of a global settlement that would not only be based on the assessment of the value of nationalized properties by the decolonizing nation but also on the comprehensive calculus of past benefits realized by private interests and chartered companies in the colonies, especially if the latter was not reemployed for the good of the colonial subjects from whom profit was extracted. Thus, only if reparations were to be calculated based on a long-term view of the historical relations between metropolis and colonial territories was Bedjaoui in favour of talking about reparations—and then, his thinking converged with solidarists' defence of the 'duty to repair' (Colonomos & Mallard, 2016). In many ways, these global settlements were exactly what Bedjaoui (1978b, p. 31) wanted the ILC to promote, as he inscribed within the article on state succession in respect to property for newly independent states a clause which mirrored the kind of settlement that the former colony had to find with the metropolis: the clause introduced 'the concept of the contribution of the dependent territory to the creation of certain movable property of the predecessor state . . . so that such property should pass to the successor state in proportion to the contribution made by the dependent territory' (Bedjaoui, 1978b, p. 31).

For instance, if Algeria was to settle claims by companies like French oil companies, French companies should also be accountable to claims by Algerian interests. In effect, Bedjaoui's (1976, p. 82) call for reciprocal settlements continued to be based upon the criticism of the philosophy and practice of 'cooperation' between former metropolis and former colony, whose permanence was most manifest in the case of French ties with former colonies from Western Africa—whether such cooperation extended to the right to issue currency, to own military bases, etc. Citing Gunnar Myrdal's criticism of the 'forced bilateralism' that such neo-colonial logics created, he opposed the logic of continued cooperation in the exploitation of oil and the recognition of an inalienable right of all nations over their 'wealth, natural resources and economic activities' (Bedjaoui, 1976, p. 89)—an inalienable right which was established in various

UN General Assembly Resolutions, like that establishing a New International Economic Order in May 1974, and which was referred to in the final version of the article on state succession in respect to property for newly independent states accepted by the ILC.

Still, the former imperial states, led by the British and the French, objected to clauses in article 15 of the UN Convention of 1983 that could open up reparation debates. The British delegate objected to the statement that newly independent states should inherit property outside their territory (in the territory of the metropolis) 'in proportion to the contribution of the dependent territory' as the determination of such property would 'require mathematical calculations that were practically impossible to carry out' (UN Conference, 1983b, p. 94), thus leading to intractable controversies about reparations—a position which the Indian delegate criticized, but which the French delegate endorsed, as the latter also claimed that 'the term "contribution" lacked precision' (UN Conference, 1983b, p. 98). The Algerian delegate tried to counterattack by arguing that the 'principle of permanent sovereignty was already embodied in the 1978 Vienna Convention on Succession of States in Respect to Treaties' and that the principles of 'equitable compensation' were well-recognized principles of international law (UN Conference, 1983b, p. 96); but from the discussion, no consensus emerged. The Swiss delegate reinforced the Western position by remarking that only in article 15, which concerned newly independent states, could we find a violation of the general principle that a transition should proceed from the agreement of all parties (UN Conference, 1983b, p. 100). As he added, 'the reference to the "fundamental economic equilibria" of the newly independent state was also open to criticism' (UN Conference, 1983b, p. 227).

8.5 Conclusion

Although the ILC Sub-Committee on state succession in financial and economic matters worked for almost twenty years to produce new wisdom on important legal principles governing the core legal questions of the NIEO, it failed to achieve consensus among its members. In many ways, by creating rigid boundaries between different types of succession (transfer, union, separation, and dissolution on one side, and newly independent states on the other side), and creating two opposite sets of rules for each group (as far as the issue of state debt was concerned), the Rapporteur to the ILC Sub-Committee restricted the principles of the NIEO to the newly independent states of Asia and Africa—most of which had already been through the process of independence at the time, which somehow doomed the resulting Convention as it prevented it from being applied to new cases. These historical and geographical restrictions thus excluded the possibility of applying the principles for 'newly independent states' to the new states that would secede, for instance, from the Soviet 'Empire', first in Eastern Europe and then in the Balkans (Craven, 2007). In addition, to the extent that Bedjaoui accepted the exclusion of the transmission of private debts from the mandate of the ILC Sub-Committee, his report lost some of its relevance for the new crises that would agitate South Asia and Latin America in the 1990s.

With these limitations in mind, it is not surprising if direct references to the work of the ILC on state succession in matters of state debts have largely been absent from debates about the sovereign debts of 'developing' nations. In many ways, the present-day revival of the doctrine of 'odious debt' by religious or left-wing activists represents a Pyrrhic victory for both Sack and Bedjaoui. First, even if the Jubilee network of legal activists—who are at the avant-garde of the fight for sovereign debt cancellation in the Third World—use Sack's name to ground their odious debt doctrine in a glorious past, they use his name inappropriately: indeed, Sack forged a doctrine whose very goal was to limit the cases in which sovereign debt cancellation would be acceptable (Gulati & Ludington, 2008), at a time when practical examples of sovereign debt cancellation seemed to abound dangerously—as with the Polish debt cancellation, recognized by the Versailles Treaty, or with the Bolsheviks' unilateral cancellation of Tsarist debts.

Second, while the present-day calls for the cancellation of the sovereign debt of Third World nations seem to converge with Bedjaoui's new international economic order, they are now expressed on moral rather than political grounds: as they are linked with denunciations of human rights abuses before, during, and after decolonization they thus fall outside the scope of the law of state succession. Besides, Bedjaoui's geographical restriction of his extended doctrine of 'odious debt' (which was much more radical than Sack's) to Asia and Africa was part of a political struggle to unite non-aligned nations of the two continents against the two Blocs who were busy fighting their Cold War in Latin America and parts of South Asia. The political aspect of his work took precedence over his willingness to form a new doctrine of 'odious debt': as some ILC members regretted, 'although the question of odious debts had been discussed by the Commission,... and the Special Rapporteur's earlier proposals [were] quite interesting, no provisions relating to it had been included in the draft articles' (Bedjaoui, 1981, p. 19). Bedjaoui had assumed implicitly that those state debts that could be deemed 'odious' were those that newly independent states could reject (since those were the non-transmissible debts) and vice versa, so there was no need to add a separate discussion of the doctrine of odious debt as related to the other categories of state succession (transfer, union, separation, or dissolution). That may well have been a tragic mistake, even though the legal work of the ILC still produced an impressive amount of documentation on the law concerning the transmission of debts from the colonial to the postcolonial context, which future studies could explore in greater detail.

Bibliography

Abi-Saab, G. (1991). 'Permanent Sovereignty over Natural Resources and Economic Activities', in M. Bedjaoui (Ed.), *International Law: Achievements and Prospects* (pp. 597–617). Dordrecht: Martinus Nijhoff Publishers.

Anghie, A. (2005). *Imperialism, Sovereignty and the Making of International Law.* Cambridge: Cambridge University Press.

Anghie, A. (2015). 'Legal Aspects of the New International Economic Order'. *Humanity: An International Journal of Human Rights, Humanitarianism, and Development* 6(1), 145–58.

Anghie, A., Chimni, B., Mickelson, K. & Okafor, O. (2003). *The Third World and International Order: Law, Politics and Globalization.* Leiden: Brill Academic Publishers, Martinus Nijhoff.

Aron, R. (1957). *La tragédie algérienne.* Paris: Plon.

Bedjaoui, M. (1961). *La Révolution algérienne et le droit.* Brussels: L'Association internationale des juristes démocrates.

Bedjaoui, M. (1968). First Report on Succession of States in respect of rights and duties resulting from sources other than treaties. International Law Commission. http://legal.un.org/docs/?path=../ilc/documentation/english/a_cn4_204.pdf&lang=EFS (Accessed 6 March 2020).

Bedjaoui, M. (1969). Second Report on Succession of States in respect of matters other than treaties. International Law Commission. http://legal.un.org/docs/?path=../ilc/documentation/english/a_cn4_216.pdf&lang=EFS (Accessed 6 March 2020).

Bedjaoui, M. (1970a). 'Problèmes Récents De Succession d'États Dans Les États Nouveaux'. The Hague: Recueil des cours de l'Académie de droit international. Vol. 130, 453–585.

Bedjaoui, M. (1970b). Third Report on Succession of States in respect of matters other than treaties. International Law Commission. http://legal.un.org/docs/?path=../ilc/publications/yearbooks/english/ilc_1970_v2.pdf&lang=EFS (Accessed 6 March 2020).

Bedjaoui, M. (1971). Fourth Report on Succession of States in respect of matters other than treaties. International Law Commission. http://legal.un.org/docs/?path=../ilc/documentation/english/a_cn4_247.pdf&lang=EFS (Accessed 6 March 2020).

Bedjaoui, M. (1972). Fifth Report on Succession of States in respect of matters other than treaties. International Law Commission. http://legal.un.org/ilc/documentation/english/a_cn4_259.pdf (Accessed 6 March 2020).

Bedjaoui, M (1973). Sixth Report on Succession of States in respect of matters other than treaties. International Law Commission. http://legal.un.org/docs/?path=../ilc/publications/yearbooks/english/ilc_1973_v2.pdf&lang=EFSR (Accessed: Accessed 6 March 2020).

Bedjaoui, M. (1974). Seventh Report on Succession of States in respect of matters other than treaties. International Law Commission. http://legal.un.org/docs/?path=../ilc/documentation/english/a_cn4_282.pdf&lang=EF (Accessed 6 March 2020).

Bedjaoui, M. (1976). Eighth Report on Succession of States in respect of matters other than treaties. International Law Commission. http://legal.un.org/docs/?path=../ilc/documentation/english/a_cn4_292.pdf&lang=EFS (Accessed 6 March 2020).

Bedjaoui, M. (1977). Ninth Report on Succession of States in respect of matters other than treaties. International Law Commission. http://legal.un.org/docs/?path=../ilc/publications/yearbooks/english/ilc_1977_v2_p1.pdf&lang=EFS (Accessed 6 March 2020).

Bedjaoui, M. (1978a). *Pour un nouvel ordre économique international.* Paris: UNESCO.

Bedjaoui, M. (1978b). Tenth Report on Succession of States in respect of matters other than treaties. Yearbook of the International Law Commission, vol. II. doc. A/CN. 4/292.

Bedjaoui, M. (1979). Eleventh Report on Succession of States in respect of matters other than treaties. International Law Commission. http://legal.un.org/docs/?path=../ilc/documentation/english/a_cn4_322.pdf&lang=EFS (Accessed 6 March 2020).

Bedjaoui, M. (1981). Thirteenth Report on Succession of States in respect of matters other than treaties. International Law Commission. http://legal.un.org/docs/?path=../ilc/documentation/english/a_cn4_345.pdf&lang=EFS (Accessed 6 March 2020).

Bedjaoui, M. (1984). 'Les Négociations Globales', in *Droits et libertés à la fin du xx*[e] *siècle: influence des données économiques et technologiques. Études offertes à Claude-Albert Colliard.* pp. 45–62. Paris: Pedone.

Blyth, M. (2013). *Austerity: The History of a Dangerous Idea.* New York: Oxford University Press.

Byrne, J. (2016). *Mecca of Revolution: Algeria, Decolonization and the Third World Order.* Oxford: Oxford University Press.

Colonomos, A. & Mallard, G. (2016). 'The *Duty to Repair* in Practice: The Hundred Years History of a Legal Concept'. in G. Mallard & J. Sgard (Eds.), *Contractual Knowledge: One Hundred Years of Legal Experimentation in Global Markets* (pp. 215–47). New York: Cambridge University Press.

Colson, J. (1972). 'Le « groupe des 77 » et le problème de l'unité des pays du Tiers Monde'. *Tiers-Monde* 13(52), 813–30.

Craven, M. (2007). *The Decolonization of International Law: State Succession and the Law of Treaties.* Oxford: Oxford University Press.

Evian Agreements (1962). in R. Malek. (1995). *L'Algérie à Evian: Histoire des négociations secrètes, 1956–1962* (pp. 313–65). Paris: Seuil, or http://imedb.blogspot.ch/2008/01/blog-post_25.html (Accessed 6 March 2020).

Grimaud, N. (1972). 'Le Conflit Pétrolier Franco-Algérien'. *Revue française de science politique*, 22(6), 1276–307.

Group of 77. (1967). 'Charter of Algiers'. http://www.g77.org/doc/algier~1.htm (Accessed 6 March 2020).

Gulati, M. & Ludington, S. (2008). 'A Convenient Untruth: Fact and Fantasy in the Doctrine of Odious Debts'. *Virginia Journal of International Law*, 48, 595–639.

International Law Commission (ILC). (1967). "Report of the ILC on the work of its nineteenth session." http://legal.un.org/docs/?path=../ilc/documentation/english/reports/a_cn4_199.pdf&lang=EF (Accessed 6 March 2020).

International Law Commission (ILC). (1970). "Report of the ILC on the Work of its Twenty-Second Session." http://legal.un.org/docs/?path=../ilc/documentation/english/reports/a_cn4_237.pdf&lang=EF (Accessed 6 March 2020).

Lachs, M. (1963). 'Report on Succession of States in respect other than treaties'. International Law Commission. http://legal.un.org/ilc/documentation/english/reports/a_cn4_163.pdf (Accessed 6 March 2020).

Ludington, S., Gulati, M. & Brophy, A. (2010). 'Applied legal history: demystifying the doctrine of odious debts'. *Theoretical Inquiries in Law*, 11(1), 247–81.

Malek, R. (1995). *L'Algérie à Evian: Histoire des négociations secrètes, 1956–1962*. Paris: Seuil.

Mallard, G. (2019). *Gift Exchange: The Transnational History of a Political Idea*. New York: Cambridge University Press.

Ozsu, U. (2015). 'In the Interest of Mankind as a Whole: Mohammed Bedjaoui's International Economic Order'. *Humanity*, 6(1), 129–43.

Pahuja, S. (2011). *Decolonizing International Law: Development, Economic Growth and the Politics of Universality*. Cambridge: Cambridge University Press.

Rajagopal, B. (2003). *International Law from Below: Development, Social Movements and Third World Resistance*. New York: Cambridge University Press.

Rist, G. (1996). *The History of Development: From Western Origins to Global Faith*. New York: Zed Books.

Sack, A. (1927). *Les effets des transformations des Etats sur leurs dettes publiques et autres obligations financières: traité juridique et financier*. Paris: Recueil Sirey.

Schrijver, N. (1997). *Permanent Sovereignty Over Natural Resources*. Cambridge: Cambridge University Press.

United Nations General Assembly (UNGA) (1974). Resolution 3201 (S-VI), May 1st. 'Declaration on the Establishment of a New International Economic Order' http://www.un-documents.net/s6r3201.htm (Accessed 6 March 2020).

United Nations General Assembly (UNGA) (1979). Resolution 34/138, Dec. 14th. 'Global negotiations relating to international economic co- operation for development'. http://www.un-documents.net/a34r138.htm (Accessed 6 March 2020).

United Nations (UN) (1983a). *Summary records of the plenary meetings and of the meetings of the Committee of the Whole*. Vol. I of Official Records of the United

Nations Conference on Succession of States in Respect of State Property, Archives and Debts. Vienna, March 1–April 8. A/CONF.117/16 (Vol. I). http://legal.un.org/diplomaticconferences/1983_succession/vol1.shtml. (Accessed 6 March 2020).

United Nations (1983b). 'Vienna Convention on Succession of States in Respect of State Property, Archives and Debts'. Vol. II of Official Records of the United Nations Conference on Succession of States in Respect of State Property, Archives and Debts. Vienna, April 8. A/CONF.117/16 (Vol. II).

9

Decolonization and Sovereign Debt

A Quagmire

Michael Waibel

9.1 Introduction

The phenomenon of state succession is one of the most complex, challenging, and politicized areas of international law and policy—covering diverse questions such as membership in international organizations, nationality, state responsibility, treaties, property, debts, and state archives. The *law* on state succession is linked to fundamental concepts of international law including personality, statehood, recognition, territory, and self-determination (particularly in the colonial context). It is secondary to the problem of identity and continuity of the state given there 'can be no succession at all' unless this problem is resolved (Marek, 1968, p. 10).

State succession into debt is an important and especially controversial subfield of the law on state succession. It is the 'original' form of succession, pre-dating the succession to treaties and to other rights and obligations (as seen, for example, with the Silesia Loans in the eighteenth century [Feilchenfeld, 1931, p. 45]). Various forms of debt (administrative, pensions, localized, general public) tended to be treated differently in different cases (e.g. in the case of Alsace-Lorraine: Feilchenfeld, 1931, pp. 439–41). This chapter contends that the contemporary law on state succession into debt remains in a quagmire.[1]

The law on state succession has traditionally distinguished between succession *to* 'public' rights and obligations (i.e., those of the state) and succession *and* 'private' rights and obligations as owed between private persons (i.e., those of non-state entities, such as individuals and companies) (Crawford, 1982, p. 16). Public debt, regardless of the identity of the creditor, belongs to the first category.

A particularly controversial aspect of decolonization after the Second World War was its effect on private property. Private property classically encompasses not

[1] On whether there is a cohesive law on state succession into debt or only a few fragmentary rules on specific points, see Arman Sarvarian, *The Law of State Succession* (Oxford University Press, forthcoming).

Michael Waibel, *Decolonization and Sovereign Debt: A Quagmire* In: *Sovereign Debt Diplomacies: Rethinking Sovereign Debt from Colonial Empires to Hegemony*. Edited by: Pierre Pénet and Juan Flores Zendejas, Oxford University Press (2021).
 DOI: 10.1093/oso/9780198866350.003.0010

only fungible and immovable assets but also contractual rights, including economic concession agreements and debt (see, generally, O'Connell, 1950, pp. 123–4).

During decolonization after the Second World War, state succession into debt became torn between the theory of universal succession and the clean-slate theory. The theory of universal succession and the clean-slate theory are extreme positions on a spectrum that came to the fore at the height of decolonization in the 1960s and 1970s. The tension between two stylizes schools on state succession into debt is the subject of this chapter.

It is particularly illuminated by the work of two distinguished scholars and practitioners of international law: Professor Daniel Patrick O'Connell (see, 1956; 1967) and Mohamed Bedjaoui, especially in his role as Special Rapporteur on State Succession at the International Law Commission. Bedjaoui's project was mostly concerned with setting aside the received doctrine and starting afresh. In Chapter 8, Grégoire Mallard shows how Bedjaoui's views on state succession were the product of education and professional experience. While the debate on state succession to debt long pre-dates O'Connell and Bedjaoui (see, generally, Feilchenfeld, 1931), the 'clean-slate' theory is a creature of the decolonization period. There was no clean-slate theory pre-Bedjaoui. O'Connell and Bedjaoui are representative of a variant of a debate on state succession into debt that has been ongoing for centuries (see the extensive review of state practice by Feilchenfeld, 1931).

9.2 Universal Succession Versus Clean Slate

Reflecting the historical development of the field, the modern literature on succession can be classified into three phases (see, Craven, 2007). In the first phase (1880–1930s), the literature attempted to formulate a general theory concerning succession; in the second and third phases (1950–74, 1990s), the context of the unfolding processes of decolonization and desovietization featured 'reactive solutions' (Sarvarian, 2016, pp. 789–90). In these phases, scholarship sought to evaluate the International Law Commission's (ILC) codification efforts and grappled with state succession cases arising from the collapse of the Soviet Union (Sarvarian, 2016, pp. 789–90; also, Craven, 2007; Eisemann & Koskenniemi, 2000; Klabbers & Council of Europe, 1999). General theorizing largely ceased with O'Connell, with the ILC electing to set aside questions of general theory when it sought to codify the law on state succession.

In the quest for a general theory on state succession, two important schools arose. On the one hand, some advocated the theory of universal succession—i.e., the automatic and complete assumption of all the predecessor state's rights and obligations by the successor state(s). Some writers held that the debt continuity norm applies in State succession, at least as a rule. For instance, Buchheit and

Gulati (2008, pp. 481–82) refer to the 'normal requirement of state/governmental succession to debt obligations', even though the theory of universal succession is based on a misleading analogy to the private law of inheritance (Crawford, 2012, p. 424; O'Connell, 1965b, pp. 367–8; 1971, pp. 156–7). On the other hand, the clean-slate (or non-succession) theory suggests that the former colony's obligations (including its debts) are extinguished upon the independence of the new state. The reasoning underpinning this theory is that, because these obligations are personal to a state, they lapse with the disappearance of the predecessor state; the successor state thus starts life with a clean slate.

Originally from New Zealand, O'Connell taught international law in Australia and the UK. The culmination of his career was his appointment as Chichele Professor of International Law at the University of Oxford from 1972 to 1979 (see, generally, Crawford, 1982; The Adelaide Law Review, 1980; Shearer, 1977). He was the leading scholar on state succession in the second half of the twentieth century (though he did not contribute to the work of the International Law Commission on this topic). He considered state succession already in his PhD at the University of Cambridge, supervised by Hersch Lauterpacht; he defended his thesis in 1951 and, subsequently, published it under the title *The Law of State Succession* with Cambridge University Press (1956). His 1967, two-volume canonical treatment of the subject, *State Succession in Municipal Law and International Law*, remains definitive, even if it is now somewhat dated. O'Connell was a socially conservative, devout Catholic and argued from natural-law positions in several publications (see, O'Connell, 1949b, 1957, 1959, 1972). Ultimately, most writers on state succession into debt have fallen back on natural law or ethics, in the absence of positive law—even arch-positivists.

Mohammed Bedjaoui was born in Algeria and studied in France. He was a practitioner and judge—serving as the President of the International Court of Justice from 1994 to 1997; in addition, he made major scholarly contributions—especially on the new international economic order (Bedjaoui, 1979), a subject proximate to the debate on state succession. Importantly, he was also legal advisor to the provisional government of Algeria prior to independence. After Algerian independence, he became Algerian Foreign Minister and also served as the state's ambassador to France and the United Nations. In his role as ILC Special Rapporteur, he came to consider the law on state succession in detail. Bedjaoui's philosophy was 'imbued with the *Nouvel Ordre Économique International* movement of the newly decolonized members of the non-aligned movement', which favoured the clean-slate theory (Sarvarian, 2016, p. 798, see further Mallard in Chapter 8).

The clean-slate theory is a product of decolonization. Even those theorists (including, for example, Keith, 1907) who were strong positivists never went so far as to say that *no* obligations could devolve through operation of law upon the successor. Keith was arguing, as a member of the UK's Colonial Office, in favour of the UK government's novel and radical rejection of debt and concession obligations arising out of its annexation of the Transvaal; they left themselves wiggle room, however, because they were also espousing claims of British investors and concessionaires in colonies such as the Philippines.

Both O'Connell and Bedjaoui's views on succession evolved considerably when confronted with the reality of newly independent states. Bedjaoui, as indicated above, favoured a clean-slate approach for such states. In his view, the free exercise by a people of its right to self-determination (which, through and by decolonization, had progressed from a mere political idea to a legal right crystallized in customary international law—notably through the production, by the United Nations, of resolutions and international conventions enshrining this right)[2] was paramount: the exercise of this right was not—and could not be—encumbered by entailed financial obligations (flowing, for example, from the acquired rights of individuals and companies) in the form of debt (Bedjaoui, 1970). In his words, '[p]olitical independence is meaningless without *economic independence*' (ILC, 1977a, p. 106)—a notion that was imbued by the 'revolutionary aims of the *Nouvel Ordre Économique International* movement to achieve economic redress for historical injustice' (2016, p. 800).

Algeria put forward this theory in other United Nations debates on self-determination. For example, in the debates preluding the Friendly Relations Declaration, the Algerian representative stated:

> The political liberation of peoples must be consummated through their economic liberation. In general, the right of self-determination should be regarded, not as a mere ideal, but as an absolute necessity to which urgent priority should be given. No restrictions must be imposed on that right, either in time or in space.
>
> (United Nations, 1966, p. 7)

This consistent message originates in Algeria's own struggle for independence, which was realized in the Evian Accords—a treaty some states have viewed as 'unjust' in light of the concessions extracted by France in exchange for Algerian independence (Dörr & Schmalenbach, 2012, p. 878).[3] Such *quid pro quos* were not uncommon in independence negotiations—with a prominent example being the Lancaster House Undertakings with respect to Mauritian independence: an Annex VII arbitral tribunal found that 'the undertakings provided by the United

[2] *See*, UNGA Res. 1514 (XV) (1960), Declaration on the granting of independence to colonial countries and peoples, UN Doc. A/RES/15/1514; UNGA Res. 2625 (1970), Declaration on principles of international law concerning friendly relations and co-operation among States in accordance with the Charter of the United Nations, UN Doc. A/RES/25/2625; International Covenant on Civil and Political Rights (1966) 999 UNTS 171; International Covenant on Economic, Social and Cultural Rights (1966) 993 UNTS 3.

[3] The idea that colonial powers imposed 'unjust' treaties resonated with former colonies throughout the world.

Kingdom at Lancaster House formed part of the *quid pro quo* through which Mauritian agreement to the detachment of the Chagos Archipelago from Mauritius was procured' (*Chagos*, para. 421).[4] In the *Chagos* advisory opinion, the International Court of Justice held that 'this detachment [of the Chagos Archipelago on the basis of the Lancaster House agreement] was not based on the free and genuine expression of the will of the people concerned.'[5]

Consequently, Bedjaoui believed that the authentic exercise of self-determination required a complementary theory of State succession to ensure that the exercise of that right by dependent peoples did not become illusory. Therefore, in his Ninth Report as Special Rapporteur, he included the following provision on State succession into debt obligations:

> When the successor State is a newly independent State:
>
> 1. No State debt of the predecessor State shall pass to the newly independent State, unless an agreement between the newly independent State and the predecessor State provides otherwise in view of the link between the State debt of the predecessor State connected with its activity in the territory to which the succession of States relates and the property, rights and interests which pass to the newly independent State.
>
> 2. The provisions of the agreement referred to in the preceding paragraph should not infringe the principle of the permanent sovereignty of every people over its wealth and natural resources, nor should their implementation endanger the fundamental economic equilibria of the newly independent State.
>
> (ILC, 1977b, p. 79)

The crucial point is that subparagraph (1) excludes pre-independence debts. The starting point is thus not continuity but rupture (which is the opposite of the position that the ILC adopted with respect to treaties).

In essence, therefore, by preventing the transfer of 'insupportable debt' to newly independent states (ILC, 1977a, p. 100), these states could freely determine their future political status (whether that meant independence, association-status, integration with another independent state or a unique political status). A clean-slate model was, in other words, essential to realizing newly independent states' freedom.

O'Connell, meanwhile, sought to mediate a path between what were, in his view, the two extremes of universal succession and the clean slate—both of which

[4] On this point, a partially dissenting opinion, authored by Judges Kateka and Wolfrum, found that, in conducting the *quid pro quo*, the UK had violated 'an obligation not to use pressure that could be acceptable in the relationship between two sovereign States, but not between a metropolitan State and a colony' (*Chagos* Dissent, p. 19).

[5] *Legal Consequences of the Separation of the Chagos Archipelago from Mauritius in 1965*, Advisory Opinion, 25 February 2019, General List No 169, para. 172.

were 'irreconcilable with political realities' (1965b, p. 367; 1971, p. 156; 1979, p. 729). He instead sought rules of law that reflected available juristic evidence and insulated the international legal structure from disorder: '[w]hatever form the change of sovereignty may take it involves a disruption of legal continuity, and rules of law are necessary to minimise the consequences of this disruption' (O'Connell, 1965b, p. 365; 1971, p. 155).

This concern for stability was a common theme throughout O'Connell's work on state succession and public debts. In his lectures at the Hague Academy, for example, he stated that 'the whole international community has demonstrated an interest in devising a settlement which will cause minimal disruption of the world's economic system' (O'Connell, 1970a, p. 148). He went on to expand that:

> Because the lenders from many countries may be affected, such a failure may have repercussions on the foreign exchange situation and even the economies of various States, and on the flow of goods and services.
>
> (O'Connell, 1970a, p. 148)

These apprehensions were reflected and developed in a discussion and report by a committee of the International Law Association on State Succession, within which O'Connell served as Rapporteur. Before listing a number of adverse effects for domestic and foreign investors and the international economic system (ILA, 1970, p. 107), the report states that:

> The Committee feels too little consideration has been given in the past to the fact that the failure to service the national debt affects not only the predecessor and successor States, but may also affect other States and the national as well as the international organisations and monetary institutions concerned with investment and a flow of capital. (ILA, 1970, p. 92)

The wholesale embrace of a clean-slate theory for decolonization could, in other words, 'precipitate the disintegration of the structure of international relations' (O'Connell, 1970b, p. 59)—something O'Connell believed to be logically incoherent in light of that fact that the law heightens 'the liberties, the security, and the dignity of new states, and it enables them to preserve the structure of trade, co-operation, and investment throughout the process of political change' (O'Connell, 1970b, p. 59). Indeed, on a theoretical level, O'Connell was of the opinion that reserving 'the argument of emancipation... for cases of [the] emergence of dependent peoples' was incongruent with the international legal philosophy that had birthed the modern world order:

> New states can hardly claim the privileges and faculties of states and yet repudiate the system from which these derive... [to do so] overlooks that a state, when

> it commences to exist as a state, does so in a structural context which gains its form from law, just as a child when born into a society becomes subjected to it by virtue of the order of being in which it is integrated. (O'Connell, 1970b, p. 58)

Thus, in a highly complex international society, 'the need for continuity and stability is more necessary than ever' (O'Connell, 1970b, p. 59; see, also, Dumberry, 2006, p. 446) and 'should not be undermined by emotional pretences to financial self-determination which have widespread, if indeterminate, repercussions' (O'Connell, 1970a, p. 148). O'Connell's contribution to this field was guided by pragmatic realities, including mixed state practice (Crawford, 1982, p. 82), without recourse to romantic or political ideals or to dogmatic loyalty to grand theories of state succession (1970a, p. 155). This stance even led O'Connell to dismiss the theories of scholars whose positions on the question of succession to public debt reflected his own. Ernst Feilchenfeld, for example, argued that there existed a 'rule of maintenance' in international law—which protects private rights as they existed at the moment of succession (1931, p. 625) and serves 'three important protective functions': (i) it secures private property rights; (ii) by promoting certainty, it insulates the international commercial and economic systems; and (iii) it protects the 'international balance sheet' and, thereby, the relative distribution of wealth among states (1931, pp. 634–5). That said, Feilchenfeld acknowledged that his proposed rule was in equity not law: he found very few rules of law applicable to state debt. In assessing this 'brilliant' thesis, O'Connell held that Feilchenfeld's rule was a *deus ex machina*—largely because, in the absence of 'the pressure exerted by equity and justice, economic considerations cannot underpin a positive rule' of law (1972, pp. 67–9). A recognized, demonstrable legal principle, in other words, was required to anchor any theory of succession.

This grounded approach, as will be seen below, led O'Connell to sharply criticize the ILC's work on state succession. O'Connell considered that, because a clean-slate theory 'had to be used in the case of decolonization for motives of politics and rhetoric', '[e]motion [had] crippled the exercise from the outset' (1979, p. 729).

O'Connell utilized this starting point to fashion his own theory. Having rejected universal succession in his 1951 PhD thesis (on the basis that successor state obligations lapsed with the predecessor state), he believed that it was clear 'that we must take the juridical bull by its horns and propose that succession should be the rule and non-succession the exception, in cases of independence of nonmetropolitan territories' (O'Connell, 1965a, p. 25). The answer, O'Connell believed, lay in the flexibility of 'equity' (see, ILA, 1978, p. 207)—though not the conception of 'equity' that is familiar to English lawyers (King, 2016, p. 36).[6] To balance the

[6] 'Equity has come to play a greatly increased role in international law. It can, at its lowest level, be an unfettered notion, but, at its highest level, it is an expression of justice, so that in one sense

respect for private property and the stability that it offered with the need for flexibility in the establishment of new relations, O'Connell proposed as a solution an equitable doctrine, grounded in acquired rights and unjust enrichment, that fell short of universal succession into pre-independence obligations:

> The legal relationship which existed between the predecessor State and the person to whom it owed a duty is something more than a mere vinculum juris; it also gives rise to a certain state of facts. Should the predecessor State have borrowed money, for example, two things are created. There is, first, the juridical link between the parties, which exists until either the money is repaid or the State itself has disappeared. There is, secondly, the factual situation which consists in the actual detention by the State of money in which the lender has an equitable interest. When the debtor State is superseded the legal duty to repay this money is not inherited ipso jure by its successor. What is 'inherited' is the state of facts which the now extinguished legal relationship has brought about. The equitable interest which the lender has in this factual situation is described variously as an 'acquired right', 'property right', and 'vested right'. The obligation of the successor State is to respect this interest. It is not an obligation derived from the predecessor, but one imposed ab exteriore by international law. It arises when the successor, through its own action in extending its sovereignty, becomes competent to destroy the title-holder's interest. The general principle in which this obligation is embodied, and which underlies the whole problem of State succession, is the principle that acquired rights must be respected.
>
> (O'Connell, 1951, pp. 205–6; also, 1950, pp. 95–6; 1965b, pp. 377–8; 1970a, pp. 134–46; 1971, pp. 162–3)

He concluded that:

> [A] successor state is under an obligation to respect those debts incurred in the ordinary routine of governmental administration in the territory acquired by it . . . Change of sovereignty does not affect the juridical character and existence of local government bodies in ceded or annexed territories, and hence debts contracted by such bodies, and the legal relationships between debtor and creditor remain intact. The creditor's interests is thus an acquired right which can be enforced against the debtor and which must be respected by the successor State.
>
> (O'Connell, 1956, pp. 180–1)

This doctrine struck a balance between the two extremes and acted as a special rule of international law regulating the transfer of debt obligations between states.

international law is restoring the natural law doctrine of the Grotian tradition to pre-eminence' (ILA, 1978, p. 207).

O'Connell thought that 'peripheral questions' (O'Connell, 1965b, p. 385; 1971, p. 167), such as 'odious' war debts or risky investments, should not distract from the overall juristic picture given that these have been '[v]irtually the only occasions on which' states have refused to succeed to debts (1951, p. 218). Consequently, his theory achieved the stability that O'Connell thought was necessary for the international financial structure (1950, p. 97).

9.3 The Quagmire of State Practice

The conflict between the two schools—and the radically different implications for the conditions under which colonial entities have been able to achieve independence—has produced a tangled law of state succession. In the context of decolonization, one school, through the international legal establishment, has produced a multilateral treaty (the Vienna Convention on the Succession of States in Respect of State Property, Archives and Debts, 1983) underpinned by an ideology whose purpose (the emancipation of dependent peoples) was achieved, in large measure, over fifty years ago, and the reflection of which was not seen, even at the time of its creation, in the practice of states. The other school (embodied by O'Connell's moderate theory), meanwhile, has seen a noticeable uptake in state practice but has, nonetheless, not yet been deemed to have secured a settled rhythm in customary international law.

Though many of O'Connell's criticisms of the ILC's work directly pertained to the 1978 Vienna Convention on Succession of States in respect of Treaties (see, O'Connell, 1979), the underlying thrust of his points apply equally to the its work on public debts (Crawford, 1982, p. 46): O'Connell opposed the codification of the law on state succession. He believed that the law of state succession was '*altogether* unsuited to the process of codification, let alone of progressive development'—preferring to let it develop as common law (O'Connell, 1979, pp. 726–7 (emphasis added)). In his view, codification risked arresting 'the historical development of the law and encapsulating it within a particular time-frame and a particular ideological milieu' (O'Connell, 1979, p. 739). Indeed, in his role of Rapporteur at the International Law Association, he was conscious that decolonization would, in all likelihood, have substantially ended before any conclusions were reached. Its work, therefore, sought to 'form the foundation for the resolution of questions of succession that would arise in new circumstances and when emotions and opinions might be quite different' (ILA, 1970, p. 335). This was achieved, in the context of the ILA's Report, by appealing to O'Connell's theory grounded on unjust enrichment (ILA, 1970, p. 108)[7]—which, O'Connell thought, introduced

[7] 'The concept of unjust enrichment has played a role in creating an obligation for the successor State with respect to the debt of its predecessor...Juridically the concept of unjust enrichment is

'a criterion of flexibility which has a respectable legal tradition behind it' (O'Connell, 1973, p. 338).

From this, one can discern the three (interconnected) bases for O'Connell's visceral criticisms of the ILC's Conventions on State Succession: marriage to a time-limited political ideology not supported by state practice, with the result that the ultimate product was unfit for purpose on arrival. The ILC's work, O'Connell argued, was marred from the beginning 'by a preoccupation with the special problem of decolonisation, around which myth and emotion [had] accumulated like mists in the marsh, so that the whole context became intellectually distorted' (1979, p. 726). This special problem was, as quickly became apparent, a historically remote episode (1979, p. 726)—meaning that the ILC's work, to the realization of O'Connell's fear, had forced 'the topic within the constraints of inflexible dogmas that [were] at once over-simple and insufficiently comprehensive' (1979, p. 727). Future work could assess to what extent O'Connell's work is responsible for the limited uptake of the two Conventions.

Similarly, Craven has noted the relationship between 'law' and 'politics' in the arena of State succession—stating that 'the failure to identify "settled" rules relating to . . . the partition of debt becomes, thereby, an *indica* of the extent to which the topic remains effectively political' (2007, p. 26). The result is that the rules differ depending on the nature of the change in question (Craven 2007, p. 39). The ILC's focus on newly independent states' clean slates meant that other important questions (including, for example, the destiny of debts excluded by the 1983 Convention in the case of independence succession) were neglected and have remained unresolved.

This result was, perhaps, even more troubling to O'Connell because the practice of newly independent States did not reflect the clean-slate theory adopted by the ILC. As he noted, 'successor states [had] generally not contested their obligations respecting debts' (O'Connell, 1973, p. 337); instead, O'Connell argued, these states had 'gone to immense lengths to maintain continuity in their internal legal systems, and . . . [were] only too aware of the implications of tearing up the traditional fabric of international law' (1970b, p. 60). Therefore, as O'Connell contended, a desire to have access to finance and capital markets and the need for recognition—by states and for the purposes of membership in international organizations—led newly independent states to quickly realize the advantages of the existing legal order (1970b, p. 59).[8] Consequently, these states sought to

utilized when there is a lapse in the formal legal relationship between two parties, as where a contract is extinguished by supervening events, and where the equities of the situation make it necessary to create a new legal relationship between the beneficiary and the potential loser' (ILA, 1970, p. 108).

[8] O'Connell contested that states had a duty of recognition, Daniel Patrick O'Connell, (1954), 'Ideology and International Law' 9 *Twentieth Century* (Melbourne), 40–50.

establish friendly relations to 'facilitate their rapid economic development' (O'Connell, 1973, p. 332).

Indeed, virtually all of the examples of state practice (see, generally, Menon, 1986; 1991) considered by the ILC in its Report were also considered by O'Connell (both individually and as ILA Rapporteur) yet they reached different conclusions. In its 1970 Report on public debts, the ILA considered state practice involving former UK, French, and Belgian colonies and concluded that the 'practice of States . . . would seem to justify the conclusion that local debts and localised debts remain the liability of newly independent States' (ILA, 1970, p. 111). This was because these metropolitan powers had structured the internal law of their colonies such that the colonies were legally separate entities capable of managing their own financial affairs (ILA, 1970, p. 108–11). India, for example, received financial obligations from the UK,[9] with province-specific debts (for Bengal and Punjab) and a specific share of the national debt passing to Pakistan as a debt to India (O'Connell, 1949a, p. 458). For the Belgium-Congo example, the ILA found that Congo was also legally separate and that attempts, by the Belgian courts, to pass debts to Belgium via the nexus of its constitutional framework had failed (ILA, 1970, pp. 110–11). Furthermore, in relation to Indonesia, the ILA found that it was the only example of a former colony assuming a repartition of the national debt—as distinct from simply continuing local debts—after it did not contest assuming debts annexed by the Netherlands to the Netherlands Indies, which were taken over by Indonesia (ILA, 1970, p. 111).[10] The subsequent repudiation of these debts had, O'Connell contended in his lectures at the Hague Academy, 'little except political relevance to the question of State Succession' (1970a, p. 144; pp. 152–3). The ILC Report, prepared by Bedjaoui, came to largely the same conclusions on these examples (ILC, 1977a, pp. 95–9) and included additional specimens—for example: the Philippines' assumption of debts contracted prior to 1 May 1934, for which the United States acted as guarantor (ILC, 1977a, p. 95) and Madagascar's assumption of debts, which had been 'self-evident' in negotiations, despite Bedjaoui questioning the extent of its financial autonomy from France (ILC, 1977a, p. 97).

The same pattern is seen with historical examples and exceptional cases of succession. Of the former, Bedjaoui found that the succession of debts from former Spanish colonies had been managed, primarily, by internal law—with the assumption of such debts acting as the 'price' for friendly relations with Spain (ILC, 1977a, p. 94). Similarly, with Cuba, the ILC Report found that debts proper to Cuba (including a mortgage for the benefit of Havana) passed to Cuba upon independence (ILC, 1977a, p. 94). O'Connell, meanwhile, found that the

[9] Indian Independence (Rights, Property and Liability) Order (1947). Gazette of India Extraordinary, §§9(a), (b), (c), and (d), 14 August 1947.

[10] Draft Financial and Economic Agreement, *Staatsblad*, No. J. 570, 21 December 1949, Article 25.

clean-slate argument had not been 'employed when Panama seceded from Colombia, Cuba from Spain, or Finland from Russia' (1970b, p. 58).

Of the latter category, both schools agreed that exceptional examples should be subtracted from the broader consideration. The ILA's 1970 Report, for instance, had concluded that exceptional cases—including Israel, Guinea, and Algeria—should not be generalized (ILA, 1970, p. 110). With Guinea, for example, the Report found that its withdrawal from the French Community had resulted in the absence of a legal mechanism for transmitting debts (ILA, 1970, p. 110); with Israel, despite all the debts being local, the absence of a legal system to manage the orderly transmission of borrowings was uncommon (ILA, 1970, p. 110). Bedjaoui, in his Report, was of a similar opinion on each example. With Guinea, for example, he suggested that the 'problem of debts [had] not assumed significant importance in the relations between the two States' (ILC, 1977a, p. 96). On Algeria, after setting out a brief overview of the history (including that Algeria's assumption of obligations under the Evian Agreement was a *quid pro quo*), he stated that his summary 'gives only the merest suggestion of the complexity of the Algerian-French financial dispute'—one interlaced with war, odious debts, and various international agreements (ILC, 1977a, p. 99). On Libya, Bedjaoui was succinct in stating that the General Assembly had intervened and resolved the problem (ILC, 1977a, p. 96).[11] Finally, on the historical example of the United States' repudiation of UK national debt, Bedjaoui concluded that, as the Revolutionary War was ignited by and fought for financial reasons, it was 'quite natural' that the United States had declined to assume any debts from the UK upon its independence (ILC, 1977a, p. 94; O'Connell, 1956, p. 160; Feilchenfeld, 1931, pp. 53–4).

In light of this divergence on state practice, O'Connell's criticism that the subject of state succession into debt was not ripe or appropriate for codification in 1970s appears warranted. Bedjaoui's Report, when analysing state practice, focuses on the financial burdens of newly independent states—conceding that there was insufficient evidence to 'determine accurately how much these countries' disastrous and extensive debt problem is due to their having attained independence and assumed certain debts in connexion with succession of States' (ILC, 1977a, p. 100).[12] For this reason, it is not surprising that O'Connell sought to juxtapose his work at the ILA with that of the ILC, which he suggested to be the 'special pleading for the minority attitude of Algeria' (1973, p. 338). He said, for example, that:

[11] *See*, UNGA Res. 388 A (V) (1950), Economic and financial provisions relating to Libya, UN Doc. A/RES/5/338 A.

[12] Though, as Bedjaoui noted in his Report, the financial capacity of the assuming state was considered in some of the practice—including, especially, the case of the Ottoman debts (ILC, 1977a Report, p. 105).

> On the subject of debts and contracts, the International Law Association Reports could solidify the law as it has been in very many areas, while the Special Rapporteur of the International Law Commission would shift it altogether on to an alternative historical and ideological course. (O'Connell, 1973, p. 338)

It is unlikely that Bedjaoui or O'Connell were best friends. Future work could look to evaluate how they engaged with each other, for example any personal correspondence between the two or systematic analysis of how they cite each other (of fail to cite each other).

9.4 A Perennial Quagmire?

In light of the above, it is understandable why these attempts by the ILC to codify the law on state succession—in the dying days of decolonization—have neither attracted broad participation nor substantially impacted subsequent state practice. O'Connell, for his part, thought it would be a 'lottery' as to when the ILC's treaties would enter into force—suggesting that the issue would not rank highly within the diplomatic priorities of states (1979, p. 726)—and he was proved correct on this point.

The 1983 Convention, in particular, is unlikely to ever enter into force and is seen as an example of the ILC's unsuccessful work (King, 2016, p. 37). It came too late to shape, to any significant degree, questions of succession in decolonization (O'Connell, 1979, p. 726; Pahuja, 2011, p. 160). Furthermore, at a deeply divided conference (see, Aldrich, 1981), Canada, the UK, and the United States, among others, voted against its adoption. The result is that, as of December 2020, the Convention had only attracted seven ratifications (with fifteen needed for entry into force) and a further seven signatures (*United Nations Treaty Collection Treaty Status* 2018). All fourteen ratifications and signatures are by states that have traditionally been capital importers, such as Liberia and Ukraine. Thus, as a matter of treaty law, the only multilateral attempt at codification in this area has ended in failure. The contribution of O'Connell to its demise is a subject for future work.

An illuminating comparison can be made with the work of the Institut de Droit International on this subject. In its 2001 Resolution on *State Succession in Matters of Property and Debts*,[13] it provided expressly for the protection of acquired rights 'so far as is possible' (Article 25) and grounded the rules of succession on equitable apportionment (Article 26). The Resolution makes provision for several forms of succession including, for example, the succession of part of the territory of a state

[13] Institut de Droit International, State Succession in Matters of Property and Debt, 2001, http://www.idi-iil.org/app/uploads/2017/06/2001_van_01_en.pdf.

(Article 26) but does not create special regimes for time-limited phenomena as the ILC's work did with decolonization.

The 1983 Convention's central provisions on newly independent states, being contrary to existing to state practice at the time, have also not become part of customary international law (see, King, 2016, p. 38; Schachter, 1993, p. 259; Shaw, 2014, p. 986; Waibel, 2011, p. 131). In addition, subsequent state practice has, for the most part, conflicted with the Convention.

On decolonization, the door remains open for further state practice (despite decolonization's heydays in the 1970s). The official position of the United Nations, for example, is that the 'process of decolonization is not complete' (United Nations, 2010, p. 2) and will remain so until there exists no Non-Self-Governing Territory that has not exercised its right to self-determination (United Nations, 2017, p. 7). However, given that, of the remaining territories, ten are administered by the UK, two by France, and three by the United States (*List of Non-Self-Governing Territories*, 2018), it is unlikely that the practice of colonial powers will divert from the previous patterns outlined by O'Connell. State practice is unlikely to evolve substantially. Therefore, as 'it is highly unlikely that Chapter XI practice might evolve to embrace non-colonial situations' like South Africa (Crawford, 2006, p. 612), practice of this hue is unlikely to shift the customary dial any further. That said, the economic repercussions flowing from a change of statute for these Non-Self-Governing Territories would be less significant than in the decolonization of the 1950–70s. Consequently, despite possible future practice (including South Sudan (Sarvarian, 2016, pp. 807–8)), the impact of further decolonization is likely to be limited.

9.5 Conclusion

After the ILC completed its ill-fated codification project, the topic of state succession disappeared for a while from the professional agenda of international lawyers. Given that the ILC's quest to formulate general rules and principles has failed, a seeming consensus has emerged, according to which state successions are to be treated in a highly fact-specific manner.

Negotiation was, and remains, the principal mode for settling succession disputes (Waibel, 2010), given the complexity of the issues and the high and low politics involved. But these negotiations take place without the benefit of well-established background rules and principles. The succession disputes involving the former Socialist Federal Republic of Yugoslavia in the 1990s (Eisemann & Koskenniemi, 2000; Klabbers & Council of Europe, 1999) principally involved negotiations but also some litigation (Stanič, 2001). The European Court of Human Rights, for instance, held that the successor states had breached the right of depositors to the peaceful enjoyment of possessions and the right to an effective domestic remedy by failing to agree on certain issues concerning succession to state debt.[14]

In recent state practice, disputes concerning succession into debt have been particularly prominent—even though the succession itself was uncontested (see, for example, Government of South Sudan, 2009). In the run-up to the Scottish Independence Referendum in 2014, the UK government commissioned a legal opinion by Professors James Crawford and Alan Boyle who endorsed the UK government's position that 'it can be expected that the weight of international opinion would favour recognizing the [remainder of the UK] as the continuator' and Scotland as the new state (Crawford & Boyle Report, 2013, p. 83). The UK government, in its own report, stated that 'there would be an expectation that an independent Scottish state would take on an equitable share of the UK's national debt'—with the quantity of an 'equitable' share to be determined in negotiations (UK Government Report, 2013, p. 57), without expressly referring to O'Connell's work. In its rival report, however, the Scottish government argued that Scotland would pass into independence with a clean slate (Scottish Government Report, 2014). The Scotland Institute, a think tank, concluded that, in any case, it would in an independent Scotland's interests to accept a portion of the UK's national debt to 'establish an international reputation as a responsible and reliable nation' (Scotland Institute Report, 2014, p. 28). Similarly, the former Vice President of Catalonia, Oriol Junqueras, suggested that Catalonia would assume a portion of Spain's national debt if Spain were willing to negotiate the transfer of its assets in Catalonia (Roger 2014). Though the reaction of Spain and the international community to Catalonia's unilateral declaration of independence suggests that its independence is unlikely to occur in the foreseeable future, the division of Spanish national debt and assets will remain a significant legal question (Dumberry, 2011, p. 3). The same is true of Belgium, the potential partition of which is likely to hinge on the position of Brussels—with the absence of salient international legal machinery making the process even more complicated (Sarvarian, 2016, p. 809).

State practice over the last several decades reflects O'Connell's appeals to grounded negotiations and the preservation of international economic balance. In this sense, his desire that the law of state succession should develop as common law—without employing 'inherently anarchic' grand theories like *tabula rasa* (O'Connell, 1965b, p. 367; 1971, p. 156–7)—has and will continue to be fulfilled.

In the end, if—as James Crawford persuasively contended—international law is an intergenerational transmission mechanism for rights and obligations (Crawford, 2014, p. 113), then it is hard to see how international law can perform

[14] App. No. 60642/08 *Ališić and others v. Bosnia and Herzegovina, Croatia, Serbia, Slovenia and the Former Yugoslav Republic of Macedonia*, European Court of Human Rights, Grand Chamber, Judgment of 16 July 2014, at paras 59–136.

this critical ordering function in frequent state succession disputes without settled principles and rules for all forms of state succession. O'Connell's view that customary international law and equity might be able to perform this function without the need for codification seems justified—largely because states have always conducted these affairs in the absence of a widely ratified international convention. His work retains a central position in contemporary debates on state succession, 'leaving many with strong and . . . continuing influences on their thinking and approaches to the law' (*The Adelaide Law Review*, 1980, p. 169). These observations, together with his overarching theory of acquired-rights succession (which remains a 'highly influential theory' (King, 2016, p. 35)), forms the bedrock of O'Connell's enduring legacy.[15]

Bibliography

Adelaide Law Review, T. (1980). 'Daniel Patrick O'Connell, 1924–1979 [In Memoriam]'. *Adelaide Law Review*, 7, 167–71.

Aldrich, G. H. (1981). 'The Thirty-Third Session of the International Law Commission'. *American Journal of International Law*, 75, 992–6.

Bedjaoui, M. (1970). 'Problèmes Récents De Succession D'états Dans Les états Nouveaux (Volume 130)', in The Hague Academy of International Law (Ed.), *Collected Courses of the Hague Academy of International Law*. Leiden: Brill.

Bedjaoui, M. (1979). *Towards an International Economic Order*. New York: Holmes & Meier.

Buchheit, L. & Gulati, G. M. (2008). 'Odious Debts and Nation-Building—When the Incubus Departs'. *Maine Law Review*, 60(2), 477–86.

Craven, M. C. R. (2007). *The Decolonization of International Law: State Succession and the Law of Treaties*. Oxford: Oxford University Press.

Crawford, J. (1982). 'The Contribution of Professor D.P. O' Connell to the Discipline of International Law'. *British Year Book of International Law*, 51, 1–87.

Crawford, J. (2006). *The Creation of States in International Law*, second edition. Oxford: Oxford University Press.

Crawford, J. (ed.) (2012). *Brownlie's Principles of Public International Law*, 8th edition. Oxford: Oxford University Press.

Crawford, J. (2014). *Chance, Order, Change: The Course of International Law, General Course on Public International Law*. Leiden: M. Nijhoff.

Crawford, J. & Boyle, A. (2013). *Opinion: Reference on the Independence of Scotland—International Law Aspects*. London: The Stationery Office.

[15] Thanks to Noémi Michel, Pierre Pénet, Arman Sarvarian, and Juan Flores for comments, Grégoire Mallard for discussions, and Caleb Kirton for research assistance.

Dörr, O. & Schmalenbach, K. (2012). *Vienna Convention on the Law of Treaties: A Commentary*. London: Springer.

Dumberry, P. (2006). 'The Controversial Issue of State Succession to International Responsibility Revisited in Light of Recent State Practice'. *German Year Book of International Law*, 49, 413–47.

Dumberry, P. (2011). *Legal Aspects of State Succession*. First Conference on Catalonia's Self-Determination: Building a New State, 3 November 2011.

Eisemann, P. M. & Koskenniemi, M. (2000). *La succession d'Etats: la codification á l'epreuve des faits/State succession: codification tested against the facts*. The Hague; London: M. Nijhoff.

Feilchenfeld, E. (1931). *Public Debts and State Succession*. New York: Macmillan.

Government of Scotland (2014). *Division of UK Public Sector Debt—Implications for Scotland and the Rest of the UK*. Edinburgh: Government Publishing Service.

Government of Southern Sudan (2009). *Southern Sudan: a guide to critical post-2011 issues*. Southern Sudan: Office of the President and Ministry of Presidential Affairs.

Government of the United Kingdom and Northern Ireland (2013). *Scotland Analysis: Devolution and the Implications of Scottish Independence* (cm. 8554). London: The Stationery Office.

International Law Association (1970). 'State Succession'. *International Law Association Reports of Conferences*, 54, 92–150.

International Law Association (1978). 'Theory and Methodology of International Law'. *International Law Association Reports of Conferences*, 58, 186–218.

International Law Commission (1977a). 'Ninth Report on Succession of States in Respect of Matters other than Treaties by Mr Mohammed Bedjaoui, Special Rapporteur (UN Doc. A/CN.4/301 and Add. 1)'. *Yearbook of the International Law Commission*, 2(1), 45–117.

International Law Commission (1977b). *Report of the International Law Commission on the work of its twenty-ninth session* (UN Doc. A/32/10). New York: General Assembly Official Records.

Keith, A.B. (1907). *The Theory of State Succession with Special Reference to English and Colonial Law*. London: Waterlow & Sons Ltd.

King, J. (2016). *The Doctrine of Odious Debts in International Law: A Restatement*. Cambridge: Cambridge University Press.

Klabbers, J. & Council of Europe (1999). *State Practice Regarding State Succession and Issues of Recognition: The Pilot Project of the Council of Europe* or *Pratique des âetats concernant la succession d'âetats et les questions de reconnaissance: le projet pilote du Conseil de l'Europe*. The Hague; London: Kluwer Law International.

Marek, K. (1968). *Identity and Continuity of States in Public International Law*. Geneva: Librairie Droz S.A.

In the Matter of the Chagos Marine Protected Area Arbitration (Mauritius v. UK) 2015 Award, 18 March 2015.

Menon, P. K. (1986). 'The Succession of States and the Problem of State Debts'. *Boston College Third World Law Journal*, 2(6), 111–41.

Menon, P. K. (1991). *The Succession of States in Respect to Treaties, State Property, Archives, and Debts*. Lewiston: E. Mellen Press.

O'Connell, D. P. (1949a). 'The British Commonwealth and State Succession After the Second World War'. *British Yearbook of International Law*, 26, 454–63.

O'Connell, D. P. (1949b). 'The Search for Ideals in Law'. *Catholic Review*, 5, 228–43.

O'Connell, D. P. (1950). 'Economic Concessions in the Law of State Succession'. *British Year Book of International Law*, 27, 93–124.

O'Connell, D. P. (1951). 'Secured and Unsecured Debts in The Law of State Succession'. *British Yearbook of International Law*, 28, 204.

O'Connell, D. P. (1954). 'Ideology and International Law' 9 Twentieth Century, 40–50.

O'Connell, D. P. (1956). *The law of state succession*. Cambridge: Cambridge University Press.

O'Connell, D. P. (1957). 'The Rational Foundations of International Law: Francesco Suarez and the Concept of *Jus Genitum*'. *Sydney Law Review*, 2, 253–70.

O'Connell, D. P. (1959). 'Natural Law and the International Community'. *Catholic Lawyer*, 5, 207–17.

O'Connell, D. P. (1965a). 'Independence and Problems of State Succession', in W.V. O'Brien (Ed.), *The New Nations in International Law and Diplomacy* (pp.7–41). New York: Praeger.

O'Connell, D. P. (1965b). *International Law* (Vol. 1). London: Stevens & Sons.

O'Connell, D. P. (1967). *State Succession in Municipal Law and International Law*. Cambridge: Cambridge University Press.

O'Connell, D. P. (1970a). 'Recent Problems of State Succession in Relation to New States', in The Hague Academy of International Law (Ed.), *Collected Courses of the Hague Academy of International Law*. Leiden: Brill.

O'Connell, D. P. (1970b). 'The Role of International Law', in S. Hoffmann (Ed.), *Conditions of World Order* (pp. 49–65). Boston: Houghton Mifflin.

O'Connell, D. P. (1971). *International Law for Students*. London: Stevens & Sons.

O'Connell, D. P. (1972). 'State Succession and the Theory of the State', in C.H. Alexandrowicz, (Ed.), *Grotian Society Papers* (pp. 23–75). Dordrecht: M. Nijhoff.

O'Connell, D. P. (1973). 'The Present State of the Law on State Succession', in M. Bos (Ed.), *The Present State of International Law and Other Essays* (pp. 331–8). Alphen aan den Rijn: Kluwer.

O'Connell, D. P. (1979). 'Reflections on the State Succession Convention'. *ZAöRV*, 39, 725–39.

Pahuja, S. (2011). *Decolonising International Law: Development, Economic Growth and the Politics of Universality*. Cambridge: Cambridge University Press.

Roger, M. (2014). 'Si España No Acepta Negociar, Cataluña No Pagará Su Deuda', El País, 1 November 2014, https://elpais.com/ccaa/2014/10/31/catalunya/1414789028_571684.html.

Sarvarian, A. (2016). 'Codifying the Law of State Succession: A Futile Endeavour?' *European Journal of International Law*, 27, 789–812.

Schachter, O. (1993). 'State Succession: The Once and Future Law'. *Vanderbilt Journal of International Law*, 33, 253.

The Scotland Institute (2014). *Debt and Destiny: An Assessment of an Independent Scotland's Fair Share of the United Kingdom's National Debt and the Impact It Could Have on Scotland's Future.* Glasgow: The Scotland Institute.

Shaw, M. N. (2014). *International Law.* Cambridge: Cambridge University Press.

Shearer, I. A. (1977). 'Obituary: Professor D.P. O'Connell'. *Australian Year Book of International Law*, 7, xxiii–xxix.

Stanič, A. (2001). 'Financial Aspects of State Succession: The Case of Yugoslavia'. *European Journal of International Law*, 12, 751–79.

United Nations (1966). *Summary Record of the Special Committee on Principles of International Law Concerning Friendly Relations and Co-Operation Among States* (UN Doc. A/AC.125/SR.43). New York: General Assembly Official Records.

United Nations (2010). *Plenary Records of the United Nations General Assembly* (UN Doc. A/65/PV.65). New York: General Assembly Official Records.

United Nations (2017). *Report of the Special Committee on the Situation With Regard to the Implementation of the Declaration of the Granting of Independence To Colonial Countries and Peoples* (UN Doc. A/72/23). New York: General Assembly Official Records.

Waibel, M. (2010). 'The Diplomatic Channel', in J. Crawford & A. Pellet (Eds.), *The Law of International Responsibility.* Oxford: Oxford University Press.

Waibel, M. (2011). *Sovereign Defaults Before International Courts and Tribunals.* Cambridge; New York: Cambridge University Press.

10
The Global South Debt Revolution That Wasn't

UNCTAD from Technocractic Activism to Technical Assistance

Quentin Deforge and Benjamin Lemoine

10.1 Introduction

> "If we look at UNCTAD in the past, and what it was between 1964 and 1980, we are now reduced to a shadow of what we were [. . .] There is a very strong opposition to the idea that UNCTAD continues to work on systemic factors, from the United States in particular, but also from Group B (group of advanced) countries in general.
>
> *Researcher: What would they like you to do?*
>
> Whether we do technical cooperation, I always say: 'count the peas somewhere'. This opposition will rather strengthen, and it does not make things any easier for us. Part of UNCTAD is the last bastion of non-neoliberal economic thinking. And that's not tolerated today".
>
> Interviewee 1. Civil servant from the Debt and Development Finance Branch (of the Division on Globalization and Development Strategies, UNCTAD)

What has become of the cooperation of developing countries for a New International Economic Order, the 'socialist globalisation', as Johanna Bockman (2015) refers to it? To address this question, we focus on the way international crises and conflicts over sovereign debt have transformed the agenda and mandate of the United Nations Conference on Trade and Development (UNCTAD), the Geneva-based organization founded in 1964 and whose history is closely linked to

Quentin Deforge and Benjamin Lemoine, *The Global South Debt Revolution That Wasn't: UNCTAD from Technocractic Activism to Technical Assistance* In: *Sovereign Debt Diplomacies: Rethinking Sovereign Debt from Colonial Empires to Hegemony.* Edited by: Pierre Pénet and Juan Flores Zendejas, Oxford University Press (2021). © Oxford University Press.
DOI: 10.1093/oso/9780198866350.003.0011

the G77 group of developing countries[1] (see Mallard in this volume). This chapter documents a historical shift in the way UNCTAD has constructed debt as a policy issue. Two 'problematizations'[2] of debt are identified, each corresponding to a specific mode of addressing the debt problems affecting developing countries: i.e. establishing a diagnosis, a set of causal relationships and identifying the preferred modes of treatment and policy instruments. The first one is what we call the *entangled* problematization of debt. Here, local contexts of over-indebtedness are interpreted within the broader, structural context of international capital flows, asymmetric trade, and power relations between nations. The second one is the *disentangled* mode of problematization that emphasizes domestic factors to explain and blame over-borrowing, which is less about structural issues and more about reckless spending, data reporting problems, and misuses of funds, all of which would relate to poor decisions by state officials. Proponents of the former problematization typically blame the international economic and financial architecture as the main issue affecting over-indebtedness while proponents of the latter often view the nation state as the sole culprit and source of its misfortune. Remedies also vary depending on the mode of problematization: the former highlights the need for a systematic debt restructuring mechanism and the rebalancing of international power relations; the latter emphasizes dedicated public policies at a domestic level, with ad hoc and 'case by case' solutions, for instance the micro-management of public finances, the need for monetary and fiscal discipline, and the building of reliable and transparent data provided to official and private creditors. This shift toward the *insulation* of the debt problem, circumscribed to the domestic sphere, is not restricted to UNCTAD. It can also be found in IMF policies emphasizing domestic blames and remedies to sovereign debt crises in lieu of structural reforms of the international financial system.[3]

This chapter traces how these modes of problematizations of debt have been debated between UNCTAD, Bretton Woods Institutions and advanced countries,

[1] Initially a group of 77 members (most of them newly independent nations), the G77 has since expanded to 134 developing countries, making this group the largest at the United Nations. Brazil, India, and South Africa are members. China participates in the G77 but is not a member.

[2] Our use of the term 'problematization' originates in Foucault's work on the History of Sexuality (Foucault, 1984). Such Foucauldian concept has made its way into more recent research in Political Science and Science and Technology Studies (STS). For instance, Brice Laurent (2017, p. 19) refers to problematization as the analysis of the 'conditions of possibility of certain qualifications of questions, the way through which they can be transformed into problems for which solutions could be proposed. The whole process is a collective production; it constitutes "the specific work of though" which cannot be separated from the practices and technologies through which it is enacted.'

[3] As Sarah Babb puts it: 'Rather than viewing external imbalances as an inherent side effect of economic globalisation, as Keynes had, the Fund placed the blame for balance-of-payments problems squarely on national governments.' 'The burden of balance-of-payments adjustment [is] placed [by IMF's rules] on debtor nations and required that governments trim their budgets and bring down inflation as condition for balance-of-payments loans' (Babb, 2003, pp. 12, 22).

and within UNCTAD since the 1960s, and most particularly within the UNCTAD's Debt and Development Finance Branch. This controversy was not simply an *intellectual* debate between rival economic doctrines but an eminently *practical* contest in which each problematization emerged incrementally and became legitimized and contested through shifting dynamics of power within and outside UNCTAD. Antagonistic debt problematizations were patterned after the rivalry between rich, western and developed nations—the so-called 'Group B' representing thirty-one members from the Western world at UNCTAD—and developing nations of the Global South (the Group of 77 [G77] at the UN).[4]

Our analysis draws on qualitative data: twenty semi-directive interviews[5] and official and unofficial archival sources, such as diplomatic cables. With this eclectic material, our aim is to unpack conflictual processes which are not typically captured in official historiographies, in particular those written by the institutions, which often centre on consensual declarations made 'on the record' in official summits (UNCTAD, 2006; Toye, 2014b). Focusing on backstage processes and diplomatic battles behind the scene, we aim to move beyond the commonly held view that the historical achievements made by developing countries have owed much to the generous concessions granted to them by advanced countries (Olson, 2013). Diplomatic cables and 'off the record' documents suggest, on the contrary, that advanced countries, in particular the US, did not always have the upper hand in international negotiations over debt. Our data reveal both the fragility of American diplomacy during the 1970s negotiations over the new international economic order and the tactics deployed by US diplomats to weaken the negotiating position of developing countries and subvert UNCTAD's tentative to combat power asymmetries between rich and poor countries and build cooperation and solidarity among developing world.

Our empirical examination centres on several UNCTAD initiatives, from its creation in 1964 to the adoption of debt restructuring principles at the United Nations General Assembly in 2015 (UNGA, 2015). UNCTAD was founded in 1964 to foster equitable principles for the integration of developing countries in the world economy. Developing countries, among which recently decolonized nations, were asking for international economic rules that would make them able to produce and trade goods equally to developed countries. In its early days,

[4] The opposition of the terms 'developed' (or 'advanced') and 'developing' countries is controversial since it reproduces, on the lexical ground, power and resources asymmetries between nations. It is also problematic since it reifies a linear and teleological reading of the economic history towards a one-path model of development (the convergence towards growth and financial capitalism). When it is possible, we prefer to use the term 'Global South' or the opposition between western, rich and creditor countries (Group B countries) versus poor, debtor and southern countries (the G77 countries). But, for practical reasons, and because actors themselves mobilize it, we also have recurse to this pair of terms in a reflexive way.

[5] Interviewees who wished to remain anonymous are mentioned with a number.

UNCTAD was a bastion of critical thinking, promoting systemic remedies on a variety of policy issues involving monetary policy, tariffs, support to industrialization, etc. However, starting in the 1980s, advanced countries waged and won a political battle to marginalize systemic financial issues from UNCTAD's mandate. UNCTAD then gradually became a technical agency, focused primarily on providing technical assistance to developing countries. This historical tension regarding the definition of the organization agenda must be understood against the background of a new division of labour among international organizations (IOs), where Bretton Woods institutions (e.g. the World Bank, IMF, and OECD) work 'upstream', providing macroscopic expertise and political analysis on how to organize debt markets and maintain debt sustainability, while IOs such as UNCTAD work 'downstream' and are often limited to supplying technical assistance (considered as a 'Global public good') to help developing states improve their management of public debt offices and 'rationalize' their financial and budgetary practices.[6] We will show that this division is a matter of controversy, both among IOs and within UNCTAD, between the Debt and Finance Development Branch and other sectors of UNCTAD.

In the next section (10.2), we show how UNCTAD's projects for structural reform of the international financial architecture, and underlying entangled problematization of debt, were contested and ultimately rejected in the 1970s. Such defeat was a blow to the transformative goals that UNCTAD had initially set to achieve. In the 1980s, UNCTAD gradually became a technical agency and its mandate was restricted to providing expert assistance and support to developing countries during their negotiations with the Paris Club. Meanwhile, the mandate to produce expertise at the macro-level was effectively transferred to the IMF and World Bank. In section 10.3, we focus on UNCTAD's technical activities and, in particular, the Debt Management Financial Analysis System (DMFAS). With DMFAS, UNCTAD went from promoting systemic change in international financial architecture to sponsoring the micro-management of domestic policies as a remedy to over indebtedness. But we also show that UNCTAD did not always restrict itself to doing 'downstream' work and technical assistance based on a country 'case by case' approach. While UNCTAD's recent project on fair principles of lending and borrowing principles conforms to the downstream work which is expected from UNCTAD, another project involving the creation of an international mechanism of sovereign debt restructuring functioned as a disturbance to this fragile upstream–downstream division of labour between IOs.

[6] The boundary and delineation of mandates between downstream and upstream levels appears in the official publications of UNCTAD, the IMF, and the World Bank. See for instance the internal audit performed by the Office of Internal Oversight Services on UNCTAD activities (OIOS, 2012).

10.2 Negotiating Debt at UNCTAD in the 1970s: A Tale of Two Competing Narratives

From the Bandung conference in 1955 to the UN resolution for a New International Economic Order (NIEO) in 1974, the Third World historically emerged as a 'political project' (Mortimer, 1980; Prashad, 2008; Rist, 2014). Key to this project were alternative economic policies designed to better integrate developing countries into the global economy. An important step in this direction was the creation of UNCTAD in 1964, initially as a conference in which measures would be discussed to reduce the trade disequilibrium at a global level between developing and developed countries. As the main international economic space for North–South 'dialogue', UNCTAD quickly became a contested site where Group B and G77 countries quarreled over a broad range of issues related to international trade and international finance.

The View From the Global South Countries: Institutional Remedies for Structural Debt Problems

A key protagonist in the early history of UNCTAD was its first Secretary General Raul Prebisch (1964–69), an Argentinean economist well known in academic and policy circles for his report *The Economic Development of Latin America and its Principal Problems* (1950). Prebisch was chiefly concerned with the effect of trade asymmetries on the economic development of the Third World. His main contribution (the 'Prebisch-Singer thesis') was to suggest that, over the long term, the price of primary goods decreases relative to the price of manufactured commodities, a decline causing the terms of trade of developing countries to deteriorate vis-à-vis developed nations. Key to his diagnostic was the observation that the 'benefits of technical progress had been distributed unequally between the center and the periphery' (Toye & Toye, 2004, p. 147). Prebisch's research gave scientific support to offset financial and trade asymmetries between nations. Combating such asymmetries and imbalances was at the heart of the battles of debt waged by some third-world economists and lawyers working within the so-called New International Economic Order (see also Dezalay, 1996).[7] While Mohammed Bedjaoui, Algerian lawyer and foremost NIEO proponent, was involved in debt issues as a reconquest for national sovereignty (and the right to nationalize natural

[7] This is reflected in this passage of the NIEO declaration requiring: 'just and equitable relationship between the prices of raw materials, primary commodities, manufactured and semi-manufactured goods exported by developing countries and the prices of raw materials, primary commodities, manufactures, capital goods and equipment imported by them with the aim of bringing about sustained improvement in their unsatisfactory terms of trade and the expansion of the world economy' (UN General Assembly, 1974).

resources of their territories industries) in postcolonial context,[8] UNCTAD economists tried to construct coordinated alternatives in international trade and financial architecture. Building on Prebisch's structural approach, over-indebtedness, incapacities of countries to repay their debts, and financial vulnerability in general were considered as a consequence of—and that could not be insulated from—structural disequilibrium between North and South in international trade.[9] Indeed, without international economic and financial regulation, developing countries were condemned to import mainly manufactured goods, and to export raw materials. Trade imbalances, monetary reserves, and developing countries states' budgets were considered as entangled in, and determined by these adverse international terms of trade, therefore making it necessary to construct South–South cooperative leverages. The Prebisch policy concepts, 'trade gap', 'saving gap', 'persistent external disequilibrium and vulnerability'[10] were closely related: international trade, monetary policies, and international flows of capital were different pieces of the same 'organic policy framework' (Pollock, 1989, p. 26).[11]

In 1964, in a confidential report to U Thant, General Secretary of the United Nations, on UNCTAD's first conference, Prebisch was 'optimistic about the prospects of the new organization', the greatest reason for optimism being the constitution of a new Third World force—the Group of 77: 'this political alliance could, he believed, exercise real pressure in pursuit of its members' interests in the years to come' (Pollock, Love & Kerner, 2006). The creation of UNCTAD raised 'a range of views within Washington's foreign-policy community' explains Edgar Dosman, Prebisch biographer:

> if some US officials were consistently negative [. . .], maintaining that domestic policies in developing countries were the entire source of the problem, there were others [. . .] who agreed that the industrial countries could not 'immunize themselves against what is happening in developing countries' and that 'a protracted polarization between rich and poor was a long-term threat to global and US security. (Dosman, 2008, p. 396)

[8] See Mallard and Waibel contributions to this volume.

[9] This is reflected in the portion of the NIEO declaration requiring: 'just and equitable relationship between the prices of raw materials, primary commodities, manufactured and semi-manufactured goods exported by developing countries and the prices of raw materials, primary commodities, manufactures, capital goods and equipment imported by them with the aim of bringing about sustained improvement in their unsatisfactory terms of trade and the expansion of the world economy' (UN General Assembly, 1974).

[10] The saving gap is the difference between mounting investment requirements and the domestic savings of the developing nations. External vulnerability refers to sudden changes in the centres' economic performance and signals, such as interest rates that can fragilize developing countries.

[11] The Prebisch Report had listed specific policies of international economic cooperation to close the trade gap: 'international commodity agreements, tariff preferences for Third World exports of manufactures, greater market access for primary products, expanded intra-Third World trade, new trade initiatives with Soviet Bloc countries, and new supplementary financing mechanisms to compensate for unexpected export shortfalls. All were too radical for Group B' (Dosman, 2008, p. 396).

In the late 1960s, UNCTAD launched a joint effort to measure the debt servicing issues facing developing countries and made recommendations regarding necessary changes with respect to the international financial architecture. During the preparation of the UNCTAD conference in Lima in 1971, proposals for a debt restructuring mechanism were discussed for the first time but were quickly rejected by developed countries represented in the Group B coalition (Rieffel, 2003, p. 137). Yet, the idea of a restructuring mechanism was not abandoned altogether. With the oil crisis of 1973, the debt position of developing countries further deteriorated and calls for international remedies to debt problems shortly returned to the table. This is evidenced in a UNCTAD report: 'It has been suggested that an examination of the characteristics of the various forms of capital flows available to developing countries would constitute a useful component of any examination of debt servicing countries.'[12] The view that debt problems were entangled with structural patterns of inequality between developed and developing countries was gaining momentum inside UNCTAD. Under a resolution adopted in 1973, UNCTAD formed a Group of experts on debt problems of developing countries. Two separate rounds of meetings took place in Geneva between May 1974 and March 1975 and between July 1977 and October 1978. A US delegate who attended the 1974–75 consultations reported to Washington that the delegates from developing countries voiced the 'proposition that there exists a general debt problem requiring international remedies', a proposition which the US delegate said produced only 'little dialogue' with developed countries.[13] Developing countries were calling for 'guidelines for debt relief and a new institutional framework for monitoring such guidelines'[14] and were adamant that, debt being a structural problem, institutional remedies were required as well as international forums to discuss the possibility of debt relief as a way to limit structural inequalities. Beyond the famous 'corridor joke' made by developed countries that understood UNCTAD to mean 'Under No Circumstances Take Any Decisions' or the rhetorical disregard of the US Assistant Secretary of State in the early years of UNCTAD—'who cares about UNCTAD? It doesn't matter in the slightest what is going on in the UN'[15]—we learn from the consultation of the diplomatic cables how developing countries' tactics of cooperation and attempts to unite, far from being neglected, were closely

[12] UNCTAD Archives, Trade and Development n°280-8, 'Ad hoc group of debt experts', 4-11-1974.

[13] US diplomacy Database, *Wikileaks*. Cable sent from the US Delegation in Geneva to the US Secretary of State in Washington DC, 13-05-1974. All cables reported in this paper were drawn from the Wikileaks' Public Library of US Diplomacy (PlusD). https://wikileaks.org/plusd/about/.

[14] US diplomacy Database, *Wikileaks*. Cable sent from the US Delegation in Geneva to the US Secretary of State in Washington DC, 13-05-1974.

[15] Thomas Mann was answering that when he received a cable asking whether the US should support Prebisch as the new Secretary-General of UNCTAD. Interview of Sternfeld, Ray, US State Department, realized by Dosman (2008, p. 396).

monitored by the US administration[16] and rich and western countries more generally.

The View From Western Countries: Technical Remedies for Domestic Debt Problems

The cables circulating between Washington DC, Geneva, and sometimes other Group B countries' capitals, show how this entangled problematization of debt was met with increasing hostile reactions from the US and Western countries between 1974 and 1978. During the negotiations, the cables—sometimes signed by Henry Kissinger himself—show a clear opposition to any mechanisms of debt restructuration. This is stated in a cable sent in 1975 by the State Department to the US Delegation in Geneva (USG): 'for the USG, debt relief is the least desirable of all approaches to the financing problem.'[17] In another cable sent by Washington to delegates in Geneva, the US manifested its intention to oppose any debt relief motions put forward by the G77: 'We see no possibility that the US could participate in schemes for generalized rescheduling of Low and Developing Countries (LDC) debt. This includes funds to refinance commercial debt as well as moratorium type proposals.'[18] This opposition extended to any initiative that could lay the foundation for any kind of framework for debt restructuring, such as an international conference on debt as asked in 1975 by G77 countries: 'The US does not support an international conference on debt. We fear that it would focus almost entirely on debt relief as a method of providing balance of payments support.'[19] With this statement, the US intended to maintain debates about debt restructuring within creditors clubs, such as the Paris Club.

Instead, the US government promoted a case-by-case approach, in which each country would take responsibility for managing its balance of payment and negotiating debt relief with its creditors. This logic of individual responsibility was entirely congruent with a *disentangled* problematization, wherein debt problems are caused by domestic factors at the local level, disconnected from international trade and

[16] For instance, Éric Helleiner (2014) explains that '*in the McCarthy years, ECLA* (Economic Commission or Latin America, former organization leaded by Prebisch that served of template for designing UNCTAD) *even fell under the scrutiny of the FBI and CIA, which considered the organization subversive*'. It is important to remember that in 1949, US opposition scuttled Prebisch's appointment at the IMF because of political suspicions: '*while no one could possibly argue that Prebisch was pro-communist, he was a Latin American who used terms such as "core" and "periphery" and was therefore not automatically "safe"*', explains Dosman (2008, p. 234).

[17] US diplomacy Database, *Wikileaks*. Cable sent from the US Secretary of State in Washington DC to the US Mission at OECD in Paris, 10-15-1975.

[18] US diplomacy Database, *Wikileaks*. Cable sent from the US Secretary of State in Washington DC to the US Delegation in Geneva, 10-31-1975.

[19] US diplomacy Database, *Wikileaks*. Cable sent from the US Secretary of State in Washington DC to the US Mission at OECD in Paris, 10-15-1975.

financial system. This alternative mode of constructing debt problems transpires in a 1974 cable sent by the US delegate in Geneva: '—internal management key to avoiding debt problem.—project evaluation very important.—collection data on and surveillance private debt essential.'[20] By erasing the structural problems affecting developing countries, this disentangled approach also helped justify market solutions to debt problems in lieu of a mechanism of debt restructuring. This is reflected in another cable from 1975: 'In our view mechanisms to increase LDC access to private capital markets should be viewed as completely different issue than debt service problems.'[21] It is in this precise context that the notion of 'creditworthiness' was first introduced in a 1975 cable in which US diplomats claimed that 'generalized debt relief could cause difficulties for those countries which currently have hopes of establishing creditworthiness adequate to borrow in the private capital markets.'[22] It is impossible to miss that the creditworthiness, an economic concept referring to the likelihood that a country will default on its debt obligations, was also used rhetorically in this debate to weaken the cohesion of the G77 coalition and promote an atomized conception of debt restructuring and rescheduling.

Hence, the main request of developing countries—an international debt restructuring mechanism—was being vehemently contested by the coalition of creditor countries led by the US. The centre stage of this debate was UNCTAD. Developed countries invested considerable effort to avoid any new role of UNCTAD regarding debt restructuring. In 1978, the US delegate in Geneva was summoned by Washington to 'forestall attempts to expand UNCTAD's limited mandate in areas such as monetary affairs, debt, and official transfers. We believe primary responsibility for these latter issues should continue to be the world bank, the IMF, and their joint development committee.'[23] This cable represents quite well the US preoccupation to make the issue of debt the exclusive preserve of the IMF and World Bank, two institutions on which the US and European countries traditionally wield considerable influence. The propositions made to extend UNCTAD's mandate also placed the Paris Club and its hosting institution, the French Treasury, in a delicate position. As reported in an emergency cable entitled 'adieu Paris for Paris club?', the French feared that the demise of the Paris Club would cause them to lose diplomatic leverage in international financial affairs.[24]

[20] US diplomacy Database, *Wikileaks*. Cable sent from the US Delegation in Geneva to the US Secretary of State in Washington DC, 13-05-1974.

[21] US diplomacy Database, *Wikileaks*. Cable sent from the US Secretary of State in Washington DC to the US Delegation in Geneva, 10-31-1975.

[22] US diplomacy Database, *Wikileaks*. Cable sent from the US Secretary of State in Washington DC to the US Missions in twenty-five countries, 02-28-1975.

[23] US diplomacy Database, *Wikileaks*. Cable sent from the US Embassy in Paris to the US Secretary of State in Washington DC and other US Missions abroad, 16-08-1977.

[24] US diplomacy Database, *Wikileaks*. Cable sent from the US Embassy in Paris to the US Secretary of State in Washington DC and other US Missions, 09-03-1976.

An interesting coalition of interests therefore emerges from examination of the diplomatic cables: the US diplomats, opposed to any new institutional arrangement on debt restructuring, teamed up with French civil servants who were concerned about the possible demise of the Paris Club in order to avoid any changes affecting UNCTAD's mandate. Mentioning the very good relations with the French Treasury officials, and impressed by the way the Paris Club worked, US diplomats agreed to strengthen the Paris Club as a method to keep UNCTAD at bay. In 1977, US officials reflected upon this Franco-American partnership in a cable portraying the French as:

> clearly preferring the creditor club mechanism to [. . .] other formal international mechanisms as the locale for debt rescheduling. These same [French] officials seem very open to ideas for strengthening the creditor club mechanism. [. . .] Now is the time to work closely with the French towards this objective.

The cable ends with the recommendation that: 'we begin a thorough discussion with the French as to the possible ways of strengthening the creditor club mechanism in general and adding to its credibility among the LDC's.'[25] Precluding any possibility of meaningful institutional change, but in need of a solution to close the discussion and avoid any further discussion on debt, the only concession made to the G77 countries was to grant UNCTAD observer access to Paris Club negotiations. This was the main gesture of goodwill from the US and Western allies to counter UNCTAD's proposals for structural rules of debt restructuring. Resolution 165 S-IX agreed on March 1975 allowed the debtor country to request UNCTAD to attend Paris Club meetings as an observer and support when the state present its case to the creditors. Before the resolution, the IMF and World Bank had routine access to Paris Club meetings, but not UNCTAD (Cosio-Pascal, 2009, p. 266). The first country to make use of this resolution was Peru in November 1978. The purpose of this resolution was twofold. First, it allowed debtor countries to use UNCTAD expertise and resources in their interactions with creditors at the Paris Club. Second, the resolution bolstered the legitimacy of the Paris Club among G77 countries.

To summarize, UNCTAD emerged weakened from the debt battles waged during the 1970s between developed and developing countries. Its objective to promote a mechanism of debt restructuration was defeated. The entangled problematization of debt was also weakened by Group B countries favouring a disentangled perspective in which the predicament of debt referred primarily to domestic problems affecting the borrowing state. Towards the end of the 1970s, UNCTAD operated under growing external pressures to tone down its

[25] US diplomacy Database, *Wikileaks*. Cable sent from the US Embassy in Paris to the US Secretary of State in Washington DC, 23-12-1977.

macro-perspective on institutional reform and focus on developing a technical expertise to assist developing countries in their negotiations with creditors and in their own management of debt. Initially an outpost of transformative change, in the 1980s UNCTAD gradually became a technical agency. This shift in mandate is not unusual because the mandate of IOs is typically ambiguous (Best, 2012), making IOs prone to 'organizational slippage' (Babb, 2003) and discretionary influence exerted on their activities by their shareholders (Pénet, 2018).[26] In the following section we examine how UNCTAD adapted to this new, restricted mandate. In particular, we examine UNCTAD's response to external pressures to separate its activities into two distinct areas of work and the request that priority be given to downstream (technical) expertise compared to upstream (structural and macro) expertise. This internal division of labour became gradually institutionalized at UNCTAD. Such priority given to technical assistance and state-borrowing capacity building is in accordance with disentangled problematization of debt and which emphasizes the need for developing states to adapt and adjust themselves (through a technical prism) to international capital market architecture, rather than an effort to reform international capital markets that would remain unchallenged and depoliticized.

10.3 'Downstream' Expertise Boundaries and the Individualization of Debtor Nations

Gradually from the 1980s, UNCTAD began to train experts in the field of 'technical assistance'. Regarding debt, technical assistance aims to improve and make credible the external debt of a borrowing country for private and multilateral investors.[27] The term became fashionable in the IO system following the 1982 Mexican debt crisis and the conditions that the IMF requested in exchange of loans (Woods, 2006). In 1981, UNCTAD launched an in-house programme of

[26] Organizational slippage can be extended, as Helleiner (2014) explains, to entities such as the US government and Bretton Woods institutions whose positions after the Second World War were actually favourable to the state-led development goals of Southern countries and the creation of a renewed international economic order. '*In its general aspirations, the NIEO proposal could be seen as an initiative that built upon the Bretton Woods foundations [...]: long-term international development finance, short-term compensatory financing for commodity export shortfalls, an international debt-restructuring mechanism, backing for infant industry trade protection, commodity price stabilization, the regulation of capital flows, and support for national autonomy in the pursuit of state-led development policies*'. The designation of such claims as 'radical' by Group B countries is a consequence of the burying process of the original Bretton Woods foundations.

[27] The 'maintenance of debt databases, debt-data validation, day-to-day debt transactions, reporting, debt statistics, operational risk management and basic debt analysis' provided by DMFAS at UNCTAD is part of the "Public debt transparency" agenda pursued by the G20, and the IMF and the World bank, and is considered as a solution role in ensuring effective risk assessment to support sustainable borrowing and lending practices.' IMF and World Bank, *G20 notes on strengthening public debt transparency*, 14 June 2018.

debt management: the Debt Management and Financial Analysis System (DMFAS) that aimed at strengthening states' individual capacities.

When 'Entrepreneurial Bureaucrats' Engage in Debt Politics

This programme was founded by Enrique Cosio-Pascal, a Mexican macroeconomist with a strong background in statistics—he was trained at ENSAE the French *Grande École* of statistics. During the interview we conducted with him, Cosio-Pascal explained that DFMAS was meant to 'assist countries in developing administrative, institutional and legal structures for effective debt management; providing technical assistance to government offices in charge of debt management; deploying and advancing debt analysis and management systems; and acting as a focal point for discussion and exchange of experiences in debt management'.[28] In funding and deploying technical assistance, UNCTAD sought to improve the information collection processes of financially strapped countries:

> The first difficulty found was the lack of information on external debt: how much did the country owe? To which creditors? In which currencies? When were the payments falling due, and in which currencies? Who were the national debtors besides the central Government? The idea of creating a computer-based debt management system emerged very naturally from this experience.[29]

Enrique Cosio-Pascal and his team performed the role of 'institutional entrepreneurs' (DiMaggio, 1988; Fligstein, 1997), designing innovative tools for debt management and methods of risk assessment. *The Economist* in 1992 deemed them 'entrepreneurial bureaucrats' for their active role in launching DMFAS, 'showing an unsuspected flair for innovation in putting computer power at the service of governments of poor countries'.[30] The newspaper was surprised to discover that 'even UNCTAD has adopted the rhetoric of enterprise, markets and "good management"', and that the 'agency is trying to live down its reputation as a sterile north-south talking shop and last bastion for those who champion an interfering state as the remedy for third-world poverty'.[31] As demands for DMFAS increased, the team's staff expanded accordingly: 'By end of the 1980s, the team was of around 20 persons and the number of countries benefiting from DMFAS technical co-operation around 30 to 40.'[32]

[28] UNCTAD website: http://unctad.org/divs/gds/dmfas/who/Pages/DMFAS- History.aspx

[29] Interview with Enrique Cosio-Pascal.

[30] 'The man from UNCTAD', *The Economist*, 4 July 1992.

[31] Ibid.

[32] DMFAS was first applied in 1981 to Bolivia, Costa Rica, Liberia, and Madagascar. The first version of DMFAS for personal computer was released in 1983. UNCTAD website: http://unctad.org/divs/gds/dmfas/who/Pages/DMFAS-History.aspx.

DMFAS was a highly technical activity involving computerized tools to produce quantitative diagnostics about debt sustainability. However, this technical turn at UNCTAD did not decrease the political statements but displaced them within the production of technical expertise itself. In the early 1980s, debt critical problematization and technical assistance coexisted inside UNCTAD as if it was a 'seamless fabric', to use William James' pragmatic philosopher concept. DMFAS experts continued to assume a critical perspective towards the expertise produced by multilateral organizations, for instance the IMF's characterization of issues of debt rescheduling as short-term 'liquidity' problems. Cosio-Pascal explains that UNCTAD perceived that the Latin American debt crises of the 1980s came from 'a long-term development problem, and not a liquidity problem as the IMF was addressing it'. But there was not much UNCTAD could do because it was not directly involved in the design of IMF lending programmes. But this technical expertise was not entirely useless either. During the 1980s, UNCTAD launched the first ('beta') version of a debt sustainability model. Cosio-Pascal explains that:

> In the 1980s, we developed a system in Lotus 1-2-3, the precursor to Excel, which could be brought to the Paris Club negotiations because laptops already existed. This module allowed us to calculate immediately if the balance of payments gap was closed after the relief granted by the Club. In a way, it was a precursor to a Debt Sustainability Model.

Turning DMFAS into a portable tool of debt sustainability analysis was the ingenious method that UNCTAD used to reclaim some of its political influence. Sociological research on quantification has showed that statistics can provide activist resources to legitimate alternative public policies (Bruno, Didier & Prévieux, 2015; Espeland, 2015). In the context of this chapter, UNCTAD tried to weaponize DMFAS and use debt sustainability analysis as 'numerical argumentation' (Deringer, 2018, p. 231) to shape the policy debate in the Paris Club. With models of debt sustainability, UNCTAD intended to bestow technical legitimacy to its political claims on the role of developmental factors in debt crises. Yet such political use of technical resources would be short-lived because UNCTAD was financially dependent upon Group B countries. DMFAS was not funded by the UN—which contributed only a fraction of UNCTAD's operational budget—but by country donors, particularly Group B and western countries which were reluctant to let UNCTAD make political use of sustainability models. Ultimately, the development of activist expertise at UNCTAD was brought to an end following a change of management in 1993. Cosio-Pascal recalls:

> Our [new] director, Roger Lawrence, an American, much less combative than our former Greek director, quickly gave up this task [computing sustainability models] for the World Bank. And I had to go to Washington to train the person

> on the module, who knew nothing about it... it was very offensive! Well, all this to get the money, but we left feathers there!

This organizational contest about who should compute sustainability models was not waged on technical but on political terms. As reflected in the quotation above, UNCTAD had sufficient technical expertise to compute debt sustainability models but its political premises and problematization of debt were seen as controversial. At the IMF and World Bank, debt sustainability models were computed under the alternative—disentangled—problematization of debt that treated debt problems not as structural problems but as domestic liquidity crises. From the 1980s onwards, statistical input prepared by the IMF and World Bank gave technical reality to the claim developed by creditor states (Group B) that 'developing countries were the "makers of their own misfortunes"' (Toye, 2014b, p. 66). According to that version, which would become hegemonic in the 1990s and 2000s, 'it was the absence of sensible economic policies that had been the cause of the debt crisis.' With UNCTAD ruled out of the preparation of debt sustainability analysis, the IMF and World Bank had free rein to spread 'Washington Consensus' policies (Williamson, 1990) in exchange for loans to countries experiencing debt problems. There is a profusion of research on IMF and World Bank conditionality (Babb & Carruthers, 2008). Critical studies have shown that, without the structural mechanism of debt restructuration, financially distressed countries in the developing world have often had no choice but to accept IMF conditional programmes and reorganize their economies and societies to conform to the neoliberal policies that Western countries favoured (Clift, 2018; Nelson, 2017; Stiglitz, 2002; Toye, 2014a). Some have linked the 1980s global diffusion of the Washington Consensus ideas to a process of 'neocolonial appropriation of the emergent global economy' (Bockman, 2015, p. 121). UNCTAD indirectly participated in this process. In line with Bockman, we show that technical expertise developed by UNCTAD was then repurposed by the group of advanced countries, the IMF, and the World Bank to give technical credence to neoliberal policies. Key to this process, we suggest, was the increasing specialization of the IO system between organizations dedicated to producing upstream expertise (e.g. the IMF and World Bank) and those confined to downstream work (e.g. UNCTAD). This boundary between mandates was further consolidated within UNCTAD in the recent years.

Disentangling the Technical Assistance from Political Claims

The initial 'politicization' of the DMFAS quickly eroded as UNCTAD began to confront pressures to distinguish clearly in its organizational structure between *upstream* (critical) and *downstream* (technical) expertise. UNCTAD's experts became progressively exclusively focused on technical assistance, detached from macro financial problematization. Debt sustainability model would inform on 'what needed to be done' without a corresponding effort to understand the broader political and historical context in which debt became a problem. This process of disentanglement of the technical from the political aspects of expertise reproduced within UNCTAD the demarcation between 'upstream' and 'downstream' that was being introduced in the IO system. This internal process was at play during the negotiations around the *Highly Indebted Initiative for Poor Countries* (HIPC). Developed countries urged UNCTAD to use input from DMFAS to calibrate programmes to ensure that poor countries would service their loans. DMFAS expert explain that the 'strong demarcation between the work of the DMFAS Program and the work of the Bretton Woods Institutions' really began to be felt in the early 2000s 'because the donors to the HIPC were very keen to ensure that the inputs that they put into HIPC were sustainable and the countries didn't end up in another situation of debt distress'. After a meeting in Oslo, it was decided that DMFAS experts would focus exclusively on downstream work (capacity-building programmes, i.e. debt data recording, reporting, debt statistics, data validation, and portfolio analysis through software) which was considered by DMFAS's executive team as UNCTAD's 'areas of comparative advantage':

> This was clear for us that we had a clear role to play in ensuring that anybody doing medium-term debt strategy or debt sustainability analysis or risk analysis would have the information, the best data available to be able to do that. We would train developing countries to understand what debt analysis was—what we call debt portfolio analysis—and what they have in their own database, and then be able to do basic debt analysis. And that was in preparation for them, following on with more sophisticated analysis and training from the Bretton Woods Institutions under, principally, the Debt Management Facility. So we became implementing partners to the Debt Management Facility. It was a small part of what we do, but it enabled us to participate in Debt Management Facility activities.[33]

Through DMFAS, UNCTAD became a technical 'partner' of Bretton Woods Institutions (the IMF and World Bank), while being financially compensated for the expertise they supplied. UNCTAD's contribution in this partnership was built around a strictly technical mandate, without trying 'to go into the areas which were demarcated as upstream', emphasizes one expert of DMFAS.

[33] Interviewee number 5, high level expert for DMFAS, UNCTAD.

To ensure that the political and the technical were segregated at UNCTAD, organizational buffers were put in place to clearly distinguish between upstream and downstream work. Upstream work is done within the Debt and Development Finance Branch, a department composed of a dozen economists. This team of researcher is what remains of the critical legacy of UNCTAD. These economists do not have access to DMFAS data for confidentiality reasons, as explained by UNCTAD officials: 'if you, people in the Branch, want the data, ask the country for it. Don't ask the DMFAS Program for it.'[34] The only data that DMFAS is allowed to share with upstream analysts are data computed by the IMF and the World Bank which now also have the monopoly over the preparation of debt sustainability analysis. This separation is also understood by DMFAS managers as a way to show to donors (long-standing donors' countries such as Norway and Switzerland) and Group B countries that DMFAS is not a political device but purely a technical one. The Debt Branch experts (upstream work at UNCTAD) interpreted this demarcation as a way to protect these financing sources: 'DMFAS wanted to sort of defend its autonomy (from the Debt Branch) to protect it.' This statement is further compounded by other Debt Branch economists explaining that DMFAS was reluctant to share data with UNCTAD's upstream level because Group B donor countries refused any UNCTAD mandate on macro questions related to debt:

> The donors, the Norwegians, but all the group of advanced economies, group B or whatever, all the group of advanced economies do not want UNCTAD to do analytical work on macro-economic issues [...] So this group of countries said: 'that's not UNCTAD mandate, that's the mandate of the IMF and the 'World Bank', so you should not do that'. So, that we got there and asked: 'how do you do your DSA?' or when we say whether Argentina or Gabon debt is sustainable: it's no! That's what really Group B countries do not want UNCTAD to do.[35]

A former expert of the Debt Branch alternatively interpreted this internal demarcation between upstream and downstream work as 'a managerial MBA-approach to the world'.[36] Other UNCTAD employees emphasized that dependence upon external sources of funding created job insecurity at DMFAS.[37] Despite these challenges, UNCTAD has sought to further insulate downstream work at DMFAS from the upstream work performed in the Debt Branch (*upstream*). By reaffirming this demarcation, UNCTAD wishes to preserve the neutrality and 'objectivity' of DMFAS against the political influence of Debt Branch experts:

[34] Interviewee number 3, expert for DMFAS, UNCTAD.
[35] Interviewee number 2. Former Debt Branch economist, UNCTAD.
[36] Ibid.
[37] Interviewee number 2 and Interviewee number 4, Expert for the Debt Branch, UNCTAD.

> DMFAS is really non-political in a sense that it happens at very low levels in terms of operational issues. But we don't get involved in the political discussions. We did see that at consecutive UNCTAD conferences, where there have been questions of UNCTAD's work in the area of finance coming from developed countries, there was never a question about the work of the DMFAS Program. And the reason being that we, what we do, is non-political. We don't get involved in the politics. It's very important for us to be able to deliver, to say: 'politics change and the wins of what's important are not changed'.[38]

The division between upstream and downstream—which Enrique Cosio-Pascal identifies as the opposition between 'those who go into the field and are in contact with people who work in ministries', and those who are 'theorists or think tankers working in University cabinet'—has further consolidated at UNCTAD in the recent years. Boundary work inside UNCTAD's Debt Branch (between upstream and downstream expertise) disentangles technical assistance from political critique. Such boundary work was how UNCTAD adapted practically to the expectations of creditors (donor countries and capital market organizations): first, the expectation that debtor countries comply with requirements of transparency and the production of 'sound' public finance data; second, the pressure to restrict the perimeter of UNCTAD activities and depoliticize its activities.

When the Debt Branch Strikes Back

Therefore, what remains of the legacy of UNCTAD and the G77 initial project for an alternate economic and financial order? The changes analysed above suggest that UNCTAD, once a bastion of critical thinking in the 1960s and 1970s, has today become almost indistinguishable from the IMF and World Bank. This process of normalization is not fully complete nor entirely accepted inside UNCTAD. In 2006, UNCTAD began to work towards the establishment of principles that would regulate and give a soft framework to sovereign debt restructuring. This project, made possible through a donation of 5 million krone from the Norwegian Government, is overseen by an economist specialist of emerging countries who joined UNCTAD in 1990 and who ran the Debt and Finance Development Branch. This project involved several high-level experts representing different UNCTAD stakeholders: lawyers, economists, the private sector, NGOs, and IOs. Important names were involved such as Anna Gelpern, Mitu Gulati, and Lee Buchheit as lawyers (offering pro-bono services) and the

[38] Interview with DMFAS expert.

economist Patrick Bolton.[39] The project also called upon a group of 'advisory countries' to provide expertise. The head of the Debt Branch mobilized diplomatic skills to bypass the reticence of the US Treasury, otherwise known as the 'guardian of the temple' against any kind of debt restructuring mechanism (Gelpern & Gulati, 2006; Weidemaeir & Gulati, 2014). The principles of 'Responsible sovereign lending and borrowing' were published in a 2010 report (UNCTAD, 2010). They comprise the principles of 'Honesty; Realistic assessments; Pre-disbursement diligence; Post-disbursement diligence; Aligned incentives; Sanctions regimes; and Renegotiation' for the lenders. The duties of the borrowers are described as 'Legal obligations; Candor; Disclosure; Internal approvals; Debt management offices; Project due diligence; Preparation for debt management'. With these principles, UNCTAD claimed that lenders, just like borrowers, have responsibilities for situations of over-indebtedness.

With new funding from the government of Norway, UNCTAD set to work in 2013 on a new institutional project on debt restructuring. The consensus-building process (reached through expert group meetings) seemed reasonably advanced, but, on August 2014, at the end of the 69th UN General Assembly, the Argentinian delegation at the United Nations went to the delegation of Bolivia, which held the presidency of the G77 in 2015, and asked for its support. Cristina Kirchner's government was then under pressure from vulture funds whose actions threatened to sabotage the restructuring agreement reached by the government with 93 per cent of bondholders (Deforge & Lemoine, 2018). In this context of economic and legal uncertainties, the Argentinian delegation forced the adoption of a resolution promoting a debt restructuring mechanism at the UN General Assembly without seeking prior consensus of the international community at large. Indeed, this discretionary move was strongly opposed by both Bretton Woods institutions and Group B countries. As a former Debt Branch head recalled:[40]

> Argentina needed help. They wanted to win the case and they said: 'Could you go and be our friend and testify?' But [at the UN] you cannot side with one country, that's the UN rule. So, I told the Minister 'I can't do that, and he was disappointed'. But I said we could always do some work, because with analytical work we supported them a great deal. They were so anxious, and they pushed for the debt resolution in the UN. [. . .] And, of course, with the US there, they didn't like that.

[39] Lee Buchheit was the Cleary Gottlieb chief lawyer in the negotiations to restructure Iraq's large foreign debts after the 2003 war. Mitu Gulati (a contributor to this volume) and Anna Gelpern are experts of collective action clauses. Patrick Bolton has worked in the beginning of the 2000s with IMF economists on research trying to apply corporate law (such as the law on bankruptcy) to international economic governance.

[40] Interviewee number 6, former Debt Branch Head.

An interviewee of the Debt Branch at UNCTAD also remembers that there was 'a fear of donors' to see DMFAS—as part of UNCTAD—associated with an Argentine initiative considered as too critical and politically radical.[41] Another former Head also recalls the surprise of the Norwegians when they discovered that the UNCTAD work on principles of responsible sovereign lending and borrowing was being used by Argentina against vultures in US courts. The head of the Debt Branch also regretted such politicization of UNCTAD expertise, which had been conceived to be used in a non-controversial 'transparent and inclusive' manner: 'I read through (the draft of Argentine resolution) and I said: "OK, that would kill our process." Because what we wanted was to gradually build support. You know, you get all these people's support, and then you can move to kind of universally accepted principles.'[42] The increasing concern of developing countries to maintain market access through measures of creditworthiness also explains the reticence to support Argentina. UNCTAD was also unwilling to sponsor a project which donors clearly disapproved of. As a result, UNCTAD backtracked and began to emphasize the principles for 'responsible borrowing', in continuation with the report issued in 2010 and restated in 2012 (UNCTAD, 2012).

In this debate over mechanisms of debt restructuring, emerging countries had to choose between defending their interest as individual borrowers seeking access to private capital markets and their collective interest in developing a restructuring process. Brazil was clearly supportive of such a project conducted by the UN—emphasizing the democratic character of the UN 'based on one country one vote'. But China voiced concerns, regretting the absence of advanced countries and international finance institutions in the process. China also stressed that

> The Committee should uphold the spirit of democracy during the process of intergovernmental negotiations and that all members should participate. [...] The Committee needs also to get support from professional institutes, as strong expertise is needed on this matter. As the work of the IMF and UNCTAD has been recognized, the World Bank and the IMF should contribute to the work of the Committee.[43]

The representative of Singapore also criticized the call to adopt a sovereign debt restructuring mechanism at the UN by reminding that 'the IMF would have been in a better position to address sovereign debt restructuring issues and such a discussion should have taken place under the auspices of the IMF.'

[41] Interviewee number 4.

[42] Interviewee number 6. Geneva, September 2018.

[43] Debates on the UN resolution on debt restructuring, September 2014 (General Assembly Sixty-eighth session, 107th plenary meeting Tuesday, 9 September 2014, 3 p.m. New York, Official Records).

Solidarity among G77 members—what James Toye (2014b, p. 167) calls the 'political façade of unity' was crumbling. The interest that developing countries shared collectively to promote international reform faced a classical collective action dilemma and a 'freeriding' temptation.[44] These countries were conflicted: on the one hand, they felt a duty to safeguard the legacy of the New International Economic Order and the solidarity principles anchored in the history of non-aligned countries and on the other hand, they were under strong economic incentives to behave selfishly by conforming to the measures of creditworthiness designed by Bretton Woods institutions. Solidarity between developing countries, in other words, was undermined by the dynamic that goes with the idea that states should become, to quote Giselle Datz (2008), 'market players'. At first glance, Argentina and the G77 won a diplomatic victory with the vote in favour of its UN resolution at the General Assembly: 134 countries voted in favour of the resolution, forty-one abstained, and six voted against (United States, Japan, Germany, Israel, the United Kingdom, and Canada). But beyond this vote, all the other Member States of the European Union abstained, 'a polite way of saying no', according to an official of the French Ministry of Foreign Affairs. Even if the UN resolution was accepted, and voted with a large majority of developing countries, it also brought to an end the 'upstream' political work of UNCTAD:

> So we support them throughout, but our ongoing work on these principles definitely shelved. Because after this you have this political impasse, because developed countries thought there was no good will to discuss, so they just withdrew, so our whole thing came to a kind of a stop after this 2014–15 UNGA Resolution.[45]

This vote on Argentina's proposal at the UN can be understood as a Pyrrhic victory, since it was adopted without the agreement of a large part of the international community and, as a result, failed to translate into any operational, policy, or concrete action. It was even interpreted as an organizational defeat, since it reproduced, rather than challenged, the distribution of mandate and activity between Bretton Woods institutions and UNCTAD. For Stéphanie Blankenburg, the current Head of the Debt Branch, it also publicly showed how costly (or even impossible) it is for developing countries to aspire to act in upstream and political areas of debt:

> It was impossible not to associate the UNCTAD principles with Argentina's initiative, but the way they managed the negotiations could have been more

[44] Already identified, for instance by Éric Helleiner on the mystery of the non-existence of a sovereign debt restructuring mechanism, SDRM.

[45] Interview with former Debt Branch Head. Interviewee number 6.

sophisticated. But on the other hand, if the advanced countries do not want it, they do not want it, you can always find an apology afterward.

The institutional defeat of UNCTAD with this resolution—compared to the mid-term and long-term consensus the organization was building—also refers to the structural impossibility for developing countries to interfere with macro issues such as debt sustainability, international financial architecture that remains the preserve of Bretton Woods institutions. UNCTAD upstream work is, at best, reduced to non-operational soft law principles and, at worse, disqualified, while giving support to the politically radical initiative of Argentina and the G77. When Mauricio Macri was elected president in 2016, Argentina's neoliberal government attempted to reconstruct its reputation in international finance by agreeing to repay all creditors, including the more aggressive holdouts, and based its economic policies and reconquest of sovereignty on foreign investment. Ironically, a few years later, the country had to comply with a new IMF bailout programme. After the election of Kirchnerist Alberto Fernandez, Argentina was once again complying with foreign creditors in order to restructure its debt.

10.4 Conclusion

The history of debt battles at UNCTAD can be seen as following the conflict between the two problematizations of debt imagined by the Global South and Western countries. In its early days, UNCTAD promoted an entangled perspective that construed debt problems in close relation with structural and historical problems affecting developing countries. This diagnostic served as the justification for an ambitious agenda for an institutional reform at international level. Evidently, this representation of debt problems ran up against the financial interests of Western creditors who favoured a disentangled perspective in which the problem of over-indebtedness afflicting the Third World was seen as a local predicament requiring domestic fixes such as the micro-management of public finances. We propose the image of a *pendulum* to suggest that these two problematizations varied in strength inside UNCTAD according to shifting dynamics of power within and outside UNCTAD. Conflicts of debt problematization (between a critical emphasis placed upstream on structural and political problems and a downstream focus on technical assistance) reflect the dilemmas that troubled the G77 group of developing countries.

From 1974 to 1978, UNCTAD invested considerable effort to link debt issues with structural problems and to propose solutions to amend the international financial architecture. The failure of such attempts led to the repurposing of a large part of UNCTAD's mandate from that of a political agency, concerned with broad and political reform of the international financial order, to that of a technical agency tasked with developing technical expertise. The separation inside the Debt Branch of UNCTAD between upstream (policy expertise) and downstream (technical expertise) has been consolidating since the end of the 1990s. Ever since, UNCTAD has been repeatedly reminded of its own illegitimacy whenever promoting upstream expertise (debt sustainability, macro financial architecture, and debt restructuring), which was viewed as the sole prerogative of Bretton Woods Institutions.

This tension over the scope of UNCTAD's mandate stresses the disappointed hopes of the agenda for a New International Economic Order and illustrates the Global South debt revolution that wasn't. Countries formerly known as Third World nations had nurtured the hope that the context of decolonization would usher in a new international era where more reciprocal financial exchange would put an end—or at least diminish—global financial asymmetries of power. Instead, developing countries, with the tacit contribution of UNCTAD, are under a neoliberal regime of continuous surveillance in which rituals of verification and forced demonstrations of accountability govern the relationships between creditors and debtors. With the failure of the NIEO, the developing world no longer presents a united front. The sense of solidarity between countries which have experienced colonial control during the nineteenth and twentieth centuries has eroded. Developing countries perceive themselves as market players whose main objective is to pursue individual strategies of debt capacity building and creditworthiness in a global capital market system. A useful perspective is provided by Giselle Datz who showed that Nigeria developed in 2000 a semi-autonomous Debt Management Office to promote the 'good image of Nigeria as a disciplined and organized nation, capable of managing its assets and liabilities' (Datz, 2008, p. 41). As a rule, since the 1980s and 1990s, developing countries are no longer prepared or even willing to promote macroeconomic alternatives, even if they have vested interest in the success of such initiatives. For developing countries, the term sovereignty has dramatically changed from the 1960s and 1970s, when sovereignty was equated with the independence movements, to the present context where sovereignty means securing access to private capital markets and conforming to international measures of creditworthiness.

Of course, twenty-first-century defaulters are no longer subject to military aggression, but they confront no less intrusive tools of international redress and pressure to conform to their international creditors. The rise of technical assistance since the 1980s has paved the way for international programmes and pedagogical tools sponsored by IOs to 'educate' developing countries and turn them into auto-disciplined and responsible market players. In the current landscape of IOs, UNCTAD retains some idiosyncratic features. The secretariat provides technical assistance to developing countries in their negotiations with creditors. But this assistance, as helpful as it might be, is a far cry from UNCTAD's historical mission to reduce asymmetries of power between developing and developed nations and promote structural reform of the international financial order. The marginalization of UNCTAD's critical work and, conversely, the developments of 'technical assistance' programmes, have contributed to the naturalization of a pro-market political agenda. Legitimate national sovereignty strategies are downplayed in terms of debt cancellation, or only marginally at the Paris Club with the technical help of UNCTAD. Sophisticated lawyers trained in global financial centres are now advising developing countries while they issue sovereign bonds governed by New York or London laws, replacing the great postcolonial legal architects in the tradition of Bedjaoui (Anghie, 2015; Mallard, 2019). Without strong cooperation in order to promote structural alternatives to the current international financial architecture, Global South countries have no other choice than pursuing individual strategies of creditworthiness to remedy debt problems.

References

Anghie, A. (2015). 'Legal Aspects of the New International Economic Order'. *Humanity: An International Journal of Human Rights, Humanitarianism, and Development*, 6(1), 145–58.

Babb, S. (2003). 'The IMF in Sociological Perspective: A Tale of Organizational Slippage'. *Studies in Comparative International Development*, 38(2), 3–27.

Babb, S. & Carruthers, B. (2008). 'Conditionality: Forms, Function, and History'. *Annual Review of Law and Social Science*, 4, 13–29.

Best, J. (2012). 'Ambiguity and Uncertainty in International Organizations: A History of Debating IMF Conditionality'. *International Studies Quarterly*, 56(4), 674–88.

Bockman, J. (2015). 'Socialist Globalization against Capitalist Neocolonialism: The Economic Ideas behind the New International Economic Order'. *Humanity: An International Journal of Human Rights, Humanitarianism, and Development*, 6(1), 109–28.

Bruno, I., Didier, E. & Prévieux, J. (2015). *Statactivisme: Comment lutter avec des nombres*. Paris: La découverte: Zones.

Clift, B. (2018). *The IMF and the Politics of Austerity in the Wake of the Global Financial Crisis*. Oxford: Oxford University Press.

Cosio-Pascal, E. (2009). 'Paris Club Intergovernmental Relations in Debt Restructuring', in B. Herman et al. (Eds.), *Overcoming Developing Country Debt Crises* (pp. 231–76). Oxford: Oxford University Press.

Datz, G. (2008). 'Governments as Market Players: State Innovation in The Global Economy'. *Journal of International Affairs*, 62(1), 35–49.

Deforge, Q. & Lemoine, B. (2018). 'Faillite d'État et Fragilité Juridique. L'Argentine Face à L'ordre Financier International'. *Actes de la Recherche en Sciences Sociales*, 221–2(1), 38–63.

Deringer, W. (2018). *Calculated Values: Finance, Politics, and the Quantitative Age*. Cambridge: Harvard University Press.

Dezalay, Y. (1996). *Dealing in Virtue—International Commercial Arbitration & the Construction of a Transnational Legal Order*, 2nd edition. Chicago: University of Chicago Press.

DiMaggio, P. (1988). 'Interest and Agency in Institutional Theory', in L.G. Zucker (Ed.), *Institutional Patterns and Organizations: Culture and Environment* (pp. 3–21). Ballinger.

Dosman, E. (2008). *The Life and Times of Raúl Prebisch, 1901–1986*. Montreal, Quebec: McGill-Queen's Press-MQUP.

Espeland, W. (2015). 'Narrating rs', in R. Rottenburg, S.E. Merry, S.J. Park & J. Mugler (Eds.), *The World of Indicators: The Making of Governmental Knowledge through Quantification* (pp. 56–75). Cambridge: Cambridge University Press.

Fligstein, N. (1997). 'Social Skill and Institutional Theory'. *American Behavioral Scientist*, 40(4), 397–405.

Foucault, M. (1984). *Histoire de la sexualité. Volume 2: L'usage des plaisirs*. Paris: Gallimard.

Gelpern A. & Gulati, M. (2006). 'Public Symbol in Private Contract: A Case Study', *Washington University Law Review*, 84, 1649–60.

Helleiner, E. (2014). *Forgotten Foundations of Bretton Woods: International Development and the Making of the Postwar Order*. Ithaca, NY: Cornell University Press.

Laurent B. (2017). *Democratic Experiments. Problematizating Nanotechnology and Democracy in Europe and the United States*. Cambridge Massachusetts: The MIT Press.

Mallard, G. (2019). *Gift Exchange: The Transnational History of a Political Idea*. Cambridge University Press.

Mortimer, R. (1980). *The Third World Coalition In International Politics*. New York: Praeger Publishers.

Nelson, S.C. (2017). *The Currency of Confidence: How Economic Beliefs Shape the IMF's Relationship with Its Borrowers*. Ithaca, NY: Cornell University Press.

OIOS (2012). 'Audit of UNCTAD Technical Cooperation Project "Strengthening the Debt Management Capacity of Developing Countries"', *Internal Audit Division* by the Office of Internal Oversights Services, 19 December 2012.

Olson, R.K. (2013). *U.S. Foreign Policy and the New International Economic Order: Negotiating Global Problems, 1974–1981*. London and New York: Bloomsbury Publishing.

Pénet, P. (2018). 'The IMF Failure that wasn't: Risk Ignorance During the European Debt Crisis'. *British Journal of Sociology*, 69(4), 1031–55.

Pollock, D. (1989). 'Raul Prebisch as a Theorician', in *Raul Prebisch: Thinker and Builder*. New York: UNCTAD, United Nations.

Pollock, D., Love J. & Kerner D. (2006). 'Prebisch at UNCTAD', in R. Prebisch, *Power, Principle and the Ethics of Development*. Buenos Aires: Institute for the Integration of Latin America and the Caribbean.

Prashad V. (2008). *The Darker Nations: A People's History of the Third World*. New York: The New Press.

Prebisch, R. (1950). *The Economic Development of Latin America and its Principal Problems*. United Nations Department of Economic Affairs.

Rieffel, A. (2003). *Restructuring Sovereign Debt: The Case for Ad Hoc Machinery*. Brookings Institution Press.

Rist, G. (2014). *The History of Development: From Western Origins to Global Faith*, 4th edition. London and New York: Zed Books.

Stiglitz, J.E. (2002). *Globalization and its Discontents*. New York: Norton.

Toye, J. (2014a). 'Assessing the G77: 50 Years after UNCTAD and 40 Years after the NIEO'. *Third World Quarterly*, 35(10), 1759–74.

Toye, J. (2014b). *UNCTAD at 50, A Short History*. Switzerland: United Nations.

Toye, J. & Toye, R. (2004). *The UN and global political economy: trade, finance, and development*. Bloomignton and Indianapolis: Indiana University Press.

United Nations General Assembly (UNGA) (1974). Resolution 3201 (S-VI), May 1st. 'Declaration on the Establishment of a New International Economic Order'. http://www.un-documents.net/s6r3201.htm (Accessed 9 March 2020).

United Nations General Assembly (UNGA) (2015). Resolution A/69/L.84, September 10. 'Basic Principles on Sovereign Debt Restructuring Processes'. https://digitallibrary.un.org/record/804641/files/A_RES_69_319-EN.pdf (Accessed 9 March 2020).

UNCTAD (2006). *UNCTAD: A brief Historical Overview*.

UNCTAD (2010). 'Responsible Sovereign Lending and Borrowing', *Discussion Papers*, n°198, April.

UNCTAD (2012). *Principles on Promoting Responsible Sovereign Lending and Borrowing*.

Weidemaeir M. & Gulati, M. (2014). 'A People's History of Collective Actions Clauses', *Virginia Journal of International Law*, 54, 1–95.

Williamson, J. (1990). 'What Washington Means by Policy Reform', in J. Williamson (Ed.), *Latin American Cadjustment: How Much Has Happened* (pp. 7–20). Washington DC: Peterson Institute for International Economics.

Woods, N. (2006). *The Globalizers: The IMF, the World Bank, and Their Borrowers*. 1st edition. Ithaca, NY: Cornell University Press.

SECTION 4

THE LEGALIZATION OF SOVEREIGN DEBT DISPUTES BETWEEN WISH AND REALITY (1990s–PRESENT)

11

Placing Contemporary Sovereign Debt

The Fragmented Landscape of Legal Precedent and Legislative Pre-emption

Giselle Datz

11.1 Introduction

Sovereign debt issuance encompasses a variety of not only fiscal and financial, but also legal manoeuvres. Although often overlooked in analyses of the political economy of debt, differences in the common 'template' of a bond contract crucially inform the legal rules of the debt game (Choi et al. 2013). Since the 1990s, and given more restricted applications of sovereign immunity laws, 'foreign governments that default on their debts can be hauled into national courts just like private debtors' (Weidemaier & Gelpern, 2013, p. 190; Weidemeier, 2014; Mustafa & Molle, 2016). As a result, beyond assumptions about reputational punishments, sovereign debt litigation has added more uncertainty and potentially high costs to the post-default scenario. This is thanks to a particular breed of creditors whose audacity and tenacity have pushed the boundaries of ad hoc sovereign debt restructurings, raising concerns among multilateral institutions, sovereign debtors, non-governmental organizations, and governments in key financial centres about their potential disruption of sovereign debt restructurings and relief programmes.

In this context, legislators in Belgium, London, and Paris have approved laws that attempt to restrict these creditors' scope of action since 2005. These initiatives were sparked by several legal battles between holdout creditors and distressed sovereign debtors, including Argentina's experience with a New York district court's ruling in favour of NML Capital (a hedge fund which chose not to participate in either the 2005 or 2010 debt restructurings of the bonds defaulted on in 2001). Because sovereign debt is notoriously difficult to enforce as sovereigns can keep their assets far from the reach of creditors, the turning point in the case came when the New York District Court judge issued an injunctive order declaring that financial intermediaries who assisted Argentina in its attempt to repay the exchanged bonds bondholders without also repaying NML would be in contempt of court. Forced to pay NML in full if it expected to have its payments to

Giselle Datz, *Placing Contemporary Sovereign Debt: The Fragmented Landscape of Legal Precedent and Legislative Pre-emption* In: *Sovereign Debt Diplomacies: Rethinking Sovereign Debt from Colonial Empires to Hegemony.* Edited by: Pierre Pénet and Juan Flores Zendejas, Oxford University Press (2021). © Oxford University Press.
DOI: 10.1093/oso/9780198866350.003.0012

creditors of exchanged bonds processed, Argentina defaulted again in 2014. The injunctive order 'cast a shockingly wide net' (Samples, 2014, p. 81) in a 'judicial gamble' that turned the tables of the sovereign debt game to the creditors' advantage (Weidemeier & Gelpern, 2013; Guzman, 2016).

It is clear that litigation between debtor governments and holdout creditors are originated from challenges to contractual stipulations and their judicial interpretations. Contracts are governed by the law of specified jurisdictions. However, despite the many judicious studies of the Argentine court saga, the role of place in debt restructurings has remained relatively neglected. While debt in its contractual form is place (jurisdiction)-specific, understandings of sovereign debt as part of the global financial machinery highlight its volatile and footloose nature. Even despite local legislative developments aiming at pre-empting 'vulture funds' from hijacking restructuring processes, the dots have yet to be connected, mapping out the salience and limitations of local authority with extraterritorial ambitions in sovereign debt processes. Judicial outcomes in holdout litigation and 'anti-vulture funds' laws, it is argued here, instantiate sovereign bond finance and shed light onto the scope of fragmentation that characterizes today's sovereign debt regime. Indeed, place matters not only when it comes to distinct sites for arbitration of and deliberations on major financial transactions; it is also indicative of specific sites of legislative innovation and diffusion. The analysis developed here reveals two paradoxical conclusions. First, while the specificity of contractual choice of law grounds debt dynamics in particular jurisdictions, they can render these dynamics more uncertain (despite the diffusion of collective action clauses) given the newly reinvigorated injunctive 'remedy' used in Argentina's legal saga and its extraterritorial ambitions. Second, debt procedures institutionalized *de facto* or *de jure* in certain jurisdictions do not do away with the need for some global coordination given the potential for jurisprudential overlap and disruptions to the payments pipeline that render custodians and clearing systems key sites for enforcement of legal orders on recalcitrant debtors.

Furthermore, the outcome of individual debt-related international litigation sets important spillover effects that spur action towards redefining contracts and restructuring frameworks to pre-empt the kind of protracted litigation that Argentina experienced in US courts. Even if holdout creditor litigation in foreign courts is not the norm in sovereign debt restructurings, beyond a legal precedent in a traditional sense, spillover effects from international litigation informally institutionalize deviant outcomes in the way debt processes are reconsidered internationally. The methodological implication is that protracted international litigation and 'anti-vulture funds' laws are revealing of instances in which outlier cases become 'trend setters', sparking new strategic arrangements that try to prevent a similar occurrence in the future (Ahram & Datz, 2014, Datz and Corcoran 2019).

11.2 Bringing Place Back In

Since the Brady Plan of the 1980s, when debts defaulted on earlier in that decade were securitized, bonds replaced bank loans as the primary instrument for emerging markets to access foreign and domestic credit (Edwards & Mishkin, 1995). This widespread process of debt securitization was part of a new phase of globalization, marked particularly by financial deregulation and capital market integration. On the one hand, emerging markets were able to access credit more broadly, securing debt deals under different laws (domestic and foreign), in different currencies and with various maturity structures. On the other hand, domestic policy autonomy was in part constrained by the whims of often overly reactive global investors (Strange, 1995; Maxfield, 1998). Deviating from the preferences of global investors for monetary stability and fiscal discipline could ignite capital outflows, increase the cost of credit, or both (Strange, 1995; Mosley, 2003; Brooks et al. 2015; Kaplan & Thomsson, 2014). In these accounts of deliberate or inadvertent convergence in market movements and policy reforms subject to overwhelming and inescapable financial volatility, place was easily blurred. Notable exceptions were studies of global cities, seen as post-Fordist 'nodes of accumulation' (Brenner, 1998) where the otherwise amorphous process of globalization could be directly scrutinized (Sassen, 1991).

To be sure, as Flandreau et al. (2009, p. 1) remark, this 'emergence of global finance was really a re-emergence'. By 1900, 'the use of modern communications to transmit prices; the development of a very broad array of private debt and equity instruments, and the widening scope for insurance activities; the expanding role of government bond markets internationally; and the more widespread use of forward and futures contracts, and derivative securities' spread to and linked major economic financial centres from Europe to the Americas, Asia, and Africa. Nonetheless, the evolution of international capital markets has not been linear. Rather, not only has broader financial integration been interrupted by domestic political imperatives that led to protectionism and capital controls, but, beyond macroeconomic policy switches, the 'microeconomics of financial globalisation' has endured marked changes (Flandreau, 2017; Obstfeld & Taylor, 2003).

When it comes to foreign debt, as Flandreau (2017, p. 160) argues, 'the way the business of originating and distributing foreign debt is organised' has gone through a 'profound transformation' in the twentieth century. Before the interwar era, underwriters functioned as 'gatekeepers of liquidity and certification agencies'. While the less prestigious underwriters originated bonds most likely to default, more reputable intermediaries dealt with less risky bonds. In contrast, thanks to the rise of rating agencies who provide assessments of sovereign risk, today 'defaults are randomly distributed across underwriters', who have 'become aggressive competitors in a new Speculative Grade market' that did not exist in the past (Flandreau et al. 2009, p. 7). The underwriting business today has become less concentrated among a few firms that, given economies of scale, charge less for their services (independently of bond spreads) than their institutional ancestors. These historical discontinuities among financial intermediaries in the sovereign bond market are also suggestive of the blurriness of place in global finance. Although 'gatekeeping' tasks are concentrated among a few rating agencies headquartered in New York City, a more diversified market where tenuous relationships between issuers and underwriters are the norm, suggests that location is often either overlooked or taken for granted when it comes to the 'microeconomics of foreign currency debt issuance' (Flandreau et al. 2009, p. 1).

For sovereign debtors, place is pertinent particularly when it comes to debt issuance and decisions about currency denomination, choice of law, and stock market listings (de Fontenay et al. 2016). Regarding the currency denomination of sovereign bonds place matters in a 'sinful' way. Eichengreen, Hausmann & Panizza (2005) explained that countries borrowing in foreign currency suffer from the 'original sin' since exchange rate depreciations make it more difficult for them to service their debts. Hausmann & Panizza (2011) report an increase in emerging market debt issued in the currency of the issuer, yet that still amounted to only 4.1 per cent of the total bonds outstanding in 2008. Although original sin declined in the first decade of the millennium, it did so 'only marginally and in a few countries'. Rather than 'redemption', some developing countries opted for 'abstinence'—i.e., lower net debt. The important implication is that financial globalization has yet to ease credit concerns for developing countries, given that market access is subject to all-too-common exchange rate risks. For a majority of sovereign debtors, foreign currency issuance remains key to the credit access game.

In addition, sovereigns that issue bonds governed by foreign law almost always submit to courts in the designated jurisdiction. Weidemeier & Gulati (2017) see this decision as one that encompasses a trade-off between credibility and flexibility. Issuing bonds in foreign currency and subject to foreign law means that emerging market nations can generally take advantage of lower interest rates than those charged for domestic-law, domestic-currency bonds, instead of contending with shocks that lead to currency depreciation and increase the costs of servicing their foreign debts (Buchheit, 2013; Olivares-Caminal, 2013; Eichengreen et al. 2003). However, foreign law bonds are likely more difficult to restructure than domestic law ones and, for this reason, are viewed as safer investments than a sovereign's domestic law bonds. The debtor hence trades debt management flexibility for a more credible commitment to repayment given stricter contract enforcement. Indeed, creditors seem to believe that 'foreign courts will more rigorously enforce sovereign debt obligations' (Weidemeier & Gulati, 2017, pp. 9–10). Overall, 'when deciding where to file a lawsuit, plaintiffs consider, among other things, which state's laws are more favourable to their claim' (Whytock, 2009, p. 100). This explains why a substantial portion of emerging market sovereign bonds are governed by New York or English law (Weidemeier & Gulati, 2017; Das et al. 2012). Far from a technicality, 'choice of law rules has significant economic consequences' not only for debtors, but also for creditors and the financial centres whose laws rule these contracts more often than not (Whytock, 2009, pp. 101–2).

During the 1980s, in order to allow New York to compete more effectively with London, attempts were made to liberalize the American Uniform Commercial Code requirement for major financing transactions (Potts, 2016). This validated the stipulations of New York law without any requirement of a reasonable connection between the transaction and New York. According to the New York Bar (2013),

> these provisions embody a legislative policy to support New York's pre-eminent position in global finance by providing legal certainty to contractual provision selecting New York laws. The New York position is a close approximate of that of English law, which may be selected by the parties even if the transaction has no real connection with the UK at all.

In effect, this meant that Euromarket contracts, which in the late 1960s had boosted London's financial status further, could select New York law, thus 'expand[ing] the financial space over which New York laws and courts would govern' (Potts, 2016, p. 533).

Given these considerations, it is when sovereign debt is seen in its most basic form—i.e., as contract—that place becomes crucial. While international law (including treaties) 'may determine such questions as whether a new government will inherit the debts of a prior government, how to allocate responsibility for debt when a country dissolves into separate states, and whether national courts must enforce judgments entered by courts of another nation', for the most part 'customary international law is mandatory', binding even those nations that do not follow it. Crucially, in the US, it is municipal law that regulates the relationship between sovereign states and the individuals and entities subject to their jurisdiction, including rules that 'define the parties' primary obligations, such as rules of contract interpretation; jurisdictional rules that determine when domestic courts may hear sovereign debt disputes; procedural and evidentiary rules that govern the details of litigation in those courts; and rules for enforcing court judgments' (Weidemaier & Gulati, 2017).

For their part, eager for lower borrowing costs, debtors often voluntarily waive sovereign immunity in debt contracts. That is to say, countries 'cede aspects of their sovereignty to provide assurances of repayment' (Weidemaier & Gulati, 2016, p. 34). This fact challenges some assumptions in the scholarship on sovereign debt both in economics and political science. First, as Weidemeier and Gulati (2017, p. 5) explain, "the assumption in some of the economics literature that contracts are irrelevant to the sovereign debt markets is premised on the belief that creditors cannot easily obtain and enforce judgments against sovereigns". Yet, sovereigns, themselves, can commit to 'promises in the bond contract that expand creditor enforcement rights. These include waivers of immunity from suit, waivers of immunity from execution, as well as a suite of contract terms, such as terms facilitating service of process, to pave the way to the courthouse.' Second, and in the same vein, political science studies on global capital as a constraining (to varying degrees) force relative to government's policy autonomy overlook the ways in which sovereigns not only expose themselves to exchange rate risk by issuing debt in foreign currency, but even more directly, agree to subject themselves to the authority of foreign courts as commercial actors no longer shielded by sovereign immunity. Therefore, sovereigns approach international bond markets voluntarily even more exposed than it is often assumed.

Contemporary dynamics involving litigation against sovereigns are informed by the 1976 passage of the Foreign Sovereign Immunities Act (FSIA) in the United States, and the State Immunity Act of 1978 (SIA) in the United Kingdom. These are the key legislative references in the transition from 'absolute' to 'restrictive' immunity. Under these laws, no longer were sovereigns 'presumptively immune from suit even when engag[ing] in commercial activity abroad'. Rather, 'under the modern, restrictive theory of immunity, sovereigns are presumptively not immune from suit for commercial acts.' In fact, while before 1976 virtually no bond contained a waiver of immunity from suit, since then all foreign issued sovereign bonds waived this immunity (Weidemeier & Gulati, 2017, p. 7; Weidemeier, 2014).[1]

Immunity waivers notwithstanding, without the means to enforce a judge's order (seizing sovereign assets or disrupting trade), a victory in litigation and profitable vindication for a holdout creditor are not one and the same. Yet, although courts 'were reluctant to enforce privately negotiated immunity waivers until relatively late in the twentieth century', the tables have turned more recently (Weidemaier & Gulati, 2016, p. 34). The *NML v. Argentina* case is the epicentre of this challenging shift. To this case and the legislative efforts sparked by holdout litigation we turn next.

11.3 Litigation, Legislation, Location

In the absence of a uniform set of procedures coordinated by a global equivalent to a bankruptcy court, sovereign debt restructurings have been ad hoc developments

[1] A similar pattern is identified in accounts of international arbitration. Waibel (2011) explains that, 'by the early twentieth century, a small handful of sovereign loan contracts allowed creditors to bring claims before arbitral tribunals. For over a century, international tribunals have also (if rarely) heard disputes arising from sovereign debt obligations.'

(Rieffel, 2003). Speaking in 2013, Lee Buchheit (2013, p. 110), one of the most seasoned lawyers in the field, reminisced: 'There has been remarkably little litigation in sovereign debt workouts in 30 years, considering the size of the affected debt stocks.' Moreover, as Marx et al. (2006, p. 69) point out, 'given the larger investor base and the diversity of debt instruments, a surprising fact is the length of time taken to resolve sovereign debt workouts [in the 1990s and the first decade of the twenty-first century] has been shorter than in the 1980s.'

Yet, in the midst of these seemingly regular patterns, outliers, such as Argentina, having experienced a much longer and more contentious international legal battle than most other debtors, are more than a statistical anomaly. Even beyond a legal precedent (in a traditional sense), spillover effects from international litigation informally institutionalize the deviant outcome in the way debt processes are reconsidered internationally (Datz and Corcoran, 2019). That is why it is all the more pertinent to track domestic decision-making with global repercussions.

'Anti-vulture funds' laws in the UK, Belgium, and France compose the so-far incipient-but-evolving landscape of judicial and legislative responses to debt disputes, which 'normalize' outlier manoeuvres through legal pre-emption. Domestic laws protecting foreign debtors from minority holdout litigation and injunctive orders in federal courts that incite contractual changes have a discernible extraterritorial impact by design or diffusion. They present some opportunities and foreclose others for sovereign creditors and debtors in particular jurisdictions.

Background: Holdout Litigation in the 1990s

In 1992, *Republic of Argentina v. Weltover* opened the door for holdout creditors to bring their cases to US courts. However, the case did not yield a clear-cut legal pathway of favourable judgments for the creditors.[2] An early suit brought against Panama by an Elliott Associates (the litigant against Argentina in the 2000s) precursor company in 1995 was dismissed on the hedge fund's unwillingness to disclose its investors, a step necessary for holdout creditors when starting litigation. By 1997, the Southern District of New York Court barred claims brought by Elliott against Peru on non-performing debt, arguing that the hedge fund was in conflict with the champerty rule—i.e., an agreement forbidding the purchase of debt with the intent to bring about a lawsuit. The Second Circuit Court of Appeals, however, reversed the District Court's opinion (Blackman & Mukhi, 2010).

[2] *Republic of Argentina v. Weltover Inc.* 504 US 607 (1992).

Elliott filed another lawsuit against Peru in US courts in 2000. This time the hedge fund's plan centred on a 'novel interpretation' of the *pari passu* ('on equal footing') clause, standard in bond contracts since the mid-nineteenth century and 'containing the borrower's promise to ensure that the obligation will always rank equally in right of payment with all of the borrower's other subordinated debts' (Blackman & Mukhi, 2010, p. 55; Gelpern, 2016; Chodos, 2016). Although most legal treatments understand the clause to mean 'ranking debt owed to different creditors ratably' (Gelpern, 2016), Elliott argued that *pari passu* in this case meant that Peru could not pay creditors of restructured debt without paying the hedge fund proportionally.[3] Elliott won a judgment of US$56 million, enforceable through Peru's assets in the US used for commercial activity (IMF, 2001). Given that Peru had virtually no such assets in New York, Elliott targeted the third parties involved with bond payments—i.e., the sovereign's fiscal agents and clearinghouses (Weidemaier et al., 2013; IMF, 2001, p. 12). With insufficient time to appeal the orders obtained by Elliott, Peru decided to settle and avoid defaulting on its Brady bond payments coming due (Blackman & Mukhi, 2010).

Elliott's success reverberated through sovereign debt litigation circles. Not only had a holdout creditor received a favourable judgment, but it was also able to obtain a restraining order to prohibit the payment of interest to other bondholders until payments were made to that holdout creditor. A chain reaction of hedge fund litigation followed, and other enforcement actions were brought to court exploring the same strategy. Yet, most did not succeed. By 2003, the *pari passu* clause was no longer receiving favourable judgments in courtrooms around the world (Blackman & Mukhi 2010; Bratton, 2004). Even so, with the Argentine default in 2001, concerns that creditor coordination problems would plague debt restructuring procedures grew significantly.

These concerns led to efforts by the IMF to establish a Sovereign Debt Restructuring Mechanism (SDRM) in 2003, heavily inspired by Chapter 11 of the US Bankruptcy Code (Miller, 2002; Buchheit, 2013). Despite the Fund's advocacy, initially backed by the Bush administration, the SDRM was halted by significant opposition from private creditors, the US government who later favoured a less 'bureaucratic' approach, and some debtor governments who worried that the mechanism would mean higher borrowing costs or lower private capital inflows into their economies (Helleiner, 2008).

[3] Gelpern (2016) finds 'three court rulings [outside the US] from the 1930s and an arbitral decision from 1980, all of which address the meaning of *pari passu* at some length, and lend qualified support to the interpretation' of rateable ranking, which underpinned the decisions about Peru and the more widely debated case of Argentina discussed here.

The Injunctive Remedy in Argentina's Battle in US Courts

Rejecting both the 2005 and 2010 exchange offers presented to creditors for bonds defaulted in 2001, NML Capital (a hedge fund subsidiary of Elliott) pursued payment in US courts. In the September 2011 hearing for the Southern District of New York (SDNY), the lawyers for Argentina argued that the Foreign Sovereign Immunities Act protected its bond payment actions. Contradicting that view, in December 2011, New York District Court Judge Griesa ruled in favour of NML. For him, Argentina violated the *pari passu* clause ('equal treatment') when it continued paying bondholders of restructured bonds while refusing to pay holdout creditors.[4] Judge Griesa hence read the *pari passu* clause as forbidding Argentina from paying its other creditors unless it also paid NML 'proportionally', and saw Argentina's regular payments to its bondholders but not to holdout creditors as a subordination of non-restructured bonds (Gelpern, 2013; Cotterill, 2013).[5]

Expecting Argentina to defy his orders, judge Griesa issued an injunction in 2012 prohibiting the country from paying its restructured debt unless it paid NML in full (Gelpern, 2013).[6] Crucially, the injunctive order threatened to sanction financial third parties working with Argentina to allow for the repayment of exchange bondholders without payment to NML as well. In fact, the amended injunction of 2012 cited each of these financial intermediaries, making clear the extraterritorial ambition of the order. Given our focus on place, it is worth quoting in full paragraph 2(f) of the injunction, extending it to entities outside of the US who could be held in contempt of the court order:

> ...(1) the indenture trustees and/or registrars under the Exchange Bonds (including but not limited to The Bank of New York Mellon f/k/a/ The Bank of New York); (2) the registered owners of the Exchange Bonds and nominees of the depositaries for the Exchange Bonds (including but not limited to Cede & Co. and The Bank of New York Depositary (Nominees) Limited) and any institutions which act as nominees; (3) the clearing corporations and systems, depositaries, operators of clearing systems, and settlement agents for the Exchange Bonds (including but not limited to the Depository Trust Company, Clearstream

[4] The *pari passu* clause, a common addition to sovereign debt contracts, was stipulated in Argentina's original 1994 debt contract as a promise to treat all payment obligations as equal 'in ranking with other unsecured external' debt commitments of the country (Gelpern, 2013, p. 3).

[5] The Argentine Congress passed a law, the Padlock Law (or, locally, *ley cerrojo*) in February 2005 prohibiting the Executive from reopening the exchange without the holdout creditors (*Clarín,* 2012). This law supported judge Griesa's reading of subordination which undermined the key premise in the *pari passu* clause (Samples, 2014).

[6] Injunctions are perceived as a remedy that should be granted when a plaintiff has no other option and only if the remedy is consistent with the equitable exercise of a court's power (Weidemaier & Gelpern, 2013).

> Banking S.A., Euroclear Bank S.A./N.V. and the Euroclear System); (4) trustee paying agents and transfer agents for the Exchange Bonds (including but not limited to The Bank of New York (Luxembourg) S.A. and The Bank of New York Mellon (including but not limited to the Bank of New York Mellon (London)); and (5) attorneys and other agents engaged by any of the foregoing or the Republic in connection with their obligations under the Exchange Bonds.[7]

Although the Supreme Court of the United States refused to respond to Argentina's challenge of the district court's interpretation of *pari passu*, it did respond to the country's second question, involving 'post-judgment discovery' of debtors' assets by the litigating creditors. After obtaining debt-collection actions against Argentina in the Southern District of New York, NML Capital sought to search for Argentina's executable (not immune) property, and subpoenaed two non-party banks for the records of the country's global transactions. In support of Argentina, the US government filed a brief with the Supreme Court stating that affirming the District Court's ruling could harm international relations by provoking 'reciprocal adverse treatment of the US in foreign courts' (quoted in UNCTAD, 2014). Despite the US government's plea, the Supreme Court held that the Foreign Sovereign Immunities Act *does not* immunize sovereign debtors against post-judgment discovery of their assets outside of the United States.[8] After all, as stated by Justice Scalia, writing for the majority, Argentina had waived its sovereign immunity from the jurisdiction of courts in the United States in the contracts it signed when it sold the bonds. Indeed, having agreed to pay its debt in New York, in US currency and having 'expansively waived immunity', Argentina 'voluntarily ceded many of the sovereign prerogatives it might reasonably expect in a wholly-domestic matter' (Weidemaier & Gelpern, 2013, pp. 18–19).

Resolution

In the presidential contest of 2015, Kirchner's challenger, Mauricio Macri, won the elections. Soon after taking office, Macri and his team negotiated a deal with holdout creditors and managed to assure the support of Argentina's lower House to repeal laws that prevented the government from paying holdout creditors. Judge Griesa then lifted his earlier injunction, and Argentina sold $16.5 billion in new bonds to international investors to help fund the promised repayment to NML and its partners in litigation. What was then 'the largest emerging market debt sale on record' (*Cronista*, 2016, *The Wall Street Journal*, 2016) would usher in

[7] FED. R. CIV. P. 65(d)(2)(c), available at: https://www.law.cornell.edu/rules/frcp/rule_65.
[8] *Republic of Argentina v. NML Capital, Ltd.* 573 U.S. (2014).

a period of increased foreign indebtedness for Argentina, which very soon—as in previous times—would prove unsustainable.

Repercussions of the Legal Battle

For some legal scholars, the case brought up against Argentina by NML set a key precedent in the history of sovereign debt restructuring. Samples qualifies this legal battle as 'a true factual outlier', explaining that even though 'the Second Circuit partially recognized Argentina as a "uniquely recalcitrant" debtor, [the] NML [case] represents the most exceptional sovereign debt situation in modern history'. In the same vein, Gelpern stated that the case ultimately yielded 'the best collection device since gunboat diplomacy and certainly the most generalizable' (quoted in *Institutional Investor*, 2015).

Understanding the Argentine case as a critical juncture in debt disputes, the US government submitted a statement to the District Court, stating that Judge Griesa's judgment had the practical and potentially dangerous effect of allowing 'a single creditor to thwart the implementation of an internationally supported restructuring plan'. The US and other governments worried that creditors would now have an incentive to litigate for a better deal rather than accept the terms of a debt restructuring as set up by the defaulting debtor. As a result, the risk of holdouts would increase (Alfaro, 2014; IMF, 2013). Indeed, this was part of an international campaign that included a 2014 United Nations General Assembly resolution calling for the establishment of a 'multilateral legal framework for sovereign debt restructuring processes' (United Nations General Assembly, 2015).

The US Court of Appeals, however, insisted that it was 'highly unlikely that in the future sovereigns w[ould] find themselves in Argentina's predicament' given the fact that collective action clauses (allowing for a majority—usually 75 per cent—of creditors to decide the outcome of a restructuring) 'have been included in 99% of the aggregate value of New York-law bonds issued since January 2005, including Argentina's 2005 and 2010 Exchange Bonds'.[9] Yet, this view has been strongly disputed by legal scholars and policymakers who assert that CACs alone do not eliminate the holdout problem. After all, 'creditors can and do target small [bond] series trading at a deep discount, where they can buy a blocking position with relative ease, holdout and threaten to sue' the sovereign debtor (Committee on International and Economic Policy Reform, 2013, p. 18; IMF, 2013).

Not only has the Argentine case set a legal precedent, it has put in motion pre-emptive reactions by other sovereigns in the form of contractual changes beyond CACs. An IMF (2015, p. 8) analysis of new sovereign bond contracts reveals that

[9] http://business-finance-restructuring.weil.com/wp-content/uploads/2012/12/NML-Capital-v-Rep-of-Argentina_12-105L-Oct-26-2012-CA2.pdf (Accessed 9 March 2020).

all post-October 2014 debt issuances that have included enhanced CACs also included modified *pari passu* clauses. Even those issuances that did not include enhanced CACs did incorporate the modified *pari passu* clause. These contractual changes reflect guidelines set up by the London-based International Capital Market Association (ICMA) as a result of the 2013 deliberations by a 'US-government orchestrated and informal group of creditors, bankers, lawyers, and government officials' that composed the 'Sovereign Debt Roundtable' meetings. Key elements in the published guidelines were the promotion of revamped CACs and the clarification of the wording of the *pari passu* clause aimed at 'neutraliz[ing its] legal importance' (Wigglesworth & Moore, 2016). The modifications, however, provide no relief to the large outstanding stock of debt that does not feature such contractual provisions. New York law-governed bonds face a higher risk of holdout disputes given NML's ultimate victory (IMF, 2015). Even with the contractual changes, this victory aggravates the moral hazard problem that has plagued sovereign debt markets. There are incentives for creditors to seek out (*sui generis*) judicial interpretations to contract provisions that now, given the precedent from Judge Griesa's injunctive order, can rely on 'remedies' that undermine sovereign debt markets' infrastructure (Guzman, 2016).

A less remarked repercussion of sovereign debt legal disputes in foreign courts are legislative initiatives aimed at restricting 'vultures funds'' litigating appetites. To those we turn next.

The UK's Debt Relief Act of 2010

In response to a successful 'vulture fund'-triggered lawsuit to recover claims on Zambian and Liberian debt at a significant discount in British courts, the UK Parliament enacted the Debt Relief (Developing Countries) Act on 8 April 2010 (Wozny, 2017; Muse-Fisher, 2014).[10] At first blocked by a Conservative representative, the 'bill was pushed through as part of the pre-election wash-up, gaining House of Lords support and making its way to royal assent' (*The Guardian*, 2010). It focuses on public and publicly guaranteed foreign debt of countries participating in the World Bank's Highly Indebted Poor Country Initiative[11] introduced in 1996. Under this legislation, commercial creditors suing HIPC debtors in foreign courts cannot recover more than the amount recoverable if the debt were reduced in accordance with the HIPC initiative. This diminishes the incentives for holdouts to pursue litigation against these particular sovereigns in UK courts. Also,

[10] Available at: http://www.legislation.gov.uk/ukpga/2010/22. The law became permanent on 16 May 2011.

[11] As of January 2018, thirty-seven countries are part of the initiative. http://www.worldbank.org/en/topic/debt/brief/hipc. [the link works].

given that 'the DRA applies to foreign judgements or arbitration awards on qualifying debt, vulture funds cannot easily shop for more favourable laws and ask UK courts to enforce the judgement' (Wozny, 2017, pp. 729–30).

The law's limitations are clear, however. It only applies to HIPC countries and does so retroactively. Muse-Fisher (2014, pp. 1696–97) explains that 'the U.K. Government feared that in the absence of similar legislation in other major financial jurisdictions (notably New York), a forward-looking application of the law, covering future indebtedness, would chill the degree to which sovereign lenders and creditors would choose English law to govern future debts.'

In 2013, the UK's Debt Relief Act sparked the same legislation in three British Crown Dependencies: the Isle of Man, Guernsey, and Jersey (Bohoslavsky & Raffer, 2017). In 2015 and 2016, Belgium and France (respectively) also passed laws attempting to limit holdout creditors' disruptive strategies in foreign courts.

The Belgian Anti-Vulture Fund Law[12]

Belgian legislation against vulture funds was first prompted by Kensington International (an international investment fund) trying to execute a foreign award against the Democratic Republic of Congo in Belgian Courts. The award amounting to US$121.4 million in 2005 was much higher than the price Kensington had paid for Congolese bonds in secondary markets, US$1.8 million (Iversen, 2015, p. 29).[13] Getting to enforcement was the next step for Kensington's lawyers, who tried to seize DRC funds worldwide, including €10.3 million of Belgian government funds that were part of an aid package targeting the construction of a thermal power station in the DRC. Belgium had also been the site of a notorious dispute between Elliott Associates (hedge fund) and Peru in 2000. The Brussels Court of Appeals sided with the creditor, and in order to press Peru to pay, it ordered Euroclear to block payments meant to reach the Brady bondholders (Nelson, 2016, p. 142). This case, which inspired the litigation strategy pursued by NML Capital against Argentina in US courts, prompted the Belgian Senate to promulgate a law in 2004 that protected Euroclear and other clearing systems from attachment and injunctive orders. In 2008, another law was passed to prevent 'vulture funds', specifically, from claiming public funds delivered as part of international cooperation (Pavlidis, 2018).[14] As in the UK, the legislators' key concern was with the 'possibility that holdout creditors could circumvent

[12] Literal translation of the original: *Loi relative à la lutte contre les activités de fonds vautours.*

[13] *Kensington International v. Republic of Congo* (2005). Available at: https://caselaw.findlaw.com/us-2nd-circuit/1113677.html

[14] Its original title was: *Loi visant à empêcher la saisie ou la cession des fonds publics destinés à la coopération internationale, notamment par la technique des fonds vautours*, 6 April 2008. Available at: http://www.ejustice.just.fgov.be/doc/rech_f.htm

multilateral efforts geared towards the reduction or cancellation of debts of very poor countries' (Iversen, 2015, p. 30). However, because this resolution did not exempt from attachment public money that was not intended for development aid another effort was put in place to broaden the scope of this initiative (Sourbron & Vereeck, 2017).

This happened in July, 2015, when the Belgian House of Representatives unanimously passed its 'anti-vulture funds' law (*Le Figaro*, 2015; Richelle, 2016; Sourbron & Vereeck, 2017). The bill's draft of April 2015 cites several cases of vulture fund-driven litigation in foreign courts as its motivation: *Elliott Associates v. Peru* in Belgium (1996–99), *Kensington International v. the DRC* in Belgium (cited above), *FG Hemisphere v. the DRC* in a Jersey Court in 2004, *Donegal International v. Zambia* in British courts (2007), and, of course, *NML v. Argentina* in New York courts (with critical judicial decisions stated in 2008 and 2012).[15] The law established that 'if a Belgian court finds a fund acting as a "vulture", the latter cannot claim more than the discounted price it paid' (Sourbron & Vereeck, 2017, p. 7). Judicial decision rests on evidence as to whether the vulture fund sought to pursue an 'illegitimate advantage', which applies in the following cases: the sovereign debtor is in a state of insolvency, payment of the claim would impact the debtor's finances negatively, the creditor's headquarters are located in a tax heaven, 'the creditor systematically uses legal procedures to recover its loans' and/or refuses to cooperate with the debtor (Wozny, 2017, p. 738). In addition, illegitimacy is determined by the 'manifest disproportion between the purchase price and the face value of the debt purchased' (Sourbron & Vereeck, 2017, p. 7).

Its political appeal notwithstanding, the law met with opposition by local financial representatives and the Institute of International Finance (Kaluma, 2015). At first, 'none of the arguments was strong enough to substantially alter, let alone repeal the law' (Sourbron & Vereeck, 2017, p. 8). Expediency, characteristic of holdout litigants' manoeuvres, was also evident in the ways legislators moved to better substantiate their pre-emptive attempts in the face of new challenges from 'vulture funds'. These creditors tried to undermine the law 'by lobbying for another bill aimed at weakening sovereign immunity and strengthening the ability to seize diplomatic goods' *within* the limit of the debt's purchase price. If these sovereign assets did not exceed the purchase price, vulture funds could state that there was no 'illegitimate advantage' in their claims.[16] Once more,

[15] Belgian Chamber of Representatives (2015), *Projet de loi relative à la lutte contre les activités des fonds vautours*, DOC 54 1057/005, Available at: http://www.dekamer.be/FLWB/PDF/54/1057/54K1057005.pdf

[16] Belgian law, in accordance with the 2004 UN Convention on Jurisdictional Immunities of States and their Property, does not allow attachment of foreign state property used for non-commercial public purposes unless an explicit waiver of immunity is part of the contract. Yet 'the Belgian law also requires that the waiver is granted in a specific way. It is the latter clause that came under attack' (Sourbron & Vereeck, 2017, p. 9). The content of the UN Convention can be found here: http://legal.un.org/ilc/texts/instruments/english/conventions /4_1_2004.pdf (Accessed 13 February 2018).

Belgian legislators acted quickly. On 24 July, 'a meticulously amended version of the bill' foreclosing this route was passed and published in the *Belgian Gazette* on 3 September 2015 (Sourbron & Vereeck, 2017, p. 9).

Yet, 'vulture funds' persisted. NML Capital Ltd and Yukos Universal Limited tried to fight the Diplomatic Immunities Law in the Belgian Constitutional Court. This time the funds' tenacity paid off to some extent. In its judgment on 27 April 2017, the Court confirmed the validity of the August 2015 Act 'whereby the immunity from execution of foreign States and international organizations was strengthened in Belgian legislation' (Theeuwes & Dopagne, 2017). Yet it 'relaxe[d] the rules of attachment as intended by the Belgian legislator', deciding 'that in accordance with the Treaty of Vienna of April 18, 1961, a specific waiver remains required for the attachment of goods for diplomatic purposes, but that in line with international law, a *general* waiver suffices for the attachment of non-diplomatic, non-commercial goods' (Sourbron & Vereeck, 2017, p. 9, emphasis added). Finally, on 31 May 2018, the Belgian Constitutional Court put to rest NML Capital's claims that the 2015 Belgian law was unconstitutional. Rather, the Court saw the law as 'non-discriminatory, respectful of Belgium's EU and international commitments and not in violation of any constitutional right'. This was a victory for the supporting public and, in particular, for the NGOs that joined the Belgium state litigating in support of the law: the Belgian coalition of French-speaking development NGOs, CNCD-11.11.11, its Flemish sister organization 11.11.11, and the Committee for the Abolition of Illegitimate Debt (CADTM, 2018).[17]

Indicative of the international diffusion of the Belgium 'anti-vultures' law, Theeuwes and Dopagne (2017) remark that 'by and large, this ruling of the Belgian Constitutional Court echoes the 8 December 2016 decision of the French Constitutional Council, which confirmed the validity of the French law adopted partially on the blueprint of the Belgian Act of 23 August 2015.'

France's Sapin II

On 8 November 2016, the Law on Transparency, Anti-corruption Measures and the Modernization of the Economy, presented by Michel Sapin, Minister for the Economy and Finance, to the Council of Ministers, was approved by the French National Assembly. After undergoing the scrutiny of the French constitutional court, French Law n° 2016-169, known as Sapin II, was finally enacted. The law was proposed by the *Agence Française Anticorruption* and reflects a broad agenda to strengthen French anti-corruption regulations (*The National Law Review*,

[17] The full decision can be found at: http://www.const-court.be/public/f/2018/2018-061f.pdf

2017).[18] Among its proposed reforms, this law 'affects the enforcement of foreign decisions and arbitral awards rendered against States' and 'seeks to clarify the protection of the property of foreign States situated in France'. Ultimately, the 'law retains a general exemption from immunity in respect to situations where the State has "expressly consented" to provisional or enforcement measures being taken'. Yet enforcement of diplomatic and consular property still does require a specific waiver by the State (Dupoirier et al., 2016).

Key to our discussion here, article 60 of Sapin II, 'provides special rules in order to avoid the seizure of the property of foreign States in France by investment funds holding debt securities that have been purchased at discounted value or in other circumstances of distress against economically vulnerable States'. However, the provision's reach is limited. It only applies to debt securities: (a) acquired *after* the entry into force of the law (11 December 2016), and (b) against sovereign debtors in default or undergoing a restructuring, which 'were recipients of the official development assistance of the OECD when the security was issued' (Dupoirier et al., 2016).

11.4 Connecting the Dots: Local Laws, Global Reach, Overlap

The local legislative and judicial decisions described above aspired to extraterritorial impact. That is not surprising. As Whytock (2009, p. 98) explains, a decision by a domestic court involving a transnational actor can transcend the case, sending 'a signal to transnational actors that the court will make a similar decision under similar circumstances in the future'. Therefore, 'the substantive function of domestic courts in global governance has not only direct effects on the litigants, but also indirect shadow effect on the strategic behaviour of transnational actors more generally' (Whytock, 2009, pp. 99–100). Holdout litigation in British, Belgian, and American courts prompted legislative pre-emptive efforts seeking to reach beyond national borders. Sourbron and Vereeck (2017, p. 7) recall that 'during their formal discussion, the Belgian members of parliament pointed out that although an international solution is preferable, a national law may set an example and expedite international action.' In fact, 'the Belgian legislators urged the Belgian government to convince its European counterparts to adopt their model-law.'

It is clear that in this new landscape of local debt governance, legislative and judicial determination may overlap, challenging one another. Such is the case of judge Griesa's injunctive order in the *NML v. Argentina* case. The order raised concerns about conflict of laws. As mentioned above, Euroclear was named

[18] The text of the law can be found at: http://www.assemblee-nationale.fr/14/pdf/ta/ta0830.pdf

among the 'third parties' involved in Argentina's payments pipeline, 'despite the Belgian law, which on its face appears to immunize [Euroclear] from court orders' like judge Griesa's injunction (Wiedemaier & Gelpern, 2013, p. 33). In the text of the Belgian Law Against Vulture Funds it was explicitly stated that:

> Regardless of the law applicable to the legal relationship between the creditor and the debtor state, no enforceable title can be obtained in Belgium, nor any measure of custody or enforcement can be taken in Belgium at the request of the creditor to obtain payment in Belgium if that payment purveys an illegitimate advantage as defined by law.

This means that Belgian courts can block payments in Belgium to vulture funds, while a foreign court order that endorses the claims by vulture funds cannot be enforced in that country (Sourbron & Vereeck, 2017, p. 7).

The rationale for the injunction issued by judge Griesa was that extraterritorial scope was needed to force Argentina to comply—a point supported by the Court of Appeals, despite vehement opposition by foreign financial intermediaries (Weidemaier & Gelpern, 2013, p. 34). In the statement it submitted the US Supreme Court, Euroclear (2014, p. 7) accused the 'lower court's exercise of jurisdiction' of being 'exorbitant' by explicitly constraining the activities of international financial intermediaries, and reaching euro-denominated bonds 'held entirely outside the US, [...] governed by English law', and whose payments 'occur outside the US'. For Euroclear's lawyers, the injunction expanded 'the authority of the US courts beyond the borders of the US to activities carried out by governmental and other institutions in Europe' (pp. 8–9). To make matters worse, the injunctive order was 'in direct conflict with Belgian law', which prohibited 'attachment or blocking of [...] any cash transfer' given its detrimental effect on 'the proper functioning of payment or settlement systems and hence to [...] the credibility and the liquidity of national and international financial markets' (p. 10). Indeed, as concluded by Weidemeier and Gelpern (2013, p. 33), the precedent of 'burden[ing] systematically important market utilities with the risk of contempt sanctions to enforce ordinary private debts' is too costly an attempt at enforcement, made even more concerning 'when it comes to foreign institutions governed by foreign law that reject this very remedy'.

11.5 Conclusion

Laws have been passed in the UK, Belgium, and France aiming at restricting holdout creditors' ability to pocket more money than they paid for the debts in contention, protecting Highly Indebted Poor Countries, and making it harder for sovereign property to be seized despite immunity waivers. Holdout creditors suing sovereigns in foreign courts, however, can continue to explore loopholes in existing legislation as well as 'shop' for less restrictive judicial forums (Sourbron & Vereeck, 2017). Since most bonds are issued under New York or English law (IMF 2013) and no legislative action has been pursued in the US yet, ample room remains for holdout creditors to attempt to conquer the perennial challenges of sovereign debt enforcement in New York courts, especially since NML Capital's remarkable victory over Argentina.

As uncoordinated efforts that are either limited in application (the UK and French laws) or overlapping in scope (the injunctive order in the *NML v. Argentina* case and the Belgian anti-vultures law), the initiatives described above are emblematic of how ad hoc mechanisms have evolved. This is a landscape of official experimentation that in some instances restricts and in others enables holdout creditors' particularly disruptive litigation in foreign courts. Contractual changes and new laws can reduce some of the risks to which sovereigns are exposed when seeking foreign bond finance, yet they do not systematically reduce the ambiguity that feeds holdouts' strategies or the uncertainty that plagues sovereign default outcomes.

Indeed, the extent to which contractual reform can help prevent the kind of costly litigation Argentina endured from 2001 to 2016 will soon become clear. At the time of writing, the country is again facing a debt restructuring process (*La Nación*, 2020). Under President Macri, public indebtedness increased by US$74 billion, jumping from 49 per cent of GDP to 94 per cent from 2015 to 2019. This was in large part the result of the cost of paying holdout creditors, the fall in economic activity, and the steep decline of the peso (*Clarín*, 2019). An IMF loan of US$57 billion in 2018, the largest in the history of that financial institution, did not ameliorate default risk (IMF 2018). Since newly defaulted Argentine bonds feature modified collective action clauses, these will be put to the test (Szymanski, 2020).

Amid public and private experimentation, place has regained prominence not simply as an element in contractual decisions or strategic site for instantiating global financial transactions, but as the (by definition, contingent) locus for domestic attempts at legislative pre-emption and its diffusion. In the absence of a statutory regime for restructurings, the notoriously imperfect world of sovereign debt can be characterized as a fragmented topography of sub-optimal local, and at times overlapping, spheres of sovereign debt governance, paradoxically embedded in a deeply integrated global financial system.

References

Ahram, A. & Datz, G. (2014). *Swimming with Black Swans: The Role of Outliers in Theory Development*. Presented at the annual convention of the American Political Science Association, Washington, DC.

Alfaro, L. (2014). *Sovereign Debt Restructuring: Evaluating the Impact of the Argentina Ruling*. Unpublished. Harvard Business School.

Blackman, J. & Mukhi, R. (2010). 'The Evolution of Modern Sovereign Debt Litigation: Vultures, Alter Egos, and Other Legal Fauna'. *Law and Contemporary Problems*, 73 (4), 47–61.

Bohoslavsky, J.P. & Raffer, K. (2017). "Conclusions: What Have We Learned?". In J.P. Bohoslausky & K. Raffer, *Sovereign Debt Crises: What Have We Learned?* New York: Cambridge University Press.

Brenner, N. (1998). 'Global City, Global States: Global City Formation and State Territorial Restructuring in Contemporary Europe". *Review of International Political Economy*, 5(1), 1–37.

Brooks, S., Cunha, R. & Mosley, L. (2015). 'Categories, Creditworthiness, and Contagion: How Investors' Shortcuts Affect Sovereign Debt'. *International Studies Quarterly*, 59(3), 587–601.

Buchheit, L. (2013). *Sovereign Debt Restructurings: The Legal Context*. Lecture from Bank for International Settlements. BIS Papers, Basel, 8 January.

Buccheit, L., Gulati, M. & Tirado, I. (2013). 'The Problem of Holdout Creditors in Eurozone Sovereign Debt Restructurings'. *Butterworths Journal of International Banking and Financial Law* (April), 191–4.

Chodos, S. (2016). 'From *Pari Passu* Discussion to the "Illegality" of Making Payments: The Case of Argentina', in J. A. Campo, & J. Stiglitz (Eds.), *Too Little, Too Late: The Quest to Resolve Sovereign Debt Crises*. New York: Columbia University Press.

Choi, S., Gulati, M. & Posner, E. (2013). 'The Dynamics of Contract Evolution'. *New York Law Review*, 88(1), 1–50.

Clarín (2012). 'Ley Cerrojo: Una Jugada Que Se volvió En Contra', 26 October 2012.

Clarín (2019). 'El País Que Deja Macri, 4 Años Despues', 2 February 2019.

Cotterill, J. (2013). 'Sovereign Pari Passu and the Litigators of the Lost Cause', *Capital Markets Law Journal*, 9(1), 18–25.

Committee for the Abolition of Illegitimate Debt (CADTM). (2018). 'Debt Justice Prevails at the Belgian Constitutional Court: Vulture funds law survives challenge by NML Capital', 6 June 2018.

Committee on International Economic Policy and Reform, Brookings Institution. (2013). *Revisiting Sovereign Bankruptcy*. Washington, DC: Brookings Institution.

Cronista (2016). 'La Corte de Nueva York despejó el camino para que la Argentina salga del default', 14 April (Buenos Aires).

Das, U.S., Papaioannou, M., & Trebesch, C. (2012). *Sovereign Debt Restructurings 1950–2010: Literature Survey, Data, and Stylized Facts*. International Monetary Fund, Working Paper 12/203.

Datz, G. & Corcoran, K. (2019). 'Deviant Debt: Reputation, Litigation and the Outlier Effects of Argentina's Debt Restructuring Saga'. *New Political Economy*, 25(2): 300–313.

de Fonteney, E., Meyer, J. & Gulati, M. (2016). 'The Sovereign Debt Listing Puzzle', Duke Law School Public Law & Legal Theory Series No. 2017–14.

Dupoirier, C., Cannon, A. & Franc-Menget, L. (2016). 'A Law on Immunity from Enforcement in France', Herbert Smith Feehills, PIL Notes, 1 December 2016.

Edwards, F.R. & Mishkin, F.S. (1995). 'The Decline of Traditional Banking: Implications for Financial Stability and Regulatory Policy'. *National Bureau of Economic Research*, n°4993.

Eichengreen, B., Hausmann, R. & Panizza, U. (2005). 'The Pain of Original Sin'. In Barry Eichengreen and Ricardo Hausmann (Eds.), *Other People's Money*. Chicago: Chicago University Press.

Euroclear Bank SA (2014). 'Brief of Amicus Curiae Euroclear Bank SA/NV in Support of Petitioner', 24 March 2014. Available at: http://www.creditslips.org/files/euroclear-amicus-brief.pdf (Accessed 9 March 2020).

Flandreau, M. (2017). 'Reputation, Regulation and the Collapse of International Capital Markets, 1920–1935', in Peter L. Rousseau and Paul Wachtel (Eds.), *Financial Systems and Economic Governance: Credit Crises and Regulation from the 19th Century to the Present*. New York: Cambridge University Press.

Flandreau, M., Flores, J., Gaillard, N. & Nieto-Parra, S. (2009). 'The End of Gatekeepers: Underwriters and the Quality of Sovereign Bond Markets, 1815–2007'. *NBER Working Paper No. 15128*.

Flores, J. (2010). 'Competition in the Underwriting Markets of Sovereign Debt: The Baring Crisis Revisited'. *Law and Contemporary Problems*, 73 (Fall), 130–50.

Gelpern, A. (2013). 'Contract Hope and Sovereign Redemption', *The Capital Markets Law Journal*, 8(2), 132–48.

Gelpern, A. (2016). 'Courts and Sovereigns in *Pari Passu* Goldmines'. *Capital Markets Law Journal*, 1(2), 251–61.

Grund, S. (2019). 'Restructuring Argentine Debt: Navigating the Legal Labyrinth', The Columbia Law School Blue Sky Blog, 3 December 2019. https://clsbluesky.law.columbia.edu/2019/12/03/restructuring-argentinas-sovereign-debt-navigating-the-legal-labyrinth/ (Accessed 3 January 2020).

Guzman, M. (2016). 'An Analysis of Argentina's 2001 Default Resolution'. *CIGI Papers No. 110*.

Hausmann, R. & Panizza, U. (2011). 'Redemption of Abstinence? Original Sin, Currency Mismatches and Counter Cyclical Policies in the New Millennium'. *Journal of Globalization and Development*, 2(1), 1–33.

Helleiner, E. (2008). 'The Mystery of the Missing Sovereign Debt Restructuring Mechanism'. *Contributions to Political Economy*, 27(1), 91–113.

*Institutional Investor (*2015). "Ukraine Struggles to Restructure Its Sovereign Debt", June 22.

International Monetary Fund (2001). *Involving the Private Sector in the Resolution of Financial Crises - Restructuring Sovereign Bonds.* Washington, DC: IMF.

International Monetary Fund (2013). *Sovereign Debt Restructuring—Recent Developments and Implications for the Fund's Legal and Policy Frameworks.* Washington, DC: IMF.

International Monetary Fund (2015). "Progress Report on Inclusion of Enhanced Contractual Provisions in International Sovereign Bond Contracts". Washington, DC: IMF.

International Monetary Fund (2018). 'IMF Executive Board Approves US$50 Billion Stand-By Arrangement for Argentina', IMF Press Release No.18/245.

Iversen, A. (2015). 'Holdout Credit Litigation: An Assessment of Legislative Initiatives to Counter Aggressive Sovereign Debt Creditor Litigators', University of Oslo Faculty of Law and Legal Studies, Research Paper Series No. 2015–13.

Jones, T. (2017). 'France Passes Law to Clip Vulture Funds' wings', Jubilee Debt Campaign, 21 March 2017.

Kaminsky, G. & Schmukler S. (2003). 'The Center and the Periphery: The Globalization of Financial Turmoil'. *NBER Working Paper No. 9479.*

Kaluma, N. (2015). 'New Belgian Law Targets "Vulture Funds" buying up Distressed Debt', European Financial Litigation Review, Allen and Overy (Belgium).

Kaplan, S. & Thomsson, K. (2014). 'The Political Economy of Sovereign Borrowing: Explaining the Policy Choices of Highly Indebted Poor Countries'. *IIEP Working Paper 2015-1.*

Kim, W. & Wei, S.J. (1999). 'Foreign Portfolio Investors before and During a Crisis'. *NBER Working Paper No. 6968.*

La Nación (2020). 'El Senado Convertió En Ley El Proyecto De Restructuración De La Deuda', 5 February 2020 (Buenos Aires).

Le Figaro (2015). 'La Belgique Vote Une Loi Contre Les "Fonds Vautour"', 1 July 2015.

Li, Y. (2015). 'The Long March towards an International Legal Framework for Sovereign Debt Restructuring', *Journal of Globalization and Development*, 6(2), 329–41.

Marx, D., Echague, J. & Sandleris, G. (2006). 'Sovereign Debt and the Debt Crisis in Emerging Countries: The Experience of the 1990s', in C. Jochnick and F.A. Preston (Eds.), *Sovereign Debt at the Crossroads.* New York: Oxford University Press.

Maxfield, S. (1998). 'Effects of International Portfolio Flows on Government Policy Choice', in Miles Kahler (Ed.), *Capital Flows and Financial Crises.* Ithaca: Cornell University Press.

Miller, M. (2002). 'Sovereign Debt Restructuring: New Articles, New Contracts—or No Change?'. *International Economics Policy Briefs, No. PB02-03.*

Mosley, L. (2003). *Global Capital and National Governments.* Cambridge: Cambridge University Press.

Muse-Fisher, J. (2014). 'Starving the Vultures: NML Capital v. Argentina and the Solutions to the Problem of Distressed-Debt Funds', *California Law Review*, 102(6), 1671–724.

Mustafa, H. A. & Molle, A. (2016). 'Waivers of Sovereign Immunity', in Frank Fariello, Laurence Boisson de Chazournes & Kevin E. David (Eds.), *The World Bank Legal Review: Financing and Implementing the Post-2015 Development Agenda.* Washington, DC: World Bank Group.

Nelson, S. (2016). 'Market rules: Social Conventions, Legal Fictions and the Organization of Sovereign Debt Markets in the Long Twentieth Century', in Grégoire Mallard and Jérôme Sgard (Eds.), *Contractual Knowledge: One Hundred Years of Legal Experimentation in Global Markets.* New York: Cambridge University Press.

New York City Bar, Committee on Foreign & Comparative Law (2013). *Governing Law in Sovereign Debt: Lessons from the Greek Crisis and Argentina's Dispute of 2012.* New York: New York Bar.

Obstfeld, M. & Taylor, A. M. (2003). 'Globalization and Capital Markets'. In Michael D. Bordo, Alan M. Taylor & Jeffrey G. Williamsom (Eds.), *Globalization in Historical Perspective.* Chicago: University of Chicago Press.

Olivares-Caminal, R. (2013). 'The Pari Passu Clause in Sovereign Debt Instruments: Developments in Recent Litigation', Bank for International Settlements, January.

Pavlidis, G. (2018). 'Vulture Litigation in the Context of Sovereign Debt: Global or Local Solutions?' *Law and Financial Markets Review*, 12(2), 93–8.

Potts, S. (2016). 'Reterritorializing Economic Governance: Contracts, Space, and Law in Transborder Economic Geographies', *Environment and Planning A*, 48(3), 523–39.

Richelle, J. (2016). *Belgium 2015 Anti-Vulture Law.* Brussels: Strelia.

Rieffel, A. (2003). *Restructuring Sovereign Debt: The Case for Ad Hoc Machinery.* Washington, DC: Brookings Institution.

Sassen, S. (1991). *The Global City: New York, London, Tokyo.* Princeton: Princeton University Press. LMU Munich.

Sourbron, L. A. & Vereeck, L. (2017). 'To Pay or Not to Pay? Evaluating the Belgium Law against Vulture Funds', *Journal of Globalization and Development*, 8(1), 1–14.

Strange, S. (1995). 'The Defective State'. *Daedalus*, 124(2), 55–74.

Szymanski, A. (2020). 'Argentina Debt Do-Over is Even Chancier than Usual', *Reuters*, 3 January 2020.

The National Law Review (2017). 'New French Anti-Corruption Law "Sapin II"', 4 January 2017.

The Wall Street Journal (2016). 'Argentina Returns to Global Debt Markets with $16.5 Billion Bond Sale', 19 April 2016.

Theeuwes, B. & Dopagne, F. (2017). 'Belgian Constitutional Court Rules in Recent Legislation Protecting Property of Foreign States and International Organizations', Kelley Drye and Warren LLP, *Lexology*, 1 May 2017.

UNCTAD (2014). 'Argentina's "Vulture Fund" Crisis Threaten Profound Consequences For International Financial System', June 25. https://unctad.org/news/argentinas-vulture-fund-crisis-threatens-profound-consequences-international-financial-system

United Nations (2015). General Assembly Resolution 69/319, 'Basic Principles on Sovereign Debt Restructuring Processes', adopted 10 September 2015.

Waibel, M. (2011). *Sovereign Defaults before International Courts and Tribunals.* New York: Cambridge University Press.

Weidemaier, W.M.C. (2010). 'Contracting for State Intervention: The Origins of Sovereign Debt Arbitration', *Law and Contemporary Problems*, 73, 335–55.

Weidemaier, W.M.C. (2014). 'Sovereign Immunity and Sovereign Debt', *Illinois Law Review*, 1, 68–114.

Weidemaier, W.M.C. & Gelpern, A. (2013). 'Injunctions in Sovereign Debt Litigation'. *UNC Legal Studies Research Paper No. 2330914.*

Weidemaier, W.M.C. & Gulati, M. (2016). 'Differing Perceptions? Market Practice and the Evolution of Foreign Sovereign Immunity'. *UNC Legal Studies Research Paper No. 2739423, Duke Law School Public Law & Legal Theory Series No. 2016–21.*

Weidemaier, W.M.C. & Gulati, M. (2017). 'Sovereign Debt and the "Contracts Matter" Hypothesis', in *The Oxford Handbook of Law and Economics, Vol. 3: Public Law and Legal Institutions.* New York: Oxford University Press.

Wigglesworth, R. & Moore, E. (2016). "Sovereign Debt: Curing Defaults", *Financial Times*, June 7.

Whytock, C. A. (2009). 'Domestic Courts and Global Governance', *Tulane Law Review*, 84, 67–123.

Wozny, L. (2017). 'National Anti-Vulture Funds Legislation: Belgium's Turn', *Columbia Business Law Review*, 2, 697–747.

Zettlemeyer, J., Trebesch, C. & Gulati, M. (2013). 'The Greek Debt Restructuring: An Autopsy', unpublished manuscript, Duke University.

12
Maduro Bonds

Mitu Gulati and Ugo Panizza

12.1 Introduction

One of the most debated questions in the literature on sovereign debt is the question of whether, when a despotic ruler is overthrown by his oppressed people, the successor government—assuming it is democratic and representative—inherits those prior debts (Pénet, 2018; King, 2016; Lienau, 2014). The general rule of governmental succession in international law is strict. Governments inherit the debts of their predecessors, regardless of political differences between the governments (Buchheit, Gulati & Thompson, 2007). Joe Biden's government inherits the debts of Donald Trump's government, no matter how odious the former thinks the latter might have been. Further, because international law conceptualizes states as infinitely lived creatures without the possibility of bankruptcy, the despotic ruler's debt stock can potentially last into infinity.[1] The current Russian and Chinese governments, for example, are still on the hook for the unpaid debts of their imperial predecessors from the early 1900s.

As a matter of theory, there are moral and economic arguments for why there should be rules restricting the obligations of successor good governments to pay the debts of prior bad ones. The primary one being that choking off a despot's ability to access the markets should reduce the incentives to be a despotic ruler in the first place (Kremer & Jayachandran, 2006; Bonilla, 2011). Put differently, the ability of the despotic ruler to externalize the costs of his despotism to future governments and populations, creates inefficiencies. There are counterarguments too—mostly focused on the difficulty of implementing such a regime under international law—the key problem being the difficulty in defining what it means to be a despotic government (Choi & Posner, 2007; Stephan, 2007; Buchheit, Gulati & Thompson, 2007). As a formal legal matter, international law can only get changed if there is widespread agreement among the countries that make up the global

[1] We are overstating the matter since debts in which the creditors do not periodically take actions to remind the debtor that a debt is owed eventually get time barred by statues of limitations in the relevant local legal jurisdictions where the creditor might wish to sue. In theory, creditors can keep their claims alive infinitely by periodically filing the relevant legal documents. But that takes effort and resources and, as debts remain unpaid for long periods of time (such as the Imperial Chinese debt and the Russian Tsarist), creditors eventually stop exerting those efforts.

Mitu Gulati and Ugo Panizza, *Maduro Bonds* In: *Sovereign Debt Diplomacies: Rethinking Sovereign Debt from Colonial Empires to Hegemony*. Edited by: Pierre Pénet and Juan Flores Zendejas, Oxford University Press (2021). © Oxford University Press.
DOI: 10.1093/oso/9780198866350.003.0013

community (Choi & Gulati, 2016). In such a case, either an international treaty could be formulated or a court could declare that a new doctrine of customary international law had arisen. However, there are enough governments in place who have either engaged in odious lending or are concerned that they might be called odious themselves that efforts to put in place an Odious Debt doctrine in international law have rarely been able to get more than a handful of governments to sign up to their cause (Michalowski, 2009a; Nehru & Thomas, 2008).

Our goal in this article is to raise the possibility of an alternate legal path to raising the costs of borrowing for despotic regimes. Specifically, an option that can be implemented now, without any need to define what it means to be a despotic government or to reform the international law rules of state succession. We propose that civil society institutions—the ones generally most willing to exert effort to deter despotic governmental behaviour—make use of domestic laws that are likely already in place in almost every legal jurisdiction that could potentially constrain the actions of misbehaving and corrupt agents.[2] All governments in the modern age, even the most despotic, are purporting to act as agents for their people. Unlike the monarchs of generations past, few leaders are claiming that their authority comes from up above (see also Michalowski, 2009b; Buchheit, Gulati & Thompson, 2007).

To illustrate our argument, we begin with a concrete and current example. That is, the Venezuelan government under President Nicolás Maduro that, while purporting to be democratic, has been widely condemned in the international community as illegitimate (Casey & Davis, 2018). We ask, in the context of the Maduro regime, whether its borrowing might be subject to legal challenge under subsequent, and presumably better, governments. If the markets perceive there to be significant enough risk of future repudiation, that will increase the cost of borrowing for the current government. The actions of civil society in identifying and loudly pointing out the potential violations of Venezuelan domestic laws in some of the borrowing that Mr Maduro's government has done have arguably already raised the borrowing costs of the Maduro government (Gulati & Panizza, 2018a).

The premise of our argument is the following: all countries, despotic or not, have systems of domestic laws that regulate agency relationships and try to deter corruption; otherwise the domestic economy would not function. Despotic governments, we conjecture, are highly likely to engage in transactions that are legally problematic—that is, that have failed to obtain proper authorizations, or where funds have been improperly spent, or where there has been some other form of corruption. The reason being that despotic governments, by definition, lack the support of the populace; meaning that there is a high likelihood that actions that they take on behalf of the populace (e.g., borrowing to buy arms that are then used

[2] On the use of domestic law to help remedy problems in the international sovereign debt market, albeit in a different context, see also Datz (2020).

to put down popular protests) can be challenged as unrepresentative and contrary to the interests of the true principals. Further, to the extent the despot is hanging on to power by the fact that they are making side payments to those who control key organs of the government (e.g., the military and the judiciary), there is bound to be a significant amount of corruption in most major government transactions. The foregoing conditions, if one translates them into the context of an ordinary principal–agent relationship, where the purported agent (the despot) is colluding with a third party (international banks, the military, the judiciary, etc.) to cheat the principal (the people), would constitute a voidable transaction in most modern legal systems. That in turn means that if opposition parties in countries with despotic governments today were to monitor and make public the potential problems with debt issuances by their despotic rulers, it would raise the cost of capital for those despots.

The remainder of the paper proceeds as follows. Section 12.2 provides a concrete illustration of our point. We describe how the efforts of civil society to point out suspicious looking aspects of a sleazy bond issue by the Maduro government both resulted in a significant increase in the market's perception of the risk of a particular bond issue and, we suspect, killed the willingness of investors to engage in other similar transactions. Those transactions, had they happened, would have helped the Maduro government. In Section 12.3, we point to a number of other legal issues that could be raised by civil society if the Maduro government attempts to do new bond issuances. Section 12.4 broadens the discussion by examining the plausibility of our core premise—that despotic governments are more likely than their 'good guy' counterparts to engage in corrupt behaviour and that lack of democracy increases the pricing penalties associated with the presence of political corruption. That, in turn, would make the government's debt more vulnerable to future repudiation under domestic laws of either the debtor country or the country whose laws are designated as governing the debt contracts. Section 12.5 concludes with a proposal for how to systematize this endeavour.

12.2 Hunger Bonds and the Hausmann Effect

As noted at the start, academics have been arguing for multiple decades as to whether international law needs an exception to the strict rule of governmental/state succession under which the debts of despotic regimes do not need to be paid by the good guys when they finally overthrow the despot (Buchheit, Gulati & Thompson 2007; King, 2017). The problem, as history teaches us, is the difficulty of defining ex ante who is a despot and who is a good guy. And, as a result, the endeavour of creating a new legal doctrine—which periodically rears its head every time some new despot is removed and civil society organizations want to enable the successor government to thrive without being burdened by the debts that the despot left behind—has consistently hit a brick wall (Gelpern, 2005).[3]

But, on 26 May 2017, Ricardo Hausmann, a professor at the Harvard Kennedy School, produced a chink in the armour. Professor Hausmann published an op-ed at the website Project Syndicate (Hausmann, 2017) which argued that investing in Venezuelan bonds was causing harm to the Venezuelan people, because it was helping finance a despotic regime that was privileging the repayment of bondholders over the welfare of people.[4] He also, the same day, went on Bloomberg Television to talk about his idea. Hausmann's target in the May 2017 piece was JPMorgan's emerging markets index (the EMBI+) (Crooks, 2017). He was advocating that JPMorgan remove Venezuela from the EMBI+ so as to make Venezuelan bonds less attractive to the markets and particularly fund managers who measure their performance as a function of how they do vis-à-vis the index.

Unbeknownst to Hausmann, two days prior, on 23 May 2017, the asset management arm of Goldman Sachs (GSAM) had purchased bonds with a face value of $2.8 billion issued by the Venezuelan state-owned oil company, PDVSA. GSAM paid 31 cents on the dollar, for a total disbursement of about $865 million. Almost simultaneously, Venezuela's international reserves increased by about $750 million (for more detail, see Gulati & Panizza, 2018a).

Adding two plus two, a series of press articles conjectured that GSAM's bond purchase looked to be providing direct funding to the Venezuelan government, flying in the face of Hausmann's plea for the government to be starved of capital. Adding fuel to the fire, GSAM appeared to have purchased its bonds at a price that was 25 per cent below what other similarly situated PDVSA bonds were trading at. *The Wall Street Journal* broke the story on 30 May—their story was followed over the next two days by articles in *Bloomberg, The Financial Times* and soon almost every other major financial network was discussing it (Vyas, Kurmanaev & Wernau, 2017; Tanzi & Zerpa, 2017; Wigglesworth & Long, 2017). The bonds got dubbed 'Hunger Bonds' (the title of Hausmann's piece) for the hardship they were causing the Venezuelan people by diverting the government's foreign exchange reserves to debt service payments.

Those news stories were then tweeted out by Ricardo Hausmann and US Senator Marco Rubio, both of whose followers number in the hundreds of thousands. Rubio's tweet, echoing Hausmann's Project Syndicate piece said 'Today we learn that @GoldmanSachs just gave the Maduro regime in #Venezuela a $2.8 billion lifeline.' Hausmann also went on CNN; this time explicitly talking about the Hunger Bond and what he saw as 'morally

[3] We have written about the specific topic of the Hunger Bonds elsewhere and the discussion in this section utilizes that that work (Gulati & Panizza 2018a & b).

[4] This was but one of many pieces that Hausmann has written over the past few years criticizing the actions of the Maduro government, including 'The Venality of Evil' and 'D-day Venezuela' in 2018. See Hausmann (2018a & b).

indefensible' behaviour by GSAM.[5] By then protests had broken out outside GSAM's office in New York, with many protesters using 'hunger bonds' on their placards, photographs of which got circulated in the news media. The term Hunger Bond became indelibly associated with the single issuance that GSAM had purchased on 25 May 2017.

This was the tip of the iceberg. Two things happened next.

First, investors began asking their lawyers about whether there was something legally problematic about the Hunger Bonds, such that it might impair future recoveries on the bond. And the lawyers replied that there might indeed be a problem. It was not an issue that had ever come up in a sovereign debt restructuring—but this transaction looked egregious enough that it could be the basis for a refusal to pay by some future government.

The issue is what is called the Original Issue Discount (or 'OID') problem. The OID issue is that the face amount of GSAM's purchase of the Hunger Bonds was artificially inflated (and the interest rate artificially deflated). In ordinary conditions, with a solvent debt, it would not matter that the face value was artificially inflated or deflated as long as the interest rate balanced things out appropriately. But, for a debtor on the brink of insolvency, this does matter. The reason is that it is the face value of the claim rather than the unaccrued interest that typically determines what the size of one's claim is when the debtor goes into a debt workout situation. So, the creditors who show up when the debtor is on the brink of insolvency are in effect artificially diluting the claims of other creditors by inflating the face amounts of their claims. It is worth reiterating here that this is not an issue that—best we are aware—has come up in any prior sovereign restructuring. But, thanks to the attention that the media focused on the Hunger Bonds, a potential legal issue got unearthed.[6] GSAM, of course, insists

[5] The CNN Money clip is available at https://money.cnn.com/2017/05/30/news/economy/goldman-sachs-venezuela/index.html Accessed on November 17, 2020.

[6] Cramer et al. (2018), write: 'OID is considered interest under New York law. Courts have held that if debt is accelerated, any unearned interest on that debt, including stated principal masquerading as interest, does not need to be repaid at the time of acceleration. Because of the stark difference between the amount paid and the face value of the bond, a court would recognize that the face value of many of these instruments is not merely principal as it claims to be, but a highly inflated interest rate posing as principal. New York courts value substance over form.[22] As such, the court looking at these transactions would not allow clever misrepresentation to obscure the true circumstances of the transaction and would recognize the inflated principal as OID.'

Drawing from Cramer et al. (2018, the relevant cases here are: *LTV Corp. v. Valley Fid. Bank & Trust Co. (In re Chateaugay Corp.)*, 961 F.2d 378, 380–1 (2d Cir. 1992); *Aardwoolf Corp. v. Nelson Capital Corp.*, 861 F.2d 46 (2d Cir. 1988) (in the event of an acceleration, the courts will only allow payment of the unpaid balance of the principal and the matured interest up to the time of payment, and will exclude unearned interest); *Atlas Fin. Corp. v. Ezrine*, 345 N.Y.S.2d 36, 38 (App. Div. 1973) (describing the 'equitable principle that the unearned part of the interest must be deducted [from the amount due] upon acceleration'); *Berman v. Schwartz*, 298 N.Y.S2d 185 (NY Sup. Ct. 1968) (holding that the mere fact that the total interest is computed in advance and added in equal proportions to and included in the face amount of the notes as a form of prepaid interest does not change the equitable principle that the unearned part of the interest must be excluded).

that its purchase of the Hunger Bonds was a legitimate and arms-length secondary market transaction—and if that is proved to be the case, the OID issue would disappear. But the fact that the Venezuelan Central Bank's foreign currency reserves rose suspiciously around the time of the GSAM purchase, and by a roughly similar dollar amount, creates smoke (for more detail, see Gulati & Panizza, 2018a).

Second, institutional investors became scared that protesters would show up at their offices if they were seen as supporting the GSAM purchase, so they avoided it. Simultaneously, a number of big broker-dealers such as Credit Suisse announced that they would not be making a market for this bond (Wigglesworth & Platt, 2017). And, Hausmann's original target, the JPMorgan index managers, while not doing what he had asked, excluded this particular bond from the EMBI+ index (for more detail, drawn from interviews with market participants, see Gulati & Panizza, 2018a).

The end result: In the first week after the Hausmann op-ed, the liquidity of the Hunger Bond was killed and its price dropped by more than 16 percent while the price of comparable PDVSA bonds barely moved. In the world of international debt finance, which is generally presumed to be relatively efficient in terms of similar instruments trading at similar prices, that's a stunning price differential. To provide a concrete contrast, big differences in the contract terms that can have a crucial impact on an investor's recovery—such as the voting threshold required to alter the payment terms on the bond (e.g., the difference between 100 per cent and 75 per cent)—generally don't generate a price differential between otherwise identical bonds of more than a few basis points. Here, the price differential that was initiated by Professor Hausmann's article was almost fifty times that much (in previous work we call this the 'Hausmann Effect'). Over a year later, in August 2018, the Hunger Bond was still being treated as a pariah by the market—trading at a yield of roughly 100 basis points below an essentially equivalent bond. To illustrate, Figure 12.1 below shows the penalty that the Hunger Bond suffered, as compared to a similar Venezuelan bond, during the week after news of the suspicious aspects of the GSAM transaction got released. Figure 12.2 shows the same relationship, except over a longer time period.

Most important, for over a year there were no other transactions similar to the GSAM purchase that were carried out, even though we have heard from market sources that multiple such deals were in the works. We know the foregoing as a result of an extensive set of conversations we had with investors in both Europe and the US about this precise matter during the period February–May 2018 (for details, see Gulati & Panizza, 2018a). GSAM itself publicly expresses regret about having come anywhere near the Hunger Bond deal (Bartenstein, 2018).

Somehow, Professor Hausmann, with his 900-word op-ed and a combination of US Senator Marco Rubio's tweet, protests by civil society, and a large number of news articles, managed to do what a century of academic and policy advocacy had failed to. That is, increase the cost of capital for an arguably illegitimate

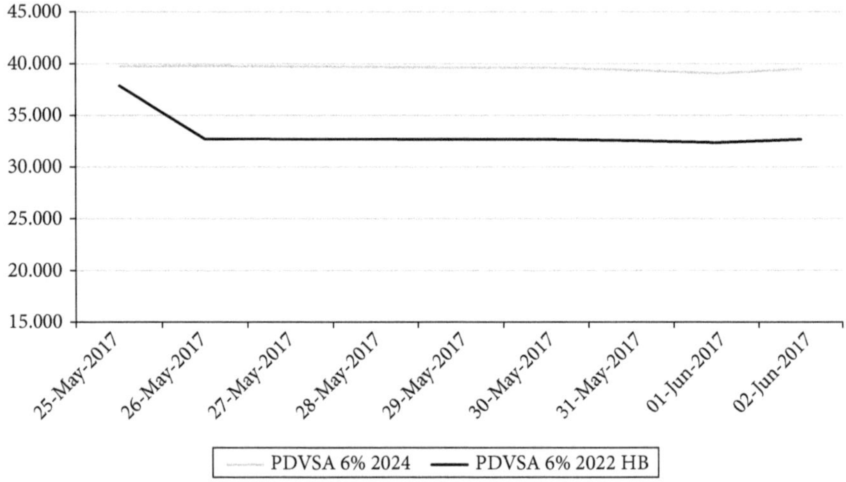

Figure 12.1. Hunger Bond and PDVSA 2024 6 per cent bond (May–June 2017)

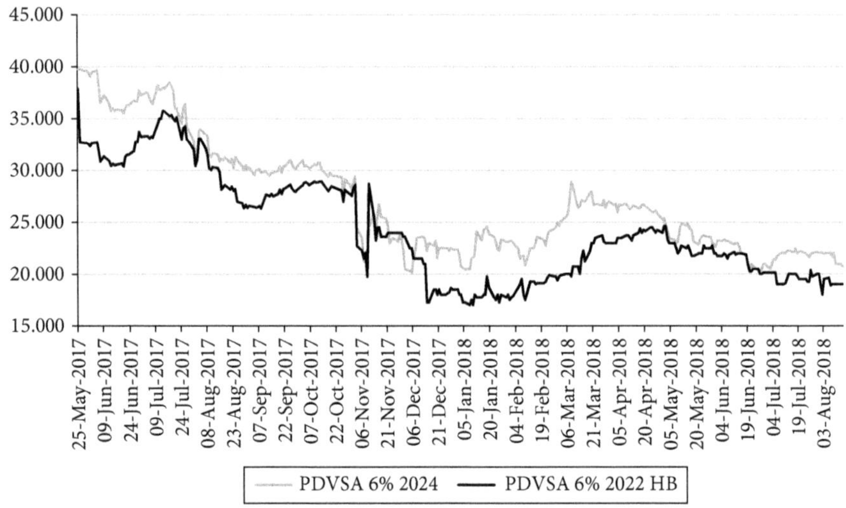

Figure 12.2. Hunger Bond and PDVSA 2024 6 per cent bond (October 2017–August 2018)

government. What we don't know, however, is what the key ingredients of this dynamic were and whether it can be replicated.[7] And a transaction that took place roughly a year later should give us reason for caution.

[7] Economic historians Kim Oosterlinck and Stephanie Collet tell a story similar to ours about one of the bonds issued by the Russian Tsar that that, in 1906, was denounced in an op-ed by the intellectual, Maxim Gorky. The result of the public outcry that followed was a sharp drop in the market value of that particular bond. See Collet & Oosterlinck (2019).

In August 2018, over a year after the Hunger Bonds event occurred, the Venezuelan government may have done something very similar to what it did with the GSAM transaction by using deeply discounted bonds to pay off an arbitration claim against it that had been brought by a Canadian mining company, Gold Reserve. *The Wall Street Journal*, again, was the first to flag this (Wernau & Scurria, 2018)—but this time there was no Hausmann article, Rubio tweet, and follow-up from other news agencies. Part of the reason for this lack of follow-up, we suspect, is that the details of the transaction are not clear; we cannot even tell what the specific bonds are that were given to Gold Reserve.

12.3 Some Possible Legal Challenges to Future Maduro Bonds[8]

Venezuela, as of this writing, in late 2020, is in default on all of its external debt. For several years now, despite having the largest oil reserves in the world, its sovereign debt has been the lowest rated debt in the JPMorgan Emerging Market Index. It has upwards of $150 billion in foreign currency denominated debt obligations that it appears to have no ability to pay (its foreign currency reserves have dwindled to under a few billion). Essentially, its sole source of foreign currency earnings is its oil industry, and a combination of government mismanagement of the oil industry and reduced international oil prices have landed the government in financial quicksand.[9]

For the Venezuelan government to be able to continue to transact in the international markets—something it needs to do since it is a single asset economy—without being under constant fear or creditor lawsuits and asset seizure, Mr Maduro has to restructure Venezuela's debt sooner rather than later. And indeed, he announced in November 2017 that that was precisely what his government intended to do (Platt & Schipani, 2017). That, in turn, since there is no money, means issuing the creditors with new debt instruments with lower promised amounts. Assuming for purposes of analysis that creditors could be persuaded to agree to a reduction of their claims, the first legal fly in the buttermilk has to do with the events of mid-2017. That was when President Maduro engineered the creation of a new legislative body (the Constituent Assembly) to approve his agenda items because the existing legislative body (the National Assembly) was controlled by the opposition parties and was not doing his bidding. This has provided us with a key event to illustrate the argument we are making.

[8] In this section, we draw in significant part from two pieces written for *The Financial Times* by one of us. See Gulati (2017) and Buchheit & Gulati (2017).

[9] *The Financial Times* has a podcast/interview with Ricardo Hausman that discusses how Venezuela landed in its current predicament. The podcast is available at https://ftalphaville.ft.com/2017/09/08/2193473/podcast-ricardo-hausmann-on-the-tragedy-in-venezuela/ accessed on 17 November, 2020.

The specific question on the table is whether the Maduro administration can now push through debt deals, with the approval of its new Constituent Assembly, that the old National Assembly would not have approved. Let us imagine, for purposes of illustration (and we are assuming that a method of getting around the US sanctions is devised), a deal in which holders of Venezuelan bonds are offered a swap. In exchange for granting the Maduro administration short-term debt relief, investors will get a new set of bonds (Maduro bonds), with more favourable terms for later payment. There would be a number of legal issues this deal might face.

Misbehaving Agent

Imagine a garden variety loan to a corporation. Would a court help the creditor get repaid if it turned out that she had made the loan through an agent who she knew was not authorized to conduct such transactions for the company? Or, if she transacted with a company representative who she knew planned to steal the funds? Basic agency law in the United States says no, and New York law governs almost all of the outstanding Venezuela debt instruments (Buchheit, Gulati & Thompson, 2007).

Along those lines, a post-Maduro government could argue that the Maduro bonds were not properly authorized by a representative body, claiming that authorization by the pro-Maduro Constituent Assembly was obviously inadequate, and that investors should have known that.

Relevant to the judge hearing the case might be the statements made by US officials in response to the election of the Constituent Assembly. President Trump said: 'Maduro is not just a bad leader, he is a dictator' (Mazzei, 2017). Similar statements about Maduro's illegitimacy are readily available from other senior US officials in the Trump administration, in addition to from senior figures in the governments of the UK, Argentina, Paraguay, Brazil, and so on.

Put all that together and a judge could find that the holders of Maduro bonds must have known that they were transacting with an unrepresentative or illegitimate agent of the people. And things could get worse. Agency law goes beyond merely voiding the contract between the principal and the third party; a third party who suborns a betrayal of trust by the agent may be answerable in tort to the principal.

The negotiations between Spain and the US after the Spanish-American war of 1898 provide an analogy. Spain, having lost and ceded Cuba to the US, argued that Spanish debts backed by Cuban revenue streams were now those of the US—citing the rule that along with a transfer of sovereignty came the transfer of sovereign obligations. The Americans rejected this claim on three grounds.

First, the loans had not been contracted for the benefit of Cuba; indeed, a portion of the proceeds had been spent to suppress rebellions on the island. Second, the Cuban people had not consented to the debts; they had been imposed by Spain. Third, the creditors knew that the pledges of Cuban revenues had been given in the context of efforts to suppress the freedom struggle. Creditors therefore, to quote a leading treatise of the time, 'took the obvious chances of their investment on so precarious a security' (for more detail, see Buchheit, Gulati & Thompson, 2007).

The foregoing argument is strong on the facts—the agents here are obviously misbehaving, and everyone knows it. The weakness is in the law. While courts readily accept the argument that a CEO is an agent of the company with legal obligations that third parties should know about, they have not yet embraced this view of the relationship between a government and its people in that fashion, except at a metaphorical level. That said, portions of international law in the post–Second World War era—starting with the Nuremberg trials, and particularly in the area of human rights—has been moving in this direction (e.g., Criddle & Fox-Decent, 2016; Fox-Decent, 2011). Plus, the political philosophy of every major modern democracy is based on the model of the government being the agent of the populace.

Unauthorized Transaction

An alternate approach might argue that the Maduro bonds are void because they were issued in violation of Venezuelan local law; specifically, the need for National Assembly approval that is specified in current law. Unlike the agency argument that has good facts, but could use stronger law, this second argument is strong on the law but might need better facts.

US law dating back to the nineteenth century says that municipal obligations issued in violation of law are void. The courts will not even allow investors to collect based on equitable principles.[10]

The facts, however, may be weak. The Maduro bonds will presumably be issued in compliance with future Venezuelan law as such law shall have been promulgated by the Constituent Assembly. It is the Constituent Assembly itself and all of its works that the post-Maduro government must argue are unauthorized, invalid, and illegitimate. And the longer the Constituent Assembly stays in power and makes the laws of the country, the more it begins to look like the real legislature.

[10] *See* Lichfield v. Ballou, 114 U.S. 190 (1885); Buchanan v. Litchfield, 102 U.S. 278 (1880). A contemporary case of debtor seeking debt relief on the ground the debt was not authorized properly is that of Puerto Rico. *See* Chari & Leary (2020).

The issue, we suspect, will come down to a question of whether new Republic of Venezuela bonds are duly 'authorized' by the Republic. Although most existing Republic of Venezuela debt instruments choose New York law as the governing law of the instruments, the bonds also contain this additional sentence: 'Authorization and execution of this security by the issuer, however, shall be governed by the laws of the Republic of Venezuela.' This sentence places the monkey squarely on the backs of the Venezuelan lawyers to opine whether a new Republic debt instrument has been authorized as a matter of Venezuelan law. That is, the matter will not be free from doubt.

Under the existing Venezuelan Constitution, as we understand it, a valid Republic debt obligation requires the prior approval of the Venezuelan legislature—the National Assembly. The opposition parties have held a majority of seats in the National Assembly since the end of 2015. The National Assembly has not given its consent to legislation approving national indebtedness since that time. This has set the stage for a three-way constitutional quarrel. President Maduro has been ruling pursuant to Emergency Decrees since September 2016. These Decrees purport to override the need for any authorizations or approvals from other branches of government. The Venezuelan Supreme Court (now packed with pro-Maduro judges) has endorsed the constitutionality of the Emergency Decrees. And, as noted, Mr Maduro has also put in place a more pliable body that he has claimed is the more representative body and, therefore, the appropriate legislative body. For its part, the National Assembly has announced that any financing transaction entered into without National Assembly blessing shall be an absolute 'nullity'.

One can sympathize with the plight of a US federal judge confronted, as she may be, with battling banjo Venezuelan legal opinions about the validity of new Republic debt instruments under Venezuelan law. The most likely fact pattern for such a case would be the issuance of new debt instruments by the current administration, followed by a change of regime, followed by a refusal of the new administration to recognize the validity of those instruments. If the instruments are governed by New York law and the action to enforce the instruments is brought in a US court, it will ultimately fall to a US federal judge to decide between competing legal opinions about the state of Venezuelan law at the time the instruments were issued.

The arguments will spin out as follows: The holders of the new bonds will argue that the Venezuelan Supreme Court—the final arbiter of constitutional law questions in Venezuela—confirmed the authorization and validity of the instruments at the time they were issued. That, the bondholders will suggest, should end the matter. The successor administration, seeking to repudiate the bonds, will argue that the Venezuelan Supreme Court has effectively become an organ of the Executive Branch. Statements, including statements by the US Government, to the effect that the Constituent Assembly is illegitimate may also be enlisted in support of the proposition that an illegitimate political body cannot authorize otherwise unconstitutional executive actions.

Bottom line: if investors considering whether to purchase of Maduro administration debt instruments ask their lawyers about whether there is a significant chance that successor governments might have defences against paying them, the answer will be yes. And, as we saw with the Hunger Bonds, opposition leaders and civil society organizations could, by the din of their objections, cause attention to focus on these matters.

12.4 Democracy, Corruption, and Sovereign Spreads

In this section, we move beyond the specific case of Venezuela—which seems to bear out our premise that despotic governments will engage in the type of illegal actions that will result in legal infirmities that later governments can utilize against creditors. The broader question is whether the positive relationship between despotism and corruption shows up more generally; i.e., wherever one finds despots in power. There are no publicly available measures of country despotism or governmental violations of internal laws in raising capital. Hence, we use as our proxies for those two variables the available measures for how democratic the country is (the least democratic being assumed to be closest to being despotic) and public corruption.

Boiled down, our idea that legal infirmities can potentially be used as a tool to limit access to credit to despotic governments is based on three assumptions: (i) that despotic regimes are more likely to be corrupt; (ii) that there is a price penalty associated with a corrupt behaviour (because it produces risks of future repudiation for those in the transaction); and (iii) that this price penalty associated with corruption is higher for despotic regimes (because the risks are higher here).

To test these assumptions, we gathered data on sovereign spreads and for two indicators measuring control of corruption and the level of democracy. Our data cover twenty-three emerging market countries for the period 1994–2017.[11] Sovereign spreads, which we collect at quarterly frequency, range between 11 and 7,100 with an average of 474 and a standard deviation of 687 (Table 12.1).

We measure democracy with the 'Level of Democracy' variable from the Quality of Government Database.[12] This variables ranges between 0 and 10 (with higher values indicating more democratic countries) and is computed as

[11] Argentina, Brazil, Bulgaria, Chile, China, Colombia, Dominican Republic, Ecuador, Egypt, Hungary, India, Malaysia, Mexico, Pakistan, Panama, Peru, Poland, Russia, Slovakia, South Africa, Turkey, Uruguay, and Venezuela. Spread data are available at quarterly frequency and the panel is unbalanced. In 1994, we only have data for five countries; from 1998, we have data for 15 countries, from 2001 20 countries, and 23 countries from 2013.

[12] The data are available at https://qog.pol.gu.se/data.

Table 12.1. Summary statistics

	Obs	Mean	Std. Dev.	Min	Max
Spread (bps)	1,805	474	687	11	7,116
Democracy	1,761	7.3	2.4	0.8	10
Control of Corruption	1,761	2.5	0.8	1	5

an average of the Freedom House indexes of civil liberties and political rights (this is the same measure of democracy used by Fortunato & Panizza 2011). In our sample, this variable ranges between 0.75 and 10, with an average of 7.3 and a standard deviation of 2.4.

Finally, we measure corruption utilizing the International Country Risk Guide (ICRG) index of control of corruption. ICRG focuses on political corruption and describes its indicator as an 'assessment of corruption within the political system' with a special focus on patronage, nepotism, secret party funding, and ties between politics and business.[13] In our sample, the indicator of corruption ranges between 1 (maximum amount of corruption) and 5 (minimum amount of corruption). The mean value is 2.5, with a standard deviation of 0.8.

As a first step, we show that there is a correlation between control of corruption and the level of democracy. The correlation between these two variables is 0.44 and statistically significant at the 1 per cent confidence level. Figure 12.3 plots cross-country averages for the period 2010–15 and shows the fit of a simple statistical model in which control of corruption is regressed over democracy. While the relationship between the two variables is positive and statistically significant, there are many countries that are far from the regression line. For instance, China is less corrupt than what is predicted by its level of democracy and the Dominican Republic and Venezuela are more corrupt than what is predicted by their level of democracy.

After having established the presence of a correlation between corruption and the level of democracy, we check the correlation between each of these variables and sovereign spreads. The first two columns of Table 12.2 show the results of simple univariate models in which sovereign spreads are regressed on corruption and democracy. They show that there is a negative correlation between control of corruption and spreads (i.e., less corrupt countries have lower spreads), but no statistically significant relationship between the level of democracy and sovereign

[13] According to ICRG, this type of corruption is particularly risky for foreign investors because it can: '...lead to popular discontent, unrealistic and inefficient controls on the state economy, and encourage the development of the black market. The greatest risk in such corruption is that at some time it will become so overweening, or some major scandal will be suddenly revealed, as to provoke a popular backlash, resulting in a fall overthrow of the government, a major reorganizing or restructuring of the country's political institutions, or, at worst, a breakdown in law and order, rendering the country ungovernable' (PRS, p. 5).

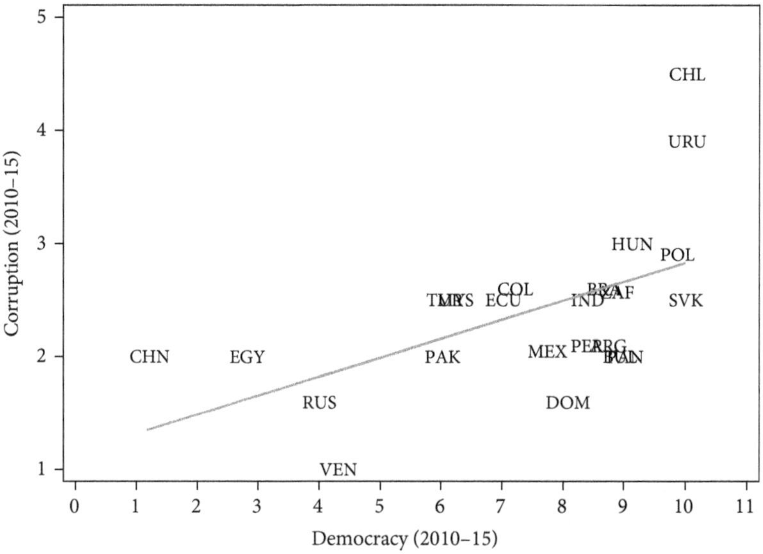

Figure 12.3. Correlation between democracy and control of corruption (2010–15)

Note: The line plots the result of the regression CORR=1.14+0.16xDEM. The t statistics on the coefficient of the democracy variable is 3.05 (p-value<0.01). The regression's R^2 is 0.31 (23 observations)

spreads. These results are robust to including both variables in the same regressions (column 3).

There are three problems with the regressions of columns 1–3. First, they do not control for a series of country-specific time invariant unobservable factors that could be jointly correlated with sovereign spreads and each of democracy and control of corruption. Second, they do not control for time-variant fundamentals which could be jointly correlated with sovereign spreads and each of corruption and democracy. Third, they do not recognize that sovereign spreads are closely correlated with credit ratings and that rating agencies take into account institutional variables such as the level of democracy and corruption when they issue their rating opinions (Panizza, 2017).

To control for these elements we augment the specification of column 3 with a set of country and time fixed effects and we also control for credit ratings.[14] Inasmuch as ratings control for all fundamentals, this specification measures if corruption and democracy are correlated with spreads even after we control for the fundamentals normally considered by credit rating agencies. Column 4 of Table 12.2 shows that, as expected, higher ratings are correlated with lower

[14] Whenever available we use Standard and Poor's sovereign ratings. When S&P ratings are not available we use Moody's rating. We convert letter ratings into a numerical scale using the same methodology described in Panizza (2017).

Table 12.2. Spreads, democracy, and corruption

	(1)	(2)	(3)	(4)	(5)	(6)	(7)	(8)
Control of Corruption	–79.51***		–86.84***	–47.72**	6.515	–52.10**	–541.42***	9.47
	(17.81)		(18.76)	(24.10)	(29.64)	(24.88)	(157.15)	(10.69)
Democracy		–7.193	5.372	–41.12**	–9.362	–33.77**	293.51	57.03
		(4.994)	(4.931)	(16.63)	(19.37)	(16.87)	(196.29)	(28.69)
Dem × Corr					17.93**	13.70**		
					(7.041)	(6.839)		
Rating				–197.4***		–197.1***	–6.86	–40.20***
				(20.27)		(20.30)	(45.13)	(2.46)
Constant	674.5***	528.7***	653.4***					
	(52.05)	(40.19)	(54.87)					
Observations	1,761	1,761	1,761	1,724	1,761	1,724	109	409
Country FE	No	No	No	Yes	Yes	Yes	No	No
Quarter-Year FE	No	No	No	Yes	Yes	Yes	Yes	Yes
Sample	All	All	All	All	All	All	DEM<3	DEM>9

Note: Robust standard errors in parenthesis,

* statistically significant at 10 per cent confidence level,

** statistically significant at 5 per cent confidence level, and

*** statistically significant at 1 per cent confidence level.

spreads. More surprising, we find that our result of a negative and statistically significant correlation between corruption and sovereign spread is robust to controlling for country fixed effects and credit rating. In this case, we also find that democracy is negatively correlated with sovereign spreads (more democracy, lower spreads). This is a strong result, as control of corruption and democratic institutions are slow-moving variables (and hence correlated with the country fixed effects), and the effect of corruption and democracy should already be captured, at least in part, by the rating score (Panizza, 2017, shows that there is a positive correlation between credit ratings and control of corruption).

Next, we test our hypothesis that corruption is especially damaging in less democratic countries by interacting democracy with control of corruption. Specifically, we estimate the following model:

$$SPREAD_{c,t} = \alpha_c + \tau_t + \delta(DEM_{c,t} - \bar{DEM}) + \kappa(CORR_{c,t} - \bar{CORR}) +$$

$$+ \chi[(DEM_{c,t} - \bar{DEM}) \times (CORR_{c,t} - \bar{CORR})] + \varepsilon_{c,t}$$

In this set up, δ measures the correlation between democracy and spreads when control of corruption is at its cross-country average (if we had not demeaned the variables, δ would have measured the correlation between democracy and spreads when control of corruption is equal to zero), κ measures the correlation between control of corruption and spreads when democracy is at its cross-country average, and χ measures how the correlation between control of corruption and sovereigns spreads varies with the level of democracy.[15] This is our key parameter of interest. If corruption is particularly damaging for democratic regimes, we expect χ to be positive and statistically significant, that is we expect that reducing corruption is more strongly correlated (in absolute value) with sovereign spreads in country-years characterized by low levels of democracy. If our hypothesis holds, instead, control of corruption should be less important in democracies.

Column 5 of Table 12.2 reports the results and shows that while neither corruption nor democracy are statistically significant when evaluated at the mean value of the other variable, the interactive coefficient (i.e., the parameter χ) is positive and statistically significant. This finding is consistent with our hypothesis that the correlation between corruption and sovereign spreads is particularly strong in non-democratic countries. And that is especially so when one isolates that subset of least democratic countries; that is the ones that are likely to be closest to being despotic.

In column 6, we control for country fundamentals by including sovereign ratings in the regression. We now find that both democracy and control of

[15] Alternatively, how the correlation between democracy and sovereign spreads varies with control of corruption.

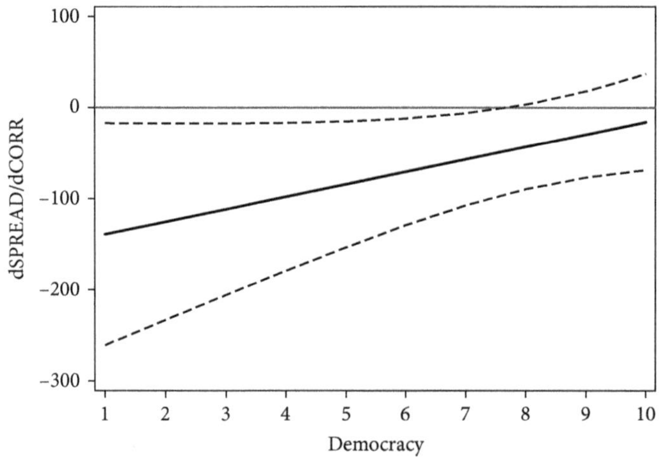

Figure 12.4. Marginal effect of corruption at different levels of democracy
Note: Based on the estimates of Table 12.2, column 6. The dotted lines plot a 95 per cent confidence interval

corruption are significantly correlated with sovereign spreads when evaluated at the mean value of the other variable; and even more interesting, we find that the interaction between corruption and democracy remains positive and statistically significant. Figure 12.4 uses the model of column 6 to plot the correlation between spreads and corruption at different levels of democracy. It shows that the correlation is negative and statistically significant up to the point at which our measure of democracy is about 7.5 (this was the level of democracy in Mexico over 2010–15), it then remains negative but not statistically significant. Figure 12.5 uses the estimates of Table 12.2 to plot the correlation between spreads and democracy conditional on the level of corruption. It shows that democracy is strongly correlated with sovereign spreads in countries characterized by high levels of corruption, but that democracy is no longer statistically significant when the index of control of corruption is above 2.5 (the level of corruption in India, Malaysia, Slovakia, and Turkey over 2010–15).

To further explore the role of corruption in countries in despotic regimes with low levels of democracy, we estimate the baseline model of column 4 by limiting the sample countries with an index of democracy below 3. Whether these are true despotic regimes or not is in the eyes of the beholder, but they are the countries in the bottom 10 per cent of our distribution of the democracy index. It should be noted that this subsample does not include countries like North Korea because North Korea does not issue bonds in the international market and therefore there are no data on spreads or sovereign rating. However, the subsample does include Venezuela starting in 2017.

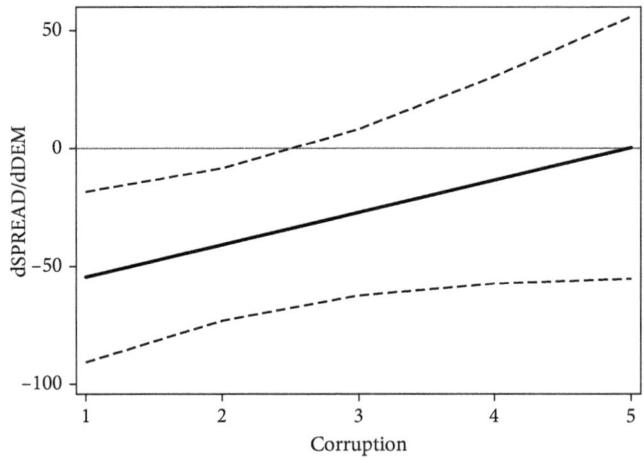

Figure 12.5. Marginal effect of democracy at different levels of corruption
Note: Based on the estimates of Table 12.2, column 6. The dotted lines plot a 95 per cent confidence interval

When we restrict the sample to non-democratic countries we find a strong negative correlation between control of corruption and spread even after controlling for sovereign ratings. Specifically, column 7 of Table 12.2 shows that a one-point improvement in the control of corruption indicator is associated with a 540-basis-point reduction in sovereign spreads. While we do not want to make too much of this result, which is based on a small sample of countries and is likely to suffer from endogeneity bias, the effect is large. It is also worth noting that for this sample of countries, sovereign ratings do not seem to matter and control of corruption is the only variable that has a statistically significant effect on spreads (note that sovereign ratings have the usual negative effect on spreads if we do not control for the level of corruption and democracy). This result is in contrast with what we find in column 8 of Table 12.2 where we limit the sample to fully democratic countries (i.e., countries in which the index of democracy is greater than 9). In this case, we find that corruption is not statistically significant while credit ratings are highly significant, with a one-notch improvement in sovereign rating being associated with a 40-basis-point reduction in sovereign spreads.

12.5 Conclusion

The foregoing suggests a new possibility towards establishing a tool that can limit access to credit by despotic regimes that goes beyond arguing for a doctrine of odious debts. What the Hunger Bonds story in particular suggests is that effectively crowdsourced disapproval of a despotic regime can raise the cost of capital for the regime. To make this crowdsourced disapproval work more systematically, perhaps a public ranking of bonds which lists potential ethical and legal problems of individual bonds would lead to price penalties for bonds with legal infirmities and increase the borrowing costs for regimes that, besides being despotic, adopt murky debt management practices. In the presence of this type of public information, few investors could claim to have bought a bond on the secondary market without knowing the illegal origin of the bond. This would depress the price of the bond in the secondary market and, hence, also increase the cost of funds in the primary market. Such a system could also help the opposition parties in countries with potentially despotic regimes announce their future plans regarding likely future investigation or even repudiation of those bonds. Indeed, to our surprise, an August 2018 *Wall Street Journal* article doing a 'one year later' update on the Hunger Bonds story from May 2017 reported that there might well be developing a market for such information among institutional investors. Apparently, a number of these firms—who, as part of their consideration of environmental, social, and governance factors, are looking to the degree of authoritarianism of a government (Wirz, 2018).

While modest, this proposal has the advantage of not requiring any legal innovation or international consensus-building because it is based on existing law and legal principles. It is readily implementable and would be a step in the right direction. At worst, it would create incentives (for all countries) to adopt more transparent sovereign debt management practices.

References

Bonilla, S. (2011). *Odious Debt: Law and Economics Perspectives*. Wiesbaden, Springer-Gabler Press.

Bartenstein, B. (2018). 'Goldman Says It's Learned From the Hunger Bonds Backlash', *Bloomberg*, 15 March 2018. https://www.bloomberg.com/news/articles/2018-03-15/goldman-says-it-s-learned-from-venezuela-hunger-bonds-backlash (Accessed 9 March 2020).

Buchheit, L. C. & Gulati, M. (2017). 'Enforcing New Venezuelan Public Debt Instruments', *FT Alphaville*, 18 August 2017. https://ftalphaville.ft.com/2017/08/18/2192462/enforcing-new-venezuelan-public-debt-instruments-maduro-bonds-part-2/ (Accessed 9 March 2020).

Buchheit, L. C., Gulati, M. & Thompson, R. (2007). 'The Dilemma of Odious Debts'. *Duke Law Journal*, 56, 1201–62.

Casey, N & Davis, J. (2018). 'As Trump Adds Sanctions on Venezuela, Its Neighbors Reject Election Results', *The New York Times*, 21 May 2018. https://www.nytimes.com/2018/05/21/world/americas/venezuela-nicolas-maduro-sanctions.html (Accessed 9 March 2020).

Chari, A. & Leary, R. (2020). 'Contract Provisions, Default Risk and Bond Prices: Evidence From Puerto Rico', in P. Pénet & J. Flores Zendejas (Eds.), *Sovereign Debt Diplomacies*: Rethinking sovereign debt from colonial empires to hegemony. Oxford University Press.

Choi, A. & Posner, E. A. (2007). A Critique of the Odious Debt Doctrine. *Law and Contemporary Problems*, 70, 33–63.

Choi, S. J. & Gulati, M. (2016). 'Customary International Law: How do Courts Do it? in Custom's Future: International Law in a Changing World Curtis A. Bradley' (Ed.), New York, Cambridge University Press.

Collet, S. & Oosterlinck, K. (2019). 'Denouncing Odious Debts'. *Journal of Business Ethics*, 160(1), 205–25.

Cramer, M., Kropp, A., Moore, K. & Saad, C. (2018). 'Lien-ing in on PDVSA: The Positive Side of Negative Pledge'. Available at: https://papers.ssrn.com/sol3/papers.cfm?abstract_id=3158780 (Accessed 10 November 2020).

Criddle, E. & Fox-Decent, E. (2016). 'Keeping the Promise of Public Fiduciary Theory', *Yale Law Journal Forum*, 26 October 2016. https://www.yalelawjournal.org/forum/keeping-the-promise-of-public-fiduciary-theory-a-reply-to-leib-and-galoob (Accessed 9 March 2020).

Crooks, N. (2017). 'Harvard's Hausmann Asks JPMorgan to Cut Venezuela from Index', *Bloomberg*, 26 May 2017. https://www.bloomberg.com/news/articles/2017-05-26/harvard-s-hausmann-calls-on-jpmorgan-to-cut-venezuela-from-index (Accessed 9 March 2020).

Datz, G. (2020). 'Placing Contemporary Sovereign Debt: The Fragmented Landscape of Legal Precedent and Legislative Preemption', in P. Pénet & J. Flores Zendejas (Eds.), *Sovereign Debt Diplomacies: Rethinking sovereign debt from colonial empires to hegemony*. Oxford University Press.

Fortunato, Piergiuseppe & Ugo Panizza. (2011). 'Democracy, Education and the Quality of Government'. *POLIS Working Paper 155*, Institute of Public Policy and Public Choice.

Fox-Decent, E. (2011). *Sovereignty's Promise: The State as Fiduciary*. Oxford, Oxford University Press.

Gelpern, A. (2005). 'Lessons That Iraq and Argentina Might Learn From Each Other'. *Chicago Journal of International Law*, 6, 391–421.

Gulati, M. (2017). 'Maduro Bonds', *FT Alphaville*, 8 August 2017. https://ftalphaville.ft.com/2017/08/08/2192263/maduro-bonds/ (Accessed 9 March 2020).

Gulati, M. & Panizza, U. (2018a). 'The Hausmann-Gorky Effect', available at: https://papers.ssrn.com/sol3/papers.cfm?abstract_id=3141389 (forthcoming *Journal of Business Ethics*).

Gulati, M. & Panizza, U. (2018b). 'A New Way to Impose Financial Sanctions on Dictators', *Oxford Business Law Blog*, 9 May 2018. https://www.law.ox.ac.uk/business-law-blog/blog/2018/05/new-way-impose-financial-sanctions-dictators (Accessed 9 March 2020).

Hausmann, R. (2017). 'The Hunger Bonds', *Project Syndicate*, 26 May 2017. https://www.project-syndicate.org/commentary/maduro-venezuela-hunger-bonds-by-ricardo-hausmann-2017-05?barrier=accesspaylog (Accessed 9 March 2020).

Hausmann, R. (2018a). 'The Venality of Evil', *Project Syndicate*, 31 July 2018. https://www.project-syndicate.org/commentary/venezuela-collapse-a-deliberate-choice-by-ricardo-hausmann-2018–07 (Accessed 9 March 2020).

Hausmann, R. (2018b). 'D-Day Venezuela', *Project Syndicate*, 2 January 2018. https://www.project-syndicate.org/commentary/venezuela-catastrophe-military-intervention-by-ricardo-hausmann-2018–01?barrier=accesspaylog (Accessed 9 March 2020).

King, J. (2016). *The Doctrine of Odious Debt in International Law: A Restatement*. Cambridge, Cambridge University Press.

Kremer, M. & Jayachandran, S. (2006). 'Odious Debt'. *American Economic Review* 96, 82–92.

Lienau, O. (2014). *Rethinking Sovereign Debt: Politics, Reputation and Legitimacy in Modern Finance*. Cambridge, Massachusetts, Harvard University Press.

Mazzei, P. (2017). 'US Slaps Sanctions on Maduro and Labels Him a "Dictator"'. *Miami Herald*, 31 July 2017. https://www.miamiherald.com/news/nation-world/world/americas/venezuela/article164575852.html (Accessed 9 March 2020).

Michalowski, S. (2009a). 'The Doctrine of Odious Debts in International Law', in M. Mader & A. Rothenbühler (Eds.), *How to Challenge Illegitimate Debt: Theory and Legal Case Studies*. Basel, Aktion Finanzplatz Schweiz Publishers.

Michalowski, S. (2009b). 'Using Private Law for the Repudiation of Odious Debts', in M. Mader & A. Rothenbühler (Eds.), *How to Challenge Illegitimate Debt: Theory and Legal Case Studies*. Basel, Aktion Finanzplatz Schweiz Publishers.

Nehru, V. & Thomas, M. (2008). *The Concept of Odious Debt: Some Considerations*. World Bank: Economic Policy and Debt Department Discussion Paper. http://siteresources.worldbank.org/INTDEBTDEPT/Resources/468980–1184253591417/OdiousDebtPaper.pdf

Panizza, U. (2017). 'The Use of Corruption Indicators in Sovereign Ratings'. IDB Working Paper. https://publications.iadb.org/handle/11319/8562 (Accessed 10 November 2020).

Pénet, P. (2018). Rethinking Odious Debts, *Books and Ideas: College de France* (March 19), at http://www.booksandideas.net/Rethinking-Odious-Debt.html (Accessed 10 November 2020).

Platt, E. & Schipani, A. (2017). Venezuela's Maduro Announces Plans for Debt Restructuring, *The Financial Times*, 2 November 2017. https://www.ft.com/content/b6abcff9-78d8-3077-b84c-a2ed1043b6ea (Accessed 10 November 2020).

Stephan, P. (2007). 'The Institutionalist Implications of an Odious Debt Doctrine'. *Law & Contemporary Problems* 70, 213–32.

Tanzi, C. J. & Zerpa, F. (2017). 'Goldman Sachs Just Ignited the Venezuela "Hunger Bonds" Movement', *Bloomberg*, 31 May 2017. https://www.bloomberg.com/news/articles/2017-05-31/goldman-sachs-gave-big-hand-to-venezuela-hunger-bonds-movement (Accessed 10 November 2020).

Vyas, K., Kurmanaev, A. & Wernau, J. (2017). 'Goldman Sachs Under Fire for Venezuela Bond Deal', *Wall Street Journal*, 30 May 2017. https://www.wsj.com/articles/goldman-sachs-under-fire-for-venezuela-bond-deal-1496100583 (Accessed 10 November 2020).

Wernau, J. & Scurria, A. (2018). 'Venezuela Uses Bonds to Pay Settlement with Mining Company', *Wall Street Journal*, 16 August 2018. https://www.wsj.com/articles/venezuelan-government-uses-bonds-to-pay-settlement-with-miner-1534411801 (Accessed 10 November 2020).

Wigglesworth, R. & Gideon L. (2017). 'Why Goldman's Venezuela Bond Trade Sparked Controversy', *The Financial Times*, 1 June 2017. https://www.ft.com/content/c2f0fc3c-466b-11e7-8519-9f94ee97d996 (Accessed 9 March 2020).

Wigglesworth, R. & Platt, E. (2017). 'Credit Suisse Institutes Trader Ban on Venezuela Bonds', *The Financial Times*, 10 August 2017. https://www.ft.com/content/ea76f1aa-7e0e-11e7-ab01-a13271d1ee9c (Accessed 9 March 2020).

Wirz, M. (2018). 'Goldman Faces Losses on Venezuelan Bond Deal That Drew Criticism', *Wall Street Journal*, 19 August 2018. https://www.wsj.com/articles/goldman-faces-losses-on-venezuelan-bond-deal-that-drew-criticism-1534683601 (Accessed 9 March 2020).

13

Contract Provisions, Default Risk, and Bond Prices

Evidence from Puerto Rico

Anusha Chari and Ryan Leary

13.1 Introduction

Puerto Rico's financial crisis, involving a debt burden of about $72 billion, marks the most significant municipal restructuring in US history. This chapter joins a growing body of literature that studies Puerto Rico's crisis.[1] We conduct a case study to investigate the pricing of key contract provisions of Puerto Rican debt. Consistent with existing literature we ask the questions: (a) do investors price contract provisions? and (b) does the pricing of contract provisions vary with credit risk? To our knowledge, this is the first study to address these questions for Puerto Rico or any municipal issuer. Puerto Rican debt offers multiple sources of variation in the contract provisions included across the different types of debt issuance.

Puerto Rico's debt crisis and default in 2016 is the latest in a long line of sovereign default crises which have raised questions about legal risk in the pricing of contract provisions and their potential modification by sovereign legislatures and domestic courts after issuance.[2] Indeed, sovereign debt is unique in that the issuer's legislature and court system have the authority to impose restructuring terms on holders of domestic law debt (Zettlemeyer et al., 2013; Chamon et al., 2018).

To address legal risk and reduce borrowing costs, sovereigns turn to debt issuance under foreign legal systems, typically in New York or London, where domestic legislative fiat and domestic courts have limited power to affect contract provisions (Carletti et al., 2019). Sovereigns have also sought to include contract provisions aimed at streamlining the restructuring process. In particular, collective action clauses (referred to as 'CACs' throughout), which allow a majority of creditors to impose restructuring terms on holdout creditors, are commonly

[1] See Feliciano and Green (2017); Chari et al. (2017); Gulati and Rasmussen (2017); Park and Samples (2017).

[2] For example, consider the case of Greece's restructuring in 2012, when Greece imposed a retroactive modification of contract terms (Zettlemeyer et al., 2013).

Anusha Chari and Ryan Leary, *Contract Provisions, Default Risk, and Bond Prices: Evidence from Puerto Rico* In: *Sovereign Debt Diplomacies: Rethinking Sovereign Debt from Colonial Empires to Hegemony.* Edited by: Pierre Pénet and Juan Flores Zendejas, Oxford University Press (2021). © Oxford University Press. DOI: 10.1093/oso/9780198866350.003.0014

included in sovereign debt since the mid-1990s (Panizza et al., 2009; Aguiar & Amador, 2014). US municipal and corporate issuers have also sought to secure debt by including provisions pledging specific assets or revenue streams.

Puerto Rico's unique status as a sub-sovereign of the United States created investor concerns about legal risk. In turn, these concerns led to the inclusion of some of the same contract provisions seen in the sovereign and municipal debt markets. First, Puerto Rico debt provides two types of legal protections that to our knowledge are unique among sovereign issuers and offer protection from the legal risk inherent in domestic law debt. First, Puerto Rico issued general obligation debt (referred to as 'GO' hereafter) which is backed by the full faith and credit of Puerto Rico and with guarantees of payment before any other obligation under Puerto Rico's constitution. Second, Puerto Rico issued debt under a related entity, the Puerto Rico Sales Tax Financing Corporation (referred to as 'COFINA' hereafter) which does not provide recourse to the full faith and credit of Puerto Rico, but rather promises by law the first lien on a sales and use tax. The pledged revenues were deemed unavailable for the payment of any other obligation, including GO debt. We ask the question: do investors price the constitutional protections of GO debt and the secured revenues offered by COFINA debt differentially? To answer this question, we match Puerto Rican law GO debt to COFINA debt along observable security issue characteristics and estimate the average yield differential in the otherwise equivalent debt.

Second, the US federal government passed PROMESA which retroactively imposed CACs on Puerto Rican debt. However, PROMESA differs from other cases of CACs because the decision was imposed post issuance by an outside government and included an option for a court-supervised restructuring process which like CACs, allows the binding of holdout creditors (Gulati & Rasmussen, 2017). On the one hand, PROMESA may create an incentive for Puerto Rico to default by making default easier, reducing individual bond-holder rights versus the prior unanimous consent clauses. On the other hand, given default PROMESA reduces negotiation inefficiencies and improves the prospects for an orderly recovery by bondholders.[3] We ask the question, how did investors price the change in the restructuring process created by PROMESA? We use an event study to measure the effect of news events indicating the law was closer to enactment to answer the question.

Third, Puerto Rico issued debt under New York law in 2014, with the typical and express aim of assuaging investor concerns about the bias of domestic courts.[4,5] However, Puerto Rico's New York law debt is interesting in that it

[3] See Ghosal and Thampanishvong (2013) for a discussion of this trade-off for CACs.

[4] https://www.publicfinancematters.com/2014/02/could-bondholders-bring-claims-against-puerto-ricobond-issuers-in-courts-outside-puerto-rico/#more-989 (Accessed 10 November 2020).

[5] New York courts are also known to be among the most protective of creditor rights.

may violate the law by exceeding Puerto Rico's legally mandated debt service limits, potentially rendering the debt unenforceable and void (Showalter, 2017). Therefore, we ask how did investors price Puerto Rican debt issued under New York law versus Puerto Rican law? To answer this question, we match Puerto Rican law debt to New York law debt along observable security issue characteristics and estimate the average yield differential in the otherwise equivalent debt using panel regression techniques. In all three cases (New York Law vs. PR Law debt, GO vs. COFINA, and PROMESA) we also investigate whether yield differentials vary with changes in Puerto Rico's credit risk.

Main Findings

We find that investors price contract provisions and law, especially when credit risk is highest. The results are consistent with the hypothesis that investors price contract provisions and that investors value them more when a restructuring becomes more likely. First, we find that GO debt trades at statistically significantly higher yields than COFINA debt. This result is consistent with the finding in the existing literature that secured debt trades at lower yields across corporate issuers (Bradley & Roberts, 2015). We also find that investors' pricing of the different legal protections of each type of debt varies significantly with changes in credit risk.

Second, we find that news of PROMESA significantly affected GO bond yields. Specifically, there was an economically and statistically significant increase in bond yields following the passage of PROMESA by the Senate and President Obama signing PROMESA. This result differs from the finding in the most recent literature that CACs reduce yields across securities (e.g. Carletti et al., 2019; Bardozzetti & Dottori, 2014). It is possible that in the case of Puerto Rican debt, individual creditors valued the right to holdout more than the streamlining of the recovery process affected by the introduction of CACs. It is also possible that investors saw the court-supervised bankruptcy process as more favourable to the issuer than the traditional standalone CACs observed in sovereign debt. The finding that investors only priced news of PROMESA when Puerto Rico was closest to default again supports the theory that legal protections are most valued when credit risk is highest.

Third, we find that New York law debt trades at statistically significantly higher yields than Puerto Rican law debt. This finding is surprising in that it differs from the existing literature that documents a foreign law premium (Chamon et al., 2018; Clare & Schmidlin, 2014). We conjecture that investors were pricing the risk that they would not be entitled to recovery in the case of Puerto Rico's New York law debt due to its potential violation of Puerto Rico's legal debt limits. We also find that the differential in the pricing of New York law and Puerto Rican law debt increases as Puerto Rico's credit risk increases. However, this result should be interpreted with caution as the New York law debt comprised a single issuance.

Background on Puerto Rico's Crisis and Puerto Rican Debt

Before Puerto Rico's default in 2016, the island benefited from decades of catch-up growth. In particular, Section 936 of the Tax Reform Act of 1976 created an incentive for investment in Puerto Rico by allowing federal tax exemptions for US companies on income originating in the territories.[6] However, Section 936 was phased out beginning in 1996, ending fully in 2006. The repeal of Section 936 led to a decline in multinational investment in Puerto Rico, a recession, and was followed by the shock of the US financial crisis. Puerto Rico's economic woes proved a strain on government finances fuelling deficits and the accompanying debt burden. The triple tax-exempt nature of the debt and the constitutional seniority of the general obligation debt made it attractive for a broad range of investors. Puerto Rico's debt differs from the unsecured bonds of recent sovereign default cases such as Greece and Argentina in that Puerto Rico's debt was issued by multiple agencies with various types of security, guarantees by the Commonwealth, and levels of priority.[7] We summarize Puerto Rico's debt load in Table 13.A.1 (see Appendix).

By 2014, Puerto Rico's credit rating reached junk status while yields spiked sharply, making it increasingly difficult for Puerto Rico to refinance its debt. Due to Puerto Rico's unique legal status, a period of uncertainty ensued regarding Puerto Rico's ability to restructure and the form a restructuring would take. Finally, the passage of the Puerto Rico Oversight, Management, and Economic Stability Act (referred to as 'PROMESA' hereafter) on 30 June 2016, established Puerto Rico's pathway to restructuring, followed by default the next day.

In the time since PROMESA passed, Puerto Rico has faced a severe challenge from a major hurricane that left much of the island without electricity for nearly a year, further battering the island's already weak economy and finances. Meanwhile, Puerto Rico has struggled to get federal aid from the Trump Administration.[8] In addition, the administration created significant uncertainty about the debt when it made, and then quickly walked back a promise to wipe out Puerto Rico's debt, causing substantial volatility in the market for Puerto Rican bonds.[9] The legal resolution of Puerto Rico's debt crisis has continued to work its way through the courts, creditors most recently arguing that PROMESA's appointment of an oversight board for Puerto Rico's finances was illegal.[10]

[6] See Collins et al. (2007).

[7] See Gulati and Rasmussen (2017) for a detailed description.

[8] https://www.nytimes.com/2018/02/08/us/puerto-rico-disaster-relief.html (Accessed 10 November 2020).

[9] https://www.nytimes.com/2017/10/04/business/dealbook/trump-puerto-rico-debt.html (Accessed 10 November 2020).

[10] https://www.reuters.com/article/us-puertorico-debt-bankruptcy/puerto-rico-creditor-aurelius-asks-u-s-judge-to-throw-out-bankruptcy-idUSKBN1EZ2UR (Accessed 10 November 2020).

Puerto Rico and the Problem of Quasi-Sovereignty

In 1898, after the Spanish-American War, Puerto Rico was ceded to the US by the Treaty of Paris. Since then, Puerto Rico's government, laws, and its relationship with the US have been defined and amended by a series of US laws. First, the Foraker Act of 1900 established a government with an executive council and governor appointed by the President of the US, an elected House of Representatives, and a judiciary. Ultimately, the US President and Congress retained authority over Puerto Rico.

The Jones-Shafroth Act of 1917 ('The Jones Act') superseded the Foraker Act. The Jones Act granted US citizenship to Puerto Ricans, created a two-house elected legislature, and exempted Puerto Rican bonds from federal, state, and local taxes. Under the Jones Act, the US President retained the authority to appoint the Puerto Rican governor. At the same time, the US Congress had the power to approve all cabinet officials and veto any laws of Puerto Rico's legislature.

Finally, a series of steps culminating in the Puerto Rico Federal Relations Act of 1950 amended the Jones Act, which finalized the current legal relationship of Puerto Rico and the United States. The Act granted Puerto Rico the authority to establish and administer its government, with a constitution and an elected governor. However, Puerto Rico's continued status as an unincorporated territory meant that Congress retained ultimate control over Puerto Rico under Article IV of the US Constitution, which empowers it to administer territories. Further, Puerto Rico operates under US monetary and tariff systems. The current legal framework classifies Puerto Rico as a quasi-sovereign.

Quasi-sovereigns or sub-sovereigns have relinquished some aspects of their sovereignty to an overall sovereign but retain some aspects of sovereignty (Gelpern, 2012). As a quasi-sovereign of the US, Puerto Rico shares some of the policy challenges faced by Greece as a member of the Eurozone. Sovereigns can respond to crises with monetary expansions and negotiate with foreign creditors primarily to maintain access to credit markets in the future. However, in the end, both Greece and Puerto Rico could not respond to their crises with monetary expansions or with strictly local legislation aimed at providing a resolution. In both cases, the path to restructuring was legally unclear. As a quasi-sovereign issuing domestic law debt, Puerto Rico made promises of repayment where the terms were subject to the uncertainty about potential modification by the issuer and potentially the US similar to the case of Greek law debt and the E.U.[11]

In both cases, the initial terms of repayment of domestic law debt were altered ultimately either by decree or negotiation with the overall sovereign after several years of uncertainty about the process of restructuring. In the case of Puerto Rico,

[11] See Gulati and Rasmussen (2017) and Zettelmeyer et al. (2013).

the US Congress passed PROMESA, which imposed CAC's on Puerto Rican debt, appointed an oversight board overseeing Puerto Rico's finances, and instituted a court-supervised process to determine the fate of Puerto Rican debt. These measures followed the US Supreme Court ruling that Puerto Rico's attempt at a domestically legislated restructuring process was unconstitutional.[12] In Greece, domestic legislation passed to impose CAC's on domestic law debt, contingent on Greece obtaining European Financial Stability Facility Bonds.[13] In both cases, the initial debt covenants present were altered, highlighting the difficulty in pricing quasi-sovereign debt where the initial contract terms may be altered in conjunction with the overall sovereign, or by the overall sovereign in ways that are determined by new legislation and negotiations.

Gelpern (2012) suggests that when on the verge of inability to meet their obligations, quasi-sovereigns raise a number of challenging questions such as whether the quasi-sovereign has the legal right to restructure or dictate the terms of restructuring; whether repayment terms of domestic law debt can be retroactively altered legislatively by the quasi-sovereign; and whether debt issued under foreign law can be treated differently under a restructuring plan.[14] The uncertainties involved with different legal systems and the potential for negotiations to be especially protracted and fraught highlight the difficulties in pricing the contract terms of quasi-sovereign debt.

Related Literature

This chapter joins a growing number of papers that study Puerto Rico's debt and economic crisis. Feliciano and Green (2017) show the significant negative effect that the repeal of Section 936 tax exemptions had on Puerto Rican manufacturing wages and the number of manufacturing establishments. Chari et al. (2017) find that increased default risk is associated with reduced economic activity in the aggregate and especially in government demand–dependent industries. Gulati and Rasmussen (2017) discuss the legal debate about Puerto Rico's rights to restructure and Park and Samples (2017) discuss the types of Puerto Rican debt and the related legal issues.

This chapter contributes to a broad debate about whether contract provisions matter. Bolton and Jeanne (2009) argue that debt that is harder to restructure is effectively senior and should trade at lower yields. On the other hand, Roubini (2000) and Weinschelbaum and Wynne (2005) argue that protections like CACs and governing law likely do not matter because investor perceptions of implicit guarantees of bailouts and because sovereigns can *ex post* render contract

[12] This process has yet to resolve issues like seniority of the various types of Puerto Rican debt.
[13] See Gulati and Rasmussen (2017). [14] See Gelpern (2012).

protections null. This chapter's investigation of the value of governing law, securing revenues, and CACs all add evidence to the debate in this literature. Our findings support the argument of Bolton and Jeanne (2009) and are inconsistent with the idea that contract provisions do not matter (Roubini, 2000; Weinschelbaum & Wynne, 2005).

More narrowly, the chapter adds to the literature that studies the borrowing costs of domestic law versus foreign law sovereign debt. With respect to Eurozone debt, existing work finds that foreign law debt trades at significantly lower yields than domestic law debt, especially when default risk is elevated (Chamon et al., 2018; Clare & Schmidlin, 2014; Choi et al., 2011).[15] Puerto Rico's issuance of New York law debt provides another case of comparable domestic and foreign law debt issued under a common currency as well as the interesting possibility that the foreign law debt could be found void and unenforceable. In addition, Puerto Rico's crisis allows us to investigate the effect of governing law in a high credit risk environment when legal protections should matter most.

The chapter proceeds as follows. Section 13.2 provides a brief historical summary of the debt contracts studied here. Section 13.3 documents the pricing differential between GO and COFINA debt. Section 13.4 shows the effect of PROMESA on bond yields. Section 13.5 examines the pricing of New York law versus Puerto Rican law debt. Section 13.6 concludes.

13.2 Background on Puerto Rican Debt

COFINA Debt

In 2007, Puerto Rico established COFINA to finance Puerto Rico's debt payable to the Puerto Rican Government Development Bank. COFINA debt is secured by the first lien on half of a 5.5 per cent sales and use tax deposited in a fund solely for the payment of COFINA debt. This guarantee is made in Puerto Rican law but not in Puerto Rico's constitution as with GO debt. There is no recourse to the Commonwealth of Puerto Rico beyond the dedicated sales tax. From July 2007 to December 2011 COFINA issued about $38 billion in debt. However, only $16 billion is senior COFINA debt, which amounts to about the same total value as Puerto Rico's total GO debt issues (Park & Samples, 2017).

The support for GO debt is a guarantee made in Puerto Rico's constitution that stipulates that Puerto Rico's full faith, credit, and taxing power back these bonds. Importantly, GO debt has the first claim on revenues over all Puerto Rico's obligations, including operating expenses like public services and the pensions

[15] The foreign law premium has also been identified for a wider set of countries. See Bradley et al. (2017).

of public employees (Park & Samples, 2017). Of course, Puerto Rico could overturn the existing Puerto Rican law and protect any of its debt with new legislation. GO debt may nevertheless provide value to investors, depending on the degree of 'partial commitment' perceived by investors (Aguiar & Amador, 2014).

PROMESA

On 30 June 2016, President Obama signed PROMESA. The law's first version passed the US Senate on 19 November 2015 and established a new framework for restructuring Puerto Rico's debt and its instrumentalities. The Supreme Court ultimately affirmed on 13 June 2016 that Puerto Rico could not pass local laws that allow restructuring and that Puerto Rico did not have access to Chapter 9 of the US bankruptcy code, reserved for the municipalities of states. Given this determination, a framework for Puerto Rican restructuring required congressional action.

PROMESA temporarily halted creditor actions against Puerto Rico until 15 February 2017 and established a seven-person oversight board with the aim of eliminating deficits and authority to approve Puerto Rico's fiscal plans. PROMESA also retroactively inserted standard CACs into Puerto Rico's debt which allowed a super-majority of creditors to bind holdout creditors to restructuring deals. The CACs replaced the unanimous consent clauses present in Puerto Rican debt before PROMESA. PROMESA allowed Puerto Rico and its instrumentalities to declare a form of bankruptcy in federal court much like Chapter 9 of the US bankruptcy code. Like CACs, the bankruptcy process allows a super-majority of creditors to bind holdout creditors (Gulati & Rasmussen, 2017).

New York Law Debt

On 11 March 2014, Puerto Rico adopted a bond resolution authorizing an additional GO bond issue of $3.5 billion, maturing on 1 July 2035. These bonds comprised Puerto Rico's final issuance of GO debt that amounted to 22 per cent of total GO debt and less than 5 per cent of Puerto Rico's total public debt. The bonds carried the same legal guarantee as for the outstanding GO debt of the Commonwealth. The significant difference between the final GO debt issue and that issued before 2014 was the agreement that the laws of the State of New York would apply to any case related to these bonds.[16] The debt issue took place in an environment where Puerto Rico had recently been downgraded to a credit rating

[16] http://www.gdb.pr.gov/investors_resources/documents/CommonwealthPRGO2014SeriesAFinalOS (Accessed 10 November 2020).

of BB+ by Standard & Poors, just one notch above junk status. The decision to issue the debt with New York governing law was to provide investors with a forum for resolving disputes seen as less partial to Puerto Rican issuers than Puerto Rican courts.

13.3 The Pricing of GO and COFINA Debt

Previous literature on the price impact of securing debt argues that secured debt may, in theory, optimally comprise any portion of total debt, depending on the relative costs of the lien imposed on the borrower versus the benefits of improved enforcement and preventing subordination (Smith & Warner, 1979). Bradley and Roberts (2015) find that including debt covenants, including securing debt, reduces yields across borrowers, especially when issued by smaller, high-risk borrowers. The investigation of COFINA versus GO debt in this section exploits the variation in the pricing of debt issued by the same issuer while previous studies of secured debt focus primarily on cross-issuer variation. Our findings are consistent with those of Bradley and Roberts (2015) who show that investors value the debt covenant of securing revenues for COFINA debt.

To identify the pricing of GO and COFINA protections in bond yields, we adopt a panel data regression model estimated with pooled ordinary least squares. This approach is based in the foreign law and collective action clause literature, both of which similarly attempt to identify the effect of a time-invariant security characteristic on yields (e.g. Becker et al., 2003; Eichengreen & Mody, 2004; Clare & Schmidlin, 2014).

The characteristics of GO and COFINA debt make it theoretically unclear which type of guarantee would be more valuable to investors. On the one hand, investors in COFINA debt have seemingly clear attachment to a specific revenue stream legally required to be sequestered in a fund. These funds cannot be used for any other purpose until COFINA debt is paid, whereas investors in GO debt do not have attachment to specific revenues. For this reason, COFINA investors may be less concerned about difficulties in attaching to revenues. On the other hand, COFINA investors entirely depend on a single revenue stream, whereas investors in GO debt have broad priority over all other expenses of Puerto Rico. For this reason, investors in GO debt may feel more secure.

It is also important to note there is a potential legal argument that COFINA debt was a violation of Puerto Rico's constitutional debt limit imposed for GO debt, an argument made by unsecured creditors in recent litigation.[17] This leaves seniority between these two types of debt uncertain. Finally, as GO debt is

[17] https://www.debtwire.com/info/legal-analysis-judge-swain%E2%80%99s-prhta-statutory-lien-decision-instructive-other-puerto-rico-bondholders (Accessed 10 November 2020).

protected by Puerto Rico's constitution while COFINA is only protected under Puerto Rican law, investors may believe that GO debt poses less legal risk. Given these competing influences, either GO or COFINA debt may theoretically be priced higher.

Therefore, we let the data speak to the market's responses signalling investor beliefs about the likely legal outcomes. The trade-off across the two types of debt make the question of whether investors value GO or COFINA protections more highly valued is an empirical one. The potential impact of credit risk on the pricing of these protections is more straightforward. If GO or COFINA protections are associated with different beliefs about recovery rates, then as the likelihood of default increases, this differential may also change. We also examine whether this is the case.

The analysis of the pricing of the legal protections of GO and COFINA debt uses two groups of bonds: GO debt issued by Puerto Rico under Puerto Rican law and senior COFINA debt; all of which is issued under Puerto Rican law. We restrict attention to GO debt issued under Puerto Rican law because COFINA debt is also issued under Puerto Rican law. We restrict our sample period to before the passage of PROMESA on 30 June 2016. As the final COFINA issuance occurred on 13 December 2011 and the final GO issuance under Puerto Rican law occurred on 3 April 2012, we further restrict the sample to the period beginning after the final issuance of GO and COFINA debt on 3 April 2012. The data used in the analysis comes from Bloomberg.

We select a sample of GO debt issued by Puerto Rico under Puerto Rican law and senior COFINA debt by filtering each baseline sample of bonds to include only bonds which are triple tax exempt, not pre-refunded uninsured, non-sinkable, non-callable, non-puttable, and fixed rate. We also restrict the matched sample to securities with between one and thirty years to maturity and that trade in at least half of the sample trading days, in this case in at least 525 of the 1,052 trading days. We include this restriction to exclude securities which do not have updated pricing information throughout the sample.

Table 13.1 reports the summary statistics for all bonds studied in the chapter in Panel A as well as the Puerto Rican law GO sample and the senior COFINA sample in Panel B. On average, GO bonds have maturities of about fifteen fewer years, have been outstanding for eight more years and have a $18 million higher face value than senior COFINA debt; all differences are significant at the 1 per cent level. The average yield to maturity on GO bonds is 8.46 per cent and is 1.11 per cent higher than for COFINA bonds, a difference significant at the 1 per cent level. Figure 13.1 shows the average yields for the selected sample of GO and COFINA bonds. The plot shows that the yields on both types of securities increase over the sample period as Puerto Rico's credit risk increased. GO and COFINA yields are relatively close for much of the sample, separating sharply as Puerto Rico approaches default and GO yields spike substantially more than COFINA yields.

Table 13.1. Summary statistics

Variable (Units)	Mean	Median	25th pctile	75th pctile	Difference
Panel A: All Bonds (49 issues, 44,088 Obs.)					
YM (years)	11.26	7.00	5.40	19.75	
Age (years)	8.70	10.17	4.17	12.67	
FV (mil. $'s)	116.12	39.29	14.74	75.02	
YTM (%)	8.68	8.07	4.82	9.63	
RISK	13.89	12.00	10.00	22.00	
Panel B: COFINA Vs. GO Bonds: GO Bonds (24 issues, 26,568 Obs.)					
YM (years)	5.66	5.08	3.67	6.75	
Age (years)	10.53	11.67	7.58	13.42	
FV (mil. $'s)	36.03	18.79	12.17	49.51	
YTM (%)	8.46	5.79	4.12	9.60	
COFINA Bonds (5 issues, 5,535 Obs.)					
YM (years)	20.65	23.67	19.17	25.92	***
Age (years)	2.42	2.42	1.33	3.50	***
FV (mil. $'s)	17.94	5.23	3.41	15.14	***
YTM (%)	7.35	7.12	5.54	8.64	***

Notes: Panel A reports the summary statistics for forty-nine security issues selected for the benchmark analyses. Panel B reports the summary statistics for senior COFINA and Puerto Rican law GO debt selected for the analysis of COFINA vs. GO debt. YM is the number of years remaining to maturity. Age is the number of years since issue. FV is the face value in millions. YTM is the daily yield. Table RISK is the S & P Long Term issuer rating measured as a categorical variable ranging from 1 (AAA) to 22 (D). The final column of Panel B reports the significance of a difference in means between the two samples, assuming unequal variances. ***, **, and * indicate significance at the 99%, 95%, and 90% levels, respectively.

With the Puerto Rican law GO and the senior COFINA sample in hand, we ask the following question: do investors price the different legal protections and security offered by GO and COFINA debt? To answer the question, we regress the daily mid-yield to maturity for different security issues on a variable indicating if a security issue is COFINA versus GO while controlling for variables capturing the credit rating of Puerto Rico, the term structure of yields, and variables controlling for issue liquidity. The regression specification also includes time (day) fixed effects to capture security invariant time effects.

The primary variable of interest captures whether or not the differing legal protections and security of COFINA and GO debt are associated with a yield differential. The risk variable captures the effect of credit ratings on yields and thus the coefficient is expected to be positive, indicating that increased risk is associated with higher yields. RISK runs from 11 (BB+) to 20 (CC) over the sample period.

We find that the average yield for Puerto Rican law GO debt is 8.5 per cent. COFINA debt has an average yield 1.1 percentage points lower than Puerto Rican

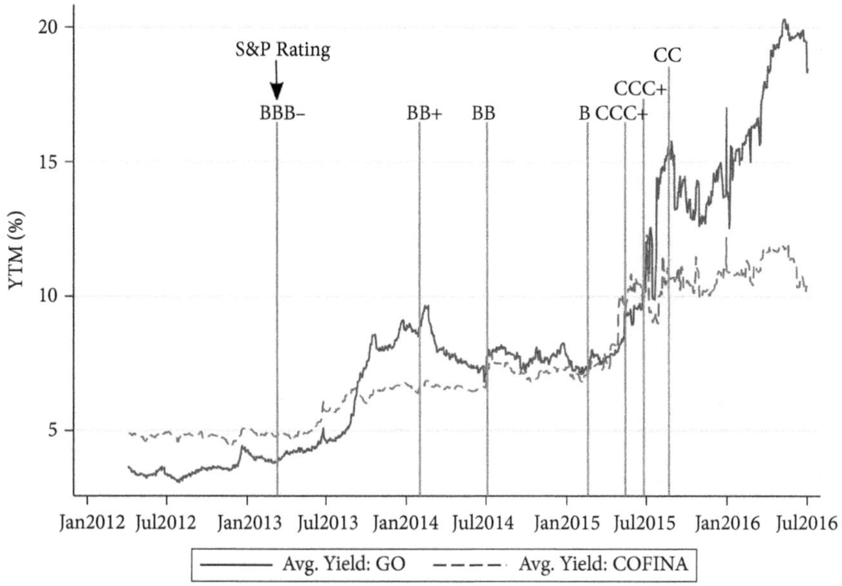

Figure 13.1. COFINA and yields

law GO debt, and the difference is statistically significant at the 15 per cent level. These results tend to indicate that investors did differentiate between the legal protections and security in GO and COFINA debt.

When we control for risk, the term structure of yields, time fixed effects, and bond liquidity, we find the predictive value of the statistical model improves. The positive and significant coefficient on *RISK* indicates that an increase in *RISK* (a one notch downgrade) is associated with a further increase in yields.

As to the economic importance of *COFINA*, we find the predicted average yield of Puerto Rican law GO debt is 7.23 per cent, while the predicted average yield of COFINA debt with the same characteristics of GO debt is 4.16 per cent or 42 per cent lower than equivalent Puerto Rican law GO debt.[18] Therefore, the additional control variables show that COFINA debt trades at yields even further lower than GO debt. This finding supports the hypothesis that investors value the legal protections and security of COFINA debt more than that of GO debt.

We turn to our next question; does the yield differential between COFINA and GO debt vary with credit risk? Figure 13.1 offers suggestive evidence that the yield differential between COFINA and GO debt widened as Puerto approached default. To answer this question analytically, we examine the yields on COFINA debt conditional on the risk rating of the debt. The results suggest that as the risk

[18] The predicted yields reported here pertain to the reference time period. The choice of time period has no effect on the per cent difference in yields.

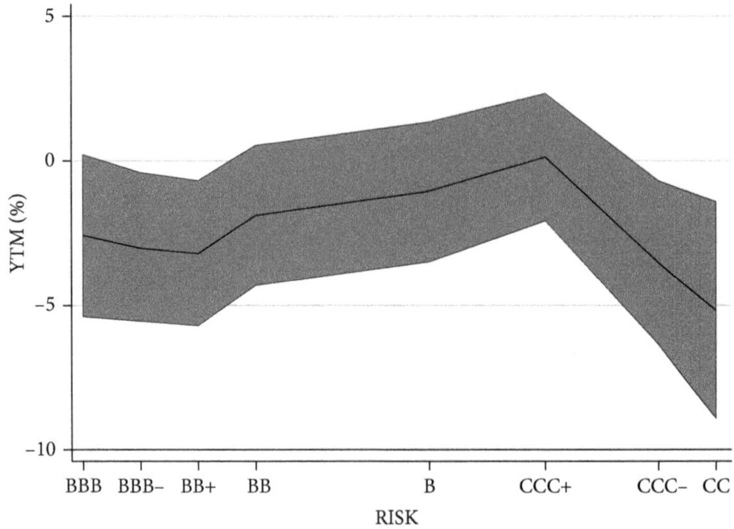

Figure 13.2. Marginal effect of COFINA across RISK with 90 per cent CI

rating of COFINA debt worsens the yields increase even more. The finding shows statistically that an increase in credit risk is associated with a larger yield differential between GO and COFINA debt.

Figure 13.2 shows that the marginal effect of *COFINA* is a 2.5 per cent decrease in yield when risk is at its lowest observed level during the sample period (BBB or 9). When the risk rating is at its highest observed level during the sample period (CC or 20), the marginal effect of *COFINA* is a 5 per cent decrease in yield, or about 1.78 times the effect at the lowest rating level in the sample.

Therefore, although COFINA yields are significantly lower than GO yields throughout the sample period, as credit risk increases, the yield differential between COFINA and GO debt widens. This finding is consistent with the hypothesis that the more likely a default is, the more investors price the differing protections offered by COFINA and GO debt due to their effect on the recovery process. Taken together, the results indicate that investors price the differing protections of COFINA and GO debt and that this difference was valued even more as default became more likely. There is a notable spike in the pricing of the differential as Puerto Rico is closest to default.

13.4 The Pricing of PROMESA

Literature that examines the price impact of collective action clauses (CACs) such as Ghosal and Thampanishvong (2013) formalizes the theoretical trade-off inherent in CACs and their impact on borrowing costs. Specifically, CACs may increase the incentive to default while also increasing recovery rates.[19] More recently, panel data models identify CACs directly and find that CACs reduce yields and that the effect varies with credit risk, although the results on how credit risk matters vary across studies (Bardozzetti & Dottori, 2014; Carletti et al., 2019). For example, data on domestic law bonds with CACs issued in the Eurozone allow a comparison of debt that is issued under the same domestic law and in the same currency. In addition, the issuance of debt with CACs was imposed on the whole Eurozone and is thus exogenous to the issuers (Carletti et al., 2019). The pricing of CACS has also been shown to depend on the presence of creditors known to be potential holdouts (Choi et al., 2018).

Puerto Rico provides an additional natural experiment to assess the effect of CACs on borrowing costs. As with the existing work on CACs, Puerto Rico allows an investigation of the effect of CACs on debt issued under the same legal system and in the same currency. In contrast to the Eurozone experiment, PROMESA provides exogenous and discrete variation in the presence of CACs within-security, rather than across securities. PROMESA is exogenous because it was imposed by the US federal government, rather than the local government. We find that CACs increase yields in contrast to the finding in the most recent literature that CACs reduce yields across securities (e.g. Carletti et al., 2019; Bardozzetti & Dottori, 2014).

To identify the pricing of PROMESA, we use news events related to PROMESA's passage and an event study approach. Event studies are the standard way to identify the effect of news events on bond yields (e.g. Krishnamurthy & Vissing-Jorgensen, 2011; Gürkaynak et al., 2004; Wright, 2012).

PROMESA imposes CACs much like those seen in sovereign debt. However, PROMESA differs in that it also temporarily halted creditor actions, introduced an oversight board for Puerto Rico's finances, and created a bankruptcy process similar to Chapter 9 to provide an alternative restructuring framework to CACs.[20] This framework was aimed at providing an orderly restructuring process in contrast to the existing unanimous consent clauses in Puerto Rican debt. Like the CACs seen in sovereign debt, PROMESA may also incentivize default by making restructuring more orderly. Thus, like the CACs present in sovereign debt, the effect of PROMESA on yields is theoretically ambiguous. However, note that PROMESA may produce different expectations about recovery prospects than the standalone CACs observed in sovereign debt. For example, investors may value the right to hold out that existed before PROMESA more in the US given the strong legal system in place to protect that right.

[19] The earlier empirical evidence about the effect of CACs on prices is mixed (Tsatsaronis, 1999; Eichengreen and Mody, 2000, 2004; Becker et al. 2003; Gugiatti and Richards, 2003a) and later work raised endogeneity concerns with respect to the proxies used for the presence of CACs and the selection of governing law for a security (Gugiatti and Richards, 2003b).

[20] Like CACs, the court-supervised process allows a majority of creditors to bind minority holdouts.

Investors may also believe that the backstop of a court-supervised bankruptcy process improves or reduces their recovery prospects versus CACs alone. In this section we let the data speak about the impact of PROMESA on bond yields.

We identify news events capturing changes in investor beliefs that PROMESA will become law. Specifically, the release of the bill's text, the reference of the bill to committee, the passage of the bill by committee, the passage of the bill by a chamber, and the President signing the bill are all key steps in the legislative process which reveal that PROMESA is closer to becoming law.

This process entailed seven events all of which indicate a greater likelihood that Puerto Rican debt will have CACs retroactively imposed by the US federal government. On 11 November 2015, the first version of PROMESA (S. 2328) was introduced in the Senate and passed. On 12 April 2016, the first House version of the bill was introduced (H.R. 4900). On 18 May 2016, PROMESA was introduced to the House Natural Resources Committee (H.R. 5278). On 25 May 2016, PROMESA cleared the committee with strong bipartisan support. On 9 June 2016, the House passed PROMESA. On 29 June 2016, the Senate passed PROMESA. President Obama signed PROMESA on 30 June 2016. Note that although there are differences in the three versions of the bill, they all include CACs for Puerto Rican debt.[21]

The analysis of the effect of PROMESA on Puerto Rican bond yields uses Puerto Rican GO debt. We use a time series beginning thirty days before the first event and ending thirty days after the last event. The data used in the analysis comes from Bloomberg. We restrict attention to bond issues with the following characteristics: bonds that are not pre-refunded, bonds that are triple tax exempt, bonds that are uninsured, bonds that are not callable or sinkable, bonds that are not puttable, bonds with maturities between one and thirty years, and bonds with fixed rate coupons. We further require that the included bonds trade during at least one hundred of the 192 trading days in the sample period. Again, we include this restriction to exclude securities which do not have updated pricing information throughout the sample. We construct the daily change in yields in basis points, censoring outliers. Table 13.1 shows the summary statistics for all bonds studied in the chapter. The selected sample includes twenty-one security issues with a total of 4,263 observations for the PROMESA investigation. Note that Puerto Rico missed its first GO payment on 1 July 2016, immediately following passage of PROMESA. The securities that defaulted were not included in the sample as they were near maturity.

We investigate the market's reaction to news about PROMESA using an event study.[22] Event studies are widely used to examine the reaction of asset prices to public news events. Recently, event studies have been used to investigate the effect

[21] There is a notable spike in the pricing of the differential as Puerto Rico is closest to default.
[22] See Mackinlay (1997).

of announcements on bond yields.[23] Assuming markets are semi-strong form efficient regarding public information, asset prices will adjust quickly to announcements about PROMESA.[24] Further, assuming that (i) such news is the dominant news during the event window, (ii) investor risk aversion is unchanged, and (iii) there is no reverse causality in PROMESA announcements with respect to bond yields at the daily frequency, changes in Puerto Rican yields during the event window will reflect the effect of the events on the expected cash flows of each bond. Expected cash flow is in turn affected by default probability, expected recovery rates, and the value of attached options. Note that the benchmark expected change in yields is zero for days where no news arrives. With the assumption that rating actions are the dominant news during the event window, the heteroskedasticity-based identification strategy of Rigobon and Sack (2004) simplifies to a standard event study.

In our benchmark results, we use a two-day window following Krishnamurthy and Vissing-Jorgensen (2011) who study agency and corporate yields. The event study seeks to investigate how yield changes differ during PROMESA announcements from non-announcement days. To do so, we regress the daily change in yields in basis points on a constant and two dummies; one indicating an announcement on this day and another indicating an announcement the previous day. The model is estimated using ordinary least squares with standard errors clustered by security. Statistical significance is assessed using an F-test of the null hypothesis that the sum of the dummies is zero.

The results are reported in Table 13.2. For the tests reported for individual events, we only include event window days for the event under investigation and non-event days.[25] The results show that only the final passage of PROMESA in the Senate and the signing of the bill by the President are correlated with significant changes in yields. Specifically, the passage of PROMESA in the Senate on 29 June 2016 was associated with a two-day increase in yields of 15.1 basis points, significant at the 10 per cent level. The signing of PROMESA by the President on 30 June 2016 is associated with a two-day increase in yields of 23.2 basis points, significant at the 1 per cent level.

Thus, only the final stages of PROMESA's passage had a significant effect on yields, and these changes were positive. Although PROMESA made it possible for Puerto Rico to restructure legally and thus would theoretically increase investor expectations of a possible default, Puerto Rico was widely expected to default and indeed missed a payment on GO debt for the first time 1 July 2016 as expected.

[23] See Krishnamurthy and Vissing-Jorgensen (2011); Gürkaynak et al. (2004); and Wright (2012).

[24] Andrade et al. (2001).

[25] Non-event days are days during the benchmark time series which do not fall in the event window of any event.

Table 13.2. The significance of PROMESA announcements varies by event

Date	Event	Two-day change in yield (basis points)
11/19/2015	First Version introduced in Senate	–3.34 (0.61)
4/12/2016	First Version released in House	–10.92 (0.23)
5/18.2016	Introduced in House Committee	–13.06 (0.20)
5/25/2016	Passed Committee	–4.58 (0.65)
6/9/2016	Passed House	–0.55 (0.92)
6.29/2016	Passed Senate	15.14* (0.10)
6/30/2016	President signs	23.26*** (0.00)
	All events	0.81 (0.84)

Notes: Table 13.2 reports the results from a panel regression of the change in the daily yield estimated using Ordinary Least Squares with standard errors clustered by security issue. Two-day changes result from the sum of dummy variables for the event day and the post-event day. Significance is determined using an F-test of the null hypothesis that the sum of the coefficients is zero. P-values from F-tests are reported in parentheses. The time series begins one month before the first event on 11/19/15 and ends one month after the last event on 6/30/16. ***, **, and * indicate significance at the 99%, 95%, and 90% levels, respectively.

In fact, this due date prompted passage of the bill on 30 June.[26] Therefore, the most plausible explanation for the effect of PROMESA on yields is that investors believed PROMESA harmed their recovery prospects relative to their earlier expectations.[27] The finding that investors only priced PROMESA when Puerto Rico was closest to default again supports the theory that legal protections are most valued when credit risk is highest.

13.5 The Pricing of New York Law Debt

In the case of typical foreign law sovereign debt, evidence from the existing literature is unambiguous that foreign law debt trades at a premium or lower yield compared to otherwise equivalent domestic law debt. This follows from the

[26] http://money.cnn.com/2016/06/29/investing/puerto-rico-debt-promesa/index.html (Accessed 10 November 2020).

[27] Again, note that the securities for which a payment was missed are not included in the sample.

fact that domestic law debt is subject to the risk that the domestic government can alter contract terms after issuance. In addition, creditor rights for foreign law debt can be litigated in relatively unsympathetic foreign courts and may result in attachment to the sovereign's assets held overseas (Chamon et al., 2018). In the case of Puerto Rico, it is theoretically unclear whether the New York Law debt should trade at higher or lower yields than the equivalent debt issued under Puerto Rican law.

Showalter (2017) presents an extensive discussion of the legal issues surrounding Puerto Rico's New York law debt, which we summarize here. Puerto Rico's New York law debt is in somewhat uncharted territory because it is not certain that the courts will enforce a clause making the debt subject to New York law. In addition, Puerto Rico's issuance of New York law debt entailed a consequence that was not foreseen by the creditors' legal counsel when the debt was issued—namely, that the New York law debt may be a violation of the balanced budgets clause of Puerto Rico's constitution. The balanced budgets clause requires that debt that would result in Puerto Rico spending more than 15 per cent of its internal revenues on GO debt service may not be issued. This was found to apply particularly to Puerto Rico' New York law debt, potentially making the debt illegal and thus unenforceable and void. Importantly, illegal debt issues have been found to be unenforceable under both New York and Puerto Rican case law. However, bondholders may have a chance of some recovery as New York courts may only consider the contract illegal if it violates New York law, rather than Puerto Rican law. Bondholders can also try and argue for quasi-contractual protection.

In summary, lawsuits pertaining to New York law debt may be heard in a venue known to be among the most protective of creditor rights, but the debt may also be in danger of being deemed void. Therefore, we let the data speak to the market's responses signalling investor beliefs about the likely legal outcomes. The question of measuring the impact of credit risk on the pricing of New York law debt is more straightforward. If the New York debt issue is associated with different beliefs about recovery rates, then an increase in the likelihood of default should widen the differential in yields between New York and Puerto Rican law debt. This follows from the fact that Puerto Rico would likely seek to avoid the potential reputation cost of default unless it decided to substantially restructure its debt. This is especially plausible given that New York law debt is a relatively small share of total Puerto Rican debt.

The analysis of the pricing of Puerto Rican debt issued under New York law versus Puerto Rican law uses two groups of bonds: GO debt issued by Puerto Rico under Puerto Rican law before the issuance of New York law debt on 11 March 2014, and GO debt issued by Puerto Rico under New York law on 11 March 2014 (Puerto Rico's final GO issuance). The data used in the analysis comes from Bloomberg. The sample of daily mid-yields we use runs between Puerto Rico's final issuance of GO debt on 11 March 2014 and just prior to the signing of PROMESA on 30 June 2016.

We filter the sample of Puerto Rican law GO bonds that match the characteristics of New York law GO bonds. We further require that the selected bonds do not mature during the sample period, have between one and thirty years until maturity, and have non-stale yield observations in at least 300 of the 598 trading days in the sample period. New York law GO bonds have the following characteristics: they mature on 1 July 2035; they are exempt from local, Puerto Rican, and federal taxes; they are not pre-refunded (which would render them essentially risk free); they are not insured; they are sinkable and callable; they are not puttable; and they have fixed rate coupons. The New York law GO debt is relatively liquid, with non-stale yields observed in each of the 598 trading days in the sample period.

Figure 13.3 shows the average yields for the selected sample of New York law and Puerto Rican law bonds. The plot shows that the yields on both types of securities increase over the sample period as Puerto Rico approaches default. New York law debt appears to trade at higher yields for the entire period. With the New York law and the Puerto Rican law GO samples in hand, we ask the following questions: first, do investors price New York law GO debt differently than Puerto Rican law GO debt?

To answer the first question, we regress the daily mid-yield to maturity for different security issues on a dummy variable indicating if New York law pertains to a security issue while controlling for variables capturing the credit rating of Puerto Rico, the term structure of yields, and variables controlling for issue liquidity. The regression specification also includes time (day) fixed effects to capture security invariant time effects.

The primary variable of interest, capturing whether or not Puerto Rican debt issued under New York law is priced differently than Puerto Rican debt issued under Puerto Rican law. The risk variable captures the effect of credit ratings on yields and thus the coefficient is expected to be positive, indicating that increased risk is associated with higher yields. RISK runs from 11 (BB+) to 20 (CC) over the sample period.

We find that the average yield for Puerto Rican law GO debt is 8.7 per cent. New York law GO debt has an average yield 1.6 percentage points or 18 per cent higher than Puerto Rican law GO debt, and the difference is statistically significant at the 1 per cent level. The finding is consistent with the hypothesis that from the perspective of investors, New York law debt was perceived to provide less protection than Puerto Rican law debt, perhaps given the possibility that New York law debt would be deemed void and unenforceable. When we control for risk and the term structure of yields to account for bond characteristics and the predictive value of the statistical model improves. We find that a one-unit increase in risk equivalent to a one notch downgrade is associated with a further increase in yields.

As to the economic significance of New York law, we find the predicted average yield of Puerto Rican law debt is 8.48 per cent, while the predicted average yield of

New York law debt that is otherwise the same as Puerto Rican law debt is 10.34 per cent, or 22 per cent higher than Puerto Rican law debt. Therefore, the additional control variables measuring risk and the term structure of yields, show that New York governing law is associated with a bigger increase in borrowing costs once we take into account key security characteristics.

For additional confirmation of the effects of New York law on bond yields, we search for the Puerto Rican law security issue from the benchmark sample with the same maturity date as the New York law issue of 1 July 2035. The maturity matched Puerto Rican law security was issued two years before the New York law issue. Figure 13.3 plots the yields of the New York law issue and the maturity matched Puerto Rican law issue. Like Figure 13.3, Figure 13.4 shows that New York law debt trades at significantly higher yields than Puerto Rican law debt and that this differential appears to widen with increased credit risk.

We turn to our next question; does the yield differential between New York law and Puerto Rican law debt vary with credit risk? Figure 13.3 provides suggestive evidence that the yield differential between New York law and Puerto Rican law debt widened as Puerto's credit risk increased. Figure 13.5 shows that the marginal effect of New York law is a 1.1 per cent increase in yield when RISK is at its lowest observed level during the sample period (BB+ or 11). When RISK is at its highest observed level during the sample period (CC or 20), the marginal effect of New York is a 2.5 per cent increase in yield, or an approximate doubling of the

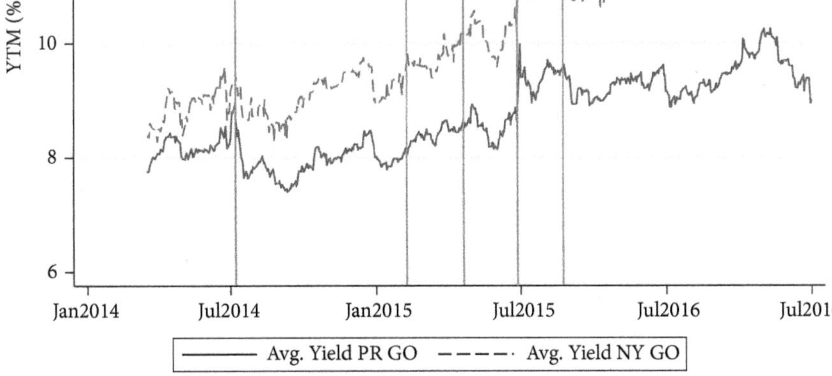

Figure 13.3. Governing law and yields

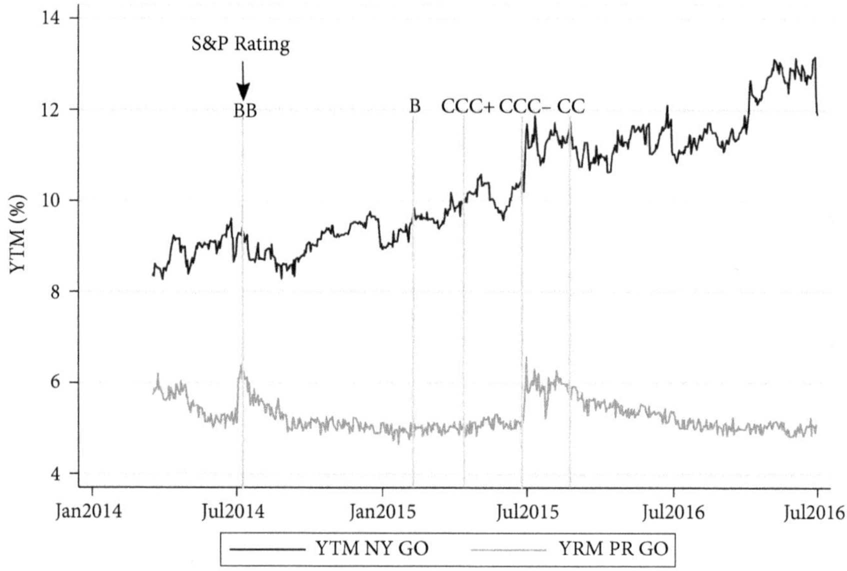

Figure 13.4. Governing law and yields: maturity matched

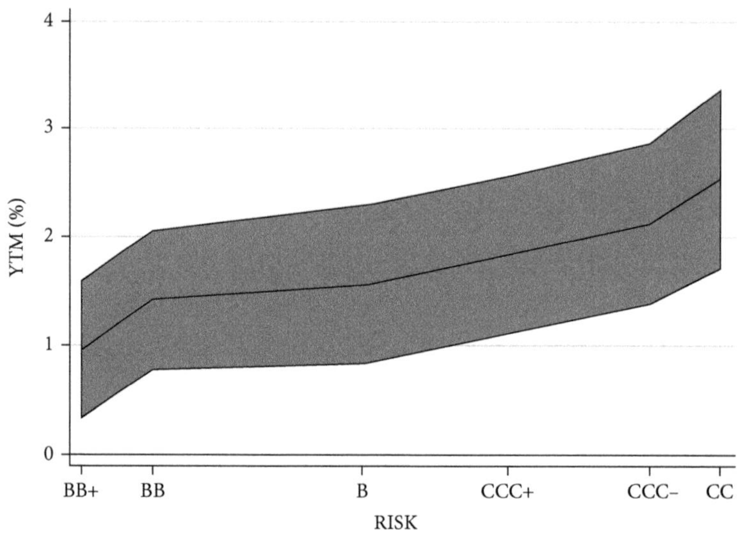

Figure 13.5. Marginal effect of New York across RISK with 90 per cent CI

effect. Therefore, although New York is associated with significantly higher yields throughout the sample period, the increase in credit risk observed over the sample period is associated with a significant increase in the positive yield differential for New York law over Puerto Rican law debt. This is consistent with the hypothesis that the more likely a default is, the more investors price the different legal environments due to their effect on the recovery process.

13.6 Conclusion

Puerto Rico presents a unique legal setting as it is a Commonwealth territory of the United States with an elected governor and legislature, while also being an unincorporated territory under the ultimate control of the US Congress. Against this backdrop, investor concern about legal risk, and the uncertainty surrounding the process for restructuring Puerto Rican debt is significant. The perceived legal risk of Puerto Rican debt, therefore, led to the inclusion of a variety of contract provisions that vary across different types of debt. Further, when restructuring became imminent, Puerto Rico was denied access to Chapter 9 of the US bankruptcy code as it was not a US state and, at the same time, prevented from creating its bankruptcy laws by the US Constitution. Ultimately, the crisis forced the US Congress to enact PROMESA to provide a framework for restructuring Puerto Rico's debt.

This chapter presents a case study to investigate the pricing of three key legal provisions of Puerto Rican debt and how these valuations vary with credit risk. In each instance, Puerto Rico offers a compelling case to study the pricing of contract provisions and law, and in all three cases, we find that investors price contract provisions and the related law.

Our findings lend support to the hypothesis that investors value contract provisions and price legal risk in debt contracts. When Puerto Rico issued debt under foreign law and secured debt with specific revenues, investors priced these protections. Investors also priced the new framework for the restructuring of Puerto Rican debt introduced by PROMESA. As credit risk increases, the yield differentials associated with all three types of contract provisions widen.

Appendix
A.1. Puerto Rican Debt Summary

Table 13.A.1. Puerto Rican debt summary as of September 2013

Issuer	Security interest	Amount (US dollars)
Commonwealth of Puerto Rico (i.e., the Puerto Rican central government)	Guaranteed/ General Obligation	16,194,333,667
	Commonwealth appropriations	2,457,501,120
Puerto Rico Electric Power Authority (PREPA)	Electric system revenue	9,052,300,000
Puerto Rico Sales Tax Financing Corporation (COFINA)	Sales tax revenue	38,374,270,000
Puerto Rico Highway and Transportation Authority	Gasoline tax and toll revenue	5,050,790,128
Puerto Rico Municipal Finance Agency	Municipal general obligation	793,000,000
Employees Retirement System of the Government of Puerto Rico	Retirement contributions	3,841,110,000
Puerto Rico Convention Center District Authority	Hotel occupancy tax	418,805,000
Puerto Rico Infrastructure Finance Authority	Federal rum tax	2,449,055,000
Government Development Bank for Puerto Rico (GDB)	Unsecured	6,161,517,000
Puerto Rico Aqueduct and Sewer Authority	Water revenue	3,437,200,000
Puerto Rico Ports Authority	Port revenue	329,215,000
Total direct debt		88,559,096,915

Notes: See Collins et al. (2007) and Lee and Jacobson (2013).

A.2. Data Appendix: Section 3

As a baseline, we also only include bonds which do not mature during the sample period. To generate a matched sample of GO and COFINA debt, we first summarize the characteristics of senior COFINA and GO debt issued under Puerto Rican law, to determine the selection of characteristics which allow the largest sample and identification of the pricing of each issuer's legal protections. These summary statistics are in Table 13.A.2. The table shows that the two samples have comparable characteristics. Most GO and senior COFINA debt are triple tax exempt, not pre-refunded, uninsured, non-sinkable, callable, non-puttable, and fixed rate. Given the comparability of the samples, we simply restrict the matched sample to securities with the characteristics that comprise the majority of both samples, with one exception—we utilize non-callable bonds in order to prevent the valuation of the option from confounding the identification of legal protections. As before,

Table 13.A.2. COFINA and GO debt have comparable characteristics, making them suitable for sample matching

Sample	COFINA bonds (86 issues, 95,202 Obs.)				PR Law GO bonds (297 issues, 328,779 Obs.)			
Variable	Mean	Median	25th pctile	75th pctile	Mean	Median	25th pctile	75th pctile
Non-triple tax exempt	0.12	0.00	0.00	0.00	0.02	0.00	0.00	0.00
Pre-refunded	0.00	0.00	0.00	0.00	0.09	0.00	0.00	0.00
Insured	0.00	0.00	0.00	0.00	0.00	0.00	0.00	0.00
Sinkable	0.14	0.00	0.00	0.00	0.27	0.00	0.00	1.00
Callable	0.80	1.00	1.00	1.00	0.81	1.00	1.00	1.00
Puttable	0.00	0.00	0.00	0.00	0.05	0.00	0.00	0.00
Fixed rate	1.00	1.00	1.00	1.00	0.93	1.00	1.00	1.00
Days issue Trades	661.63	990.50	195.00	1,042.00	352.73	228.50	1.00	594.00
Years to maturity	21.16	19.75	14.33	25.50	10.75	9.25	5.58	15.33
Years since issue	5.32	5.58	3.92	7.08	8.92	8.67	4.58	12.58
Face value (millions)	71.36	26.53	7.43	91.01	45.58	20.63	11.52	52.95

Notes: Table 13.A.2 reports the summary statistics for senior COFINA and Puerto Rican law GO debt which do not mature during the sample period. The time series begins on 3 April 2012 when the last issue of such debt occurred and ends on 30 June 2016. Note that the first seven variables are dummies. For example, 100% of COFINA bonds are fixed rate while 93% of GO bonds are fixed rate.

Table 13.A.3. The filtering process produces a sample of twenty-nine securities

	GO # Issues	GO: Face value ($ mln)	COFINA # Issues	COFINA: Face value ($ mln)
Baseline	294	13,506	86	6,137
Triple tax Exempt	289	13,473	76	5,575
Non-pre-refunded	263	12,462	76	5,575
Uninsured	263	12,462	76	5,575
Non-sinkable	189	5,453	68	3,353
Non-callable	50	2,420	15	948
Non-puttable	44	1,444	15	948
Fixed rate	43	1,411	15	948
Maturity between 1 and 30 years	43	1,411	13	841
Trades in at least 525 days	24	1,411	5	90
Final sample	24	865	5	90

Notes: Table 13.A.3 summarizes the number of bond issues and the total maturity amount at each phase of the screening process for construction of the PR law GO sample for comparison to New York law GO debt. The baseline sample includes all GO debt with an observed yield during the sample period (which runs from 12 March 2014 to 29 June 2016) issued under Puerto Rican or New York law where the maturity amount is available. The remaining rows summarize the sample after each filter is applied.

we also restrict the matched sample to securities with between one and thirty years to maturity and that trade in at least half of the sample trading days, in this case in at least 525 of the 1,052 trading days.[28]

Table 13.A.3 shows the breakdown of security characteristics in the filtering process to select a sample of Puerto Rican law GO debt and COFINA debt that have matching characteristics. The filtering process results in twenty-four Puerto Rican law GO security issues with a total maturity value of $865 million and five senior COFINA security issues with a total maturity value of $90 million. The two most important filters which serve to reduce the size of the final sample versus the baseline sample are callable securities and securities which traded in fewer than 525 of the 1,052 trading days.

References

Aguiar, M. & Amador, M. (2014). 'Sovereign Debt'. *Handbook of International Economics*, 4, 647–87.

Andrade, G., Mitchell, M., & Stafford, E. (2001). 'New Evidence and Perspectives on Mergers. *Journal of Economic Perspectives*,' 15(2), 103–20.

[28] Again, we include this restriction to exclude securities which do not have updated pricing information throughout the sample. As 525 trading days is an arbitrary requirement, we relax this assumption for robustness.

Bardozzetti, A. & Dottori, D. (2014). 'Collective Action Clauses: How Do They Affect Sovereign Bond Yields?' *Journal of International Economics*, 92(2), 286–303.

Becker, T., Richards, A., & Thaicharoen, Y. (2003). 'Bond Restructuring and Moral Hazard: Are Collective Action Clauses Costly?' *Journal of International Economics*, 61(1), 127–61.

Bolton, P. & Jeanne, O. (2009). 'Structuring and Restructuring Sovereign Debt: The Role of Seniority'. *The Review of Economic Studies*, 76(3), 879–902.

Bradley, M., Fontenay, E., Salvatierra, I., & Gulati, M. (2017). 'Pricing Sovereign Debt: Foreign versus Local Parameters'. *European Financial Management*, 24(2), 261–97.

Bradley, M. & Roberts, M. R. (2015). 'The Structure and Pricing of Corporate Debt Covenants'. *Quarterly Journal of Finance*, 5(2), 1–37.

Carletti, E., Colla, P., Gulati, G. M., & Ongena, S. (2019). 'The Price of Law: The Case of the Eurozone Collective Action Clauses'. Available at SSRN: https://ssrn.com/abstract=2817041.

Chamon, M., Schumacher, J., & Trebesch, C. (2018). 'Foreign Law Bonds: Can they Reduce Sovereign Borrowing Costs?' *Journal of International Economics*, 114(C), 164–79.

Chari, A., Leary, R., & Phan, T. (2017). 'The Costs of (sub)Sovereign Default Risk: Evidence from Puerto Rico'. NBER Working Paper, 24108. Available at: http://www.nber.org/papers/w24108.

Choi, S., Gulati, M., & Posner, E. A. (2011). 'Pricing Terms in Sovereign Debt Contracts: A Greek Case Study with Implications for the European Crisis Resolution Mechanism'. *Capital Markets Law Journal*, 6(2), 163–87.

Choi, S., Gulati, M., & Scott, E. (2018). 'Hidden Holdouts: Contract Arbitrageurs and the Pricing of Collective Rights'. Columbia Law and Economics Working Paper, 586. Available at SSRN: https://ssrn.com/abstract=3203949.

Clare, A. & Schmidlin, N. (2014). 'The Impact of Foreign Governing Law on European Government Bonds Yields'. Case Business School. Available at SSRN: https://ssrn.com/abstract=2406477.

Collins, S. M., Bosworth, B. P., & Soto-Class, M. A. (2007). *The Economy of Puerto Rico: Restoring Growth*. Brookings Institution Press, Washington, D.C.

Eichengreen, B. & Mody, A. (2000). 'Would Collective Action Clauses Raise Borrowing Costs?' NBER Working Paper, 7458. Available at: http://www.nber.org/papers/w7458.

Eichengreen, B. & Mody, A. (2004). 'Do Collective Action Clauses Raise Borrowing Costs?' *The Economic Journal*. 114(495), 247–64.

Feliciano, Z. M. & Green, A. (2017). 'US Multinationals in Puerto Rico and the Repeal of Section 936 Tax Exemption for US Corporations'. NBER Working Paper, 23681. Available at: http://nber.org/papers/w23681.

Gelpern, A. (2012). 'Bankruptcy, Backwards: The Problem of Quasi-Sovereign Debt'. *The Yale Law Journal*, 121(4), 888–942.

Ghosal, S. & Thampanishvong, K. (2013). 'Does Strengthening Collective Action Clauses (CACs) Help?' *Journal of International Economics*, 89(1), 68–78.

Gugiatti, M. & Richards, A. (2003a). 'Do Collective Action Clauses Influence Bond Yields? New Evidence from Emerging Markets'. *Journal of International Finance*, 6(3), 415–47.

Gugiatti, M. & Richards, A. (2003b). The Use of Collective Action Clauses in New York Law Bonds of Sovereign Borrowers." Available at SSRN: https://ssrn.com/abstract=443840.

Gulati, M. G. & Rasmussen, R. K. (2017). 'Puerto Rico and the Netherworld of Debt Restructuring'. *Southern California Law Review*, 91(1), 133–62.

Gürkaynak, R., Sack, B., & Swanson, E. (2004). The Effects of Monetary Policy on Asset Prices: An Intraday Event-study Analysis. Manuscript.

Krishnamurthy, A. & Vissing-Jorgensen, A. (2011). 'The Effects of Quantitative Easing on Interest Rates: Channels and Implications for Policy'. NBER Working Paper Series, 17555. Available at: http://nber.org/papers/w17555.

Lee, C. & Jacobson, E. (2013). Morningstar Special Report: Puerto Rico Fiscal Strain: Implications for Investors. Morningstar.

Mackinlay, C. (1997). 'Event Studies in Economics and Finance'. *Journal of Economic Literature*, 35(1), 13–39.

Panizza, U., Strurzenegger, F., & Zettelmeyer, J. (2009). 'The Economics and Law of Sovereign Debt and Default'. *Journal of Economic Literature*, 47(3), 651–98.

Park, S. K. & Samples, T. R. (2017). 'Puerto Rico's Debt Dilemma and Pathways Toward Sovereign Solvency'. *American Business Law Journal*, 54(1), 9–60.

Rigobon, R. & Sack, B. (2004). 'The Impact of Monetary Policy on Asset Prices'. *Journal of Monetary Economics*, 51(8), 1553–75.

Roubini, N. (2000). 'Bail-in, Burden-sharing, Private Sector Involvement (PSI) in Crisis Resolution and Constructive Engagement of the Private Sector. A Primer: Evolving Definitions, Doctrine, Practice and Case Law'. Mimeo, NYU.

Showalter, J. C. (2017). 'The Consequences from Issuing Invalid Municipal Debt: Examining the Voidable Debt Issues in the Detroit Bankruptcy and Puerto Rican Debt Crisis'. *North Carolina Banking Institute*, 21(1).

Smith, C. J. & Warner, J. B. (1979). 'Bankruptcy, Secured Debt, and Optimal Capital Structure: Comment'. *Journal of Finance*, 34(1), 247–51.

Tsatsaronis, K. (1999). 'The Effect of Collective Action Clauses on Sovereign Bond Yields'. *BIS Quarterly Review*: International Banking and Financial Market Developments, November 1999, 22–3.

Weinschelbaum, F. & Wynne, J. (2005). 'Renegotiation, Collective Action Clauses and Sovereign Debt Markets'. *Journal of International Economics*, 67(1), 47–72.

Wright, J. (2012). 'What Does Monetary Policy do to Long-term Interest Rates at the Zero Lower Bound?' *The Economic Journal*, 122(564), 447–66.

Zettelmeyer, J., Trebesch, C., & Gulati, M. (2013). 'The Greek Debt Restructuring: An Autopsy'. Economic Policy, 28(75), 513–63.

Concluding Remarks. (Neo)Colonialism, (Neo)Imperialism, and Hegemony

On Choosing Concepts in Sovereign Debt

Odette Lienau

Occasionally, concluding chapters are indeed conclusive, complete with a totalizing argument. But, given the variation and complexity of the material in this volume, such an approach would hardly be appropriate here. Instead, I aim to raise questions that are at least implicitly hinted at by this volume's contributions. In particular, how consciously should scholars use politically charged and historically embedded terms in their writing about sovereign debt—how 'diplomatic' should we be? And what are the reasons for and the ramifications of taking some of the themes and terms in this book beyond the pages of an academic manuscript? What is the continued appeal of one or another term, even if it doesn't quite fit the situation?

The title of this volume is 'Sovereign Debt Diplomacies' and, in describing a sovereign debt diplomacy, the editors highlight that central to the concept is a 'resolutely pragmatic' set of analytical premises. They note that 'a diplomatic perspective suggests that financial disputes cannot be easily reduced to legal contracts or any standardized blueprint of action.'[1] I would add that implicated in colloquial understandings of the terms 'diplomacy' and 'diplomatic' is an attentiveness to language itself—to the careful selection of words and narratives and an understanding of the power that these choices have to change perspectives and set events in motion.

This volume's introduction presents with great care an analytical approach to sovereign debt that speaks to the concepts of colonialism, neo-colonialism, imperialism, and hegemony. And each of the substantive chapters pushes the analysis forward in some way, drawing from different disciplines and historical periods. As befits a scholarly endeavour, these arguments are presented with a degree of analytical detachment. The concepts as used through these pages are primarily intended to be descriptive, to the extent possible, analytically capturing relationships between debtors and creditors and allowing for comparisons across cases and time. But, of course, the terms themselves are heavily politically

[1] Pierre Pénet and Juan Flores Zendejas, Introduction to this volume, [currently p. 6].

Odette Lienau, *Concluding Remarks. (Neo)Colonialism, (Neo)Imperialism, and Hegemony: On Choosing Concepts in Sovereign Debt* In: *Sovereign Debt Diplomacies: Rethinking Sovereign Debt from Colonial Empires to Hegemony.* Edited by: Pierre Pénet and Juan Flores Zendejas, Oxford University Press (2021). © Oxford University Press.
DOI: 10.1093/oso/9780198866350.003.0015

charged—for sovereign borrowers, their populations, and private and public creditors alike. The terms can be used instrumentally—with a view to eliciting a response in others to further a goal or policy. And, in addition, such language, like all linguistic action, can be expressive as well: communicating a particular and internally relevant meaning without concern for how it is perceived or reacted to by an external audience. This is no less the case in international financial relations than any other sphere.

As such, in these concluding remarks, I consider the political salience of choosing words and characterizations when discussing sovereign debt. I suggest that, particularly in popular usage, the selection among these terms is often intended less as an accurate description than as an expression of the desire to identify a responsible actor, highlight the unequal burdens of restructuring, or emphasize or construct a national narrative. This conclusion also raises the question of the degree to which scholars should be mindful in using these terms, and of whether this fraught terminology can ever be left behind in the sovereign debt arena. Indeed, given the continued political salience of sovereign debt issues and the emotion they engender, it can sometimes be difficult to disentangle the scholarly from the popular, the descriptive from the performative, and the instrumental from the expressive.

*

The continuum of terms from 'colonial' to 'hegemonic' frequently makes its way into widespread discussions, or accusations, in sovereign debt. In recent memory, the Greek crisis led it to be called a 'debt colony', Argentina's tribulations in US courts have been decried as 'judicial colonialism', and China's financial interests in Africa flagged as potential 'debt colonialism' (Chang, 2012; Daniel, 2019). And academic assessments too have sometimes invoked these terms (e.g., Giannacopoulos, 2016). Aside from their analytical usefulness, presented ably in this volume's introduction, why do these terms have such popular power? How do we conceive of colonial, neo-colonial, imperial, or hegemonic developments and what do contemporary speakers seek to convey in selecting these terms? I begin these concluding remarks with a quick review of how these terms seem to feature in the popular imagination, returning at points to themes introduced at the beginning of this volume.

At one end of the spectrum is the term colonial, by which we often mean the domination of one nation-state or polity by another, generally for the explicit benefit of the dominating polity or, more likely and more precisely, an elite subset of that polity. Although the ideal-type understanding of colonial domination involves a direct military occupation of a foreign geographic area, the term and the practice itself is of course flexible. Colonial control has occurred, and can occur, not only through military but also political, economic, social, and cultural means, or any combination thereof. Often there is a dyadic implication—a clear colonizer and colonized, although of course the colonizer may be involved in dyadic relationships with a number of polities or geographic areas. Also embedded in the term 'colonial' tends to be a clear will to control: an effort to subdue a foreign entity, in which the conquest and subjugation itself may be one of the end goals rather than merely a means to some other goal. The term 'neo-colonial' weakens the element of direct political and military control but can still retain the suggestion of wilful domination and an active effort to thwart the independent trajectory of the subjected region and population.

Imperialism is sometimes used as a synonym for colonialism but tends to be understood as a looser and more diffuse term, encompassing a broader variety of practices and intensities of subjugation. The element of direct control may be less immediately present, and variations of imperial rule might include direct as opposed to indirect rule and deliberate as opposed to incidental oppression. Hegemony perhaps lies at the far end of the continuum in the popular understanding. It can be understood as the univalent domination of a society or community—up to and including global society—by a single set of practices and principles. This may be associated with a hegemonic political power, but the term itself is conventionally less tethered to traditional forms of political organization. The volume's editors take a similar approach, calling a 'hegemonic debt diplomacy' one characterized by deterritorialization, universality, and uniformity.

Still, do we *need* to come up with a common terminology or set of definitions? What can be understood even without a coherent shared approach? Certainly, for an academic endeavour it is helpful to develop a joint framework. But it is also important to acknowledge that these concepts are moving targets, evoking a sensibility without offering a fully satisfying degree of precision. To use a Wittgensteinian analogy, concepts or linguistic terms imply a family resemblance—like ropes, they are made of many strings without any one string offering the single, core essence of the whole.[2] Particularly if this is the case, it is even more important to understand the impetus behind the use of one term as opposed to an alternative when other possible words might serve just as well or even be more technically accurate. This is particularly the case when the speaker is an individual, and perhaps a political representative, who believes they suffer under some variant of (neo)colonialism, (neo)imperialism, or oppressive hegemony. It is clear that, although these terms are viewed as anachronistic in some circles, they retain a rhetorical attraction that, for many, connects to deep-seated feelings of powerlessness.

So what is evoked when such language is used in the sovereign debt arena, regardless of accuracy per se or of the degree to which that use fits with traditional definitions or applications? One source of the ongoing appeal of the terms (neo)colonial and (neo)imperial no doubt connects to the search for a responsible actor in international financial relations. In popular imaginings of a traditional

[2] For more on the idea of family resemblance as a way to think through the notion or concept of a 'game', see Wittgenstein (1968, paras. 66–7).

colonial or imperial relationship, there is a clear colonial agent or actor—a ruler or ruling class and a hierarchy of officials imposing their wishes on an unwilling populace. But finding a responsible governing actor—or, in other words, separating out a clear acting agent from a background structure—is less clear in the international economic arena today, particularly in sovereign debt. The unwilling populace remains, believing that its own agency and future projects have been undermined: often the population of a sovereign borrower caught in controversy feels trapped in a system over which it has little say—bearing a burden that should be shared more evenly across debtor and creditor, subjected to austerity measures that appear unreasonable or punitive, sometimes in order to repay debt burdens for which it received little benefit and over which it had little control.

However, it can be somewhat harder or more controversial to identify the principally responsible actor in the contemporary sovereign debt arena. At least in ideal-type understandings of colonialism and imperialism, the colonial centre was unlikely to deny the fact of its control, its choice, and the benefit it derived from the arrangement. In contemporary sovereign debt, however, there is hardly an eagerness to accept agency. If there is neo-colonialism or neo-imperialism in sovereign debt, it is one without a self-acknowledged neo-colonialist. Even those actors that we may think of as active, controlling agents—international financial institutions (IFIs), investors, and major state actors—claim that they too are limited by structures beyond their control. Investors see themselves as constrained by the need to make profits or be overtaken in a competitive market and the IFIs view themselves as merely providing sage advice on the basis of these market realities. If anything, these actors may agree that there is a hegemonic approach in sovereign debt—a uniform set of practices and principles requiring repayment in all instances, at least as a background expectation. But some are likely to claim that this hegemony is largely inevitable, given the spread of capital markets across the globe. And even acceptance of the language of hegemony is likely to be an acceptance of the un-agentic form—of a hegemony freed from a political centre of gravity, in which these actors too are constrained by the broader and univalent exigencies of markets.

To some degree, the decision to use the language of neo-colonialism or neo-imperialism in sovereign debt seems to be an effort to resist this move away from agency. These terms are used not so much to suggest a tight analogy with the traditional definitions but to insist on the continued existence of responsibility and control. Yes, perhaps there is a hegemony of the market to which all are subjected, but there are moments of control and action even within this uniformity—of strengthening as opposed to weakening particular (and potentially problematic) market principles. I have written elsewhere about how market principles that appear objective or inevitable in a given historical moment may in fact be variable over time; in this, they are more like conventional 'law' than is often acknowledged (Lienau, 2014; 2017). In clinging to an arguably anachronistic language of neo-colonialism or neo-imperialism in sovereign debt, speakers may be making an inchoate claim about the continued relevance of agency, choice, and responsibility in this realm of principles and rules with no clearly identifiable rule-maker.

Related to this claim of the ongoing relevance of narratives of agency and control is an insistence on attending to the distributional consequences of the current system. The language of (neo)colonialism and (neo)imperialism implies that one group has benefited at the expense of another. In the popular imagination of colonial regimes, the uneven capture of benefit is indeed the central goal. Of course, a number of participants (or perpetrators) in certain variants of colonialism and imperialism may have genuinely imagined a benefit for the colonized, especially in their so-called 'gifts' of civilization: new forms of law, religion, economy, and political organization (Mallard, 2019). But uneven benefit and, indeed, blatant exploitation are far more commonly associated with these terms. Thus, employing this language in the contemporary era insists not only on the presence of agency and control but also on the existence of uneven benefit. And using language to invoke an anticolonial or anti-imperial struggle calls for the identification and correction of these unequal outcomes.

As for the term hegemony, such a system presumably benefits the hegemon. But what of the less agent-centric notion of a hegemony of ideas and principles that make up international capital markets? While particular groups associated with these ideas may be understood to benefit from the system, others (one can think of the IFIs) refute the notion that it is designed for their benefit, per se. Instead, they contend that they merely support, and improve upon, a system that for all its faults should eventually come to serve the greater good. To the extent that the benefits that result from such a system fall unevenly across the global population, this pattern of inequality can be presented, at least by some, as more neutral and therefore less politically problematic and objectionable.

How does this translate to sovereign debt? The distributional implications in contemporary sovereign debt can be difficult to paint with a broad political brush, even as compared to several decades ago. The traditional North–South distinction that is historically central in international finance has at least partially broken down. To begin with, the increase of South–South capital flows, with steep rises beginning in the early 2000s, has arguably made the distinction less salient (World Bank, 2006). This traditional dividing line has been blurred further as countries traditionally associated with the Global South have increased their investment in the US and Europe. The more explicit acknowledgement of distributional variation among the countries of the Global North has also confused this distinction (Pénet 2018), including recently with the intensive (and sometimes derisive) discussion of the so-called PIIGS countries of Europe (Portugal, Italy, Ireland, Greece, and Spain). And of course, especially in recent years, there has been greater political attention paid to inequality within countries of the Global North as well, and an acknowledgement that the fruits of a global capitalist system are unequally shared even within its ostensible centre. In the US, for example, the language of colonialism and imperialism has recently been used to reconceptualize the internal American experience at both a broad historical level (Rana, 2010) and as a way of discussing contemporary issues of racial inequity and criminal justice (Hayes, 2018).

In short, it is complicated to use accepted geographic and political boundaries as a shorthand to clearly delineate between those exploited by and those who benefit from sovereign debt. While these boundaries have always been more problematic than popularly imagined, the more open contemporary discussion of class in even the traditional centres of post–Second World War international finance has deepened such ambiguity in recent years. Still, the use of the terms (neo)colonial and (neo)imperial in particular express a genuine yearning for an identification of those unduly benefited from the current system of sovereign debt and for restitution for those unduly harmed—even if the map of benefit and burden fits less neatly onto traditional nation state geographies than it once did.

Finally, it is important to note briefly the ongoing appeal of (neo)colonial, (neo) imperial, and even hegemonic narrative frames in shoring up national support for regimes of wavering popularity or legitimacy. This effort to identify or construct an external adversary in times of political difficulty is of course hardly new. Neither is it unique to countries in financial trouble; indeed, it is among the most popular weapons in the arsenal of public officials seeking to strengthen domestic support. But the use of such terms for internal political ends can take on particular urgency in a sovereign debt context, especially for those debtor countries whose histories include control by foreign actors through financial means or debt burdens inherited from colonial or externally imposed rulers. Although such history may be considered long irrelevant by creditors, it can seem vivid for vulnerable groups burdened by austerity measures, making them more susceptible to populist appeals based in part on narratives of challenging neo-colonialism and neo-imperialism. These appeals may be even more likely to connect with a debtor state's population if the international community leaves unanswered the other demands that can motivate the contemporary use of these narratives—in particular, the calls for identifying agency and accountability and for a more explicit recognition and redress of the uneven benefit and burden that emerges in sovereign debt practices.

*

In short, in thinking through sovereign debt in light of these terms, it is important to keep in mind that such narrative frames do not belong to history or academic analysis alone. They are very much alive in the contemporary world, regularly used by activists and politicians and still resonant with broader populations. This is especially so in many of those countries dealing with sovereign debt problems, some of which have historical memories of past forms of colonial and imperial financial control. Given that this is the case, scholars have a special responsibility to think carefully about the multiple layers in which their terms of analysis have meaning: they face not just the bare facts of sovereign debt practice past and present but also the reality of how they are perceived and discussed in the wider world. This raises an additional question worth brief consideration: what are the ways in which scholars themselves might deal sensitively with this popular engagement?

To begin with, as demonstrated by many of the contributions in this volume, scholars can fill in the historical and analytical narrative in light of a conceptual framework that explicitly takes into account the concepts of (neo)colonialism, (neo)imperialism, and hegemony. They can put these broader political concepts at the centre of sovereign debt analysis in a way that is done all too infrequently. Such an approach would not only improve our understanding of the past but also might make it accessible and legible in terms that resonate with non-expert populations. This type of project could connect to creditor-side actors as well, who may be resentful of the accusatory rhetoric sometimes associated with these narratives on the borrower side. In demonstrating how sovereign debt historically and conceptually connects to these terms in a measured and less inflammatory way, scholars can try to bridge this divide and start breaking down some of the resistance to such analysis that occasionally exists. Of course, a significant portion of the creditor-side objection may result from a concern that even marginally shifting the conceptual or normative valence of sovereign debt discussions could adversely impact these creditors' material interests over the long run. Thus, resistance may stem less from an objection to the popular use of language per se than from a suspicion that even a more careful use of such terms could shift the playing field. Nonetheless, to the extent that a mismatch or resentment of language is one factor that undermines good faith cooperation, this form of scholarly intervention may help.

Scholars can also take up more directly the project of translation that I hinted at above. When politicians or activists speak of (neo)colonialism, (neo)imperialism, or hegemony, what, more precisely, do they aim to take to task? What, in any given instance, is being asserted or sought through this terminology? Such language in popular usage can be understood as an invitation to study more explicitly, and in finer detail, the demands and concerns for which these terms sometimes serve as shorthand. These scholarly projects would involve an effort to think through the claims and arguments implied by the linguistic usage on the ground in a more specific case. Such a practice of translation could assist not only the external targets or audience of this language. It might also help speakers within the sovereign debtor political community clarify for themselves the problems or concerns that they identify and perhaps articulate the connections between these problems and previous country experiences. Although these terms will no doubt continue to have blunt rhetorical appeal, helping to convert them into more precise language could encourage broader engagement and more successful communication on the ground.

Of course, while engaging in such projects or analysis, it is also important to keep in mind the question of appropriate scope. At what point and under what circumstances does it make sense to introduce analyses of sovereign debt that use the politically laden terms at the centre of this volume? And, particularly for those scholars more attuned and sympathetic to these narratives, is there a point at which the narrative or conceptual framing can go too far? It might be asserted that sovereign debtors cannot engage in even plain vanilla commercial bond transactions without raising the spectre of neo-colonialism or neo-imperialism, for example. If this is so, is it the transaction itself that is problematic, and is *any* commercial transaction involving sovereign states problematic? Is it when there is a clear asymmetry of power, such as in situations where the sovereign state is historically a less developed country or perhaps a state at the 'margins' as with Greece in recent memory? Or is any state necessarily less powerful than the hegemonic global financial markets writ large?

Alternatively, perhaps what makes such terminology more or less apt rests not so much with the characteristics of particular states as with the historically contingent nature and the varying practical application of a broader institutional or legal framework. For example, do changes in the understandings and legal approaches to sovereign immunity shape the appropriate boundaries for these terms? Or does the absence of something like a global bankruptcy regime or another collective safety net render the initial transactions more demanding of scrutiny? Of course, the introduction of particular policy tools to address these issues is unlikely to eliminate these dynamics and narratives. For example, if a more institutionalized sovereign debt restructuring framework existed, it is not difficult to imagine that its procedures and staff would suffer the charge of acting in a neo-imperial fashion, at least from some quarters. Certainly there is no clear or single answer to these questions—or to the more general question of when the use of such concepts becomes so broad as to lose meaning and power—and there will likely be as many opinions as commentators. But the questions themselves are worth explicit and careful consideration; they should not be merely an afterthought.

*

In short, I suggest that there may be value in asking two layers of questions that align with the idea of sovereign debt diplomacies. The first, taken up more directly by this volume's contributions, involves a study of sovereign debt in light of the concepts of (neo)colonialism, (neo)imperialism, and hegemony in ways that blur disciplinary boundaries and that adopt pragmatic rather than formalistic approaches to these issues. A second layer, implicitly suggested by these chapters and highlighted through these concluding remarks, takes up more explicitly the matter of how these politically laden terms themselves frame discussions of sovereign debt in ways that have impact in the world. Especially in the public sphere, these concepts frequently are used not strictly to describe an event but rather to express the desire to identify a responsible actor, to emphasize the unequal burdens of restructuring, and to shore up support for a domestic government. Given this popular salience, it is important for scholars to be aware of their own use of these terms, and of how they might participate in a project of translation or clarification when these narratives arise. Although such attentiveness is not likely to shift the underlying material issues and inequities that so profoundly impact the sovereign debt arena, it might nonetheless contribute to greater understanding and collaboration. In other words, there is and should be a diplomacy to speaking and writing about sovereign debt diplomacies themselves.

References

Chang, H. (2012). 'How Could Greece and Argentina—the New "Debt Colonies"—be set Free?', *The Guardian*, 25 November 2012.

Daniel, L. (2019). 'Debt Colonialism: Is China Trying to Buyout Africa's Resources?' *The South African*, 22 October 2019. www.thesouthafrican.com (Accessed 10 November 2020).

Giannacopoulos, M. (2016). 'Sovereign Debt Crises, Referendums and the Changing Face of Colonial Power'. *Continuum: Journal of Media & Cultural Studies*, 31(1), 33–42.

Hayes, C. (2018). *A Colony in a Nation*. New York and London, W.W. Norton.

Lienau, O. (2014). *Rethinking Sovereign Debt: Politics, Reputation, and Legitimacy in Modern Finance*. Cambridge, Massachusetts, Harvard University Press.

Lienau, O. (2017). 'Law in Hiding: Market Principles in the Global Legal Order'. *Hastings Law Journal*, 68, 541–608(3).

Mallard, G. (2019). *Gift Exchange: The Transnational History of a Political Idea*. Cambridge, Cambridge University Press.

Pénet, P. (2018). 'Rethinking Odious Debts', *Books and Ideas*, 19 March 2018. http://www.booksandideas.net/Rethinking-Odious-Debt.html (Accessed 10 November 2020).

Rana, Aziz (2010). *The Two Faces of American Freedom*. Cambridge, Massachusetts, Harvard University Press.

Wittgenstein, L. (1968). *Philosophical Investigations*. London, Macmillan.

World Bank (2006). *Global Development Finance 2006: The Development Potential of Surging Capital Flows*. Washington, International Bank for Reconstruction and Development / The World Bank.

Index

Note: Figures and Tables are indicated by an italic '*f*' and '*t*' following the page number.

The manufacturer's authorised representative in the EU for product safety is Oxford University Press España S.A. of el Parque Empresarial San Fernando de Henares, Avenida de Castilla, 2 – 28830 Madrid (www.oup.es/en or product.safety@oup.com). OUP España S.A. also acts as importer into Spain of products made by the manufacturer.

www.ingramcontent.com/pod-product-compliance
Ingram Content Group UK Ltd.
Pitfield, Milton Keynes, MK11 3LW, UK
UKHW020850150926
475595UK00003B/99
* 9 7 8 0 1 9 8 8 6 6 3 5 0 *